Max Stirner and Nihilism

Studies in German Literature, Linguistics, and Culture

MAX STIRNER AND NIHILISM

Between Two Nothings

Tim Dowdall

CAMDEN HOUSE

Rochester, New York

Copyright © 2024 Tim Dowdall

All Rights Reserved. Except as permitted under current legislation, no part of this work may be photocopied, stored in a retrieval system, published, performed in public, adapted, broadcast, transmitted, recorded, or reproduced in any form or by any means, without the prior permission of the copyright owner.

First published 2024
by Camden House

Camden House is an imprint of Boydell & Brewer Inc.
668 Mt. Hope Avenue, Rochester, NY 14620, USA
and of Boydell & Brewer Limited
PO Box 9, Woodbridge, Suffolk IP12 3DF, UK
www.boydellandbrewer.com

ISBN-13: 978-1-64014-170-4

Library of Congress Cataloging-in-Publication Data

CIP data is available from the Library of Congress.

The publisher has no responsibility for the continued existence or accuracy of URLs for external or third-party internet websites referred to in this book, and does not guarantee that any content on such websites is, or will remain, accurate or appropriate.

This book is dedicated to me.

Between two nothings
Huddled up,
A question-mark,
A weary riddle,
A riddle for vultures. . . .
They will "solve" thee
    —Nietzsche, *Dionysus-Dithyrambs*

Contents

Acknowledgments		ix
Notes on Sources, Abbreviations, Translations, and Spelling		xi
Introduction	Stirner: Sinner or Saint?	1
Chapter 1	The Origins of Disrepute: Stirner in Context	6
Chapter 2	The Meaning of Nothing: Nihilism's Complex Etymology	26
Chapter 3	The Tragic Age for Europe: Nihilism from Nietzsche to Now	54
Chapter 4	The Use and Abuse of Nihilism: Stirner under Fire	87
Chapter 5	The State of Denial: Stirner and Political Nihilism	124
Chapter 6	The Absence of Absolutes: Stirner and Moral Nihilism	154
Chapter 7	The Fear of Nothing: Stirner and Existential Nihilism	186
Conclusion	Stirner: The Happy Nihilist?	234
Bibliography		249
Index		269

Acknowledgments

My profound thanks go to the three great mentors in my academic journey: firstly, to Professor Wilfried van der Will, without whose enduring support and good counsel, spanning a longer time than either of us would care to dwell on, this book would never have been written; secondly, to the late Professor J. P. Stern, who gave me precious insights and endless inspiration during my short time at UCL; and, finally, to Dr. Nicholas Martin, whose unfailing encouragement and expert guidance along the way have been invaluable. I am grateful to my publishing team at Camden House for helping me at every turn and answering my every question, and especially to my editor, Jim Walker, for his shrewd advice and congenial manner. I should also like to make special mention of Kurt W. Fleming, the director of the Max Stirner Archive in Leipzig, who has given me both moral support and unrestricted access to the Archive's documents.

Notes on Sources, Abbreviations, Translations, and Spelling

Quotations from Stirner are given both in the original German and in English translation. Unless otherwise stated, I have used the following editions of Stirner's magnum opus:

Max Stirner, *Der Einzige und sein Eigentum: Ausführlich kommentierte Studienausgabe*. Edited by Bernd Kast. Freiburg and Munich: Verlag Karl Alber, 2016, referred to as *Der Einzige* in the main text and *EE* in footnotes.

Max Stirner, *The Ego and Its Own*. Edited by David Leopold and translated by Steven T. Byington. Cambridge: Cambridge University Press, 2006, referred to as *EO* in footnotes.

All translations for which an English-language source is not mentioned are my own.

Sources for books and scholarly journals are given in full in the bibliography and in shortened or abbreviated form in the footnotes. Online sources, as well as those for reference works and newspaper and magazine articles, are only cited in the footnotes.

Typographical errors in quotations from primary or secondary sources have not been corrected.

German orthography throughout corresponds to that in the original source. Thus, for instance, Stirner's magnum opus is sometimes referred to as *Der Einzige und sein Eigenthum*, as in the first edition, and sometimes *Der Einzige und sein Eigentum*, as in subsequent editions.

Italicized words in quotations correspond to emphasis in the source.

INTRODUCTION

Stirner: Sinner or Saint?

PHILOSOPHY, IN ATTEMPTING TO EXTEND the boundaries of human thought, is inevitably divisive, but few philosophers have polarized opinion as much as Max Stirner (1806–1856). This might be thought remarkable considering the fact that he only published one original full-length work, *Der Einzige und sein Eigentum*, but this singular book is so explosive in terms of both its style and substance that the strong reactions it has evoked ever since its publication in 1844 are hardly surprising. More so, perhaps, is how little known it remains despite the interest it has attracted from admirers like Max Ernst, Herbert Read, and Benjamin Tucker, as well as from detractors like Marx and Engels, Martin Buber, and Albert Camus. For his supporters, Stirner's lack of standing has often been a matter of bemusement, a disturbing example of the wasted talent in human intellectual evolution, that has been the lot of so many thinkers in history who, like Stirner, swam against what was, or would become, the prevailing tide. Among other things, this study aims to explain some of the factors that have inhibited the popularity of Stirner's ideas, although, it should be pointed out for those who have followed this discussion in more recent times, the emphasis here is on the incompatibility of those ideas with the broad patterns of human development rather than on advancing a theory of coordinated marginalization.

There has been a recurrent tendency in Stirner criticism over the years to view his thought from the contextual perspective of the commentator rather than of Stirner himself. This applies particularly to the time between 1880 and 1914 that encompassed both the flowering of anarchism and Nietzsche's initial, enthusiastic reception in Germany and beyond, as well as to the broad periods of post–World War II existentialism and late twentieth-century postmodernism. This inquiry, conversely, endeavors to assess the staunchly unpartisan Stirner, as far as is possible, on his own terms and in the light of his own historical and sociocultural environment. It is not, however, a general account of Stirner's life and work, but tackles instead the specific question of the relationship between Stirner's thought and nihilism.

There are several reasons for adopting this particular focus. Firstly, although the allegation of nihilism has frequently been leveled at Stirner, even involving, at times, a meticulous exposition of the justification for so doing, the charge has only ever been challenged in passing, rather than being subjected to robust critical analysis. Especially as Stirner's status as a nihilist has developed over time into something of a truism, it deserves, at last, to undergo systematic scrutiny. Secondly, of all the many accusations made against Stirner, including his being an egoist, anarchist, individualist, and solipsist, none is arguably more controversial than that of his being a nihilist. As this study will chronicle, the history of Stirner's reception shows that his link to nihilism has been self-evident to some but unthinkable to others. Even allowing for the axiom of there being two sides to every story, such polarization requires explanation. And, thirdly, there is a common opacity to nihilism as a term and Stirner as a thinker, which, paradoxically, makes them mutually illuminating topics, especially as they also have in common some of the fundamental reasons for their obscurity. I shall argue that these shared reasons are essentially ideological in nature and, thus, the apparently narrow question about Stirner and nihilism sheds a broad light on both the reception of Stirner's thought and his true place in the history of philosophy.

As regards the term nihilism, there are few routinely used words in the English language that are so imprecisely employed or ill understood. In order therefore to tackle the question in hand, a proper investigation into the meaning of the term is indispensable. Indeed, there are so many interconnected but distinct definitions that a comprehensive etymological history is necessary to understand exactly what Stirner's detractors have in mind. For, while it may be an exaggeration to say there are as many definitions as accusations, it transpires that there is an extraordinary variety in the nature of the incriminations against Stirner subsumed under the heading of nihilism. Unfortunately, despite the large body of literature on the subject, no one reference work about nihilism adequately serves the purpose of explaining all the different meanings of the term that have been employed over the years in relation to Stirner. Moreover, the lack of consensus between authors on nihilism makes it doubly important that a specific, tailor-made analysis be included in this study.

Stirner's own obscurity is equally profound. The reasons for this are manifold, starting with the limited nature of his literary output, and proceeding through his unconventional style of writing, unusual vocabulary, and almost malicious wit, to the inherent bias of many of his critics, whose various accounts of Stirner often say more about their own ideological animus than about Stirner's thought. The picture of Stirner that has therefore built up over time is bedeviled by accidental misunderstandings and willful misrepresentations, creating a ghostly composite figure displaying symptoms of both sociopathy and dissociative identity disorder. It certainly has not helped Stirner's image that one of the most important and influential thinkers of modern times, Karl Marx, pilloried Stirner, ridiculing him as Saint Max and depicting him as an effigy of the petty-bourgeois individualist. Marx, however, is just an extreme case; Stirner spared all other ideologies as little as he did communism, and each one has attempted to take its revenge in its own particular way.

There is one aggravating factor in the anglophone world as far as comprehending Stirner is concerned, namely the difficulty of translating his idiosyncratic prose that mimics Hegel, creates its own internal definitions, and is replete with incendiary slogans, immoderate italicization, and the brazen over-use of hyperbole. His peculiar terminology results in apparently simple words possessing a complexity of meaning that renders them essentially untranslatable. The problem becomes immediately apparent with the title of his major work, *Der Einzige und sein Eigentum*. The first and still most widely read translation, by Steven T. Byington (1869–1957), first published in 1907, renders the title as *The Ego and His Own*, which was the self-confessed brainchild of the publisher, the individualist anarchist, Benjamin Tucker (1854–1939). In the publisher's preface, Tucker acknowledges the inaccuracy of this translation, suggests *The Unique One and His Property* as a more literal but also more clumsy title, and commends *The Ego and His Own* for its euphony and (borrowing one of Stirner's terms, *Einzigkeit*) its uniqueness.[1] The choice is nonetheless a problematic one; neither of the substantives captures the precise meaning of the original and both have misleading connotations, the former psychological and ethical, the latter sociopolitical.

The debate around the title has continued to this day. The revised, annotated version of the Byington translation, edited by David Leopold, which first appeared in 1995, amended the title to *The Ego and Its Own*, in order to demonstrate that, for Stirner, the individual ego precedes gender—a small but nonetheless worthwhile improvement.[2] Leopold identifies a slightly different title to Tucker's literal alternative as the more accurate translation, namely *The Unique Individual and Its Property*, but opts for the gender-neutral version of the original for the actual book title, for reasons of euphony, familiarity, and fidelity. A new translation, meanwhile, by the pseudonymous anarchist, Wolfi Landstreicher, which appeared in 2017 declaring the express intention of correcting the numerous inaccuracies of the Byington version, replaces the original English book title with another modification of the more literal translation, namely *The Unique and Its Property*, on the basis of the unacceptable looseness of Byington's variant.[3] Without trying to detract from the value of Landstreicher's project as a whole and especially its stated aims, by rendering *Der Einzige* as "The Unique," this translation arguably

---

1 See Tucker, "Publisher's Preface," x.
2 See Leopold, "Introduction," xxxix–xl.
3 See Landstreicher, "Introduction," 8.

realizes the worst of both worlds in being neither particularly catchy nor readily understandable.

An alternative heading might be *The Unique Individual and Its Possessions*, which, although hardly mellifluous or immune from misinterpretation, at least conveys the essential meaning and avoids both wading straight into the various debates about egoism and the ego and diverting attention away from the core elements of the book to the status of property in anarchist thought. These may well be issues that the reader would like to consider, but it is potentially misleading to flag them up in the title, as this runs the risk of planting prejudices and preconceptions in the reader's mind. In any case, in view of the unresolvable controversy surrounding the English translation of the title, I have chosen to refer to Stirner's book henceforth as *Der Einzige*. Using either of the abbreviated English versions, *The Ego* or *The Unique*, would involve too much of a compromise. *The Ego* would be a constant reminder of a secondary issue for the purposes of this study, and it would make no sense to mention *The Unique*, as it is Leopold's scholarly edition of Byington's translation from which the quotations are taken. It is to be hoped that using the shortened German title throughout this study will not prove to be an irritation for the non-German reader. For the sake of consistency, references in the text to other German titles are also in the original, with the English translation in brackets on the first occurrence.

The problem of translation does not stop with the title of *Der Einzige* but continues in the text of Stirner's writings, and I therefore include the original German texts in square brackets immediately after long quotations from the English versions. I trust this will be more of a boon for readers who understand German than it will be a bane for those who do not. For short quotations, the German original is in a footnote. This monograph is meant for both German and non-German readers, and the benefit to the former of being able immediately to access the original should outweigh the inconvenience caused by the additional, and, for some, unintelligible, text. The book is also written for the inquisitive as well as the initiated, which is why it includes a biographical outline, even though similar information is included in numerous other books on Stirner. This narrative helps to place the discussion of Stirner and nihilism in its historical perspective and is invaluable for those who arrive at reading this book without prior knowledge of Stirner, because, for instance, of an interest in nihilism.

In his short preamble to the second section of *Der Einzige*, Stirner implies that his aim is to complete the Enlightenment's task of overcoming the divine. If, as can reasonably be claimed, Stirner's prime interest was to eradicate myths, abstractions, and absolutes, and thereby to liberate the individual from the shackles of dogmatic hegemony in all its guises, then this study is an attempt to extend the spirit of Stirner's endeavor to the criticism of his work, and specifically to the specter of nihilism that hangs over it. This is not meant to anticipate the outcome of this investigation, but rather to affirm commitment to the principle of unbiased analysis in order to allow a balanced assessment of the role of nihilism in Stirner's thought to emerge and, in the process, to free the original text of *Der Einzige* from the suffocating waves of critical dogma that threaten periodically to engulf it.

CHAPTER 1

The Origins of Disrepute: Stirner in Context

Max the Obscure

STIRNER IS COMMONLY REGARDED as no more than an insignificant, but nonetheless irksome, footnote in the history of German philosophy, a perception, I shall argue, that deserves reconsideration. His influence on subsequent thinkers can often only be surmised, leading at least one observer to suspect a clandestine conspiracy to keep him firmly in the shadows.[1] There are many possible reasons for Stirner's disrepute, not least of which is the explosive nature of his iconoclastic message, which is too unconventional for some and too dangerous for others. Another is that, unlike many of his German predecessors, he makes no attempt to construct a grand philosophical system, but instead articulates the great majority of his ideas in a single work, leading perhaps to their appearing less weighty or significant. Or, equally, it could be because *Der Einzige* is written in a style that is far from the abstruse complexity found in the work of his predecessor, Hegel, on the one hand, and equally far from the rich, expressive lyricism of his successor, Nietzsche, on the other. In other words, his writing may appear too pellucid to those used to reading Hegel and too dull for admirers of Nietzsche. Whatever the reason, or combination of reasons, for his unpopularity—an issue that will be addressed in more detail in the course of this study—the fact is that Stirner is largely unknown or ignored outside a relatively small circle of anarchists, post-anarchists, Marxists, and scholars of (anti-)Hegelianism.

Stirner's lack of prominence is curious when one considers that, even for a time of such intellectual upheaval as the post-Hegelian *Vormärz* (pre-March period) from 1831 to 1848, *Der Einzige* is a remarkably radical work. It explicitly rejects as hegemonic myths and fictions (or, in Stirner's terminology, spooks [*Spuke*] and *idées fixes*) all the man-made causes to which humans commonly devote themselves, be they institutionalized systems like religion, communism, nationalism, and monarchy, or abstract principles like goodness, truth, freedom, and justice. Rarely, if

---

1 See Laska, *Ein dauerhafter Dissident*, 73–77.

ever, in the history of ideas has there been such a comprehensive assault on man's convictions and beliefs. Individually, Stirner's Young Hegelian colleagues confronted different elements of the prevailing ideology, as did Feuerbach, for instance, with Christianity and Marx with capitalism, but Stirner assails the entire edifice of human dogma. It is, perhaps, understandable that such wholesale destruction of the ideological landscape has been interpreted by some as being the epitome of nihilism.

Despite his relative anonymity, however, a growing number of voices in recent years have argued that Stirner is still relevant today. John Welsh, in his recent book on Stirner, goes so far as to say that "Stirner's most important contribution in the history of ideas is his unique description of modernity and the problems it poses to individuals and social relations."[2] Such a claim rests largely on the radicalism of Stirner's philosophical message: he dared to go where no thinker had gone before, or, arguably, has since, in proposing the complete dismantling of all sacred heteronomous abstractions which, in his opinion, enslave the individual to extraneous causes and inhibit her or his potential for egoistic self-fulfillment. This extreme proposition encourages Stirner's readers not only to question authority in all its manifestations but also to confront the validity of their own and others' convictions and beliefs. This in turn implicitly calls into question the ultimate aim of the Enlightenment challenge to dogma that was famously expressed by Immanuel Kant (1724–1804) in the opening line of his essay "Was ist Aufklärung?" (What Is Enlightenment? 1784), where he writes: "Enlightenment is man's exit from his self-incurred minority."[3] In a postmodern Western world of seemingly unlimited skepticism and unbridled individualism, the issues that are raised by Stirner's philosophical undertaking, by undermining the entire ideological fabric of mankind and, however inadvertently, opening up to scrutiny the *telos* of the Enlightenment project with regard to the eradication of dogma, are arguably as crucial today as they were in Stirner's own time.

The exposition of Stirner's explosive ideas is confined, in the main, to the pages of his magnum opus, which was the only original book he published, his other publications being translations, compilations, and newspaper or journal articles. *Der Einzige* contains two main sections sandwiched between a short synoptic introduction, which stretches to just four pages in the first edition, and an only slightly longer, seven-page conclusion. The first section, entitled "Man" (*Der Mensch*), presents Stirner's assessment of human history, proposing a quasi-Hegelian triadic process of teleological development that governs an individual human life—from the realism of childhood through the idealism of youth to the egoism of adulthood—and, analogously, the course of mankind—from

---

2 Welsh, *Max Stirner's Dialectical Egoism*, 280.
3 Kant, *Basic Writings of Kant*, 133.

the pre-Christian ancients through the Christian moderns to the "free ones" of the future. This process is presented as an error-strewn work in progress, moving gradually towards the liberation of the individual from the tyranny of fictions, abstractions, and dogma.

The second section, entitled "I" (*Ich*), describes the principles of egoism towards which the process of enlightened emancipation aims, dissecting various themes, like freedom, power, and love, in an effort to identify autonomy in terms of the concepts of ownness (*Eigenheit*), ownership (*Eigentum*), and self-enjoyment (*Selbstgenuss*). What this means in practice is the rejection of externally imposed causes in favor of individual consciousness stripped back to its essential egoistic foundations. Stirner proposes a radical reevaluation of human existence, divested of what he views as the implausible nonsense of religious mythology and reduced, in quasi-Cartesian fashion, to the bare bones of what can be taken to be self-evident, namely the self-conscious ego, which, once disabused of the supposed advantages of subjection (for example, the benefits conferred by political or spiritual authority), inevitably comes to recognize the primacy of the self. This enlightened, autonomous person is the "unique individual" (*der Einzige*, also translated as the unique one or just the unique) of the book's title, while its possessions (*Eigentum*) consist of everything that can be brought under its dominion through the exercise of will. In keeping with the intellectual discourse of his time, Stirner also addresses in some detail, though hardly conclusively, the question of social organization, by postulating what one might term his egosystem, the so-called "union of egoists" (*Verein von Egoisten*), as a model for the cooperative coexistence of enlightened individuals, free from heteronomous influence or coercion.

While it may be unclear how so radical a viewpoint as that expressed in *Der Einzige* can have been ignored or forgotten, it is all the more apparent why it should have acquired a reputation for notoriety among many of those observers who do at least acknowledge Stirner's existence. His self-proclaimed egoism, which, as a concept, is sufficiently taboo in itself, has thus regularly been lumped together with the, to many, disreputable doctrines of anarchism or nihilism. It comes as no surprise that those who have dismissed Stirner as a nihilist (who include among their number such luminaries as Tomáš Garrigue Masaryk, Hugo Ball, Karl Löwith, Albert Camus, and Gilles Deleuze) have invariably belittled his contribution to Western philosophy, while those few (like the far less illustrious Anselm Ruest, Bernd Kast, and Bernd Laska) who have denied any such connection have tended towards a more positive assessment of his achievements.

This polarization with regard to the issue of Stirner and nihilism is particularly pronounced in the world of anglophone scholarship, where what was for many decades after its publication in 1971 the only full-length monograph on Stirner, R. W. K. Paterson's *The Nihilistic Egoist:*

Max Stirner, adopts, as the title suggests, an uncompromisingly negative approach towards the man and his ideas, portraying Stirner as a modern Antichrist, apparently for the primary purpose of corrective education rather than the impartial dissemination of knowledge. It is an unsatisfactory state of affairs when the unsuspecting student's main or only source of information presents a view so partisan that it obscures the sense and substance of the work which it professes to describe and analyze. The present book will attempt to redress the balance by offering an alternative appraisal of Stirner's thought and legacy, which seeks to uncover the meaning and significance of his philosophy, stripped of the self-perpetuating accumulation of nearly two centuries of obloquy.

The Life and Death of Max Stirner

Before embarking on the investigation into the nature of Stirner's thought and its relationship to nihilism, it is important to put his ideas into their historical and biographical perspective, in order properly to understand the environment in which they were generated, and thereby to avoid the all-too-common error of interpreting his thought anachronistically. Knowledge of Stirner's biography also helps to explain the use to which the chronicle of his life has been put in the process of discrediting him, a tendency which, as will be discussed below, dates back to the period immediately following the publication of *Der Einzige*.

The life and death of Max Stirner, viewed through the long lens of the ensuing century and a half of human history, can appear almost comical in its ineffectualness. Much of what is known of his biography is contained in the hagiographical account written by his chief disciple and devotee, the egoist anarchist writer and poet, John Henry Mackay (1864–1933). Reflecting on Stirner's modest grave, which lies in a forgotten corner of the Cemetery II of the *Sophiengemeinde* (Sophia Parish) in central Berlin, Mackay writes with immoderate pathos:

> New graves have enclosed the old one, and whoever wants to find it today must laboriously seek it through their narrow rows.
>
> The golden letters of the name on the slab are losing their luster. But while they fade there, this name shines its victorious gleam through the night of our time and announces the morning, the morning of the freedom of the human race.[4]

Mackay's almost fanatical enthusiasm does not, however, persuade him to conceal the actual, dismal chronicle of Stirner's life. He was born Johann Caspar Schmidt, the only child of a flute-maker and a postman's

---

4   Mackay, *Max Stirner*, 213.

daughter, in provincial Bayreuth on October 25, 1806—the birth month of the modern age according to Stepelevich, coinciding with Napoleon's victory over Prussia at the Battle of Jena and Hegel's completion of his magnum opus, *Die Phänomenologie des Geistes* (The Phenomenology of Mind).[5] Stirner's father died six months after his birth, while his mother survived her son by three years, dying in a lunatic asylum in 1859. He spent his childhood in Bayreuth and Kulm, living for most of that time with his mother and stepfather, whose only child together, Stirner's half-sister, died at the age of two. He finished his schooling at the *Gymnasium* in Bayreuth, followed by intermittent periods of study at the universities of Berlin, Erlangen, and Königsberg, during which time he was given the nickname "Stirner" by his classmates, on account of his unusually high forehead (*Stirn*).[6]

While in Berlin, from 1826 to 1828, Stirner attended Schleiermacher's lectures on ethics and Hegel's on the philosophy of religion, but his studies ended in 1835 with no more than a second-class teaching certificate (*bedingte facultas docendi*). According to Mackay, Stirner nonetheless occasionally included the title of *Dr.* on his compulsory police registrations.[7] Stirner's first wife, Agnes Clara Kunigunde Burtz, who was his landlady's illegitimate granddaughter (or niece—Mackay was unsure), died in childbirth eight and a half months after their wedding in 1837, an event which, though sadly not uncommon at that time, might be expected, along with the deaths of family members during his childhood, to have had a lasting effect on Stirner's disposition.[8] Mackay, however, insinuates that the marriage was not based on deep love or passionate intimacy, by repeating a piece of hearsay, namely that Stirner had told a friend, who in turn informed Mackay, "that his first wife had once uncovered herself unconsciously in sleep, and that it had been impossible for him from that moment on to touch her again."[9]

Having been refused employment as a grammar school teacher, Stirner worked for five years from 1839 as a private school teacher at Madame Gropius's Lehr- und Erziehungs-Anstalt für höhere Töchter (Pedagogical and Educational Institution for Higher Daughters). He resigned from this position shortly before the publication of *Der Einzige* in 1844, perhaps quite rightly fearing scandal, or in confident but entirely misguided expectation of the book's popular and commercial success. Instead, it was immediately proscribed by the censors of

---

5   See Stepelevich, "Max Stirner and the Last Man," 1–2.
6   See Mackay, *Max Stirner*, 85.
7   See Mackay, *Max Stirner*, 48.
8   See Mackay, *Max Stirner*, 50.
9   Mackay, *Max Stirner*, 88. The friend was Edgar Bauer. See Stepelevich, "Letter from Edgar Bauer," 171.

various German states and added to the *Index Librorum Prohibitorum*, the Roman Catholic Church's infamous list of forbidden books.[10] For a radical Young Hegelian like Stirner, it was almost more damaging, at least in reputational if not in financial terms, that the ban was lifted a week later in Saxony (where *Der Einzige* was published) because the authorities could not imagine anyone would take it seriously. The officials, according to one of the most important political dailies of the time, the *Allgemeine Zeitung Augsburg* (Augsburg General Newspaper), were of the opinion that religion and morals could hardly be better promoted than by the book's repellent impudence.[11] The ban nevertheless remained in place in Prussia.

One year prior to the publication of his magnum opus, and five years after the death of his first wife at the age of twenty-two, Stirner entered into his second marriage, to a beer-drinking, pipe-smoking, billiard-playing, cross-dressing young woman of independent means twelve years his junior called Marie Daehnhardt, to whom he dedicated his masterwork with the words, "to my sweetheart."[12] Mackay writes with unsubstantiated certainty and undisguised contempt of her being "without any special intellectual gifts" and that "a beauty she was not."[13] A few years before her death in 1903, in answer to Mackay's inquiries, she said of Stirner that he was "very sly," "too selfish to have true friends," and that she had neither respected nor loved him.[14] Nonetheless, their wedding seems to have been a riotous affair, or at least a highly unconventional one. On the arrival of the officiating church councilor, who went by the name of Marot, one of the guests, Ludwig Buhl, of Young Hegelian fame, had to be compelled to put his workaday coat over his shirtsleeves; the game of cards they had been playing was reluctantly put to one side; the bride, who was delayed, finally appeared in a simple, everyday dress without the traditional myrtle crown and veil; and it was ascertained that no Bible could be found for use in the ceremony.[15] Mackay states indignantly, and apparently without the slightest irony, that those who were gathered there were not in a festive mood, and had certainly not recently arrived from the local pub, as was sometimes claimed. When the ceremony finally got underway, the guests stared out of the window, rather than follow the pastor's arid address. To top it all, it transpired that no one had thought of purchasing wedding rings, so a fellow Young Hegelian, Bruno Bauer,

---

10   *Index Librorum Prohibitorum*, 28.
11   See *Allgemeine Zeitung* (Augsburg), November 12, 1844: 2533.
12   *EO*, 3; *EE*, 10: "Meinem Liebchen." For a character profile of Marie Daehnhardt, see Mackay, *Max Stirner*, 118–20.
13   Mackay, *Max Stirner*, 118.
14   Mackay, *Max Stirner*, 12.
15   See Mackay, *Max Stirner*, 116–17.

had to help out by dismantling his purse and extracting the two brass rings that held it together, which served as impromptu, and no doubt ill-fitting, substitutes. Marot was invited to the celebratory dinner but made his excuses and promptly departed.[16]

The marriage lasted for two and a half years, during which time the couple managed to lose Marie's entire handsome fortune, as Mackay describes it, of ten, or, according to one account, thirty thousand thalers, chiefly, it seems, through the instigation and operation of a dairy business, which achieved little more than filling Berlin's public sewers with gallons of sour milk.[17] Stirner subsequently thought of trying his hand at investing in the stock market but was (perhaps luckily) dissuaded by a friend. Marie, meanwhile, removed, in her own words, their rings from *his* fingers (the rings presumably having been bought in the meantime with *her* money), and ran away to London, whence she made her way to Melbourne and became a washerwoman, married a laborer, and fled "[in] to the arms of the Catholic Church."[18] Her former husband spent the last decade of his life, from the time of his separation from Marie in 1846 till his death in 1856, living from hand to mouth; he was even reduced in the summer of 1846 to placing an advertisement in a Berlin newspaper for a loan of 600 thalers.[19] Friedrich Engels (1820–1895) wrote in a letter dated October 22, 1889, to Max Hildebrand, who had requested information from him about his erstwhile acquaintance: "For the rest I know nothing about Stirner; I never found out what subsequently befell him, except that Marx told me he had almost literally starved to death."[20] Stirner moved home frequently, sometimes after only a few months, in an attempt to evade his creditors, and resided for the last five years of his life in various rented accommodations as a lodger, having had to sell his own furniture.[21] His efforts to escape justice were not entirely successful and he twice served time in debtors' prison, in 1853 and 1854.

Stirner died in poverty on June 25, 1856, at the age of forty-nine, of complications arising from a common carbuncle on the neck, which was caused, according to some accounts, by an insect bite that had become infected.[22] Just twelve years earlier he had written in *Der Einzige* with seemingly naïve insouciance: "Finally, the old man? When I become one, there will still be time enough to speak of that."[23] Stirner's death was

16 See Mackay, *Max Stirner*, 117.
17 See Mackay, *Max Stirner*, 121, 186.
18 Mackay, *Max Stirner*, 190.
19 See Mackay, *Max Stirner*, 192.
20 Marx and Engels, *Collected Works*, 48:394.
21 See Mackay, *Max Stirner*, 202.
22 See Mackay, *Max Stirner*, 205.
23 *EO*, 18; *EE*, 24: "Endlich der Greis? Wenn Ich einer werde, so ist noch Zeit genug, davon zu sprechen."

largely ignored in the press. One of the few newspapers that did report it, a local supplement from the Bavarian town of Würzburg, dedicated about one column inch to the announcement, which ended by notifying its readers of the fact that Stirner had died "in very straitened circumstances."[24] Marx wrote to Engels on September 26, 1856 (a full three months after the event) with what appears to be a yawn of casual indifference: "No news apart from what you may already know, namely that *Stirner* has died."[25] The only account that remains to us otherwise is Mackay's sober description of the circumstances of Stirner's demise, which relates the somber details of his suppurating abscess. It reads like a prosaic antipode to the myth of Rilke's death from an infection resulting from the prick of a thorn, sustained while gathering roses for the Egyptian beauty, Nimet Eloui Bey.[26] In death, as in life, Stirner stayed true to his demythologizing principles.

Thus the grim reality of Stirner's life seems to have confirmed Hobbes's dictum; it was solitary and poor, quite probably nasty on occasion and possibly brutish too, and certainly short even by the standards of the time, at least for those lucky enough to escape death in infancy.[27] Despite his unfailing admiration for Stirner, Mackay does not shy away from confronting the truth; on the contrary, he faces his own manifest disappointment head on: "Not only a deep discouragement, but also a great disappointment gripped me, as . . . I became more and more convinced how simply and uneventfully this life had been lived."[28] He had told Marie Daehnhardt, when he finally located her in 1897, that he was only interested in finding out the truth about Stirner, and he seems to have remained true to his word as far as the bleak, tragicomic catalog of biographical events is concerned, though he undoubtedly does his best to present the cold facts of Stirner's life in the best possible light:[29]

> His life is a new proof that it is not those who make the big fuss of the day, the darlings of the crowd, but rather the solitary and restless researchers, who in quiet work point the way to the fate of mankind, who in truth are immortal.

---

24 "Rubrik: Vermischtes," *Würzburger Anzeiger: Beiblatt zur Neuen Würzburger Zeitung*, July 2, 1856: 2.
25 Marx and Engels, *Collected Works*, 40:70.
26 See Gass, *Reading Rilke*, 3. See also Oswald, "Introduction," 7–23, where he writes of "Rilke's transformation of death into a personal mythological event" (19). Rilke in fact died of leukemia.
27 See Hobbes, *Leviathan*, 186.
28 Mackay, *Max Stirner*, 6.
29 See Mackay, *Max Stirner*, 11.

Among them stands Max Stirner. He has joined himself to the Newtons and the Darwins, not to the Bismarcks.[30]

This is the exalted company in which, in Mackay's opinion, Stirner belongs.

Stirner and *Die Freien*

The company Stirner actually kept is considerably less eminent and acclaimed in the history of ideas, but nonetheless consisted of some of the most radical thinkers of his time. Collectively, they were known as *Die Freien* (the Free Ones), the Berlin branch of the Young Hegelians, who gathered in various taverns, but most notably in Hippels Weinstube at Friedrichstrasse 94, in order to converse, debate, and revel.[31] *Die Freien* was an informal circle of young writers and poets, journalists and editors, and teachers and students, who, according to Mackay, had only one thing in common: being "more or less dissatisfied with the political and social conditions of the time."[32] Mackay stresses that they cannot be considered a union or a society, having had no chairman, constitution, or articles of association.[33] Instead, he labels them the "extreme left" and "the scattered volunteer corps of radicalism."[34] Engels, together with Edgar Bauer (1820–1886), published a satirical epic poem in 1842 entitled *Der Triumph des Glaubens* (The Triumph of Faith), where its members are lampooned as demons, atheists, and rebels. Stirner is described as follows:

> See *Stirner* too, the thoughtful moderation-hater;
> Though still on beer, he'll soon be drinking blood like water.
> And if the others shout a wild: *à bas les rois!*
> *Stirner* is sure to add: *à bas aussi les lois!*[35]

Perhaps the two most important thinkers associated with Young Hegelianism were the renowned biblical scholars David Friedrich Strauss (1808–1874) and Ludwig Feuerbach (1804–1872). Although they were not members of *Die Freien* at any time, their influence on the group was considerable. Strauss and Feuerbach, with their magnum opuses *Das Leben Jesu* (The Life of Jesus, 1835) and *Das Wesen des Christenthums* (The Essence of Christianity, 1841), respectively, initiated a period of

---

30 Mackay, *Max Stirner*, 24.
31 See Mackay, *Max Stirner*, 57.
32 Mackay, *Max Stirner*, 57.
33 See Mackay, *Max Stirner*, 58.
34 Mackay, *Max Stirner*, 57, 59.
35 Marx and Engels, *Collected Works*, 2:336.

profound and prolific polemical attack on Christianity, which was unprecedented both in its scale and significance. The philosophical challenge to religion had been bubbling under for a number of decades, as demonstrated by the atheism dispute between Jacobi and Fichte from 1798 to 1800 (which will be considered in more detail in chapter 2), but its roots stretched back to the Scientific Revolution, which began in the middle of the sixteenth century, and which was followed by the dawn of the Enlightenment in the second half of the seventeenth century. After more than a hundred years of Enlightenment thinkers seeking to reconcile philosophy with religion (or at least to establish their separate realms) and to paper over the ever-widening cracks in the relationship between philosophy and theological orthodoxy created by skeptical inquiry, the first half of the nineteenth century was the time when the inevitable conflict between the two sides finally broke through the surface. This first manifested itself in Strauss's sensational debunking of biblical miracles, and indeed of Christian mythology as a whole, followed by Feuerbach's humanistic evaluation of Christianity as an anthropological phenomenon.

Unlike Strauss and Feuerbach, the most important Young Hegelian in historical terms, Karl Marx (1818–1883), was at least an informal member of *Die Freien*, though only during the early years of its existence. Mackay states, based on information in Engels's letter to Hildebrand, that Marx had left Berlin by the time Stirner appeared on the scene, which was probably around the middle or end of 1841, and thus the two never met.[36] In 1845–1846, by which time he was living in Brussels, Marx wrote *Die deutsche Ideologie* (The German Ideology), a savage critique of his Young Hegelian colleagues. Nearly two thirds of the book is devoted to Stirner, but it seems that his enmity was based on his knowledge of *Der Einzige* rather than on personal acquaintance. But regardless of whether Stirner knew them personally or not, the waves created by Strauss, Feuerbach, and Marx were intensely felt by the entire company of *Die Freien*, whose vigorous exchanges of information and wide knowledge of subversive publications ensured quick access to the latest intellectual developments of the time.

The only known sketch of *Die Freien*, by Engels, shows from left to right: Arnold Ruge, Ludwig Buhl, Karl Nauwerck, Bruno Bauer, Otto Wigand, Edgar Bauer, Max Stirner, Eduard Meyen, and Carl Friedrich Köppen.[37] Although Engels, in a letter to Marx of November 19, 1844 claimed that "Stirner is the most talented, independent and hard-working of the 'Free,'" it was Bruno Bauer (1809–1882) who, according to Karl

---

36   See Mackay, *Max Stirner*, 90.
37   See Wikipedia, s.v. *Die Freien by Friedrich Engels*, c. 1842, pen & ink, accessed June 30, 2023, https://de.m.wikipedia.org/wiki/Datei:Die_Freien_by_Friedrich_Engels.jpg.

Löwith (1897–1973), was "the intellectual center of the Berlin 'free spirits.'"[38] Initially, Bauer was considered a Right Hegelian according to the classification of David Strauss, in which Strauss sought to differentiate between those conservative members of the Hegelian school who accepted Hegel's position on religion, the Right Hegelians, and the progressive radicals who rejected it, the Left Hegelians.[39] Throughout his career as a theologian, historian, philosopher, and social theorist, Bauer floated between these ill-defined and fluctuating groupings, engaging in lengthy and at times hostile disputes with David Strauss and Marx and Engels. He is remembered above all for his biblical criticism, most notably for the denial of the existence of Jesus Christ as a historical person. He argued that the New Testament was a fictional, literary work, owing more to the Greek tradition than to Judaism.[40] Although in later life Bauer remained a theological radical and atheist, politically he became increasingly conservative and antisemitic with age. Clearly, like Buhl, he had a friendly relationship with Stirner. Writing about Bruno Bauer's request for him to make a drawing of the dead Stirner, the painter and writer Ludwig Pietsch commented in his memoirs: "Bauer's tenderness and intimacy of feeling . . . was particularly evident in his behavior towards the few people for whom he harbored true affection or love. One was his old, widowed father. . . . The other was Max Stirner, a lonely, world-despising, courageous, profound, and astute thinker."[41]

As for the other members of *Die Freien*, Ruge was a philosopher and writer, a follower of Feuerbach, politically a democratic liberal and a supporter of the 1848 revolutions, as well as the founder of the *Hallesche Jahrbücher* (Halle Yearbooks), which, from 1838 to 1843, was the most important mouthpiece of the Young Hegelian movement. Ruge was not an actual member of *Die Freien*; he visited them just once, at Hippels in November 1842, departing in a fit of indignation at the coarse tone of his interlocutors.[42] Later, he nonetheless paid Stirner the compliment of calling *Der Einzige* "the first readable philosophical book in Germany."[43] Buhl was a writer, journalist, and translator and, although Mackay says Stirner was not really intimate with anyone, Buhl does seem to have been one of his few friends.[44] Of *Die Freien*, only he and Bruno Bauer attended both Stirner's second wedding and his funeral. It was Buhl who inherited Stirner's literary estate, which, according to Mackay, disappeared after

---

38 Marx and Engels, *Collected Works*, 38:13; Löwith, *From Hegel to Nietzsche*, 343.
39 See Strauss, *Streitschriften*, 95–126.
40 See Bauer, *Christus und die Caesaren*.
41 Pietsch, *Wie ich Schriftsteller geworden bin*, 257–58.
42 See Mackay, *Max Stirner*, 73.
43 Ruge, *Briefwechsel*, 386.
44 See Mackay, *Max Stirner*, 90.

Buhl's death (supposedly by suicide).[45] Wigand, who like Ruge was just a visitor, was the Young Hegelians' principal publisher, and he included Bruno Bauer, Ruge, Engels, and Stirner among his clients. Nauwerck, journalist, orientalist, and revolutionary, Meyen, editor, journalist, and democrat, and Köppen, historian, teacher, and political journalist, have all fallen even further into obscurity than the other members of *Die Freien* depicted by Engels. Edgar Bauer, who went from freedom fighter in his youth to founding editor of a Christian-conservative newspaper, *Die Kirchlichen Blätter* (The Church Gazette) at the age of fifty, is now perhaps known for little more than having been the younger brother of Bruno Bauer.

Also included by Mackay in the inner circle of *Die Freien* are Engels, Dr. Adolf Rutenberg, Mussak (Eduard Mushacke?), Hermann Maron, and six others.[46] Of the "inestimable" number comprising the outer circle, he lists well over fifty men (including Nauwerck and Marx) and five women (including Marie Daehnhardt and Louise Aston, the author and feminist). He mentions some other guest visitors as well, including the poets Georg Herwegh and Hoffmann von Fallersleben.[47] *Die Freien* was, in other words, a large, boisterous, vociferous gathering of progressive freethinkers, representing the avant-garde of political, social, and philosophical thinking in the period of the *Vormärz*. Mackay's characteristically extravagant assessment reads as follows: "Hardly ever in the history of a people—unless it was at the time of the French Encyclopedists—has a circle of men met as significant, as unique, as interesting, as radical, and as unconcerned about every judgment as 'The Free' at Hippel's formed in the fifth decade of the nineteenth century in Berlin."[48]

Despite Mackay's tendency towards hyperbole, this claim deserves to be taken seriously. The Young Hegelians, of which *Die Freien* was an important element, can be seen as representing one of the most significant directional adjustments in the post-Cartesian history of ideas, insofar as they employed philosophy both for the purposes of open sedition against the established order and for the uncompromising propagation of atheism. It is only, broadly speaking, after Hegel that modern, Western atheism came into the open and, as such, the Young Hegelians can be said to have been active at a watershed moment in the emergence of secularism.[49] Prior to this, European atheists had been isolated and/or secretive,

---

45   See Mackay, *Max Stirner*, 210.
46   For a discussion of Mussak and Mushacke, see Laska, "Nietzsches initiale Krise," 127.
47   See Mackay, *Max Stirner*, 73–74.
48   Mackay, *Max Stirner*, 81.
49   The reference to modern, Western atheism is as opposed, above all, to classical atheism. See Whitmarsh, *Battling the Gods*. My intention is not to perpetuate the "modernist mythology" (12) that "atheism is a modern invention, a

like Kazimierz Łyszczyński (1634–1689), whose retraction and abjuration did not save him from becoming the only historical victim of a Polish auto da fé;[50] Matthias Knutzen (1646–1674 or thereafter), who was a fugitive until his trail disappeared abruptly; Jean Meslier (1664–1729), whose 633-page *Testament* was published posthumously; and Baron d'Holbach (1723–1789), whose atheistic writings were published anonymously or pseudonymously.[51] Even as progressive a thinker as David Hume (1711–1776) did not openly admit to atheism and indeed defended himself in writing against such accusations.[52]

By the beginning of the nineteenth century, adherence to atheism was sufficiently widespread, its persecution so much less severe, and the social taboos surrounding it so much more relaxed, that radical thinkers no longer felt compelled to conceal their lack of belief. Gone, by this time, were the Enlightenment's countless attempts to reconcile reason and faith, as was the general reluctance to offend social mores or risk the wrath of church and state. Instead, there occurred a liberation not just of thought, but also of expression, which paved the way for the unfettered ideas of Nietzsche and his successors. Löwith, in his seminal work on the revolution in nineteenth-century thought, is routinely disdainful of the Young Hegelians, accusing them of being insipid and monotonous, and tending to view them as mere epigones of the master.[53] But however much he plays down their individual contributions to the history of philosophy, Löwith nonetheless recognizes the significance of their collective role in challenging both the principles and dominance of Hegelian philosophy and initiating the radical philosophical changes of that epoch.[54]

In *Der Einzige*, Stirner dedicates a sub-section to *Die Freien*, dividing the group into three main ideological blocs—political liberalism (represented by Ruge and Meyen), social liberalism (Hess, Marx, Engels), and humane liberalism (Bauer)—all three of which he rejects as abstractions that replace the class system with the state, personal possessions with the property of society, and the religious God of Christianity with the earthly faith in humanity, thus subjugating the individual anew and alienating it from its self-interest.[55] According to Stirner's analysis,

---

product of the European Enlightenment" (4), but to concentrate on the period that is relevant to this study. As Whitmarsh states: "The Christianization of the Roman Empire put an end to serious philosophical atheism for over a millennium" (238).

50   See Hoffmann, "The Development of Religious Studies in Poland," 88.
51   See Schröder, "Introduction," 7–32. Onfray, *Atheist Manifesto*, 29–31.
52   See Hume, *A Letter from a Gentleman to His Friend*.
53   See Löwith, *From Hegel to Nietzsche*, 67.
54   See the section entitled "The Overthrow of Hegelian Philosophy by the Young Hegelians," in Löwith, *From Hegel to Nietzsche*, 65–121.
55   See *EO*, 128–29; *EE*, 151–52.

all forms of liberalism, among which he includes communism under the name of social liberalism, are based on the same teleological principles and ethical precepts as Christianity, in other words on the very *idées fixes* he aims to eradicate in the name of the sovereign individual. But however vehement his attacks on his fellow Young Hegelians may have been, there can nonetheless be little doubt of the importance of the prevailing intellectual climate of unrest, upheaval, and rebellion, for the development of his own ideas.

The period immediately following Hegel's death in 1831 was characterized by an unprecedented splintering of the hitherto discernible, if by no means linear, progression of Western philosophy into countless conflicting directions. It was as if the colossus of philosophy, Hegel, were demonstrating the proof of his dialectical theory using his own self as evidence, by inducing a similarly colossal antithetical reaction, which exploded the boundaries of rational inquiry and emancipated the critical mind.[56] He bequeathed to his successors, including Stirner, both the weapons—in the form of his analytical methodology—and the motivation—in the form of the impetus for an equal and opposite reaction. Hegel's conservative political views, based on the guiding principles of caution, discipline, diligence, and order, as manifested in his apparent exaltation of the authoritarian state, must have seemed like a provocation to the more radical young students attending his university lectures, and, unsurprisingly, it didn't take long after his death for intellectual pandemonium to break out.[57] The backlash was spearheaded by the Young Hegelians, who, in the words of Paterson, "stood for a destruction of all inherent authority, doctrinal and institutional, by a critical analysis of the presuppositions and functions of accepted beliefs and practices."[58]

However simple and uneventful Stirner's life was otherwise, it was his contemporaneity with and proximity to the Young Hegelians, through his knowledge of their publications and his attendance at the discussions and debates of their Berlin chapter, *Die Freien*, that gave him the opportunity to transcend his challenging circumstances and make a statement in the form of his major work, *Der Einzige*, which is recognized by some as having far-reaching philosophical significance.[59] One of these is Laska, who

---

56   See Stepelevich, "Hegel and Stirner," 278: "Stirner's thought represents the final dialectical inversion of Hegelianism"; Stepelevich, *Max Stirner on the Path of Doubt*, 8: "[Stirner] is the fate of Hegelianism"; Basch, *L'Individualisme anarchiste*, 101: "Stirner est l'Anti-Hegel."

57   For Hegel and the state, see Hegel, *Hegel's Philosophy of Right*, 244–45: "The state . . . is the ethical whole and the actualization of freedom. . . . The state is the spirit, which abides in the world and there realizes itself consciously."

58   Paterson, *The Nihilistic Egoist*, 28.

59   It is nonetheless a minority opinion. McLellan offers an alternative view: "Stirner's book was to a large extent an amalgam of current clichés." McLellan,

sees in Stirner a "key figure in modern intellectual history," asserting that "thorough and targeted research shows that Stirner's ideas . . . have had an impact that can hardly be overestimated."[60] Another is Mackay, who takes every opportunity to express his admiration, bordering on adulation, for Stirner the philosopher.

Saul Newman cautions against drawing too close a parallel between Stirner's biography and his philosophy. Referring to Leopold's essay "A Solitary Life," he writes: "Leopold . . . has the decency to avoid drawing too close a link between Stirner's life and personality and his philosophy, as though the latter were merely a reflection of the former. . . . With Stirner, we witness the immolation and disappearance of the author behind the text, like, as Foucault once said, a face drawn in sand at the edge of the sea."[61] Despite the risk of drawing false inferences, the scrutiny of Stirner's biography is nonetheless instructive for the understanding of his work, firstly because it lends support to the evidence from his writings of a man who eschewed self-glorification (and glorification in general), and secondly because it illuminates the significance of the radical, intellectual environment of which he was a part. Newman is clearly concerned by the apparent paradox of a philosophy based on freedom through ownership being propounded by a man who manifestly failed to own very much, at least materially, in his own lifetime. He is not alone in this; Mackay was also worried that Stirner's detractors, once they knew his life story, would say that "the teacher of egoism followed his teaching poorly in his own life or that following it bore bad fruit."[62] Such fears are borne out by Marx and Engels's savage, ad hominem attack on Stirner in the relentlessly sardonic and inordinately long (329-page) "Sankt Max" section of *Die deutsche Ideologie*, where their adversary is depicted as a petty-bourgeois bigot of limited experience and narrow horizons: "In the case of a parochial Berlin school-master or author, . . . whose relations to this world are reduced to a minimum by his pitiful position in life, when such an individual experiences the need to think, it is indeed inevitable that his thought becomes just as abstract as he himself and his life."[63]

This sort of exultant denunciation of Stirner has been repeated throughout the nineteenth and twentieth centuries, perhaps most

---

The Young Hegelians, 136.

60 Laska, *Ein dauerhafter Dissident*, 120, 8. Laska's thesis is that Stirner had a significant "subcutaneous" and largely unrecognized effect on subsequent thinkers, first and foremost on Marx and Nietzsche, but also on Max Adler, Ernst Jünger, and Carl Schmitt, among others. For more information on Stirner and Schmitt, see Laska, *"Katechon" und "Anarch"* and Jorn Janssen's forthcoming book on *Stirner and the Political Theology of Fanaticism*.

61 Newman, "Introduction: Re-encountering Stirner's Ghosts," 11–12.

62 Mackay, *Max Stirner*, 212.

63 Marx and Engels, *Collected Works*, 5:263.

spectacularly by the avantgarde Marxist critic, writer, and composer, Hans G. Helms (1932–2012), in *Die Ideologie der anonymen Gesellschaft* (The Ideology of the Anonymous Society, 1966), where he went to great lengths (and book length, at 619 pages) to associate Stirner with the most dangerous elements of the modern sociopolitical landscape. In the process, Stirner has been characterized in many different, often contradictory, and usually derogatory ways. This is illustrated by the fact that Marxists tend to classify him as a proto-fascist, while conservatives label him a proto-anarchist.[64] Yet, as Newman has noted: "He has been described as a nihilist, existentialist, individualist, liberal, psychological egoist—but all such labels are inadequate. Just as we think we have Stirner in our conceptual grasp, just as we think we have pinned him down, he slips away again like one of his own spectres."[65] To put it another way, so many of the labels applied to Stirner are mutually exclusive that they cannot possibly all be true.[66]

The Debate Surrounding Stirner and Nihilism

The label of nihilist is, along with egoist and anarchist, the epithet most commonly applied to Stirner, perhaps because, of all the accusations leveled against him, it is the most malleable and least specific. Egoists, anarchists, solipsists, fascists, existentialists, and individualists can all be described as nihilistic, insofar as their ideas involve negation, be it in the form of denial of morality or reality, purpose or personal salvation. It only took a few months after the publication of *Der Einzige* for Stirner to be accused of nihilism, even though, at the time, the word *Nihilismus* was a relative neologism in German. The Old Hegelian philosopher and pedagogue, Karl Rosenkranz (1805–1879), wrote in his journal in late 1844 or 1845:[67]

---

64 See Laska, *Ein dauerhafter Dissident*, 41–52 and 84–87.
65 Newman, "Introduction: Re-encountering Stirner's Ghosts," 2.
66 See Laska, *Ein dauerhafter Dissident*, 5. Laska gives a comprehensive overview of the labels that have been applied to Stirner, listing twenty-two in the table of contents alone. Stulpe arrives at a similar number: "The 'Unique One' appears . . . as an anarchist, superman, psychopath, socialist, petty bourgeois, intellectual, fascist, genius, paranoiac, bohemian, Satanist, existentialist, individualist, terrorist, member of the middle-class, critic of totalitarianism, solipsist, prophet, nihilist, metaphysician, and all of these with various meanings, evaluations, and combinations." Stulpe, *Gesichter des Einzigen*, 19.
67 In general usage, the term Old Hegelian is almost interchangeable with Right Hegelian, similarly to Young Hegelian's equivalence with Left Hegelian. For further detail and explanation, see the chapter entitled "Old Hegelians, Young Hegelians, Neo-Hegelians," in Löwith, *From Hegel to Nietzsche*, 53–135.

> Stirner's book . . . is evidently the pinnacle of the one-sided, subjective tendency in which the Young Hegelian school has lost itself. In this work, it has transitioned from atheism to social radicalism. It has arrived at the state of nature, at brutal tyranny, at ruthless license for all desires and passions, at the apotheosis of egoism and nothingness. . . . Theoretically, such nihilism in relation to all ethical pathos cannot develop into anything; it could only be followed by the practice of egoistic fanaticism, by revolution.[68]

The historical condemnation of Stirner's philosophy as nihilistic commenced at this juncture, defined, in this case, as a form of ethical nihilism that derives from atheistic subjectivism and ends in revolutionary destruction. The next known usage of the term in relation to Stirner came soon afterwards, in 1847, when a short, anonymous article entitled "From Berlin" appeared in *Die Grenzboten* (The Border Messenger), a weekly national-liberal magazine, where the term is again associated with Stirner as a representative of a school of thought, and oblique reference is made to his desultory life (thus providing substance for Mackay's and Newman's later concerns): "Another writer of this school of nihilism, Max Stirner . . . did not realize his principle of egoism with particular success in his life, because he only dreamed about it, only played with it in abstractions, wrestled with it in logical visions."[69] It is from these beginnings, shortly after the publication of *Der Einzige*, that the association of Stirner with nihilism evolved.

It can perhaps be assumed that once Rosenkranz, who, at the time, was widely read and often highly regarded, had used the term nihilism to describe the unpalatably radical position of the Young Hegelians, it became to some extent an established view, at least in those intellectual circles in Germany where the debate over Hegel's legacy continued to rage. Later on, the connection was further reinforced by the fact that the so-called first Stirner renaissance, in the 1890s, coincided with, and was to some extent fueled by, Nietzsche's sudden and explosive popularity. In this context, Stirner was often viewed as a precursor of Nietzsche, and it was only natural that nihilism, as an important theme in Nietzsche's

---

Stepelevich denies the claim that Stirner was a Young Hegelian, calling him instead a synthesis of Old and New Hegelianism. This is an interesting and valid objection, but for the purposes of this study, I have persisted in referring to him as a Young Hegelian to indicate his radical intellectual environment and orientation. The Young Hegelians were, in any case, a highly heterogeneous bunch. See Stepelevich, *Max Stirner on the Path of Doubt*, 2–8.

68   Rosenkranz, *Aus einem Tagebuch*, 132–33. The individual entries are not dated, but the journal ends in the spring of 1846. It was first published in 1854.

69   "Tagebuch. III. Aus Berlin," *Grenzboten: Zeitschrift für Politik und Literatur* 6, no. 1 (1847): 563. Rosenkranz was a contributor to this journal.

philosophy, should also be identified with Stirner. This idea subsequently became almost a commonplace, and it has only recently been consistently challenged by various writers and scholars, chiefly by figures associated with the Max Stirner Society, which was established in 2002 in Hummeltal, near Stirner's birthplace, Bayreuth, and had as its mission the publication of a journal and the advancement of research into Stirner's life and work. Remarkably, they represent, apart from a few solitary exceptions, the first real proponents of Stirner's ideas since the initial Stirner renaissance, which was championed by Mackay and carried forward by Anselm Ruest (1878–1943) and Rolf Engert (1889–1962). The Stirner Society made it one of its principal aims to expose significant misinterpretations of Stirner's work through analysis of the history of its reception, and one of the labels its members have challenged as a misconception is that of Stirner as a nihilist.

The chief originator of the modern reevaluation of Stirner is Bernd Laska, whose 1996 work, *Ein dauerhafter Dissident* (An Enduring Dissident), contains a short chapter entitled "Der Nihilist" that lists some examples of the recurrent accusation of nihilism, culminating in Hermann Schmitz's description of Stirner as "the only perfect nihilist in the history of modern philosophy."[70] Although Laska does not offer a direct refutation, he suggests that the various—in his opinion—inappropriate labels attached to Stirner are evidence of the inadequate reception of Stirner's work till now, resulting in its maverick status as a *hapax legomenon* in the text of Western philosophy.[71] Bernd Kast revisits the theme of Stirner's mislabeling in the afterword to his 2009 study edition of *Der Einzige*, where he writes of the "five eradicable misunderstandings with regard to *Der Einzige*," including a section on the accusation of nihilism, in which he asserts that: "if nihilism . . . represents the absence of any meaning and purpose, then Stirner's 'Unique One' is anything but a nihilist."[72] Yet it is precisely here that the problem lies, namely, which definition of nihilism is being applied to Stirner's philosophy, for, as Kast observes, the term is extremely unclear.[73]

The term nihilism is, in effect, an insubstantial catch-all devoid of specificity. The reasons for this are both etymological and historical. Etymologically, it derives from the Latin *nihil*, meaning nothing, but adding only the (Greek) suffix -ism means there is no indication of what

70 Schmitz, *Selbstdarstellung als Philosophie*, 309. Schmitz is echoing Nietzsche's description of himself as "the first perfect European nihilist." Nietzsche, *The Will to Power*, 7.
71 See Laska, *Ein dauerhafter Dissident*, 117.
72 Kast, "Afterword," in *EE*, 380.
73 See Brock, *Nietzsche und der Nihilismus*, 8: "The word 'nihilism' belongs to that group of terms that are generally used as a matter of course, without one actually knowing clearly what they really mean."

that nothingness refers to, leaving it open to interpretation, unlike, for instance, the word atheism, which has a clearly delineated field of application. As a result, there are as many forms of nihilism as there are principles that can be denied. Historically, the term was used initially by critical commentators in an undefined manner as a polemical device, which indicated little more than the hopeless heterodoxy of the accused. Since then, its status as the ultimate expression of negativity has led to its being freely used and adapted within numerous different fields, and, in the process, it has only to a very limited extent shaken off its stigmatic quality, and that mainly in a countercultural context. Definitions of nihilism have thus multiplied unchecked over the course of the last two centuries.

The next step, therefore, in this study is to trace the complex genealogy of the word nihilism in order to be able to evaluate the applicability of each of its distinct definitions to Stirner's ideas. While doing so, it is perhaps worth bearing in mind that although nihilism has only ever been used—to a greater or lesser degree—pejoratively in connection with Stirner, this does not, of course, mean that positive connotations are impossible. Nowadays there are a few philosophical voices that embrace the notion that the term nihilism does not in itself possess inherently malign qualities. James Tartaglia, for instance, writes about "the false assumption that nihilism is *bad*";[74] elsewhere, he asserts that, "if nihilism is true, it cannot be good or bad. Rather, nihilism's implication that life is meaningless is best viewed as simply a fact about life, not fundamentally different in kind from the fact that life evolved on Earth; except that the former is a philosophical fact."[75]

Stirner never employed the words nihilism or nihilist in his published works, and there is no record of his having referred to himself as a nihilist; but the word nothing, from which it derives, is a significant, if overinterpreted, term in *Der Einzige*. Intriguingly, Stirner twice mentions the word in the form of "the creative nothing," that is with an apparently positive implication.[76] In order to understand this concept of creative nothingness and to determine whether it can be seen as representing some form of affirmative nihilism, it is necessary to remove the baggage of a hundred and eighty years of critical negativity associated with Stirner's alleged nihilistic tendencies and to analyze objectively his ideas in relation to the

---

74 Tartaglia, "Nihilism and the Meaning of Life," v. See Tartaglia, *Philosophy in a Meaningless Life*, 5: "Religious leaders still espouse the idea that without the meaning God gives to life, there can be no standards of moral conduct; but few non-believers find this equation of atheism with moral chaos remotely plausible. Despite this, however, the assumption that nihilism is bad has exerted massive influence within secular culture." See also, Brassier, *Nihil Unbound*, xi: "Nihilism is not an existential quandary but a speculative opportunity."
75 Tartaglia, *Philosophy in a Meaningless Life*, 5.
76 *EO*, 7; *EE*, 15: "das schöpferische Nichts."

innumerable meanings of nihilism, while keeping an open mind about the predominantly negative interpretations of his thought. What will become apparent during this process is that, up until now, there have largely been just two opposing opinions, namely that Stirner is, or is anything but, a nihilist. It is my contention that the truth is more nuanced and that a proper understanding of the various definitions of nihilism will throw up both connections and disparities within Stirner's thought.

CHAPTER 2

The Meaning of Nothing: Nihilism's Complex Etymology

Definitions and Interpretations of Nihilism

THE VAGUENESS INHERENT in nihilism's nonspecificity presents the first obstacle to assessing its relevance to Stirner's thought. Although the word has, since its invention, been in increasingly common usage, there is a remarkable amount of confusion about what nihilism actually means, and only a few of Stirner's accusers on the subject make their definitions clear. Instead, many of them seem to treat its meaning as a given, which only serves to deepen the confusion and misunderstanding. Indeed, far from leading to a reduction in occurrence, the general uncertainty around the interpretation of nihilism has resulted in its liberal and, at times, almost indiscriminate use, thus increasing both the number of possible definitions and their ambiguity. Unless this complex web of meanings is untangled, it is impossible to determine whether Stirner can reasonably be called a nihilist, a task which is made no easier by the fact that standard textbooks on nihilism fail to reach a consensus view on the question of the term's definition. In the absence of clarity, both about nihilism generally and about how it applies to Stirner, it is imperative that this study provide a comprehensive, if relatively brief, account of the history of nihilism, against which Stirner's thought can be measured.

The next two chapters will therefore be concerned with the etymology of nihilism, examining its various definitions, and tracing its development as a concept over time. The focus will be on two central and closely connected themes around which the discussion about Stirner and nihilism often revolves, namely, the relationship between atheism and nothingness on the one hand, and Nietzsche's conception of nihilism on the other. The current chapter will commence with an overview of the interpretations and connotations of nihilism and proceed to an assessment of the evolution of the concept of nihilism from its origins as a polemical term used for the excoriation of irreligion, up until Nietzsche's assimilation of the word into his philosophical project. The following chapter will then concentrate on the formation and development of Nietzschean nihilism and examine the possibility that Stirner's ideas contributed to its genesis.

Armed with this knowledge, it will be possible in the following chapters to gain an insight into the different historical perspectives of Stirner's accusers and to understand the implications, and judge the veracity, of their accusations.

While general works of reference all agree about the derivation of the word nihilism from the Latin word for nothing, there is significant variation in the definitions they provide. *The New Oxford Dictionary of English* offers the following: "the rejection of all religious and moral principles, often in the belief that life is meaningless," adding sub-definitions for philosophical nihilism ("that nothing in the world has a real existence") and historical nihilism ("the doctrine of an extreme Russian revolutionary party *c*. 1900").[1] *Merriam-Webster* covers similar ground, listing "a viewpoint that traditional values and beliefs are unfounded and . . . existence is senseless," as well as a "19th century Russian party advocating revolutionary reform . . . using terrorism," and adding "a doctrine that denies any objective ground of truth and esp. of moral truths."[2] *Collins Cobuild Advanced Learner's Dictionary* provides a simple description that almost seems to have Stirner in mind: "a belief which rejects all political and religious authority and current ideas in favour of the individual."[3] However, *Collins English Dictionary* augments this with a string of further definitions including "a complete denial of all established authority and institutions," "an extreme form of scepticism that systematically rejects all values, belief in existence, the possibility of communication," "a revolutionary doctrine of destruction for its own sake," and "the practice or promulgation of terrorism."[4]

Britannica Concise Encyclopedia proposes a relatively straightforward, generic definition: "any of various philosophical positions that deny that there are objective foundations for human value systems," while the *Internet Encyclopedia of Philosophy* asserts similarly that it "is the belief that all values are baseless and that nothing can be known or communicated."[5] The *Penguin Dictionary of Philosophy* offers an even more general assessment, namely that "any view which contains a significant denial can be described as nihilistic, but when the term is used there is often a suggestion of loss or despair."[6] It then lists, more specifically, the views that are labeled as nihilistic as "those which deny the existence of a God, the

---

1 *The New Oxford Dictionary of English*, 1st ed. (2001), s.v. "nihilism."
2 *Merriam-Webster's Collegiate Dictionary*, 11th ed. (2006), s.v. "nihilism."
3 *Collins Cobuild Advanced Learner's Dictionary*, 8th ed. (2014), s.v. "nihilism."
4 *Collins English Dictionary*, 4th ed. (1998), s.v. "nihilism."
5 *Britannica Concise Encyclopedia* (2006), s.v. "nihilism." *Internet Encyclopedia of Philosophy*, "Nihilism," by Alan Pratt, accessed June 30, 2023, https://www.iep.utm.edu/nihilism/.
6 *The Penguin Dictionary of Philosophy*, 2nd ed. (2005), s.v. "nihilism."

immortality of the soul, the freedom of the will, the authority of reason, the possibility of knowledge, the objectivity of morals, or the ultimate happy ending of human history." The sheer volume of divergent definitions, far surpassing the customary inconsistency of dictionary interpretations, demonstrates the magnitude of the problem of understanding and evaluating the allegations of Stirner's nihilism.

As with works of reference, studies devoted specifically to the subject of nihilism fail to present a uniform picture. In *The Banalization of Nihilism*, Karen L. Carr recognizes the "wide variety of usages" and attempts to simplify the different definitions by ordering them under five headings: epistemological, aletheological, metaphysical or ontological, ethical or moral, and existential or axiological.[7] These cover respectively: denial of the possibility of knowledge, denial of truth, denial of empirical reality, denial of absolute values, and denial that life has a meaning (along with the concomitant feelings of emptiness and hopelessness). As Carr readily acknowledges, these distinct forms of nihilism are far from being mutually exclusive and, instead, they "overlap and intermingle."[8] This is not, however, an exhaustive list of the manifestations of nihilism owing to the innumerable possible applications of the action of denial. Nihilism, after all, effectively means the negation of whatever it is connected with.

Donald A. Crosby, in his study of nihilism, also identifies five types, but they differ from Carr's, in that aletheological nihilism is subsumed under the epistemological variety, while metaphysical nihilism is excluded, and these two are replaced by political and cosmic nihilism. Political nihilism can be defined as the denial of the legitimacy of certain sociopolitical structures; it is chiefly, if not exclusively, associated with nineteenth-century Russian nihilism.[9] Cosmic nihilism is the denial of an intelligible and moral cosmic order discoverable in nature and is characterized by a view of the universe as alien, chaotic, and oblivious to the cares, aspirations, and values of humanity.[10] Elsewhere, one can find at least five further forms of nihilism: aesthetic nihilism, or the implicit denial of God through subjective aesthetics;[11] mereological nihilism, or

---

7   See Carr, *The Banalization of Nihilism*, 16–18.
8   Carr, *The Banalization of Nihilism*, 18.
9   See Crosby, *The Specter of the Absurd*, 9–11. Also, Slocombe, *Nihilism*, 7.
10   See Crosby, *The Specter of the Absurd*, 26–30. Also, *Concise Routledge Encyclopedia of Philosophy*, 1st ed. (2000), "NIHILISM," by Donald A. Crosby: "Cosmic nihilism regards nature as either wholly unintelligible and starkly indifferent to basic human concerns, or as knowable only in the sense of being amenable to scientific description and explanation." H. P. Lovecraft is a prime example of a cosmic nihilist. A self-confessed cosmic nihilist is David Benatar. See Benatar, *The Human Predicament*, 62–63.
11   See, e.g., Koepke, "Nothing but the Dark Side of Ourselves?" 143–63.

the denial of composite objects;[12] semantic nihilism, or the denial of linguistic meaning;[13] logical nihilism, or the denial of absolute logic;[14] and theological nihilism, or the denial of God in terms of His unknowability or undiscoverability (i.e., it is not simply a redundant synonym for atheism).[15] The list could go on and on, but the twelve definitions above cover the most frequent occurrences of the term, and it is almost certainly to one or more of these twelve types of nihilism that each of Stirner's accusers is referring, even if they may be unforthcoming about the specific type.

Carr tries to delineate nihilism's boundaries further by examining its relationship to other, similar concepts. There is an obvious link between nihilism and atheism, but, according to Carr, neither one necessarily entails the other, except in the case of alethiological nihilism, "which seems to lead irrevocably to atheism."[16] Nonetheless, atheism is usually implied by nihilism in its various guises, with the possible exceptions of mereological and semantic nihilism, which are both sufficiently self-contained not to require any reference to God's existence or non-existence. Carr also distinguishes between nihilism on the one hand, and skepticism and relativism on the other, on the basis of the latter two being more "innocuous."[17] Thus, skepticism entails uncertainty, while nihilism, like atheism, makes a substantial (negative) claim; and similarly, relativism questions the validity of a statement by viewing it in relation to its context, but nihilism involves a further "deterioration" into complete rejection.[18] Even so, skepticism and relativism are usually essential components of a nihilistic outlook, as is pessimism, which, like nihilism, involves the negation of some aspect of human existence.[19] All of these connections are relevant to the question of Stirner's alleged nihilism, insofar as one would expect to see some corroborative evidence of their presence in his writings.

There have been numerous other books dedicated to the subject of nihilism since the early twentieth century, some of which have made significant contributions to the modern understanding of the word, above all by augmenting nihilism's negative connotations. Perhaps the most

---

12   See, e.g., Inwagen, *Material Beings*, 72–73.
13   See, e.g., Slocombe, *Nihilism*, 7. Robert Kirk calls Willard van Orman Quine a semantic nihilist in Kirk, *Translation Determined*, 29–30.
14   See, e.g., Milkov, *A Hundred Years of English Philosophy*, 94: "Wittgenstein's logical nihilism was clearly expressed in . . . the assumption that the propositions of logic are tautologies."
15   See, e.g., Slocombe, *Nihilism*, 7. See also Lütkehaus, *Nichts*, 644–55.
16   Carr, *The Banalization of Nihilism*, 21.
17   Carr, *The Banalization of Nihilism*, 20.
18   Carr, *The Banalization of Nihilism*, 21.
19   Nietzsche saw pessimism "as a precursor of nihilism" and even suggested "that the term should be replaced by nihilism." Nietzsche, *The Will to Power*, 32.

important of these is Hermann Rauschning's (1887–1982) *Die Revolution des Nihilismus* (The Revolution of Nihilism, 1938), in which he analyzes the National Socialists' rise to, and consolidation of, power, in terms of a political nihilism that had grown out of the intellectual nihilism of the *fin de siècle*.[20] Rauschning's book represents the voice of the disinherited conservative bourgeoisie, which, as his own biography shows, was initially seduced by the Nazi message, only to become disillusioned by the concrete results of its ideology. His branding of Nazism as nihilistic tied nihilism irreversibly to the horrors of the twentieth century. It is a viewpoint that has gone on to win wide acceptance; in his first interview in Germany after the Second World War, Thomas Mann declared: "According to my way of thinking, nazism [*sic*] was entirely devilish nihilism."[21]

Rauschning's book, in turn, influenced the Protestant theologian, Helmut Thielicke (1908–1986), who, in *Der Nihilismus. Entstehung, Wesen, Überwindung* (Nihilism: Its Origin, Nature, and Overcoming, 1950), presents nihilism as the ultimate ism, whose only message is "that ... nothingness prevails and the world is meaningless."[22] Seemingly oblivious to the existence of the word Protestantism (or evangelism, or Catholicism), he maintains that adding the suffix -ism absolutizes the principle to which it is applied, leading inevitably to intolerance and totalitarianism, and a distorted perspective on God's creation.[23] He then proceeds on what amounts to an evangelical crusade against all modern manifestations of nihilism, culminating in the following dubious claim: "'Without God, everything is lawful,' ... nobody can depend upon anybody. / This is the reason why all atheistic state systems necessarily become police states: the people can be held in check only by stronger controls and by terror.... The police state and the dual police system are necessary consequences of nihilism."[24] Thielicke is extrapolating here from the abbreviated version of Dostoevsky's famous assertion, "without God, everything is permitted," in order to underpin his sweeping statement about the nature of the secular state.[25] He thus combines

---

20 See Rauschning, *Die Revolution des Nihilismus*, 150.
21 Howard Kennedy, "Author Thomas Mann distinguishes between Nazism [and] pure communism," *Stars and Stripes*, July 26, 1949: 1.
22 Thielicke, *Nihilism*, 27.
23 See Thielicke, *Nihilism*, 20–21.
24 Thielicke, *Nihilism*, 116–17.
25 Jean-Paul Sartre is complicit in the popularization of the abbreviated form of the phrase. In his well-known lecture, *L'Existentialisme est un humanisme*, delivered in 1946, he states: "Dostoievsky once wrote 'If God did not exist, everything would be permitted'; and that, for existentialism, is the starting point." Sartre, *Existentialism and Humanism*, 33. Dostoevsky's actual statements, at least in translation, are less concise: "If there is no immortality of the soul, then there is no virtue, and therefore everything is permitted." "Without God and the future

Dostoevsky's notion of atheism engendering amorality, which is repeated ad nauseam in *The Brothers Karamazov*, with Rauschning's analysis of Nazism as nihilistic, to produce a compelling, if flawed, argument for religion's monopoly on morality.[26]

Essentially, for Thielicke, nihilism has two forms. On the one hand, it is the acknowledgment that life has no meaning, expressed through anxiety, or *horror vacui*, while, on the other, it is a descriptive term for moral emptiness, in other words, existential and ethical nihilism respectively.[27] He considers both forms to be pathological conditions, examples of modern man's alienation from God. The medical theme continues in another important work on the subject, *Nihilism* (1969), by Stanley Rosen (1929–2014). Rosen describes nihilism as a "perennial pestilence," for which he attempts to provide "protective inoculation" in his advocacy of Platonic reason.[28] His starting point is the ordinary language philosophy of Wittgenstein, of whom he writes: "Wittgenstein and his philosophical progeny are nihilists because they cannot distinguish speech from silence."[29] He then moves on to the fundamental ontology of Heidegger, which, he states, "is nihilism because it makes the ostensible speech of Being irrelevant to human action."[30] Moreover, in Heidegger's case, "what began as the attempt to overcome nihilism was transformed into a profound resignation in the face of nihilism."[31]

Rosen argues that nihilism is the result of the collapse of belief in objective moral truths, which has led to the contemporary crisis of reason. His aim is to reveal the nihilistic essence of both the continental and analytical branches of contemporary philosophy, in order to illustrate and emphasize "that the Platonic-Aristotelian conception of the relation between reason and the good is superior to the modern, or predominately modern, conception," as well as, effectively, to reverse Heidegger's claim "that Plato is responsible for nihilism in the western tradition."[32]

---

life? It means everything is permitted now, one can do anything?" Dostoevsky, *The Brothers Karamazov* (2002), 82, 589. Alternatively: "Without God and without a life to come? After all, that would mean that now all things are lawful, that one may do anything one likes." Dostoevsky, *The Brothers Karamazov* (2003), 753.

26 This assertion has since been thoroughly discredited. See, e.g., Harari, *21 Lessons*, 200: "Though Gods can inspire us to act compassionately, religious faith is not a necessary condition for moral behaviour. . . . Morality of some kind is natural." See also Dawkins, *The God Delusion*, 226–33 and Hitchens, *God Is Not Great*, 173–93.
27 See Thielicke, *Nihilism*, 36–39.
28 Rosen, *Nihilism*, xx.
29 Rosen, *Nihilism*, 17.
30 Rosen, *Nihilism*, 42.
31 Rosen, *Nihilism*, 103.
32 Rosen, *Nihilism*, 138.

Regardless of the merits of his argument, his exposition hardly treats the causes of nihilism. Just as Thielicke says that Christianity is preferable to modern nihilism, Rosen offers eternal Platonic values as the better option. Rosen was clearly indebted to his teacher, Leo Strauss (1899–1973), for the general tenor of his thesis, in terms of his praise of Platonism, as well as his abhorrence of nihilism and the danger it poses for humanity. Strauss had previously tackled the issue of nihilism in a lecture he delivered in 1941 entitled "German Nihilism," which is largely concerned with the assertions and implications of Rauschning's book. Having failed to find a definition of nihilism there, he offers his own, namely that "nihilism is the rejection of the principles of civilization."[33] This forms the basis for Rosen's analysis: nihilism is rooted in the chaos and destruction of the Second World War, and his response to it reflects a longing for a return to moral certainty.[34]

It is clear that Rauschning, Thielicke, and Rosen are all referring to a fundamentally similar phenomenon, though each has his own political, theological, or philosophical axe to grind. For all of them, nihilism is, to some degree, a conveniently negative description of the enemy, be it Nazism, atheism, or anti-Platonism. Each of these works is thus an anti-nihilist polemic, and although the specific target of their criticism may vary, they all agree with, and reinforce, Rauschning's analysis of Nazism as the ultimate apotheosis of nihilism. This view has inevitably colored the modern perception of nihilism and supported the tendency to demonize those historical figures considered to have been nihilists, Stirner among them.[35] What these books fail to do, however, is to provide an account of the etymology of nihilism, treating the word instead as a static term, dependent, to a greater or lesser extent, on the author's input for its definition. This conceals the fact that the word nihilism has had a fluid and dynamic history, which needs to be understood in order fully to grasp the different meanings of Stirner's accusers. Subsequent publications about nihilism have gone some way towards rectifying this, but significant disagreement between authors still exists, and it is therefore important for the purposes of this study to trace the tangled ancestry of the term and follow its complex evolution, especially during the period of Stirner's critical reception, from the publication of *Der Einzige* to the present day.[36]

---

33 Strauss, "German Nihilism," 364.

34 See Strauss, *The City and Man*, 1: "It is not self-forgetting and pain-loving antiquarianism nor self-forgetting and intoxicating romanticism which induces us to turn with passionate interest . . . toward the political thought of classical antiquity. We are impelled to do so by the crisis of our time, the crisis of the West."

35 For a discussion of Stirner and fascism, see Laska, *Ein dauerhafter Dissident*, 84–87.

36 Some examples of subsequent books on nihilism are Arendt, ed., *Der Nihilismus als Phänomen der Geistesgeschichte*; Weier, *Nihilismus. Geschichte,*

The Antecedents and Origins of Nihilism

All sources agree that nihilism is a relative neologism insofar as it did not exist in an identical or similar form in ancient times. *Midenismos*, which is the current Greek equivalent, was created specifically as a direct translation of the modern word nihilism. The philosophy of Gorgias (483–375 BCE) has been considered an example of ontological nihilism, because of the intriguing trilemma in *Concerning the Non-existent*, namely, "firstly, that nothing exists; secondly, that even if anything exists it is inapprehensible by man; thirdly, that even if anything is apprehensible, yet of a surety it is inexpressible and incommunicable to one's neighbour."[37] However, as Higgins contends, "this argument . . . can also be interpreted as an assertion that it is *logos* and *logos* alone which is the proper object of our inquiries, since it is the only thing we can really *know*."[38] Moreover, Gorgias is recognized as one of the founders of sophism, and his trilemma can be viewed in this light more as a rhetorical exercise than a doctrinal statement, especially as the assertion that nothing exists, if taken literally (i.e., not as "nothing" exists), is seemingly self-defeating.

Similarly, the radical skepticism of Pyrrho of Elis (360–270 BCE), which is based on suspension of judgment and the implicit understanding that nothing can be considered to be true, has been interpreted, by Nietzsche among others, as epistemological nihilism.[39] However, the point of Pyrrho's reasoning is not so much to comment on the nature of knowledge, but to find a way of achieving ataraxia in life. Both of the above examples represent the historically misleading application of a modern term to an archaic idea. Indeed, the ancient Greeks may not have entertained anything like the concept of nihilism even in its simplest form (thus explaining why they had no word for it), because they shunned the idea of nothingness. Nowhere is this clearer than in the philosophy of Parmenides (515–? BCE), who "set out to exorcize negative notions such as 'nothing' and 'what is not' from his account of the world."[40] It is further demonstrated by the failure of the ancient Greeks to accommodate, or even contemplate, zero in their system of mathematics, as Charles Seife explains:

System, Kritik; Goudsblom, *Nihilism and Culture*; Gawoll, *Nihilismus und Metaphysik*; Vercellone, *Einführung in den Nihilismus*; Cunningham, *Genealogy of Nihilism*.

37 Sextus Empiricus, *Against the Logicians*, 35. Gorgias's original text is no longer extant.

38 *Internet Encyclopedia of Philosophy*, "Gorgias (483–375 B.C.E.)," by C. Francis Higgins, accessed June 30, 2023, https://www.iep.utm.edu/gorgias/.

39 See Nietzsche, *Werke*, 8.3:70.

40 Gottlieb, *The Dream of Reason*, 61.

Zero clashed with one of the central tenets of Western philosophy, a dictum whose roots were in the number-philosophy of Pythagoras and whose importance came from the paradoxes of Zeno. The whole Greek universe rested upon this pillar: there is no void.

The Greek universe, created by Pythagoras, Aristotle, and Ptolemy, survived long after the collapse of Greek civilization. In that universe there is no such thing as nothing. There is no zero.[41]

Seife goes on to assert that the dominance of Aristotelian philosophy, having successfully fended off the challenge of atomism, held back the progress of Western thought, above all in science and mathematics, for two thousand years, with its reluctance to accept infinity and its emphatic rejection of the void. It was only in the Renaissance, after the adoption, mainly because of trade and commerce, of Arabic numerals (which included zero) in the Late Middle Ages, that the ascendancy of Aristotelian philosophy was finally overthrown and both the void and the infinite became a part of European thinking, thus facilitating the Scientific Revolution.[42] While the word nihilism did not, and arguably could not, appear until after this paradigm shift in Western conceptual thinking, it is nonetheless relevant to the discussion of Stirner's alleged nihilism that man's problematic relationship with the concept of nothingness stretches back to antiquity. The magnitude of this issue may help to explain the emphasis Stirner's accusers have attached to the word *Nichts* (nothing) in *Der Einzige*, a subject that will be discussed at length in later chapters. There are few words able to inspire such horror in the human mind as nothingness, and Europeans' gradual acceptance of zero in the thirteenth and fourteenth centuries opened up to scrutiny an idea that had remained largely hidden from view until that time.[43] It also prepared the ground for the emergence of a new word, nihilism, that served as an encapsulation of the negative qualities of nothingness.

Standard reference sources are nonetheless as unclear on the origin of the word nihilism as they are on the question of its definition, reconfirming the general impression of confusion that surrounds the topic. *Merriam-Webster's Collegiate Dictionary* and the *Online Etymology Dictionary* both agree, however erroneously, that its first usage was in 1817, coined by Friedrich Heinrich Jacobi (1743–1819) shortly before his death.[44] *Merriam-Webster Online*, on the other hand, gives its first known use as 1812, while *The New Oxford Dictionary of English* and the

41   Seife, *Zero*, 25.
42   See Seife, *Zero*, 83.
43   See Seife, *Zero*, 78–81.
44   See *Merriam-Webster's Collegiate Dictionary*, 11th ed. (2006), s.v. "nihilism." *Online Etymology Dictionary*, s.v. "nihilism," accessed June 30, 2023, https://www.etymonline.com/word/nihilism.

Internet Encyclopedia of Philosophy are more vague, placing its inception in the early nineteenth century.[45] *Collins Online Dictionary* is vaguer still, stating only that it originated in the nineteenth century.[46] Other works of reference, like Pan's *A Dictionary of Philosophy* and the first edition of the *Penguin Dictionary of Philosophy*, do not mention any date prior to the advent of Russian nihilism in the 1850s and the popularization of the term by Ivan Turgenev (1818–1883) in his book *Fathers and Sons*, published in 1862.[47] The corresponding entry in the second edition of *The Penguin Dictionary of Philosophy* is updated to include the sentence: "Jacobi seems to have been the first to use the word in his 'Sendbrief' (open letter) to Fichte in 1799."[48] The online version of the *Encyclopedia Britannica*, meanwhile, states that: "The term is an old one, applied to certain heretics in the Middle Ages."[49] Which heretics and who applied it, it fails to reveal. The *Historisches Wörterbuch der Philosophie* (Historical Dictionary of Philosophy) is more forthcoming, mentioning nihilism's connection to the word *Nihilianismus*, which was used by Walter of St. Victor in the second half of the twelfth century to describe a heretical movement in Christology.[50] It traces the first use of the word nihilism, albeit in Latin, to Friedrich Lebrecht Götze's tractatus of 1733 entitled *De nonismo et nihilismo in theologia*.

As for the first appearance of nihilism in a work in Stirner's mother tongue, the *Digitales Wörterbuch der deutschen Sprache* (Digital Dictionary of the German Language) and German Wikipedia offer the earliest dates, namely c. 1786 and 1787, respectively, when the "pietistic Christian of mystical bent," Jacob Hermann Obereit (1725–1798), allegedly coined the term to describe "the methodologically necessary annihilation of a common global certainty," caused by Kant's "hypostatization of the subjective individual as a guarantor of knowledge."[51] Although care needs to

---

[45] See *The New Oxford Dictionary of English*, 1st ed. (2001), s.v. "nihilism." *Internet Encyclopedia of Philosophy*, "Nihilism," by Alan Pratt, accessed June 30, 2023, https://www.iep.utm.edu/nihilism/.

[46] See *Collins Online Dictionary*, s.v. "nihilism," accessed June 30, 2023, https://www.collinsdictionary.com/dictionary/english/nihilism.

[47] See *A Dictionary of Philosophy*, 2nd ed. (1984), s.v. "nihilism." *The Penguin Dictionary of Philosophy*, 1st ed. (1999), s.v. "nihilism."

[48] *The Penguin Dictionary of Philosophy*, 2nd ed. (2005), s.v. "nihilism."

[49] *Encyclopedia Britannica Online*, "Nihilism," by Adam Augustyn, accessed June 30, 2023, https://www.britannica.com/topic/nihilism.

[50] See *Historisches Wörterbuch der Philosophie*, "*Nihilismus*," by Wolfgang Müller-Lauter and Wilhelm Goerdt, accessed June 30, 2023, https://www.schwabeonline.ch/schwabe-xaveropp/elibrary/start.xav#__elibrary__%2F%2F*%5B%40attr_id%3D%27verw.nihilismus%27%5D__1524502191047.

[51] *Digitales Wörterbuch der deutschen Sprache*, s.v. "*Nihilismus*," accessed June 30, 2023, https://www.dwds.de/wb/Nihilismus. Wikipedia, s.v. "*Nihilismus*,"

be exercised with online sources, there is indeed a dramatic dialogue by Obereit of 1787 called *Der wiederkommende Lebensgeist* (The Returning Life Spirit), whose characters include *Nihilisme*, along with Metaphysics, Humanity, and Eternity. As the introduction proclaims, the book's objective is for the spirit of Cebes, the disciple of Socrates and archetypal seeker after truth and virtue, to illuminate and scrutinize the philosophical orientation of Kant, Moses Mendelssohn, Thomas Wizenmann, and Johann Georg Heinrich Feder, in other words of the leading contemporaneous Enlightenment thinkers.[52] It does this through the elucidatory debate between its abstract characters, in the course of which *Nihilisme* appears as the negative essence of transcendental idealism, born out of the subjectivist urge to supplant God with the noumenon, and thus ultimately representing everything that is not God: "For he is the only one there, all else is nothing, nothing without him, nothing before him."[53] The discourse wades into the ongoing pantheism or Spinoza controversy between Jacobi and Mendelssohn, attempting to devise a synthesis of current Enlightenment ideas with Obereit's own version of hermetic mysticism, and failing, in the process, to be either convincing or coherent.

It is perhaps not surprising that Obereit uses the French spelling of the word, as there is evidence of its existence in French as early as 1761 in Jean-Baptiste Louis Crevier's *Histoire de l'Université de Paris*, where *nihiliste* is used to mean a heretic who doubts Jesus Christ's existence as a man.[54] The first known use of the word in the German spelling, *Nihilismus*, was thirty-five years later in 1796, just ten years before Stirner's birth, when the Lutheran theologian Daniel Jenisch (1762–1804) employed it to discredit the subjectivist tendencies of German idealism, deploring the diminution of God's realm implicit in transcendental idealism, and the ramifications for the Christian promise of eternal life. Jenisch wrote indignantly: "The idea of the idealistic nihilism of human perception . . . is almost more horrifying to me than the idea of the eternal destruction of my own existence."[55] The next appearance of *Nihilismus* in the historical textual record comes in 1799, with Jacobi's open letter to Fichte, which, as with the examples of Obereit and Jenisch above, is the product of a religious thinker's reaction to the perceived dangers of Enlightenment thought. Just as Obereit's above-mentioned work develops out of the pantheism controversy, so Jacobi's letter is a response

---

accessed June 30, 2023, https://de.wikipedia.org/wiki/Nihilismus. The description of Obereit is from Garland and Garland, *The Oxford Companion to German Literature*, 647.

52 See Obereit, *Der wiederkommende Lebensgeist*, 3.
53 Obereit, *Der wiederkommende Lebensgeist*, 15.
54 See *Centre National de Ressources Textuelles et Lexicales*, s.v. "*Nihiliste*," accessed June 30, 2023, http://www.cnrtl.fr/definition/nihiliste.
55 Jenisch, *Ueber Grund und Werth*, 273.

to the atheism dispute, which revolved around Johann Gottlieb Fichte (1762–1814) and his refinement of Kantian metaphysics and ethics, above all in his magnum opus, *Grundlage der gesamten Wissenschaftslehre* (Foundations of the Entire Science of Knowledge, 1794/1795), where Kant's mind-independent thing-in-itself is rejected, leaving the I, or Ego, at least implicitly, as the sole, ultimate reality.

The specific catalyst for this dispute was a piece entitled "Ueber den Grund unseres Glaubens an eine göttliche Weltregierung" (On the Basis of our Belief in a Divine Governance of the World), published in December 1798, in which, despite the benign title, Fichte's views clearly reflect his subjectivism and pantheism bordering, theoretically at least, on solipsism and atheism. What Fichte identifies as the absolute being is simply the world itself, for, "to assert that an intellect is the creator of the sensible world . . . possesses not the least intelligibility."[56] Fichte's essay was a response to and defense of Friedrich Karl Forberg's article, "Entwicklung des Begriffs der Religion" (The Development of the Concept of Religion), which was published in the same edition and in which God seems to be portrayed as no more than a useful fiction for the encouragement of good moral behavior.[57] There followed the publication of an anonymous accusation of atheism against both authors, which led ultimately to Fichte being forced to resign his professorship at the University of Jena. Jacobi's response was to produce his open letter to Fichte in March 1799, in which he writes: "Truly, my dear Fichte, I should not be annoyed if you, or whoever else it may be, want to call chimerism that which I oppose to idealism, which I rebuke as nihilism."[58]

This oft-quoted sentence has frequently been cited as the birth of the word *Nihilismus* in German and, indeed, of nihilism in philosophy, but such a claim ignores the antecedent dispute, which had been running for more than a decade. As Wolfgang Müller-Lauter has observed: "Jacobi did not invent the word nihilism. Nor was he the first to make philosophical use of it."[59] Müller-Lauter goes on to suggest the term *Annihilation* as a possible influence on the genesis of the word *Nihilismus*, the use of which was not uncommon in the period prior to the latter's appearance (he cites F. Nicolai's 1798 polemic against Fichte as an example). Commenting on Müller-Lauter's assumptions, Susanna

---

56 Fichte, "On the Basis of our Belief," 145.
57 See Forberg, "Entwicklung des Begriffs der Religion," 21: "Religion is nothing other than a practical belief in a moral world government."
58 Jacobi, *Jacobi's Werke*, 3:44. Jacobi's comment is a direct response to Fichte's statement that "what is grounded in reason is purely and simply necessary, and what is not necessary is—precisely for this reason—contrary to reason. To hold something of this latter sort to be true is an illusion and a dream, no matter how pious the dream may be." Fichte, "On the Basis of our Belief," 144–45.
59 Müller-Lauter, "Nihilismus als Konsequenz des Idealismus," 113.

Kahlefeld advocates the idea put forward by H. Timm, that Jacobi discovered the word nihilism in the writings of Obereit and used it in a very similar way.[60] Regardless of other influences, this is almost certainly the case, as there was an inevitable cross-fertilization of ideas within the debate around German idealism. It is no surprise to find Obereit praising Jacobi in his book *Der wiederkommende Lebensgeist*, Jacobi having fired the opening salvo in the pantheism dispute by publishing *Ueber die Lehre des Spinoza in Briefen an den Herrn Moses Mendelssohn* (Concerning the Doctrine of Spinoza in Letters to Mr. Moses Mendelssohn) in 1785, in which he attacked Mendelssohn's (and Gotthold Ephraim Lessing's) support for Spinozism.[61] For Jacobi, Spinozism revealed the direct causal relationship between rationalism, materialism, and the inevitable end result of atheism, to which he offered with proselytizing zeal the antidote of faith and revelation, a solution that would have appealed to Obereit, and which seems to anticipate Thielicke's response to nihilism a century and a half later.

There has also been a suggestion that Jacobi came across the word *Nihilianismus* (in relation to the condemnation of the heretics Peter Lombard and Peter of Poitiers) in 1786 in a reference work by J. A. Cramer about medieval philosophy, which he was using for the second edition of his Spinoza letters.[62] Be that as it may—and Müller-Lauter is generally skeptical about the idea—it would probably only have reinforced in Jacobi's mind the importance of the term introduced to a German audience for the first time by Obereit.[63] It was a word that suited his purposes perfectly: it was derogatory, it was cautionary, and it illustrated the dichotomy between the lonely emptiness of Fichte's subjective I and the eternal plenitude of the Christian promise of the Kingdom of Heaven. He sums up the latter as follows: "Man has such a choice; this single one: nothingness or God. By choosing nothingness he makes himself God; that is, he makes a ghost into God; for it is impossible, if there is no God, that man and all that surrounds him should not be mere ghosts."[64] For Jacobi, nihilism represents the void that he imagines would be left by

---

60 See Kahlefeld, *Dialektik und Sprung in Jacobis Philosophie*, 108. Timm, "Die Bedeutung der Spinoza-Briefe für die Entwicklung der idealistischen Religionsphilosophie," 80.

61 See Obereit, *Der wiederkommende Lebensgeist*, 125–26: "So, the noble Jacobi was perfectly right, with all the men of God, that only through a divine life can one become aware of God, that divine life, God's image in man, living religion, are the only source of insight into truth and of love of goodness, as the only, best, and united form of humanity."

62 See Bonsiepen, *Der Begriff der Negativität*, 46. Also, Baum, *Vernunft und Erkenntnis*, 42.

63 See Müller-Lauter, "Nihilismus als Konsequenz des Idealismus," 114.

64 Jacobi, *Jacobi's Werke*, 3:49.

the absence of his particular interpretation of God. Although Fichte had his own concept of God as the embodiment of moral order and is thus unlikely to have considered himself an atheist, his position was clearly heretical in the eyes of Jacobi, thus making a term whose ultimate derivation could be traced back to a twelfth-century theological dispute all the more appropriate.

Georg Wilhelm Friedrich Hegel (1770–1831), who was the dominant philosopher of his—and Stirner's—time in Germany, made his contribution to the atheism dispute in one of his early works, in which he addresses, among other things, the issue of the ontological status of nothingness and uses the word *Nihilismus* in Jacobi's sense of the term in the process of undermining Jacobi's accusation against Fichte:

> We have already shown why Jacobi so violently abhors the nihilism he finds in Fichte's philosophy. As far as Fichte's system itself is concerned, nihilism is certainly implicit in pure thought as a task. . . . So the Ego is for ever and ever affected by a Non-Ego. This has to be the case because infinity, or thought, which is only one *relatum* in the antithesis, is to be posited as being *in itself*.[65]

Hegel's downplaying of nihilism, combined with his scathing attack on Jacobi, only served to prolong the debate. In the summer of 1802, Jacobi wrote three letters to his student and friend, Friedrich Köppen (1775–1858), in which he responded to Hegel's rebuke, as well as commenting on Schelling's identity philosophy.[66] These letters were to appear the following year as an appendix to Köppen's book, *Schellings Lehre oder das Ganze der Philosophie des absoluten Nichts* (Schelling's Teaching or the Complete Philosophy of Absolute Nothingness), in which he proceeds to transfer to Schelling Jacobi's denunciation of Fichte's philosophy as nihilism, using the following eccentric logic:

> Schelling's system is neither realism nor idealism, indeed the issue is meaningless: but for this reason, it is nihilism.
>
> Proof: if it were realism, it would have to begin with the predominance of objectivity; if it were idealism, with the predominance of subjectivity. . . . Now, everything arises as a plus, every something, ideal or real, through the predominance of the one or the other; so, the system begins only with the minus of something = nothing.[67]

---

65   Hegel, *Faith & Knowledge*, 168.
66   See Müller-Lauter, "Nihilismus als Konsequenz des Idealismus," 152. Friedrich Köppen is not to be confused with the Young Hegelian, Karl Friedrich Köppen (1808–1863).
67   Köppen, *Schellings Lehre*, 85.

In this first phase of the existence of *Nihilismus* as a term in German—which occurred in the two decades immediately preceding Stirner's birth in 1806 and revolved around the world of German idealism to which the Young Hegelians would later react—the word's usage was confined to a philosophical debate about the conflict between reason and faith, where nihilism denoted the nothingness that supposedly follows once solipsistic subjectivism has rendered the postulation of God unnecessary. In nearly all cases, with the sole exception of Hegel's, the word is used during this period as an extreme form of condemnation. From this highly specialized definition, a more wide-ranging concept would develop over time. The phase that followed in the checkered history of nihilism has the added significance for this study that it took place largely within Stirner's own lifetime.

The Evolution of Nihilism in Germany before Nietzsche

In 1804, just two years before Stirner was born, the concept of nihilism spilled over from the philosophical to the literary scene when Jean Paul (1743–1819), a friend and correspondent of Jacobi's, included in his book *Vorschule der Ästhetik* (School for Aesthetics) a section entitled "Poetische Nihilisten" (Poetic Nihilists). Adopting the terminology of his mentor, Jean Paul attacks the German Romantics, who were students and followers of Fichte, censuring them for their subjectivism, just as in *Clavis Fichtiana seu Leibgeberiana* (The Key to the Thought of Fichte or Leibgeber)—which was written in 1799, published in 1800, and dedicated to Jacobi—he condemns Fichte for his egoism. As Müller-Lauter observes: "Jacobi's understanding of Fichte's idealism as egoism that ends in nihilism impressed his contemporaries."[68] The introductory statement of "Poetische Nihilisten" declares: "It follows from the lawless, capricious spirit of the present age, which would egoistically annihilate the world and the universe in order to clear a free space for free *play* in the void, and which tears off the *bandage* of its wounds as a *bond*, that this age must speak scornfully of the imitation and study of nature."[69] The image of the wounds bandaged presumably by the consolations of religion, and the notion of these dressings being willfully and witlessly ripped off, demonstrate the extent of Jean Paul's opposition to the fashionable subjectivism of the *Frühromantik* (early Romanticism).

---

68   Müller-Lauter, "Nihilismus als Konsequenz des Idealismus," 142.
69   Jean Paul Richter, *School for Aesthetics*, 32.

The term *Nihilismus* (or *Nihilist*) is not, however, part of the vocabulary of the early Romantics.[70] This is hardly surprising as, up to this time, the word had generally only been used for polemical purposes as a means of condemning an opponent's philosophical position or point of view. In other words, it was exclusively employed by the accusers and not the accused. Carr's assertion that nihilism is not reflectively articulated may no longer be true today, but it certainly was at the turn of the nineteenth century.[71] Nonetheless, the connection between nihilism and the despair-ridden subjectivism of early Romanticism is self-evident, as numerous publications on the subject have asserted.[72] The (anti-)hero of Ludwig Tieck's epistolary novel *William Lovell* (1795), which appeared in the same year as Fichte's *Grundlage der gesamten Wissenschaftslehre*, has been called "the first real nihilist in German literature."[73] The book charts the descent of the young, eponymous, English gentleman and romantic dreamer from the harmony of family life and young love, through debauchery, seduction, and murder, to a self-willed dueling death. Comparing him to other Romantic heroes, Gillespie writes: "Lovell is particularly important, not merely because he is a more radical Romantic hero but because he becomes such a complete egoist, so utterly absorbed by the demonic potentialities of the I."[74] Lovell subjects the world as object, or not-I, to his own desire for freedom, with complete disregard for established moral or religious values, thereby leading himself into a tragic spiral of discovery and destruction. As Gillespie puts it: "In William Lovell, we see the birth of nihilism out of the spirit of a Romanticism that is decisively informed by the thought of Fichte."[75]

If William Lovell is the first nihilist in German literature, then *Nachtwachen des Bonaventura* (The Night Watches of Bonaventura), a satirical tale dated 1804 and reliably attributed to August Klingemann (1777–1831), is, according to Kohlschmidt and Vordtriede, a "nihilistic Gesamtkunstwerk," "whose entire content is ultimately nothingness and nihilistic despair."[76] *Nachtwachen* is an episodic novel narrated by the night watchman, Johannes Kreuzgang, foundling, outsider, poet, actor, and fool, who wanders the dark streets in the dead of night, calling

---

70   Kohlschmidt and Schenk both claim that Novalis uses the term *Nihilismus*, though neither cites a source. See Kohlschmidt, "Nihilismus der Romantik," 83 and Schenk, *The Mind of the European Romantics*, 49.

71   See Carr, *The Banalization of Nihilism*, 22.

72   See, e.g., Arendt, *Der "poetische Nihilismus" in der Romantik*. See also Ponomarev, *Der Nihilismus und seine Erfahrung in der Romantik*.

73   Vordtriede, "Das nihilistische Geburtstagskind," 210.

74   Gillespie, *Nihilism before Nietzsche*, 106.

75   Gillespie, *Nihilism before Nietzsche*, 109.

76   Kohlschmidt, "Nihilismus der Romantik," 94; Vordtriede, "Das nihilistische Geburtstagskind," 211.

out the intervals of the passage of time. In a series of stories, fragments, letters, fantasies, observations, and reflections divided into sixteen night watches, he parodies all conceivable aspects of human life including poetry, literature, love, marriage, the law, the state, religion generally, and Christianity specifically. Using irony as his chief weapon, he engages in a radical, systematic devaluation of all contemporary norms, resulting in self-conscious disorientation and despair: "Then I saw myself alone with me alone in the Nothing; only the late earth was still flickering far out in the distance, as an extinguishing spark—but it was only a thought of mine which was just ending."[77] The novel culminates in a devastating image of all-pervading nothingness, as Kreuzgang, on being shown his father's grave in the churchyard, opens the lid of the coffin and prises the praying hands apart, only for the body to disintegrate into ash. Kreuzgang exclaims: "I strew this handful of paternal dust into the air and it remains—Nothing! / On the grave beyond, the visionary is still standing and embracing Nothing! / And the echo in the charnel-house cries for the last time—*NOTHING!*"[78]

In ending *Nachtwachen* with the threefold repetition of the word nothing, Klingemann was mimicking the end of Jean Paul's *Clavis Fichtiana*, where the author contemplates ironically the implications of the subjectivist worldview: "I, so completely alone, nowhere a pulse, no life, nothing around me and without me nothing but nothing—. . . Thus I come from eternity, thus I go to eternity—And who hears the lamentation and knows me now? I. Who hears it and who knows me after eternity?—I."[79] The confrontation with nothingness is a central theme of German Romanticism and represents the source of its malady of the soul. Friedrich Hölderlin (1770–1843), for instance, has Hyperion write to Bellarmin: "Oh, you wretches . . . who, even as I, are so utterly in the clutch of the Nothing that governs us, so profoundly aware that we are born for nothing, that we love a nothing, believe in nothing, work ourselves to death for nothing only that little by little we may pass over into nothing."[80] It is clear where this skeptical insecurity originates; as an imaginary Hamlet writes in his correspondence with Ophelia in *Nachtwachen*: "for this time I am really mad—so very much does all reside in ourselves and outside of us there is nothing real; indeed, according to the newest school we do not know whether we are in fact standing on our feet or on our heads."[81]

Provoked, unsettled, and emboldened by Fichte's idealism, the German Romantics carried out a literary investigation of the charge of

---

77 Gillespie, ed., *Nachtwachen*, 213.
78 Gillespie, ed., *Nachtwachen*, 247.
79 Jean Paul Richter, *Clavis Fichtiana*, 1056.
80 Hölderlin, *Hyperion*, 57.
81 Gillespie, ed., *Nachtwachen*, 205–7.

nihilism (without actually mentioning the term) by plumbing the depths of a subjectivist worldview, where individual consciousness is left on its own to confront the internalized external realities of life and death without recourse to a savior of last resort. Kreuzgang dares to say: "Praise God there is a death, and afterwards no eternity!"[82] With characteristic boldness, the Romantics explored the ancient horror of nothingness as none had done previously in the history of Western thought. It should perhaps be mentioned in passing that, although Stirner is fond of name-dropping in *Der Einzige*, the German Romantics are noticeably absent, except for one oblique reference to Tieck and a disdainful characterization of Romantic writers as somnambulists and visionaries who defend belief in spirits and ghosts for fear of losing God.[83]

Dieter Arendt observes that nihilism is "the reverse side of idealism. Nihilism can only evolve where an ontological nothingness precedes it in the conceptual idea of the world."[84] By the beginning of the nineteenth century, it had become, according to Pöggeler, a fundamental concept in the discussion around German idealism, and was employed in this sense not only by Fichte and Hegel but also by Friedrich Wilhelm Joseph Schelling (1775–1854), Friedrich Schlegel (1772–1829), and Wilhelm Traugott Krug (1770–1842), Kant's successor in the chair of logic and metaphysics at Königsberg.[85] It continued to be used polemically by Catholic theological reactionaries and supporters of Jacobi, like Franz Berg (1753–1821), Professor of Ecclesiastical History in Würzburg, Cajetan Weiller (1761–1826), Professor of Philosophy and Pedagogy at the Lyzeum in Munich, and Jakob Salat (1766–1851), Professor of Philosophy in Landshut, culminating in the essays, speeches, and letters of Franz von Baader (1765–1841), in which he repeatedly questions the limits of human reason as a way of undermining the assertions of enlightened idealism, and offers the following as a felicitous description of nihilism: "the misuse of intelligence in a manner that is destructive to religion."[86]

On the Protestant side, the religious philosopher and professed theist Christian Hermann Weiße (1801–1866) used the term *Nihilismus* in his 1833 work *Die Idee der Gottheit* (The Idea of Deity) to describe Hegel's pantheistic idealism.[87] He goes on to extend this criticism to deism, by asserting that "deism, like pantheism, leads to nihilism: for it

---

82 Gillespie, ed., *Nachtwachen*, 215.
83 See *EO*, 230, 35; *EE*, 264, 44.
84 Arendt, "Die Überwindung des Nihilismus," 350.
85 See Pöggeler, "Hegel und die Anfänge der Nihilismus-Diskussion," 312–13.
86 Baader, "Über die Freiheit der Intelligenz," 288.
87 See Weiße, *Die Idee der Gottheit*, 225.

too establishes only an extra-temporal, metaphysical category of deity, but not the knowledge of a God who is real from eternity to eternity for all time."[88] As with all of the above examples, from Obereit onwards, the formula is essentially the same, connecting pantheism and Spinozism with idealism and subjectivism, which ultimately equates to atheism and ends in the nothingness of nihilism. It is this concept of nothingness, with all the fear and trembling it induces, which can be found at the heart of many of the accusations of nihilism leveled against Stirner.

The word *Nihilismus* also continued to appear and to evolve in the literature of the time. In Karl Leberecht Immermann's (1796–1840) *Die Epigonen* (The Epigones, 1836), a romantic satire on the decline of the nobility during the Biedermeier epoch, the word appears to be used in a way that comes closer to what would become known as existential nihilism. The protagonist, Hermann, is introduced to the reader as a world-weary cynic, who declares: "I have finished with life. . . . I wish for nothing, I ask for nothing."[89] We are subsequently informed that he considered himself "a precocious prophet of nihilism."[90] The gradual transition in the meaning of nihilism that is here in evidence was, to some extent, made possible by the fact that idealism had (in the main) had its day, the feud between philosophical idealism and theology had all but petered out, and the term nihilism as a specific denunciation of atheist subjectivism was thus becoming increasingly redundant.

What the history of the struggle had shown, however, was that there is more to nothingness than meets the eye (or the I, for that matter) and that nihilism, on both a philosophical and literary level, had started to establish its own identity and take on a life of its own. Its remit shifted from the narrow confines of a philosophico-theological debate to a wider sociopolitical sphere.[91] Thus, in the 1830s, the word *Nihilismus* was finally beginning to demonstrate an incipient universality that transcended the strict limits of its earlier usage. Rosenkranz's adoption of the

---

88   Weiße, *Die Idee der Gottheit*, 247.
89   Immermann, *Die Epigonen*, 5.
90   Immermann, *Die Epigonen*, 125.
91   The theological debate surrounding nihilism has not completely disappeared, as is evidenced by Hans Wiersma's 2012 article on the controversial 1979 film *Monty Python's Life of Brian*, where, following in the footsteps of the legendary Malcolm Muggeridge and Mervyn Stockwood, Wiersma concludes: "To proclaim from the cross—that sign of eternal hope for two billion Christians—that 'death's the final word' is a sort of *absconditus et revelatus sub contrario*: Nihilism hidden and revealed under its opposite. . . . Like it or not, you have to hand it to Monty Python for their collective stroke of genius, for crafting a last word to beat all last words. Or you can simply point out one final irony, namely, that as the chorus winds down, nihilism itself is crucified." Wiersma, "Redeeming *Life of Brian*," 176.

word to condemn Stirner in 1844 or 1845 is one of the last recorded uses of the term in something close to its original sense, insofar, at least, as he continues to employ it as a derogatory epithet, although the point of reference is now clearly starting to evolve beyond the framework of idealism. Two years earlier, in 1842, the Protestant theologian Johann Wilhelm Hanne (1813–1889) had published a book attacking the pantheistic nihilism of philosophy, from Spinoza, through Fichte, Schelling, and Hegel, and extending the lineage to Strauss, Feuerbach, and Bauer.[92] Such examples constitute a link between the original definition and the new one that was developing as a result of the enormous social changes associated with the *Vormärz* and the 1848 revolutions.

In literature, these changes were reflected in the group known as *Junges Deutschland* (Young Germany), a loose collection of young, politically progressive, secular writers, who deplored the apolitical introspection of German Romanticism and drew their ideological inspiration from the Young Hegelians. Of the authors associated with this group, the best known today are Heinrich Heine (1797–1856) and Georg Büchner (1813–1837). However, the main reason Heine is numbered among them is because he was included in the Frankfurt Bundestag's resolution banning publication of their works, while Büchner explicitly distanced himself from the movement, although he did consider Heine a member of the "literary party."[93] One undisputed member of the group was Karl Gutzkow (1811–1878), who was born into a poor family in Berlin, studied at the University of Berlin, attending Hegel's and Schleiermacher's lectures, and was profoundly influenced by Strauss's *Das Leben Jesu*. Gutzkow was undoubtedly familiar with Stirner, whose first article under his own name was published in Gutzkow's journal *Telegraph für Deutschland* (Telegraph for Germany) in 1842.[94]

Among Gutzkow's many literary and dramatic works is the novella *Die Nihilisten* (The Nihilists), published in serial form in 1853 and as a book in 1856. It is the story of a group of young radicals around the emancipated heroine, Hertha Wingolf. The tone is set in the first chapter, where she is seen to be studying Feuerbach's *Das Wesen des Christentums*.[95] The nihilists in question are her suitor, Constantin Ulrichs, and his bosom friend Jean Reps (originally Johann Repse, but renamed at university as a token of the overcoming of Jean Paul), who are designated nihilists because "nothing is proven to them, . . . nothing

---

92 See Hanne, *Der moderne Nihilismus*.
93 See Büchner, *Werke und Briefe*, 188.
94 See Mackay, *Max Stirner*, 93.
95 See Gutzkow, *Gesammelte Werke*, 3:152: "Feuerbach's *Essence of Christianity* cannot be read but only studied."

fixed."[96] But the term also reflects their failure to realize their revolutionary ideals (Ulrichs becomes a respected, well-to-do lawyer and Reps a textile manufacturer) and, as such, the book can be seen as an expression of disillusionment at the failure of the 1848 revolutions. What is significant, however, from a terminological point of view, is that by the middle of the nineteenth century the term *Nihilist* was sufficiently familiar in Germany to be used in the title of a novella and sufficiently nuanced to incorporate different aspects of moral skepticism and political radicalism.[97]

The word *Nihilismus* was not only becoming relatively common at this time but was also being used in various contexts. Joseph von Radowitz (1797–1853), a conservative Prussian statesman, employed the term in 1846 to describe the lax morals of contemporary society: "If . . . in politics as in life, the duties imposed by justice and honor are completely disregarded, even common sense fails to deter the insistence on nihilism."[98] In the same year, the popular novelist Berthold Auerbach (1812–1882) made a similar observation: "A modern trend is attempting repeatedly to spread atheistic despair among the people. . . . This modern nihilism is philosophically on a par with subjective Romanticism, against which it fought so hard; it has no sense of moderation or direction; it merely adheres to subjective pleasure, whose momentary desires are all supposed to be justified."[99]

In a letter of November 28, 1860, Feuerbach writes about how "Schopenhauer's quietism and nihilism had numerous followers, particularly among the young."[100] Another philosopher, Eduard von Hartmann (1842–1906), was also familiar with the term, using it in his *Philosophie des Unbewussten* (Philosophy of the Unconscious, 1869) in relation to mystics like Jakob Böhme: "We find among the largest number of mystics a turning away from active life, . . . even a striving after mental and bodily annihilation [*Nihilismus*]."[101] In the same year, a book was published by Max Müller (1823–1900) with the title *Ueber den Buddhistischen Nihilismus* (On Buddhist Nihilism). Victor Hugo (1802–1885), meanwhile, was still using the word as a condemnation of the rejection of transcendence,

---

96   Gutzkow, *Gesammelte Werke*, 3:252.

97   The term was also spreading to other countries. The Scottish metaphysician Sir William Hamilton (1788–1856), who visited Germany in 1817 and 1820 and was influenced by the philosophy of Kant, wrote in his *Lectures on Metaphysics*: "This doctrine [that all our knowledge of mind or matter, is only a consciousness of various bundles of baseless appearances], as refusing a substantial reality to the phaenomenal [*sic*] existence of which we are conscious, is called Nihilism." Hamilton, *Lectures on Metaphysics and Logic*, 294.

98   Radowitz, *Gespräche*, 328.

99   Auerbach, *Schrift und Volk*, 304.

100 Feuerbach, *Gesammelte Werke*, 20:314.

101 Hartmann, *Philosophy of the Unconscious*, 1:354.

declaring that "denial of the infinite leads directly to nihilism."[102] Hugo endows the word with the anti-subjectivist overtones of Jacobi's denunciation of Fichte, combined with the heavy irony of *Nachtwachen*: "With nihilism no discussion is possible. For the logical nihilist doubts the existence of his interlocutor, and is not quite sure he exists himself."[103] At the same time, by way, apparently, of logical proof of his opinion, he repeats the thoroughly discredited Pythagorean-Aristotelian denial of the existence of zero: "Nihilism has no scope. There is no nothing. Zero does not exist. Everything is something. Nothing is nothing."[104]

By the middle of the nineteenth century, use of the term nihilism was becoming more and more widespread, with an ever-increasing diversity of meanings. Despite this, as noted above, neither the word *Nihilismus* nor any of its derivatives appears in Stirner's published works; nihilism's growing prominence does not seem to have made much of an impression on Stirner. It is nonetheless conceivable that the fact that he lived during a time when nihilism was a developing issue of intellectual interest and died shortly before its dramatic popularization (which is the next topic to be addressed) may have had some influence on the opinions of his readers and critics.

Nihilism's Transformation in the Latter Half of the Nineteenth Century

The decisive developments in the etymology of nihilism occurred after Stirner's death in 1856. The first of these came about with the publication of Turgenev's *Fathers and Sons* in 1862, which, for the first time, introduced the word nihilist to a mass audience. In his postscript to the 1869 edition, Turgenev even claimed to have invented the word, despite its increasing prevalence prior to that in Germany, where Turgenev had lived from 1838 to 1841 while studying in Berlin (where he became acquainted with the Young Hegelians, including Bruno Bauer and Stirner) and from 1863 to 1870 in Baden-Baden. His claim is especially remarkable, not to say disingenuous, as, according to Tomáš Masaryk, the word nihilism had been used previously in Russia as well, apparently since at least 1829. This leads Masaryk to conclude: "Accusations of nihilism were rife at this time, Turgenev thus discovered not only the new character type for his novel, but also its name."[105]

---

102 Hugo, *Les Miserables*, 438.
103 Hugo, *Les Miserables*, 438–39.
104 Hugo, *Les Miserables*, 439.
105 Masaryk, *Zur russischen Geschichts- und Religionsphilosophie*, 2:93. My translation, as the existing English translation by Eden and Cedar Paul mistranslates this line.

What Turgenev undeniably did do, however, was popularize the word, which had till then been largely confined to a specific philosophical debate and to literature of limited readership, as well as give it a clear and elaborate definition. Arkady, in *Fathers and Sons*, explains: "A nihilist is a person who does not take any principle for granted, however much that principle may be revered."[106] He does not "recognize any authorities," repudiates everything, and is interested only in destruction because "the ground must be cleared first."[107] Turgenev's personification of nihilism is, tellingly, a man of science, a medical student named Bazarov. He is arrogant, aggressive, argumentative, and disrespectful to his elders, and yet, paradoxically, it is he who commands the reader's deepest sympathy. If Turgenev's remarks about his (anti-)hero are to be believed, this is completely intentional. He called Bazarov his "beloved child" and said "that he shared almost all Bazarov's views, all save those on art." He declared to a group of radical Russian students in Heidelberg that "if the reader does not love Bazarov, as he is—coarse, heartless, ruthlessly dry and brusque—... the fault is mine; I have not succeeded in my task." He also "told the anarchist, Kropotkin, that he loved Bazarov 'very, very much, ... I will show you my diaries—you will see how I wept when I ended the book with Bazarov's death.'"[108] It is hard to deny that Turgenev did succeed in his task, giving the word nihilism its first truly, if by no means exclusively, positive slant in the process.

Perhaps the main reason why Bazarov elicits sympathy is because he confronts directly and without compromise the core problems of modern, post-religious man. The first of these is the fundamental meaninglessness of existence that is implied by a relativistic outlook:

> The tiny bit of space I occupy is so minute in comparison with the rest of the universe, where I am not and which is not concerned with me; and the period of time in which it is my lot to live is so infinitesimal compared with the eternity in which I have not been and shall not be ... And yet here, in this atom which is myself, in this mathematical point, blood circulates, the brain operates and aspires to something too ... What a monstrous business! What futility![109]

---

106 Turgenev, *Fathers and Sons*, 94.
107 Turgenev, *Fathers and Sons*, 123, 124.
108 Berlin, "Fathers and Children," 38–39.
109 Turgenev, *Fathers and Sons*, 208. A similar sentiment can be found in Levin's statement to Oblonsky, brother of the title character in *Anna Karenina*: "This whole world of ours is only a speck of mildew sprung up on a tiny planet; yet we think we can have something great—thoughts, actions! They are all but grains of sand! / If you once realize that to-morrow, if not to-day, you will die and nothing will be left of you, everything becomes insignificant!" Tolstoy, *Anna Karenina*, 375.

The second human problem Bazarov tackles is the illusory nature of love as a product of human imagination and fantasy. He says to Anna Sergeyevna, the object of his unrequited affection: "And besides, love . . . is a purely imaginary feeling."[110] And the third, and most devastating, problem he addresses is the finality of personal extinction:

> "Farewell," he said with sudden force, and his eyes flashed a last gleam. "Farewell. . . . Listen. . . . You know, I never kissed you then. . . . Breathe on the dying flame and let it go out . . ."
> Anna Sergeyevna touched his forehead with her lips.
> "Enough!" he murmured, and sank back on the pillow. "Now . . . darkness . . ."
> Anna Sergeyevna went softly out of the room.
> "Well?" Vassily Ivanych asked her in a whisper.
> "He has fallen asleep," she replied, almost inaudibly.
> Bazarov was not destined to wake again.[111]

This simple dialogue is a supreme example of understated pathos, a demonstration of Turgenev's mastery of his art, and a challenge to the reader's stoic fortitude. Life, love, and death: this is the new matrix within which the word nihilism would now operate.

Turgenev not only gave the term a far wider audience than ever before, both in and beyond Russia, but he also effectively christened the radical political movements of the time in his homeland, insofar as Dmitry Pisarev (1840–1868) assimilated and adopted the epithet nihilist after having read *Fathers and Sons*, and it was extended by association to his rival Nikolay Chernyshevsky (1828–1889) despite the latter's vehement protestations.[112] Pisarev and Chernyshevsky were the ideological leaders of the two branches of Russian nihilism in the late 1850s and 1860s, each faction having its own mouthpiece in the periodicals *Russkoe Slovo* (Russian Word) and *Sovremennik* (The Contemporary), respectively. What they both had in common was atheism, materialism, positivism, scientism, and the demand for social change. They differed, however, in their vision of the latter: Chernyshevsky was a utopian socialist who advocated revolution for the purposes of the democratization and westernization of Russia, while Pisarev was an uncompromising extremist, taking social utilitarianism so far that he infamously justified matricide. While it is impossible to prove a direct link between Stirner and either Pisarev or

---

110 Turgenev, *Fathers and Sons*, 262.
111 Turgenev, *Fathers and Sons*, 289.
112 See Slocombe, *Nihilism*, 13.

Chernyshevsky, the distinct phenomenon of Russian nihilism is relevant to this study, firstly because there is some evidence of Stirner's influence on its forefathers, and secondly because Stirner has been accused of similar tendencies to those of the Russian nihilists. These issues will be discussed in more detail in chapter 5 below.

Once nihilism had been identified—thanks to Turgenev—with subversive political movements in Russia, the term was handed on, again by association, to the next generation of radicals, most notably to Sergey Gennadiyevich Nechaev (1847–1882), the author of the infamous "Revolutionary Catechism" written in 1869, which opens with the chilling words:

> 1. The revolutionary is a doomed man. He has no personal interests, no business affairs, no emotions, no attachments, no property, and no name. Everything in him is wholly absorbed in the single thought and the single passion for revolution.
>
> 2. The revolutionary knows that in the very depths of his being . . . he has broken all the bonds which tie him to the social order and the civilized world with all its laws, moralities, and customs, and with all its generally accepted conventions. He is their implacable enemy, and if he continues to live with them it is only in order to destroy them more speedily.[113]

For Nechaev, the Machiavelli of Russian nihilism, the end always justified the means. Three months after completing the "Catechism" he carried out, with the help of his comrades, the brutal murder of the student Ivan Ivanov, a dissenting former member of his revolutionary group Narodnaya Rasprava (People's Retribution).[114] The profoundly religious Dostoevsky was deeply disturbed by the political climate in Russia, and the murder of Ivanov was a powerful inspiration for one of his great anti-nihilist novels, *Demons* (1871–72). Ivanov is the model for the character Ivan Pavlovich Shatov, who is assassinated by Pyotr Stepanovich Verkhovensky, the villain of the piece, modeled on Nechaev. Unlike in *Fathers and Sons*, what sympathy there is is for the victim, Shatov, although he is little more than a pathetic effigy of reborn innocence whose role, it seems, is largely to

---

113 Sergey Gennadiyevich Nechaev, "The Revolutionary Catechism," *Marxists Internet Archive*, accessed June 30, 2023, https://www.marxists.org/subject/anarchism/nechayev/catechism.htm. Even Bakunin, the father of collectivist anarchism, who collaborated with Nechaev on the "Catechism," felt compelled to condemn Nechaev's extremism. See Confino, ed., *Daughter of a Revolutionary*, 244, 277.

114 See Hingley, *Nihilists*, 58–59.

contrast, offset, and exaggerate the malignant depravity of the nihilists, his murderers.[115]

Fyodor Dostoevsky (1821–1881) and his fellow anti-nihilist authors, Nikolai Leskov (1831–1895) and Aleksey Pisemsky (1821–1881), but also Turgenev and Leo Tolstoy (1828–1910), helped, each in his own different way, to immortalize Russian nihilism as a radical political movement related to anarchism and terrorism, bent on the violent destruction of all forms of authority. The association with terrorism was fed by events on the ground. In 1866 there had been an unsuccessful assassination attempt on Tsar Alexander II by Dmitry Karakozov. A decade later a whole series of political shootings and stabbings of military, police, and government officials took place, including Vera Zasulich's attempt on the life of Colonel Trepov, which was the inspiration behind Oscar Wilde's first play, *Vera; or, the Nihilists* (1880). Meanwhile, the unsuccessful attempts on the Tsar's life had continued; there were five in total—in 1866, 1867, twice in 1879, and 1880—culminating in his assassination by a bomb in 1881, which was carried out by a group called Narodnaya Volya (People's Will). In the aftermath, the nihilist movement in Russia was brutally suppressed by the imperial authorities, at the head of which was the autocratic new Tsar, Alexander III, who had witnessed first-hand the gruesome death of his father.

Russian nihilism never recovered. However much its successor might have owed to it, it was entirely superseded in the sociopolitical arena by the more potent and constructive force of revolutionary communism. Nihilophiles need not have worried, though. Back in Western Europe, the birthplace of nihilism, the germination of its greatest redefinition and reevaluation was already underway, which would cement forever nihilism's place in the history of ideas and create a version of the word which corresponds to many of the most entrenched opinions about Stirner's nihilism. Nietzsche first mentions *Nihilisten* in his writings in the summer of 1880: "The consolation of Luther, when matters didn't move forward, 'the end of the world.' The nihilists had Schopenhauer as a philosopher. All of the extremely active ones want to let the world go to pieces, once they realize their will is impossible (Wotan)."[116] By Nietzsche's standards, this is a relatively innocuous start to his treatment of a word which would become so fundamental to his philosophy. The next appearance

---

115 Dostoevsky's abhorrence of nihilism is also evident in his satirical caricature of Turgenev in *Demons* as the flamboyant Karmazinov, who is ridiculed for his support for and legitimation of nihilism. See Dostoevsky, *Demons*, 236: "The great writer was mortally afraid of the rising generation of young revolutionaries, and . . . sucked up to them shamelessly, mainly because they paid absolutely no attention to him."

116 Nietzsche, *Werke*, 5.1:455.

comes just five fragments later, this time specifying the type of nihilism to which he is referring: "Nowadays, one generally answers the question of whether Russian nihilists are more immoral than Russian officials, in favor of the nihilists."[117] The word *Nihilismus* follows soon afterwards in a letter of March 13, 1881, to Heinrich Köselitz (pseudonym for Peter Gast, 1854–1918): "I need all types of health—it has gone a little too deep into my heart, this 'heartbreaking nihilism.'"[118]

From these unremarkable beginnings emerged a concept which has played a major role in the philosophy and literature of the twentieth century and beyond. Six and a half years later, Nietzsche was writing in apocalyptic style: "What I relate is the history of the next two centuries. I describe what is coming, what is inevitable: *the rise of nihilism.*"[119] In an earlier fragment, he offers a definition of the phenomenon which he predicts will convulse humanity: "*Nihilism*: there is no goal, no answer to the question: why? What is the significance of nihilism?—*that the highest values devalue themselves.*"[120] The result of this upheaval in people's minds is the conviction that "all that happens is gratuitous and meaningless."[121] Here, finally, is nihilism in a form that is instantly recognizable today; no longer is it just a term of critical rebuke or a simple embodiment of the negativity that the word implies.

While Turgenev may have been responsible for the initial popularization of the term nihilism, the most significant turning point in its etymological development is to be found in Nietzsche's formulation of a sophisticated and elaborate concept based on the prophecy of a growing spiritual malaise at the heart of Western civilization. Thus, the word changed in the course of the nineteenth century from being a two-dimensional, exclusively negative label, whose meaning depended wholly on its specific reference, to a potentially positive (or at least not necessarily negative), three-dimensional, free-standing conceptualization of a pervasive sociocultural phenomenon. Having started as little more than a

---

117 Nietzsche, *Werke*, 5.1:457–58. Alexander Herzen and Mikhail Bakunin are mentioned in Nietzsche's letters and fragments starting from 1872 and 1873, respectively. See Nietzsche, *Briefwechsel*, 2.3:41 (Herzen); *Werke*, 3.4:182 (Bakunin). He does not refer to Turgenev, Dostoevsky, or Tolstoy in his published works and/or fragments and/or letters until early 1887. See Nietzsche, *Briefwechsel*, 3.5:21 (Dostoevsky); *Werke*, 8.2:73 (Tolstoy); *Briefwechsel*, 3.5:92 (Turgenev).

118 Nietzsche, *Briefwechsel*, 3.1:68. Nietzsche's comment is a response to Köselitz's letter of March 10, in which he comments "that in a letter to Wagner, Schuré described your current opinions as 'heartbreaking nihilism.'" *Briefwechsel*, 3.2:144.

119 Nietzsche, *The Will to Power*, 7.
120 Nietzsche, *The Will to Power*, 15.
121 Nietzsche, *The Will to Power*, 30.

polemical device, albeit one of utterly judgmental condemnation, it developed into a complex and commonly used concept, focused above all on the profound crisis caused by the erosion and collapse of religious certainty concerning absolute truth and personal immortality, itself precipitated by advances in science and reason.

Nihilism in this new sense is essentially the result of the head-on clash of enlightened human consciousness with the apparent fact of its own ephemerality; and, as such, "the danger of nihilism," as Rosen points out, "is a permanent human possibility."[122] Such a definition, which can engender an overwhelming denial of meaning and purpose, has the potential to remain actual for as long as man has critical self-awareness and dies, unless a believable myth is created that can defuse the crisis by making immortality credible or oblivion attractive. Rosen is more pessimistic: he declares that nihilism "cannot be 'solved' without the dissolution of human nature."[123] Certainly it is an intractable problem, which, if secularization theory is correct, is likely to become worse as the sophistication of human thought grows in inverse proportion to human credulity.[124]

One of the principal aims of this study is to ascertain how and where Stirner fits into this bleak picture. Indeed, the Nietzschean definition of nihilism plays such a key part in this investigation, especially because of the frequent association of Stirner with Nietzsche, that the next chapter will be dedicated to dissecting its multiple layers of meaning, tracing its development since Nietzsche's death, and considering what connections it may or may not have with Stirner's philosophy. This will also afford the opportunity to examine the relationship between these two nineteenth-century German philosophers, whose lives and ideas both overlap and contrast with one another.

---

122 Rosen, *Nihilism*, xiv.
123 Rosen, *Nihilism*, xx.
124 For information on secularization theory, see Bruce, *God is Dead*.

CHAPTER 3

The Tragic Age for Europe: Nihilism from Nietzsche to Now

Nietzsche's Uncanny Guest

IN ORDER TO UNDERSTAND the relevance of nihilism to Stirner's thought, there is no more important definition of the term than the one fashioned by Friedrich Nietzsche (1844–1900) in the course of his last nine years of lucidity, from 1880 to 1889. In the nearly two and a half centuries of nihilism's semantic evolution up to the present day, Nietzsche plays the pivotal role; the concept of nihilism that bears his name has colored, to a greater or lesser degree, all but the first fifty years of the discussion around Stirner and nihilism. Nietzsche took a word that had recently undergone rapid development, both in its prevalence and complexity, and transformed it into a radical new concept that encapsulated the crisis of Western modernity. Ever since, the common perception of nihilism has been based to a large extent on Nietzsche's diagnosis, not least because of the extraordinary influence he has had on subsequent generations of thinkers, artists, and writers.[1] As Gillespie says: "When it comes to our understanding of nihilism, we are almost all Nietzscheans."[2]

It is, in a sense, Stirner's misfortune to have been so closely linked to Nietzsche at the time of the decisive, so-called first Stirner renaissance, which was largely brought about by the coincidence of three events: firstly, Hartmann's attack on Nietzsche in 1891 (discussed in more detail below), in which he employed Stirner as a weapon; secondly, the publication of Lauterbach's new edition of *Der Einzige* in 1893 in Reclam's low-priced, high-circulation *Universal-Bibliothek*, where he compares the two philosophers in his short introduction; and, thirdly, Nietzsche's meteoric rise to fame in the last decade of the nineteenth century, which

---

1 See Stern, *A Study of Nietzsche*, x. Stern lists Rilke, Yeats, Valéry, H. G. Wells, D. H. Lawrence, Thomas Mann, George Bernard Shaw, and Gottfried Benn among those influenced by Nietzsche, although the full list is of course considerably longer (and constantly growing).

2 Gillespie, *Nihilism before Nietzsche*, xii.

inadvertently shone a light on Stirner.[3] One of the abiding outcomes of this concurrence is the assumption that Nietzsche's thought and Stirner's share characteristics and concerns, including those relating to nihilism, a belief that is reinforced by apparent similarities in their writings.

The question that arises from this supposed association is not simply whether there is a fundamental similarity between Nietzschean nihilism and Stirner's thought, but whether such an affinity derives from Nietzsche having known Stirner's writings, and then used, or even plagiarized, them as a component in or an inspiration for his description of the sinister cultural condition that he believed to be engulfing European civilization. While dissecting Nietzsche's definition serves to illuminate the question of whether Stirner's thought can be viewed as nihilistic in a Nietzschean sense, evidence of Stirner's direct influence on and contribution to the genesis of Nietzschean nihilism—which is an idea put forward most emphatically by Laska—would make it hard, if not impossible, to deny the charge that Stirner is a nihilist according to Nietzsche's definition, or, at least, that his thought possesses some (proto-)nihilistic elements.[4]

Before addressing this issue, however, it is necessary to determine the full meaning of Nietzschean nihilism, an undertaking which is not as straightforward as it might seem, owing both to the complexity of his ideas on the subject and how those ideas are presented. Nietzsche writes in a distinct "hybrid mode" of language that Stern calls "literary-philosophical" and which is replete with metaphor.[5] Thus, nihilism is famously introduced to the reader in the dramatic opening line of the expanded 1906 edition of *Der Wille zur Macht* (The Will to Power, 1901/1906) as a mysterious and shadowy figure: "Nihilism stands at the door; whence comes this most uncanny of all guests?"[6] Although *Der Wille zur Macht* is a largely discredited and often derided attempt by Nietzsche's sister and her philological henchmen in the Nietzsche Archive on the *Lügenhügel* (hill of lies) to produce, or fabricate, a systematic philosophical magnum opus by disingenuous and unscholarly means based only loosely on Nietzsche's own abandoned plans, the book's popularity since publication is undeniable.[7] Indeed, as far as nihilism is concerned, it is Nietzsche's most important work, even if he never envisaged it in such

3   See Mackay, *Max Stirner*, 10.
4   See Laska, "Nietzsches initiale Krise," 109–33.
5   See Stern, "Nietzsche and the Idea of Metaphor," 64–82.
6   Nietzsche, *The Will to Power*, 11.
7   *Lügenhügel* was Köselitz's nickname for the Nietzsche Archive. See Hoffmann, ed., *Franz Overbeck, Heinrich Köselitz: Briefwechsel*, 771. Concerning the popularity of *Der Wille zur Macht*, Heidegger even went as far as to say: "[Nietzsche's] philosophy proper was left behind as posthumous, unpublished work." Heidegger, *Nietzsche*, 1:9.

a form; it has been described by one commentator as "the most influential book never to have been written."[8] What is significant for the purposes of this study is not the credibility of this posthumous collection of notes as a publication, but how effectively it has propagated the haunting image of nihilism as a sinister, uninvited guest.

Concerning the reason for nihilism's appearance, in a fragment from the "Lenzer Heide" text (also included in *Der Wille zur Macht*), Nietzsche ties it inextricably to "that lurid metaphor," as Stern calls it, the death of God:[9] "Thus the belief that nature is utterly immoral, that everything is purposeless and meaningless, is a psychologically inevitable sentiment, when belief in God and in an essentially moral world order is no longer tenable. Nihilism appears at this point."[10] Nietzsche's best-known account of God's demise, once again expressed in figurative language, is his parable of the madman (*Der tolle Mensch*) in section 125 of *Die fröhliche Wissenschaft* (The Gay Science, 1882), in which the madman, like Diogenes the Cynic, wanders around the marketplace in broad daylight with a lamp, searching in vain not, as Diogenes had, for a man (or an honest man in later interpretations), but for God, before revealing to the bystanders: "*We have killed him.* . . . All of us are his murderers."[11] He then proceeds to outline the consequences of this act of deicide in a crescendo of increasingly terrifying questions:

> Whither are we moving? Away from all suns? Are we not plunging continually? . . . Is there still any up or down? Are we not straying as through an infinite nothing? Do we not feel the breath of empty space? Has it not become colder? Is not night continually closing in on us? . . . Do we hear nothing as yet of the noise of the gravediggers who are burying God? Do we smell nothing as yet of the divine decomposition? Gods too decompose. God is dead. God remains dead. And we have killed him. . . . Is not the greatness of this deed too great for us? Must we ourselves not become gods simply to appear worthy of it?[12]

This powerful parable is one of the most frequently cited passages from Nietzsche's oeuvre, though not, as its notoriety might lead one to believe, because it is the first historical appearance of the distinct idea of the death of God (as opposed to the simple fact of God's non-existence). This honor should arguably be bestowed more correctly on Hegel, although Hegel uses the concept to refer to the crucifixion as part of the

---

8   Schaefer, *Im Namen Nietzsches*, 188.
9   Stern, *A Study of Nietzsche*, 53.
10 Nietzsche, *The Will to Power*, 43.
11 Nietzsche, *The Gay Science*, 181.
12 Nietzsche, *The Gay Science*, 181.

dialectical process resulting in the emergence of God's complete revelation as Absolute Spirit.[13] Hegel's is, in other words, a quite different concept to the finality of Nietzsche's pronouncement.

A generation after Hegel, Stirner—who, unlike Hegel, was a self-confessed and uncompromising atheist—employed the image of man's murder of God to describe the transformation of Christian morality into secular humanism, initiated by Feuerbach's anthropologization of theology. Like Nietzsche after him, Stirner remarks on man's inclination not only to kill but also to supplant God: "They did not notice that man has killed God in order to become now—'*sole* God on high.'"[14] Those who have asserted that Nietzsche plagiarized Stirner have made much of the similarity between their depictions of deicide, but Stirner is far from being Nietzsche's only possible source for the idea, if, indeed, a source were needed. In the generation after Stirner, the notion of the death of God resurfaced in the philosophy of the radical, anti-natalistic pessimism of Philipp Mainländer (1841–1876), a writer whom Nietzsche had certainly read, and whom he disdainfully describes as "that mawkish apostle of virginity."[15] In his 1876 magnum opus, Mainländer writes of the death of God as a welcome liberation: "God has died and his death was the life of the world."[16]

However, Nietzsche makes no claim to originality regarding the postulation of the death of God. In 1882, neither the concept of atheism itself nor its metaphorical vehicle in the image of the death of God was a novel idea. Nietzsche's point in the parable of the madman is not to make a radically new revelation concerning God's absence but rather to highlight man's failure to appreciate and understand the nihilistic consequences of what Nietzsche considered to be the foregone conclusion of God's demise as a result of the processes put into motion by the

---

13 See Hegel, *Faith and Knowledge*, 190: "But the pure concept or infinity as the abyss of nothingness in which all being is engulfed, must signify the infinite grief [of the finite] purely as a moment of the supreme Idea. . . . Formerly, the infinite grief only existed historically in the formative process of culture. It existed as the feeling that 'God Himself is dead,' upon which the religion of more recent times rests."

14 *EO*, 139; *EE*, 162: "man hat nicht gemerkt, dass der Mensch den Gott getötet hat, um nun—'alleiniger Gott in der Höhe' zu werden."

15 Nietzsche, *The Gay Science*, 309.

16 Mainländer, *Die Philosophie der Erlösung*, 108. Stern considers Schopenhauer's phrase, "religion is almost entirely dead," and Heine's, "it is the old Jehovah himself preparing for death . . . they are bringing the sacraments to a dying God," as the antecedents of Nietzsche's "God is dead." Stern, *A Study of Nietzsche*, 144.

Enlightenment.[17] The deeper significance of this passage is therefore to be found in the series of questions that are posed, which paint a picture of a dark, cooling, sunless world without a horizon, where the seas have dried up and the air reeks of atrophy and decay. Even more terrifying, perhaps, is the Lovecraftian vision of this world traveling through the empty space of infinite nothing.[18]

Nietzsche's madman nonetheless strikes a note of optimism by exclaiming with reference to God's murder: "There has never been a greater deed; and whoever is born after us—for the sake of this deed he will belong to a higher history than all history hitherto."[19] The death of God is thus depicted as a catastrophe but also as an opportunity and a historical necessity, analogous to the destructive clean break advocated by the Russian nihilists; but immediately after conveying the good news, the madman announces dejectedly that his time has not yet come, and that God's murderers—i.e., the unbelievers of secular society—are not able to comprehend the true import of their new, godless world. In another passage in the same work, Nietzsche offers an alternative version, or perhaps the prototype, of the later image of the uncanny guest standing at the door:

> The greatest recent event—that "God is dead," that the belief in the Christian god has become unbelievable—is already beginning to cast its first shadows over Europe. . . . The event itself is far too great, too distant, too remote from the multitude's capacity for comprehension even for the tidings of it to be thought of as having *arrived* as yet. Much less may one suppose that many people know as yet *what* this event really means.[20]

What lies ahead for humanity, which he later defines as the history of the next two centuries, is "this long plenitude and sequence of breakdown, destruction, ruin, and cataclysm."[21] Having endowed this incipient period in the development of man with a cause, an essence, and a

---

17   In *Menschliches Allzumenschliches* 1 (Human, All Too Human, 1878), Nietzsche had already given the nonmetaphorical explanation: "the growth of the Enlightenment undermined the dogmas of religion and inspired a fundamental distrust of them." Nietzsche, *Human, All Too Human*, 81.

18   See Tongeren, *Friedrich Nietzsche*, 134–35: "Should we not start by recognizing that the text doesn't so much want to tell us that God is dead, or that this would be shocking when taken on its own; doesn't it instead seek to tell us something about humankind rather than God?"

19   Nietzsche, *The Gay Science*, 181.
20   Nietzsche, *The Gay Science*, 279.
21   Nietzsche, *The Gay Science*, 279. See Nietzsche, *The Will to Power*, 7.

duration, he also gives it a name: "The tragic age for Europe: caused by the struggle with nihilism."[22]

It would be a mistake, however, to regard Nietzsche's concept of nihilism as no more than a characterization of the upheaval associated with society's transition from belief to unbelief. The "versatility and liveliness of his philosophical imagination," as Stern describes it, is such that Nietzsche weaves an intricate web of meanings around the term, which, in its totality, represents his vision of the spiritual crisis of modernity.[23] As Edith Düsing writes: "Nietzsche's nihilism complex is multi-dimensional. Nietzsche argues in sometimes muddled lines of thought as a diagnostician, a secular prophet, a cultural critic, a therapist of senselessness, and a biopsychological strategist."[24] He appropriates and assimilates the word nihilism, develops and extends its realm, and endows it with a multitude of associations and connotations, taking full advantage of its nonspecific malleability, to create a concept of protean complexity. Goudsblom sums up the elusiveness of Nietzsche's definition as follows: "In the 1880s Nietzsche bestowed a pregnant new significance on the word nihilism. The concept is central to his philosophy, but the meaning he attaches to it is difficult to capture in a single definition; it changes according to the context in which he uses it."[25] It is, metaphorically speaking, this shadowy monster of nihilism that has succeeded in capturing the collective Western imagination and against which the thought of Stirner is to be measured.

Features of Nietzsche's Nihilism

There have been many studies of the typology of Nietzschean nihilism, which examine the different usages of the term, their relationships to one another, the periods of Nietzsche's productive life in which they appear, and the interconnected phases of nihilism they reveal.[26] Goudsblom identifies six pairs of opposite meanings: as a divine way of thinking versus an expression of decadence; as a characteristic of morality versus morality as an antidote to nihilism; as strength versus weakness; as complete versus

---

22 Nietzsche, *Werke*, 8.1:314.
23 Stern, *A Study of Nietzsche*, 126.
24 Düsing, "Gottestod-Nihilismus-Melancholie," 48–49.
25 Goudsblom, *Nihilism and Culture*, 10.
26 Concerning the phases of nihilism, Tongeren writes: "Nietzsche can be said to distinguish four phases or stages of nihilism. . . . Nihilism is (4) the conscious experience of an antagonism, that is the result of (3) the decline of (2) the protective structure that was built to hide (1) the absurdity of life and world." Tongeren, *Friedrich Nietzsche*, 100.

incomplete; as active versus passive; and as theoretical versus practical.[27] Carr paints a similarly heterogeneous picture: "Nihilism [in Nietzsche] is described as a historical process, a psychological state, a philosophical position, a cultural condition, a sign of weakness, a sign of strength, as the danger of dangers, and as a divine way of thinking."[28] She concludes that the only certainty is its ambiguity. This ambiguity, however, is to some extent the natural product of the word's semantic vagueness. Nietzsche exploits its potential for wide applicability, bestowing on it a universality that is a key feature of its modern usage. The fact remains, though, that Nietzschean nihilism cannot be viewed as a singularity, but rather as a complex of interrelated ideas.

For Nietzsche, perhaps the most important differentiation to be made within the amorphous intricacy of nihilism is between its active and passive forms:

> It [nihilism] can *mean two different things:*
> (a) Nihilism as a sign of an increase in mental power, as *active nihilism* . . .
> (b) Nihilism as a decline and retrogression of mental power: *passive nihilism.*[29]

Even though he does not see nihilism as an end in itself, active nihilism, while it is a manifestation of destructive strength, is also a cleansing force capable of questioning, rejecting, and eliminating ancient dogma, established authority, and dilapidated systems of values. It is the crowning achievement of skepticism, "the logical outcome of our greatest values and ideals," and a "revaluation of all values," which sweeps away the old and prepares the ground for an entirely new set of values.[30] As Zarathustra exclaims: "That which is falling should also be pushed!"[31] One is again reminded of the rebellious energy and defiance of the Russian nihilists, who, both in their real-life and literary forms, acted as an inspiration for Nietzsche's conception of nihilism.

Passive nihilism, on the other hand, is presented as an expression of weakness, decadence, exhaustion, and resignation, exemplified in the negativity of Buddhism's view of the universe. Schopenhauer represents the personification of passive nihilism for Nietzsche, while the prime example of an active nihilist could be construed, according to his own confessions, as Nietzsche himself, who writes of being "the first perfect

---

27   See Goudsblom, *Nihilism and Culture*, 10.
28   Carr, *The Banalization of Nihilism*, 27.
29   Nietzsche, *The Will to Power*, 24.
30   Nietzsche, *The Will to Power*, 8.
31   Nietzsche, *Thus Spoke Zarathustra*, 226.

European nihilist, but as one who has already outlived the nihilism he contains within himself—who has left it behind him, considers it beneath him, no longer a part of him."[32] Nietzsche's confrontation with the nihilist problematic leads to his rebirth as an anti-nihilist. His liberation from the thrall of nihilism is based above all else on the realization of the logical fallacy inherent in the assumption of the meaninglessness of life. In another fragment from the "Lenzer Heide" text, he explains: "*One* interpretation has failed, but since it was considered *the* interpretation, it now seems as if there is no meaning in existence at all, as if all is *in vain*."[33]

Even after becoming an arch-enemy of nihilism, Nietzsche persists with the annihilation of conventional beliefs, by challenging Christianity, religion in general, Western values, and the notion of absolute truth, as demonstrated by the titles and sub-titles of two of his last works, *Götzen-Dämmerung oder wie man mit dem Hammer philosophirt* and *Der Antichrist. Fluch auf das Christenthum* (Twilight of the Idols or How to Philosophize with a Hammer and The Anti-Christ: A Curse on Christianity, both 1888). In the former, he rejects the legitimacy of morality and religion: "Morality and religion fall entirely under the psychology of error."[34] In the latter, he does full justice to his self-appointed role as "an opponent of Christianity de rigueur," attacking Christianity with a viciousness that is unprecedented in the history of Western philosophy:[35]

> I *condemn* Christianity, I bring against the Christian Church the most terrible charge any prosecutor has ever uttered. To me it is the extremest thinkable form of corruption.... The Christian Church has left nothing untouched by its depravity, it has made of every value a disvalue, of every truth a lie, of every kind of integrity a vileness of soul.[36]

Nietzsche's acts of iconoclasm certainly find parallels in the unorthodox opinions of Stirner. It is one of the aims of this study to ascertain whether Stirner, like Nietzsche, is driven by an actively nihilistic impulse, or whether such similarities are superficial or coincidental in nature.

Nihilistic statements of one form or another—destructive, skeptical, or simply amoral—abound in Nietzsche's writings, providing the building

---

32 Nietzsche, *The Will to Power*, 7. See Nietzsche, *The Will to Power*, 25: "The courage to face what we already *know* only comes late in life. I have only quite recently admitted to myself that I was the quintessential nihilist all along: the energy and radicalism with which I progressed as a nihilist deceived me about this fundamental fact."
33 Nietzsche, *The Will to Power*, 43.
34 Nietzsche, *Twilight of the Idols and The Anti-Christ*, 52–53.
35 Nietzsche, *Ecce Homo*, 48.
36 Nietzsche, *Twilight of the Idols and The Anti-Christ*, 186.

blocks for his elaborate, multifaceted concept of nihilism. In one of his earliest unpublished works, *Ueber Wahrheit und Lüge im außermoralischen Sinne* (On Truth and Lie in an Extra-Moral Sense, 1873), one finds in its opening sentences, couched in language that anticipates the parable of the madman, the relativism which acts as the foundation of Nietzschean nihilism:

> In some remote corner of the universe, poured out and glittering in innumerable solar systems, there once was a star on which clever animals invented knowledge. That was the haughtiest and most mendacious minute of "world history"—yet only a minute. After nature had drawn a few breaths the star grew cold, and the clever animals had to die.—One might invent such a fable and still not have illustrated sufficiently how wretched, how shadowy and flighty, how aimless and arbitrary, the human intellect appears in nature. There have been eternities when it did not exist; and when it is done for again, nothing will have happened.[37]

Relativism is an essential element of Nietzsche's philosophical outlook, as is conveyed by one of his most celebrated phrases: "facts are precisely what there are not, only interpretations."[38] Having discarded facts, Nietzsche proceeds to question the interpretations that replace them, leading to the articulation of a range of nihilism types that coalesce to form his overarching concept. One of the first casualties in his campaign against the traditional certainties of human thought is the notion of right and wrong: "He who considers more deeply knows that, whatever his acts and judgments may be, he is always wrong."[39] The idea of universal order suffers a similar fate: "The total character of the world . . . is in all eternity chaos—in the sense not of a lack of necessity but of a lack of order, arrangement, form, beauty, wisdom, and whatever other names there are for our aesthetic anthropomorphisms."[40] At the root of this perception of existential uncertainty is the Scientific Revolution, which created conditions conducive to the descent into the spiritual void: "Since Copernicus, man seems to have got himself on an inclined plane—now he is slipping faster and faster away from the center into—what? into nothingness? into a '*penetrating* sense of his nothingness?'"[41]

---

37 Nietzsche, *The Portable Nietzsche*, 42.
38 Nietzsche, *The Will to Power*, 287.
39 Nietzsche, *Human, All Too Human*, 182.
40 Nietzsche, *The Gay Science*, 168.
41 Nietzsche, *On the Genealogy of Morals*, 155. The phrase in German is "in's '*d u r c h b o h r e n d e* Gefühl seines Nichts.'" The quote is from Friedrich Schiller, *Don Karlos, Infant von Spanien* (Don Carlos), 2.1: "der in seines Nichts durchbohrendem Gefühle so dazustehen sich verdammt" (Condemned to stand

Such examples of moral, cosmic, and existential nihilism combine to form a conceptual edifice that constitutes the basis of the modern notion of nihilism, according to which Stirner has most often been adjudged a nihilist in the period since World War II. The heterogeneity of Nietzschean nihilism no doubt contributes to the ease with which it can be and has been applied to Stirner and others. Nonetheless, one crucial ingredient can be distilled from the nihilist concoction, what one might call the spirit of Nietzschean nihilism, namely the idea of the meaninglessness of human life, which is expressed in numerous pithy slogans that litter the posthumous fragments: "This is the most extreme form of nihilism: nothingness (that is, 'meaninglessness') for ever";[42] "(What does nihilism mean?) Purposelessness";[43] "Nihilism: there is no goal, no answer to the question: why?"[44] The absence of any meaning or purpose to human life is the unstable bedrock upon which the elaborate structure of nihilism is built.

Perhaps the most paradoxical feature of Nietzschean nihilism is its portrayal as the result of the emptiness caused by the death of God, at the same time as its being inextricably linked to the history of Christianity itself. While, on the one hand, Christian morality is described as "the great *antidote* to practical and theoretical *nihilism*," on the other hand, it is precisely the Christian exaltation of the truth that, according to Nietzsche, has led to the dismantling of Christian dogma:[45]

> Christianity's downfall comes about through its morality, which is inseparable from it and which turns us against the Christian God. Our sense of truthfulness, which has been highly developed by Christianity, is *disgusted* with the falsehood and hypocrisy of the whole Christian interpretation of the world and its history. And so we swing from the extreme of believing that "God is truth" to the opposite extreme of fanatically believing that "all is false."[46]

Thus, Christianity carries within itself the seeds of its own destruction, in the form of the skeptical potential of the will to truth to

---

there in the piercing sense of his nothingness). Stirner quotes part of Schiller's phrase unaltered in *Der Einzige*, except he writes *nichts* in lowercase. Stirner uses the quotation to describe the leveling effect of socialism. See *EE*, 136; *EO*, 115.

42 Nietzsche, *The Will to Power*, 43. This is also from the "Lenzer Heide" text, referring specifically to eternal recurrence as the most extreme form of nihilism because it perpetuates senselessness.
43 Nietzsche, *Werke*, 8.1:324.
44 Nietzsche, *The Will to Power*, 15.
45 Nietzsche, *The Will to Power*, 16.
46 Nietzsche, *The Will to Power*, 11.

undermine its claim to veracity and disprove what Nietzsche describes as its true world theory.[47]

Moreover, Nietzsche identifies a link between Christianity as the religion of the weak and oppressed and the passively nihilistic values of slave morality that are inspired by the negative energy of the herd instinct. The first and most fundamental of these values is the Platonic denial of the value of temporal life in favor of a mythical, noumenal true world. In *Ecce Homo*, he describes Christianity as "this denial of the will to life become religion!"[48] But the value for which Nietzsche reserves his deepest scorn is compassion, which he calls "practical nihilism":[49]

> Christianity is called the religion of *pity*. . . . Pity persuades to *nothingness*! . . . One does not say "nothingness": one says "the Beyond"; or "God"; or "*true* life"; . . . This innocent rhetoric from the domain of religio-moral idiosyncrasy at once appears *much less innocent* when one grasps *which* tendency is here draping the mantle of sublime words about itself: the tendency *hostile to life*. . . . Nothing in our unhealthy modernity is more unhealthy than Christian pity.[50]

For Nietzsche, compassion, which he sees as the ethical quintessence of both Christianity and Buddhism, is born of weakness, "an expression of physiological décadence";[51] it leads inevitably, he claims, to depression and ill health, both literally and metaphorically.[52] Here we find the origin of the association of nihilism with sickness, which, as noted in the previous chapter, is a recurring theme in studies of the subject throughout the twentieth century.[53] Nietzsche has a chronic propensity for employing medical terminology to express, among other things, his disgust with the nihilistic principles of religion.[54] Pathology, symptom, sickness, decay, decadence, depression: this is the vocabulary he uses to describe nihilism

---

47 See, e.g., Nietzsche, *Twilight of the Idols and The Anti-Christ*, 40–41.
48 Nietzsche, *Ecce Homo*, 320.
49 Nietzsche, *Twilight of the Idols and The Anti-Christ*, 118.
50 Nietzsche, *Twilight of the Idols and The Anti-Christ*, 118–19.
51 Nietzsche, *The Will to Power*, 32.
52 See Huszar, "Nietzsche's Theory of Decadence," 259: "According to Nietzsche, all philosophies, religions and arts which spring from weakness are decadent. He combats them not as one would refute an error, but as one would fight against a disease. His critique is not that of a philosopher but that of a physician. Physiology is to him the criterion of value, the sole arbiter of what is good or bad."
53 See, e.g., Thielicke, *Der Nihilismus*, 72 and Vercellone, *Einführung in den Nihilismus*, 8.
54 This is especially true from 1875 onwards. See Pasley, "Nietzsche's Use of Medical Imagery," 136.

and its debilitating effects. In 1887, he writes: "Nihilism represents an *intermediate* pathological state";[55] and in a later fragment: "What they do not understand, ... is that pessimism is not a problem but a symptom, that the term should be replaced by *nihilism*, that the question of whether it is better to be or not to be, is itself an illness, a decline in strength, a kind of hypersensitivity."[56]

Mainländer, who openly proclaimed the utter worthlessness of life, was undoubtedly one of Nietzsche's targets in this regard. But it is Mainländer's mentor, Arthur Schopenhauer (1788–1860), who, in Nietzsche's middle and later writings, bears the brunt of his opprobrium. Both philosophers are listed by Nietzsche, together with Leopardi and Baudelaire, in a group he calls "the modern pessimists as decadents."[57] In Nietzsche's vision of the world, they belong with the unbelievers in the marketplace who mock the madman and fail to understand his message; they reappear in *Also sprach Zarathustra* (Thus Spoke Zarathustra, 1883–1885) as the last men, satiated and comfortable, but also empty, miserable, and resentful, without goals and aspirations.[58] They are the atheists who reach an accommodation with the nihilism that surrounds them, accepting it as an undeniable reality and even welcoming it, but are unable to appreciate its significance for mankind or fully grasp the meaning of its meaninglessness. An argument could also be and indeed has been made that Stirner, the egoistic atheist—carefree, assertive, and blissfully unaware of the serious consequences of the death of God—is the true model for Nietzsche's last man, despite the fact that he seems to be anything but miserable.[59] As noted above, were this to be the case, it would make the accusation of nihilism against Stirner difficult to refute and must therefore be considered in more detail.

The Stirner-Nietzsche Question

It could be conjectured that Nietzsche had in mind phrases of Stirner's, such as "it is only as this unique I that I take everything for my own," when he put the following words into Zarathustra's mouth:[60] "Our way is upward, from the species across to the super-species. But the degenerate

---

55   Nietzsche, *The Will to Power*, 20.
56   Nietzsche, *The Will to Power*, 32.
57   Nietzsche, *Werke*, 8.3:187, 223.
58   See Nietzsche, *Thus Spoke Zarathustra*, 45.
59   See Stepelevich, "Max Stirner and the Last Man," 1: "Stirner can be considered, and would be pleased to present himself, as the 'Last Man.'"
60   *EO*, 319; *EE*, 365: "nur als dieses einzige Ich nehme Ich Mir alles zu eigen."

mind which says 'All for me' is a horror to us."[61] If true, it would underpin the idea that Stirner has nihilistic credentials, by presenting him as one of Nietzsche's original nihilists. But before accepting such a version of events, it must first be asked whether Nietzsche actually knew of Stirner. The debate about this issue has smoldered on, and occasionally burst into flames, ever since Hartmann published an essay, "Nietzsches 'neue Moral'" (Nietzsche's New Morality, 1891/1898), in which he declared that Nietzsche's so-called new morality was not new at all, but was presented by Stirner "in masterly form" in 1845 in *Der Einzige*.[62] In comparing the two philosophers, Hartmann leaves no doubt about his preference for Stirner: "Whoever acclaims Nietzsche's puzzling masks as a new and deep wisdom should . . . above all not fail to revert to Stirner's brilliant masterpiece, which in terms of style is not inferior to Nietzsche's writings, but towers above them in philosophical content."[63]

Having acknowledged that Nietzsche does not mention Stirner in his writings, Hartmann argues that Nietzsche must have known about him, as Nietzsche's polemical criticism of Hartmann, in *Vom Nutzen und Nachteil der Historie für das Leben* (On the Use and Abuse of History for Life, 1874), focuses precisely on the chapter in Hartmann's *Philosophie des Unbewussten* in which Stirner is mentioned. Hartmann considers it highly improbable that Nietzsche would subsequently not have felt compelled to get to know so congenial a thinker, not least, perhaps, because of Hartmann's candid recommendation of *Der Einzige* as a book "that nobody interested in practical philosophy should leave unread."[64] This is then followed by a thinly veiled accusation of plagiarism, identifying a shift in Nietzsche's thinking, which, in Hartmann's opinion, is best explained by his having read and, by implication, assimilated Stirner, without publicly acknowledging the fact.[65]

One should not forget, however, that Hartmann had a score to settle, for which the timing of this assault was opportune. Nietzsche's growing

61   Nietzsche, *Thus Spoke Zarathustra*, 100.
62   Hartmann, *Ethische Studien*, 60. The essay was first published in *Preussische Jahrbücher* (Prussian Yearbooks) in 1891. The heated debate that followed can be considered the catalyst for the first Stirner renaissance. See Laska, "Nietzsches initiale Krise," 118.
63   Hartmann, *Ethische Studien*, 61. Hartmann was not the only commentator to champion Stirner over Nietzsche, but most writers on the subject have done the opposite. Alois Riehl says that comparing Nietzsche and Stirner is like setting works of genius against a literary curiosity. See Riehl, *Friedrich Nietzsche*, 81. Lévy writes: "Stirner is a critical spirit; Nietzsche is an artist." Lévy, *Stirner et Nietzsche*, 35. Fritz Mauthner called Nietzsche a poet, and Stirner just a thinker. Mauthner, "Hat Nietzsche Stirner's *Einzigen* gekannt?" 22.
64   Hartmann, *Philosophy of the Unconscious*, 3:97.
65   See Hartmann, *Ethische Studien*, 61.

popularity was threatening to eclipse Hartmann's, but the former's mental breakdown in 1889 rendered him incapable of responding to criticism. Seventeen years before the first publication of Hartmann's essay in 1891, Nietzsche had viciously attacked Hartmann's ideas as a "philosophical joke," his thought as "philosophy of unconscious irony," and Hartmann himself as "the unconscious parodist" and "rogue of rogues."[66] In just a few paragraphs, Nietzsche had made himself an implacable enemy. It is therefore reasonable to assume that Hartmann's prime motivation in comparing Nietzsche unfavorably with Stirner was to discredit Nietzsche by associating him with an *enfant terrible*, rather than to venerate Stirner.[67] Stirner was little more to Hartmann than a weapon in the war against his detractor, Nietzsche, though this, in itself, does not necessarily disprove Hartmann's argument.

In fact, Hartmann's theory was as speculative as it was vindictive, but it nonetheless started a discussion that rumbles on more than a century and a quarter later. During that time, further indications of Nietzsche having been acquainted with Stirner, considered by some as evidence—circumstantial, anecdotal, thematic, or textual—have appeared. Included in the first category is the fact that Nietzsche is known to have read Lange's *Geschichte des Materialismus* (History of Materialism, 1866), in which Stirner is also briefly mentioned.[68] The reference to Stirner is so fleeting that it covers no more than half a page out of more than five hundred and fifty pages. Nonetheless, the nature of the description is such that one can imagine that had he read it, Nietzsche's interest might possibly have been piqued.[69] Lange's few words about Stirner include the following: "Stirner went so far . . . as to reject all moral ideas. . . . What a pity that to this book—the extremest that we know anywhere—a second positive part was not added. . . . Stirner lays so much stress on the

66   Nietzsche, *Thoughts out of Season*, 2:77–79.
67   See Laska, *Ein heimlicher Hit*, 20: "Hartmann's intention was clear, . . . he wanted to expose, denounce and disavow Nietzsche."
68   Nietzsche referred to Lange in letters to Gersdorff in 1866 and 1868 and to Mushacke in 1866, and in three fragments in 1884 and 1885. See Nietzsche, *Briefwechsel*, 1.2:159, 184, 257; *Werke*, 7.2:90, 119; *Werke*, 7.3:173.
69   Mackay's interest was apparently aroused in precisely this way. According to his biography of Stirner, he learnt about Stirner while reading Lange's book in the British Museum Reading Room. See Mackay, *Max Stirner*, 5. Laska doubts the veracity of Mackay's claim, speculating instead that Mackay read *Der Einzige* soon after publication of the second edition in 1882, during the period of his close friendship with Hermann Conradi, but that, after their acrimonious split in 1885, he concealed this in order not to have to credit Conradi with Stirner's rediscovery. See Laska, *Ein dauerhafter Dissident*, 34–36.

will . . . that it appears as the root force of human nature. It may remind us of Schopenhauer."[70]

Nietzsche apparently knew Lange's book well enough to recommend it both to his schoolfriend Carl von Gersdorff (1844–1904) and to his fellow student Hermann Mushacke (1845–1905) in 1866, the year of its first publication (around the time Nietzsche was embarking on his detailed study of Schopenhauer), calling it "excellent in its own way and very instructive," and "the most important philosophical work to have been published in the last few decades . . . about which I could write a full-length panegyric."[71] Admittedly, one thousandth of a book is not very much, but Nietzsche's warm and unequivocal recommendations suggest he read it in sufficient detail to have been able to absorb Lange's portrayal of Stirner, and above all Lange's rather surprising association of Stirner's ideas with those of Schopenhauer, in which case it is conceivable that Nietzsche would have been unable to resist the temptation to read Stirner's work.[72] Albert Lévy (1844–1907) suggests as much in his book *Stirner et Nietzsche,* published in 1904: "Lange only devotes about ten lines to Stirner; . . . There is . . . in this short analysis a word that must have caught Nietzsche's attention: Lange declares . . . that Stirner may remind us of Schopenhauer."[73] Four years later, Carl Albrecht Bernoulli (1868–1937) asks in *Franz Overbeck und Friedrich Nietzsche—eine Freundschaft* (Franz Overbeck and Friedrich Nietzsche—a Friendship), while referring to the same passage: "Was Nietzsche satisfied with this comment? Did he not reach for the book himself?"[74]

Anecdotal evidence that Nietzsche was acquainted with Stirner's work includes, firstly, Nietzsche's student Adolf Baumgartner (1855–1930) saying he borrowed *Der Einzige* from the Basel library in 1874 on

---

70   Lange, *The History of Materialism,* 256.

71   Nietzsche, *Briefwechsel,* 1.2:159, 184.

72   Although the association with Schopenhauer may, at first sight, seem far-fetched, the Stirner scholar Anselm Ruest considered it a perceptive observation: "there are deeper connections . . . between Schopenhauer's and Stirner's worldviews. . . . Albert Lange instinctively sensed and envisaged as much." Ruest, *Max Stirner,* 266–67. Anselm Ruest was the anagrammatic pseudonym of Ernst Samuel.

73   Lévy, *Stirner et Nietzsche,* 12.

74   Bernoulli, *Franz Overbeck und Friedrich Nietzsche,* 1:149. It is certainly true that Nietzsche was fascinated with Schopenhauer, whose works he devoured voraciously around this time. See Nietzsche, *Thoughts out of Season,* 2:114: "I belong to those readers of Schopenhauer who know perfectly well, after they have turned the first page, that they will read all the others, and listen to every word that he has spoken."

his teacher's recommendation;[75] secondly, Ida Overbeck (1848–1933), wife of Nietzsche's friend, Franz Overbeck (1837–1905), recalling a private conversation with Nietzsche where he at first expressed enthusiasm for Stirner, but then immediately backpedaled and asked her to forget it, for fear of accusations of plagiarism;[76] and, thirdly, her also remembering Nietzsche recommending Stirner's book to Baumgartner as "the boldest and most consistent since Hobbes."[77] All of these hearsay reports, based on memories dating back some twenty years, are presented by Bernoulli in defense of his erstwhile professor, Franz Overbeck, against the venomous attacks of Elisabeth Förster-Nietzsche, the director of the Nietzsche Archive and self-appointed guardian and shaper of her brother's legacy.[78]

Bernoulli also puts forward an idea originally proposed by Karl Joël (1864–1934), author of the celebrated work, *Nietzsche und die Romantik* (Nietzsche and Romanticism, 1905), that the conductor and first husband of Cosima Wagner, Hans von Bülow, who knew of both Stirner and Nietzsche and gave a speech singing Stirner's praises after a performance of Beethoven's "Eroica" in 1892, may have introduced Nietzsche to Stirner's ideas.[79] However, Bernoulli considers it more likely that

75 See Bernoulli, *Franz Overbeck und Friedrich Nietzsche*, 1:135–36. In a text inserted into the work, Franz Overbeck writes: "Mrs. El. Förster claims unhesitatingly that Nietzsche was unfamiliar with Stirner. The whole issue is settled, however, since, in February 1899, I found out from an old loan register of the Basel Library that Baumgartner had borrowed Stirner's work there on 14 July 1874. . . . [Baumgartner] had belonged to Nietzsche's most intimate acquaintances for the whole term, and, as I have now had him personally confirm to me, he only got to know Stirner's work on Nietzsche's warmest recommendation."

76 See Bernoulli, *Franz Overbeck und Friedrich Nietzsche*, 1:239. Ida Overbeck reported Nietzsche having said: "Klinger was a philistine, no, I feel no relation to him; but Stirner, yes! . . . Now I have said it to you after all, and I did not want to speak about it. Forget it again. People will talk of plagiarism."

77 Bernoulli, *Franz Overbeck und Friedrich Nietzsche*, 1:239. Ida Overbeck does not say whether she heard this first or second hand. See Safranski, *Nietzsche*, 124–25.

78 For further details of the acrimonious relationship between Förster-Nietzsche and the Overbecks, see Bernoulli, *Franz Overbeck und Friedrich Nietzsche*, 2:334–453, especially 429–35 ("Ecce Femina!") and 435–38 ("Overbeck über Nietzsches Schwester").

79 Nietzsche's correspondence with von Bülow lasted from January 1872, when he sent the conductor a copy of *Die Geburt der Tragödie* (The Birth of Tragedy, 1872), to the beginning of January 1889, when von Bülow was the recipient of one of Nietzsche's last, pathetic letters from Turin: "In view of the fact that you started and have been the first Hanseatic citizen, I, in all modesty, only the third Veuve Cliquot-Ariadne, may I not spoil the game for you: instead I condemn you to be the 'Lion of Venice'—may he devour you . . . Dionysos." Nietzsche, *Briefwechsel*, 3.5:573–74. Concerning the "Eroica" concert, see

Nietzsche knew Stirner from his student days, as, so he reports, Théophile Droz, a fellow student of Nietzsche's, had intimated in his reminiscences.[80] Nonetheless, Bernoulli stops short of accusing Nietzsche of plagiarizing Stirner's philosophical ideas. He inserts in the text of his book an essay by Overbeck, where the latter concludes that Nietzsche had read Stirner but, in what is more likely to be a gesture of loyalty to his old friend than a sign of appeasement to Nietzsche's sister, he declares that, for those who knew Nietzsche, plagiarism would be the last thing of which they would imagine him to be capable.[81]

Another theory, offered by Lévy, is that it may have been Wagner who introduced Nietzsche to Stirner: "The question ... arises as to where Nietzsche encountered the name of Stirner. This name may have been uttered in front of him at the home of Richard Wagner; Wagner had perhaps heard of Stirner at the time of the 1848 revolutions, through his friend Bakunin, for example."[82] Based, as it is, on two assumptions, namely that Wagner had heard of Stirner during the 1848 revolutions (in which Stirner was not remotely involved) and that Wagner subsequently talked about him in Nietzsche's company some twenty years later, there is even less evidence for Lévy's theory than there is for the corresponding one about Bülow, who is at least known to have been an admirer of Stirner. Unlike the claims of Baumgartner and Ida Overbeck though, neither of these theories has even unsubstantiated hearsay to back it up.

The same can be said about Laska's deliberations on the possibility that Nietzsche's meeting in October 1865 with the teacher Dr. Eduard Mushacke, father of his student friend Hermann Mushacke and, according to Laska, a veteran of the Young Hegelians, resulted in his becoming acquainted with Stirner's thought, which, in turn, led to a profound crisis in Nietzsche's intellectual development.[83] Laska's reasoning is as follows:

Mackay, *Max Stirner*, 8. It was von Bülow who supported Mackay in his efforts to erect a commemorative plaque on the wall of Stirner's last abode in Berlin and place a headstone on his grave. For Bernoulli's theory, see Bernoulli, *Franz Overbeck und Friedrich Nietzsche*, 1:151.

80 See Bernoulli, *Franz Overbeck und Friedrich Nietzsche*, 1:153. "It says there, ... 'It is possible that a book, which at the time was considered a novelty, exerted a certain influence on Nietzsche's spirit. It was *Der Einzige und sein Eigentum* by Max Stirner, a gospel of the most ruthless individualism, of intellectual and social anarchism without barriers.'"

81 See Bernoulli, *Franz Overbeck und Friedrich Nietzsche*, 1:137. "I maintain ... that Nietzsche did read Stirner.... For opponents this may ... justify the conclusion that he was a plagiarist. For those who knew him closely, it is the last thing they would think."

82 Lévy, *Stirner et Nietzsche*, 10.

83 See Laska, "Nietzsches initiale Krise," 127. Laska claims that Mushacke was misspelled phonetically as Mussak by Engels in his letter to Max Hildebrand

"It is hard to imagine that Mushacke did not tell the deeply interested Nietzsche about his friend Stirner; that he did not have his *Der Einzige* in his bookcase; that Nietzsche did not devour the book there and then."[84] Whether the non-occurrence of any or all of these three related events is really inconceivable or not, Laska's idea is certainly a shrewd one, tying together various details of Nietzsche's biography, his notorious mental instability, and his later preoccupation with the problem of nihilism. Laska effectively replaces the conventional view that Nietzsche's reading of Schopenhauer was the impetus for his "serious mental-psychological life crisis," with the possibility that it was instead the undocumented confrontation with the ideas of Stirner that resulted in his conversion from philologist to philosopher.[85]

Although there is clearly no definitive proof that Stirner did not play any role in Nietzsche's crisis, it would seem odd in that case that Nietzsche wrote to Hermann Mushacke of all people in July of the following year (1866): "Since Schopenhauer removed the bandage of optimism from our eyes, we see more clearly. Life is more interesting, even if it is uglier."[86] Laska's explanation for Nietzsche's failure to acknowledge that he knew, and was influenced by, Stirner, can be found in his theory of "primary repression," an expression that Laska borrows from Freud, and which he defines thus: "Primary repression occurs when someone fails to examine rationally and master thoughts that worry them, but instead removes them from their consciousness by means of a mainly unconsciously controlled psychic dynamic, i.e. in an irrational manner."[87] According to this theory, Nietzsche's letter to Mushacke about Schopenhauer could conceivably be part of an elaborate subconscious attempt to banish Stirner from his mind. It is an intriguing idea, but one that it is impossible either to prove or disprove. It nonetheless makes a strong if, once again,

---

of October 22, 1889. See Marx and Engels, *Collected Works*, 48:394. Mackay received a copy of the letter and, Laska surmises, adopted the misspelling unquestioningly in his biography of Stirner. See Mackay, *Max Stirner*, 64, 90. Mackay states that Stirner and "Mussak" were good friends, although Engels's letter does not imply this. For Nietzsche's meeting with Mushacke senior, see Nietzsche, *Briefwechsel*, 1.2:77, 87–88, 90.

84   Laska, "Nietzsches initiale Krise," 128.
85   Laska, "Nietzsches initiale Krise," 129. For the orthodox view of Nietzsche's discovery of Schopenhauer having precipitated his crisis, see Safranski, *Nietzsche*, 36.
86   Nietzsche, *Briefwechsel*, 1.2:140.
87   Laska, *Ein dauerhafter Dissident*, 73. Laska uses the adjective "primary" not, as in Freud, to denote the first clinical phase, but to distinguish it from secondary repression, which is, in his terminology, when a follower unquestioningly adopts the position of the master.

speculative case for the reevaluation of Stirner's significance in the history of ideas, which is, after all, Laska's intention.[88]

Arguing from the other end of the spectrum is Nietzsche's sister, Elisabeth Förster-Nietzsche (1846–1935), who, having returned to Germany from Paraguay in 1893 after the suicide of her Aryan-supremacist, anti-Semitic husband, had established herself as literary executor of her deranged and bed-ridden brother, and set up the Nietzsche Archive, initially in Naumburg in 1894, moving it in 1897 to its permanent location in Weimar. Förster-Nietzsche seems to have been determined to stamp out any suspicion that Nietzsche had ever heard of Stirner. Resa von Schirnhofer (1855–1948), the Austrian philosopher and feminist who was acquainted with Nietzsche, reports how, during a visit to Weimar in 1897, she felt like a criminal as she was repeatedly interrogated by Förster-Nietzsche about whether she could categorically confirm that Nietzsche had never mentioned Stirner to her by name.[89] In her introduction to Henri Lichtenberger's *Die Philosophie Friedrich Nietzsches* (The Philosophy of Friedrich Nietzsche), published two years later, Förster-Nietzsche, who sounds as if she could be protesting too much, puts her case authoritatively, though without any corroboration: "It has . . . often been claimed that my brother must have read Stirner. For certain external and internal reasons, I can say with complete certainty that he never held his book in his hand, and all the research I have made in this direction has yielded the same result."[90]

In an article in 1907, Förster-Nietzsche does provide some evidence for her conviction that her brother had been unacquainted with Stirner. Her intention therein is to undermine the testimony of Franz Overbeck, by contrasting it with the declaration of Joël concerning the Baumgartner incident.[91] Unfortunately, she misquotes Joël, apparently intentionally, who corrected her in an article in the same journal just three weeks later, confirming that Baumgartner had written to him about Nietzsche recommending Stirner's book, not Lange's *Geschichte des Materialismus*, as Förster-Nietzsche had claimed.[92] Even though Joël reaffirmed his belief that Stirner had not had any serious influence on Nietzsche, and although Gast came to Förster-Nietzsche's rescue in an article soon afterwards—which sought to question the reliability of Overbeck's defective memory in old age, declaring, again with no evidence, that Nietzsche had definitely

---

88 See Laska, *Ein dauerhafter Dissident*, 120.
89 See Schirnhofer, "Vom Menschen Nietzsche," 250–60 and 441–58; Prideaux, *I am Dynamite!*, 247–52; Gilman, ed., *Conversations with Nietzsche*, 238.
90 Förster-Nietzsche, "Introduction," LXVII.
91 See Förster-Nietzsche, "Nietzsche und Stirner," 407–8.
92 See Joël, "Nietzsche und Stirner," 34–35.

not read Stirner—the damage to her already tarnished credibility had been done.[93] Moreover, Gast's mauling of the late Franz Overbeck is particularly dubious, considering that he had written to Overbeck in a letter fourteen years earlier: "The kinship between Stirner and N. is striking!"[94]

As a postscript to this discussion of the contretemps between the Weimar tradition (Förster-Nietzsche) and the Basel tradition (Overbeck) of preserving and promoting Nietzsche's legacy, it is, I think, worth mentioning one other circumstantial piece of evidence, which could possibly support Overbeck's side of the argument.[95] In a letter to Nietzsche of April 15, 1883, Franz Overbeck refers to the line "Ich hab' Mein' Sach' auf Nichts gestellt" (All things are nothing to me; or, more literally, I have set my affair on nothing), which features prominently in *Der Einzige*.[96] What he writes is: "Ich schreibe Dir diess zu mehrerem Genusse des 'Nichts' auf welches Du 'Dein' Sach' gestellt' hast" (I am writing you this that you take much pleasure from the "nothing" on which you have "set your heart").[97] If he were indeed quoting from Stirner, this might suggest that both sender and recipient were familiar with him and, moreover, the fact that Nietzsche makes no reference whatsoever to the comment in his reply of April 17 could conceivably be considered a reinforcement of Ida Overbeck's assertion that Nietzsche was making a self-conscious effort to prevent any association being construed between himself and Stirner.[98]

Johann-Christoph Emmelius, in his scholarly article on the subject, makes an excellent, though nonetheless ultimately unprovable, case for the reference being to Goethe's poem "Vanitas! vanitatum vanitas!" (the

---

93 See Gast, "Nietzsche und Stirner," 146. Förster-Nietzsche's reputation had been tarnished above all by an article by Rudolf Steiner, where he wrote: "The private lessons I had to give Mrs. Förster-Nietzsche taught me above all one thing: that Mrs. Förster-Nietzsche is a complete layman in everything concerning her brother's teaching. She does not have any sort of independent opinion about the simplest aspects of this teaching . . . [and lacks] any sense of finer, or even for coarser logical distinctions." Steiner, "Das Nietzsche-Archiv," 519. He concludes with the words: "Perhaps I have done too much out of courtesy and consideration in praising her qualities. Now I declare that this was a great stupidity on my part, and that I am most willing formally to take back any praise I have bestowed on Mrs. Förster-Nietzsche." 528.

94 Hoffmann, ed., *Franz Overbeck, Heinrich Köselitz: Briefwechsel*, 376.

95 For further information on the Weimar and Basel traditions, see Hoffmann, "Zur Geschichte des Nietzsche-Archivs," 94–96.

96 See *EE*, 13, 370; *EO*, 5, 324. An alternative translation offered in a footnote in the first English edition is: "I have set my affair on nothing." See *EO* (1907), 3.

97 Nietzsche, *Briefwechsel*, 3.2:366.

98 See Nietzsche, *Briefwechsel*, 3.1:361.

first line of which Stirner had shamelessly appropriated for the opening and closing lines of his book), citing among other things a letter from Overbeck to Gast (Köselitz) of February 24, 1893, where the former says he cannot recall Nietzsche ever having mentioned Stirner in their conversations.[99] Emmelius fails, however, to notice one piece of textual evidence, which indicates that Stirner might be the more likely source after all, namely that Overbeck wrote *Dein* capitalized (though admittedly he generally capitalized second person singular pronouns in the text of his letters), and, more importantly, he wrote both *Dein* and *Sach* followed by apostrophes, which Stirner did and Goethe did not.[100] However, even if it was Stirner that Overbeck was quoting in the letter, it does not of course necessarily mean that Nietzsche recognized it as such, or that he deliberately ignored it. This, therefore, is no more than another tantalizing but entirely speculative clue, which, even together with all the other evidence, does not allow an unbiased observer to come down decisively on one side or the other.

From Nescience to Plagiarism

Between the poles of Förster-Nietzsche's unwavering denial on the one hand, and Hartmann's insinuation of plagiarism on the other, various other shades of opinion have appeared in the numerous commentaries on the subject. Lichtenberger himself writes about the inescapable similarities between the two thinkers' ideas: "One finds in an almost forgotten thinker, Max Stirner, nearly just as strongly as in Nietzsche, the unrelenting individualism, the cult of the ego, the hostility towards the state, the protest against the dogma of equality, so that to compare his magnum opus, *Der Einzige*, from this point of view with Nietzsche's writings is very curious."[101] Robert Schellwien (1821–1900), in his book *Max Stirner und Friedrich Nietzsche* (1892), follows a similar line, describing the two thinkers jointly as prophets of individualism, and concluding: "The literary activities of these two thinkers lie more than thirty years apart, but, however great their disparity, their congruity is no less."[102]

---

99 See Emmelius, "'Ich hab' mein' Sach' auf nichts gestellt.'" 311.

100 In both Goethe and Stirner, the possessive pronoun is, of course, *mein*, not *dein*. *Mein* is capitalized in the title of the prologue to *Der Einzige*, but not in the book's last line. Mysteriously, there is no apostrophe after *Mein* in the prologue of the first edition of *Der Einzige*, though this is corrected in some later editions, including Lauterbach's Reclam edition and Kast's study edition. There is, however, an apostrophe after *mein* in the final line of the first edition and the Lauterbach and Kast editions, though not in the Wigand edition of 1901.

101 Lichtenberger, *Die Philosophie Friedrich Nietzsches*, 192.

102 Schellwien, *Max Stirner und Friedrich Nietzsche*, 7.

Unsurprisingly, Mackay was less even-handed than Lichtenberger and Schellwien, asserting that "wanting to compare this eternally vacillating, muddled spirit, who is repeatedly self-contradictory, almost helplessly tumbling from truth to error, with the deep, clear, calm, and superior genius of Stirner is an absurdity not worth serious refutation."[103] In a later, revised edition of Mackay's biography of Stirner, he declares it beyond doubt, since the posthumous publication of Overbeck's reminiscences, "that Nietzsche knew *Der Einzige* and shyly buried in himself the overwhelming force of its influence, until he was able to free himself of it in his own creating."[104]

Anselm Ruest, writing in 1906 between the first and second editions of Mackay's work, maintained that Nietzsche had read Stirner and was sympathetic towards him, but had avoided referring to him because he was concerned that Stirner's ideas were too dangerous for human consumption.[105] Benedict Lachmann (1878–1941), an acquaintance of both Mackay and Ruest, was no less convinced: "It has long been argued among interested parties whether Nietzsche knew Stirner. The question is almost certainly decided in the affirmative."[106] Löwith, though less partisan than Mackay, Ruest, and Lachmann, seems to have accepted the Overbecks' testimony, also believing that Nietzsche knew of Stirner: "And so it is easy to imagine that Nietzsche was so 'economical,' as Overbeck called it, with his knowledge of Stirner because he was both attracted to and repelled by him, and did not want to be confused with him."[107] More recently, Safranski has expressed a similar view: "Given the unfavorable reputation of Stirner, one could easily imagine that Nietzsche had no desire to be mentioned in the same breath as this philosophical outcast."[108]

Outside Germany, various opinions have been voiced. Herbert Read (1893–1968) wrote that "it is easy to detect the influence it [Stirner's text] had on Nietzsche's *style* (its influence on his thought is still more obvious)," while Leszek Kołakowski (1927–2009), in his handbook on Marxism, proclaimed that Nietzsche "had read Stirner's work though he nowhere expressly refers to it."[109] John Carroll, in his introduction to the 1971 abridged English translation of *Der Einzige*, echoed Lichtenberger's analysis concerning their similarities: "The bounds of coincidence are strained by the degree to which Stirner anticipates Nietzsche both in

---

103 Mackay, *Max Stirner*, 18.
104 Mackay, *Max Stirner*, 19.
105 See Ruest, *Max Stirner*, 306. "Nietzsche liked Stirner's teachings, but he found the way in which they were promulgated too unscrupulous, . . . for far too many people—unsuitable, too dangerous."
106 Lachmann, *Protagoras, Nietzsche, Stirner*, 12.
107 Löwith, *From Hegel to Nietzsche*, 187.
108 Safranski, *Nietzsche*, 126.
109 Read, *The Tenth Muse*, 76; Kołakowski, *Main Currents of Marxism*, 1:163.

ideas and prose style; . . . they have too many key concepts in common—Antichrist, immoralism, priest-morality, irrationalism, and superman/egoist. Stirner also wrote about the 'death of God', the enervating curse of democracy, and the State as the new idol."[110]

Likewise, Gilles Deleuze (1925–1995) was in no doubt about the link between the two, though he identifies Stirner as one of the prime embodiments of Nietzschean nihilism, making the relationship between Nietzsche and Stirner one of antagonism rather than affinity:

> We have every reason to suppose that Nietzsche had a profound knowledge of the Hegelian movement, from Hegel to Stirner himself. . . . We will misunderstand the whole of Nietzsche's work if we do not see "against whom" its principal concepts are directed. . . . Nietzsche never stops attacking *the theological and Christian character of German philosophy* . . .—*the powerlessness of this philosophy to extricate itself from the nihilistic perspective* (Hegel's negative nihilism, Feuerbach's reactive nihilism, Stirner's extreme nihilism). . . . It is clear that Stirner plays the revelatory role in all this. It is he who pushes the dialectic to its final consequences.[111]

In Deleuze's view, Zarathustra's rallying cry to overcome man is clearly directed at the ultimate manifestation of nihilism, exemplified by Stirner's demythologizing egoist. "The allusion to Stirner is obvious," he writes, referring to Zarathustra's appeal to the "Higher Men."[112] Finally, in the ledger of those convinced of Stirner's influence on Nietzsche, one finds perhaps the most extreme example of misinformation in the airy assertion of George Woodcock (1912–1995) that "Nietzsche himself regarded Stirner as one of the unrecognized seminal minds of the nineteenth century."[113]

There are, however, others, for whom, as Lévy declares, "it does not appear that Stirner had a decisive influence on Nietzsche."[114] Georg Simmel (1858–1918) is one of these, contrasting Stirner's sophism with Nietzsche's nobility.[115] Another is Rudolf Steiner (1861–1925), whose assessment is almost diametrically opposed to Mackay's, at least as far as Stirner's influence on Nietzsche's thought is concerned: "What path might Nietzsche not have taken if, instead of Schopenhauer, his teacher had been Max Stirner! In Nietzsche's writings, no influence of Stirner whatsoever is to be found. By his own effort, Nietzsche had to work his

110 Carroll, "Introduction," 24.
111 Deleuze, *Nietzsche and Philosophy*, 162.
112 Deleuze, *Nietzsche and Philosophy*, 163.
113 Woodcock, *Anarchism*, 94.
114 Lévy, *Stirner et Nietzsche*, 19.
115 See Simmel, *Schopenhauer und Nietzsche*, 234.

way out of German idealism to a Stirner-like world conception."[116] In the anglophone world, Paterson takes the view that Nietzsche probably only knew vaguely of Stirner and that "he never felt moved to enlarge this . . . knowledge for utilization in his own philosophical programme."[117] More recently, Glassford, while addressing the Stirner-Nietzsche question, recognizes a "startling similarity in the basic outlook," and notes the parallels in both the style and content of their writings, but finally suggests that "Stirner and Nietzsche's work is similar simply because of the inevitable logic of post-Hegelian philosophy."[118] Brobjer, responding to Glassford's article, considers the similarities between Nietzsche and Stirner noteworthy, but "general" rather than "staggering," and rejects accusations of plagiarism outright and suggestions of influence as "inappropriate."[119]

In the wide spectrum of the plagiarism debate, a significant majority of commentators seem to have believed that Nietzsche at least knew of Stirner, though the degree of the latter's influence on Nietzsche is hotly disputed. The reason for this overwhelming tendency in favor of familiarity may lie in the nature of the question itself, which is generally more interesting to those who recognize some form of connection, but it is noticeable that even those who deny Stirner's direct influence on Nietzsche (with the exception of Förster-Nietzsche and her associate, Köselitz) nonetheless point to their affinities. Paterson calls attention to the biographical coincidences: both thinkers were solitary; both cut short their teaching careers to dedicate themselves to philosophy; both had sudden ends to their philosophical careers; and both died relatively young. He also notes the basic similarities in their *Weltanschauungen*—the focus on individualism, the denial of transcendent solutions, the tendency towards moral skepticism, the antipathy towards all manifestations of institutional authority, and the recognition of conflict as the basic feature of human intercourse.[120] Löwith says of their fundamental kinship: "Both can be separated by an entire world and yet belong together through the inner consistency of their radical criticism of Christian humanitarianism."[121]

Apparent similarities in their ideas can be readily discovered through textual comparisons. Perhaps the most conspicuous of these concerns the resemblance of their pronouncements on the death of God, which was alluded to earlier in this chapter. With regard to the underlying cause behind the act of deicide, Stirner, like Nietzsche, notes the crucial role played by truth: "The truth wears longer than all the gods; for it is only

---

116 Steiner, *Friedrich Nietzsche*, 122.
117 Paterson, *The Nihilistic Egoist*, 149.
118 Glassford, "Did Friedrich Nietzsche Plagiarize from Max Stirner?," 78.
119 Brobjer, "A Possible Solution to the Stirner-Nietzsche Question," 109–14.
120 See Paterson, *The Nihilistic Egoist*, 146.
121 Löwith, *From Hegel to Nietzsche*, 187.

in the truth's service, and for love of it, that people have overthrown the gods and at last God himself."[122] Stirner also anticipates Nietzsche in recognizing Christianity's antipathy towards earthly life: "In all this there is room made for the Christian proposition that the world is empty, for the Christian *contempt of the world*."[123] Generally, Stirner's anti-Christian polemic can often sound proto-Nietzschean, both in tone and in style, as, for instance, in the observation that "all thinking that does not sin against the holy spirit is belief in spirits or ghosts."[124]

Stirner's and Nietzsche's views on Feuerbach as a peddler of secularized Christianity are also remarkably similar. Stirner declares "how thoroughly theological is the liberation that Feuerbach is labouring to give us," while Nietzsche states "Hegel Feuerbach Strauss—it all stinks of theologians and church fathers."[125] Both thinkers express a profound skepticism towards the notion of truth. Nietzsche writes: "What are man's truths ultimately? Merely his *irrefutable* errors."[126] In a similar vein, Stirner declares: "The truth is dead, a letter, a word, a material that I can use up."[127] Morality fares likewise, with Nietzsche writing a book entitled *Jenseits von Gut und Böse* (Beyond Good and Evil, 1886), and Stirner proclaiming: "I am neither good nor bad."[128] Nicholas Martin, writing about Nietzsche's contempt for established sociopolitical ideologies, observes: "Nietzsche spurns all the 'isms' of political thought: nationalism, communism, liberalism, socialism, and so forth. By the same token, he rejects universalizable ethical value systems: Christianity, utilitarianism, the belief in human and material progress, and egalitarianism."[129] Something very similar could be said of Stirner, the opening lines of whose magnum opus

---

122 *EO*, 311; *EE*, 356: "Die Wahrheit hält länger vor, als alle Götter; denn nur in ihrem Dienste und ihr zu Liebe hat man die Götter und zuletzt selbst den Gott gestürzt."

123 *EO*, 85; *EE*, 102: "In alledem ist für den christlichen Satz, daß die Welt eitel sei, für die christliche *Weltverachtung* der Raum geöffnet."

124 *EO*, 306; *EE*, 351: "Alles Denken aber, das nicht gegen den heiligen Geist sündigt, ist Geister- oder Gespensterglaube."

125 *EO*, 33; *EE*, 42: "Wie durchaus theologisch, d.h. gottesgelahrt, die Befreiung ist, welche Feuerbach Uns zu geben sich bemüht." Nietzsche, *Werke*, 7.2:260.

126 Nietzsche, *The Gay Science*, 219. See Nietzsche, *Beyond Good and Evil*, 88: "Perhaps no one has ever been sufficiently truthful about what 'truthfulness' is."

127 *EO*, 312–13; *EE*, 358: "Die Wahrheit ist tot, ein Buchstabe, ein Wort, ein Material, das Ich verbrauchen kann."

128 *EO*, 7; *EE*, 15: "Ich bin weder gut noch böse."

129 Martin, *Nietzsche and Schiller*, 196.

bemoan the causes to which a person is supposed to be dedicated, including those of God, mankind, humanity, truth, and justice.[130]

The list of similarities is a long one. Nietzsche writes "Become what you are!"[131] Stirner declares: "Over the portal of our time stands not that 'Know thyself' of Apollo, but a '*Get the value out of thyself!*'"[132] Nietzsche develops his social theory from the concepts of "*master morality* and *slave morality*."[133] Stirner declares: "*Victory* or *defeat*—between the two alternatives the fate of the combat wavers. The victor becomes the *lord*, the vanquished one the *subject*: the former exercises *supremacy* and 'rights of supremacy', the latter fulfils in awe and deference the 'duties of a subject.'"[134] Nietzsche is dynamite, philosophizes with a hammer, and creates the concept of the Will to Power as the fundamental principle of human motivation and of life itself.[135] Stirner's writing is littered with dictums that appear to support such a worldview. He lays emphasis on following the dictates of the will, as opposed to the normative values of acquired knowledge: "Proper knowledge perfects itself when it stops being knowledge and becomes a simple human drive once again, the will."[136] He elevates might over right: "Right—is a wheel in the head, put there by a spook; power—that am I myself, I am the powerful one and owner of power."[137] And he extols the virtues of power: "My freedom becomes complete only when it is my—*might*."[138]

Yet despite the many apparent similarities, there is no incontrovertible evidence of Nietzsche having read, or even known of, Stirner. It is quite possible, as Glassford implies, that their affinities are based on the inevitable consistency of thought which is bound to exist between two radical, nineteenth-century German thinkers. Nietzsche's nihilistic and anti-nihilistic ideas are clearly a response to the perceived miasmic spirit of

---

130 See *EO*, 5; *EE*, 13.
131 Nietzsche, *Thus Spoke Zarathustra*, 252.
132 *EO*, 278; *EE*, 319: "Über der Pforte unserer Zeit steht nicht jenes apollinische: 'Erkenne Dich selbst,' sondern ein: *Verwerte Dich!*"
133 Nietzsche, *Beyond Good and Evil*, 175.
134 *EO*, 13; *EE*, 19: "*Siegen* oder *Unterliegen*,—zwischen beiden Wechselfällen schwankt das Kampfgeschick. Der Sieger wird der *Herr*, der Unterliegende der *Untertan*: jener übt die *Hoheit* und 'Hoheitsrechte,' dieser erfüllt in Ehrfurcht und Respekt die 'Untertanpflichten.'"
135 See Nietzsche, *Ecce Homo*, 126, 116.
136 Stirner, *The False Principle of Our Education*, 20; Stirner, *Max Stirner's Kleinere Schriften*, 20: "Das rechte Wissen vollendet sich, indem es aufhört Wissen zu sein, und wieder ein einfacher, menschlicher Trieb wird,—der Wille."
137 *EO*, 187; *EE*, 215: "Recht—ist ein Sparren, erteilt von einem Spuk; Macht—das bin Ich selbst, Ich bin der Mächtige und Eigner der Macht."
138 *EO*, 151; *EE*, 174: "Meine Freiheit wird erst vollkommen, wenn sie meine—*Gewalt* ist."

Western modernity, but there are many possible philosophical personifications of his "last man," including Schopenhauer, Mainländer, and Julius Bahnsen (1830–1881), all of whom are specifically identified by Nietzsche as products of the shadow cast over Europe by the death of God. The latter two occupy, like Stirner, only minor positions in the received history of ideas, so it would seem strange for Nietzsche to have mentioned them but not Stirner, had he known of him. The Austrian polymath Egon Friedell (1878–1938) acknowledges this when he asserts: "Nietzsche himself, it is patent, never read Stirner; otherwise, with his love for all literary 'outsiders,' he would certainly have mentioned him more than once."[139]

Nietzsche does not hesitate to write about those thinkers who supplied elements of the terminology he used for his most important concepts. God is dead is a phrase used by Hegel; Apollonian-Dionysian, as a philosophical dualism, came from Schelling (among others);[140] the Will was central to the philosophy of Schopenhauer;[141] "Become what you are" is from Pindar's Pythian Ode 2, 72;[142] Eternal Recurrence (the idea for which, so Nietzsche reports in *Ecce Homo*, came to him in a flash of inspiration "'6,000 feet beyond man and time,' . . . walking through the woods beside the lake of Silvaplana") appears in various forms in ancient Indian and Egyptian religions, as well as in the philosophy of Pythagoras, Empedocles, Zeno of Citium, and the Stoics.[143] Overman (*Übermensch*) was a term used in the sixteenth- and seventeenth-century theological prose of certain followers of Luther, later to be adopted and modified in meaning by Herder, from whom Goethe acquired it.[144]

There is no escaping the fact that Nietzsche is a highly inventive assembler of eclectic concepts. Even such essential Nietzschean characters as Zarathustra and Dionysos are adaptations of historical or

---

139 Friedell, *A Cultural History of the Modern Age*, 3:114.
140 See Vogel, *Apollinisch und Dionysisch*.
141 See Schopenhauer, *The World as Will and Representation*.
142 Nietzsche, *Thus Spoke Zarathustra*, 252. See Stern, *A Study of Nietzsche*, 115.
143 See Nietzsche, *Ecce Homo*, 99; *Encyclopedia.com*, "Eternal Return," by Milič Čapek, accessed June 30, 2023, https://www.encyclopedia.com/humanities/encyclopedias-almanacs-transcripts-and-maps/eternal-return; *Stanford Encyclopedia of Philosophy*, "Pythagoras," by Carl Huffman, accessed June 30, 2023, https://plato.stanford.edu/entries/pythagoras/; *Stanford Encyclopedia of Philosophy*, "Stoicism," by Dirk Baltzly, accessed June 30, 2023, https://plato.stanford.edu/entries/stoicism/.
144 See *Digitales Wörterbuch der deutschen Sprache*, s.v. "Übermensch," accessed June 30, 2023, https://www.dwds.de/wb/dwb/%C3%9Cbermensch. *Übermensch* was also employed in an anthropological sense by Feuerbach and subsequently by Moses Hess, who used it to describe Bruno Bauer. See Löwith, *From Hegel to Nietzsche*, 187.

mythical figures. As Martin remarks: "He is an impatient, inveterate, and incorrigible borrower and rejecter of ideas."[145] He does not, however, make any obvious attempt to conceal his sources: he mentions Schopenhauer in his writings about a thousand times, Goethe five hundred times, and Hegel and Luther more than a hundred times each; Fichte, Schelling, Schleiermacher, Feuerbach, and Strauss are lumped together as theologians;[146] Herder also appears, as do Pindar, Pythagoras, Empedocles, and Zeno, as well as Bahnsen, Mainländer, and Hartmann. He even refers to the obscure Afrikan Spir (1837–1890), whose work Nietzsche is known to have read around the time that Hartmann alleges Stirner's influence to have occurred.[147]

It is of course possible that any evidence there was that Nietzsche knew Stirner has in some way or other been tampered with (Laska speaks of "obliterated traces of Stirner in Nietzsche's work and estate"), and that Nietzsche and, subsequently, his sister were indeed concerned about charges of plagiarism, as the testimony of Ida Overbeck would suggest.[148] The self-styled "atheist who loves God," Paul Carus (1852–1919), considered the accusation of plagiarism irrelevant, because, if Nietzsche was beyond good and evil, then he must be beyond plagiarism as well.[149] But the fact is that the lack of any concrete evidence of Nietzsche ever having encountered Stirner's work means that such an allegation is pure speculation anyway. Stirner cannot be considered a component of the Nietzschean understanding of nihilism on the basis of factual proof and thus cannot be accorded the title of nihilist on this account. Instead of being the model for Nietzsche's uncanniest of all guests, as has been suggested, Stirner may not even have been the shadow of its shadow. If the accusation of nihilism against Stirner is to stand up, the evidence must be sought elsewhere.

---

145 Martin, *Nietzsche and Schiller*, 6.

146 See Nietzsche, *Werke*, 7.2:150.

147 See Nietzsche, *Werke*, 3.4:318. See also Safranski, *Nietzsche*, 161: "In the mid-1870s, Nietzsche studied a treatise called *Denken und Wirklichkeit* [Thought and Reality, 1877], by the philosopher Afrikan Spir. This work had long been consigned to oblivion, but it had a lasting impact on Nietzsche. Section 18 of *Human, All Too Human* cited Spir, not by name, but by presenting a 'proposition by an outstanding logician.'"

148 See Laska, "Nietzsches initiale Krise." Glassford, for one, considers Ida Overbeck's evidence to be dubious. See Glassford, "Did Friedrich Nietzsche Plagiarize from Max Stirner?" 78.

149 See Carus, *Nietzsche*, 100–101: "Nietzsche has been blamed for appropriating Stirner's thoughts; . . . but we must concede that the common rules of literary ethics can not apply to individualists who deny all and any moral authority."

The Existential Dimension

Returning to the task of defining Nietzschean nihilism as an alternative means of establishing whether Stirner can reasonably be called a nihilist, it is important for the purposes of this analysis to trace the etymology of the term after Nietzsche's death, in order to determine its full range of characteristics. Strange though it may sound, Nietzschean nihilism, as a concept, continued to evolve throughout the twentieth century; following its development helps to build up a picture of its shifting appearance against which to measure, and better understand, the different, and often anachronistic, senses in which the label of nihilist is used by Stirner's accusers.

Frederico Vercellone, in his introduction to nihilism, observes that "Nietzsche's distorted, newly discovered thinking forms a kind of common thread that runs through the nihilism debate in our [i.e., the twentieth] century."[150] The effect of Nietzsche's concept of nihilism on subsequent thinkers, writers, and artists has been considerable, which has contributed greatly to the word becoming part of common usage. The list of those associated, in some form or other, with nihilism after Nietzsche constitutes a who's who of modern Western culture, including: Wittgenstein and Heidegger; Sartre and Camus; Derrida and Baudrillard; Cioran and Bataille; Conrad and Kafka; Beckett and Ionesco; Duchamp and Munch; Berg and Stravinsky; Stevens and Yeats.[151] There is no major field of culture that Nietzschean nihilism has left untouched. It has seeped into some minor ones as well: take, for instance, without necessarily having to listen to it, the type of popular music known as Death Metal.[152]

In the 135 years since the onset of Nietzsche's mental derangement in 1889, the most important developments in the evolution of the concept of nihilism have come from the cultural movement known as existentialism. To all intents and purposes, the type of nihilism associated with Nietzsche, that is nihilism based on the assumption of meaninglessness, is nowadays described as existential nihilism. However, existentialism has not just adopted the term, it has also helped to shape its meaning by developing ideas not fully explored by Nietzsche. Although Reginster argues that "Nietzsche conceives of nihilism primarily in terms of despair," this begs the question of whether Nietzsche ever expresses

---

150 Vercellone, *Einführung in den Nihilismus*, 89.

151 See Martin, *From Nietzsche to Wittgenstein*, where Heidegger, Sartre, Camus, Derrida, Baudrillard, Conrad, Kafka, Cioran, Bataille, Beckett, Ionesco, and Duchamp are all mentioned. Also, see Prideaux, *Edvard Munch: Behind the Scream*, 68–90; Adorno, *Die musikalischen Monographien*, 326; Fay, *Shostakovich*, 173; Bloom, *Wallace Stevens*, 62; Gillis, *Irish Poetry*, 148.

152 See Brett Stevens, "On Death Metal and Nihilism," *Death Metal Underground*, August 19, 2016, http://www.deathmetal.org/article/on-death-metal-and-nihilism/.

personal despair, except perhaps in his final semi-lucid moments during the equine embrace.[153] Despair (*Verzweiflung*) is a word that does not play a significant role in Nietzsche's writings; even when he is articulating an idea which in itself is horrifying, the wit and wisdom of the phrase often forestalls the emotional response of the reader, as in the remark: "And when you gaze long into an abyss the abyss also gazes into you."[154] In this and other similar instances, we are confronted more with the concept of emptiness as an underlying potentiality than with the iconic scream of anguish depicted by Munch. Munch's painting may have been a direct response to Nietzsche's ideas, but it needed the artist's sensibility to express the full visceral impact of their implications.[155]

This subjective element within the modern concept of nihilism surely postdates Nietzsche, although its antecedents are to be found in Søren Kierkegaard (1813–1855), who addresses the issue of existential despair in *Fear and Trembling* (1843): "If there were no eternal consciousness in man, . . . if an unfathomable, insatiable emptiness lay hid beneath everything, what would life be but despair? . . . If an eternal oblivion always lurked hungrily for its prey and there were no power strong enough to wrest it from its clutches—how empty and devoid of comfort would life be!"[156] In *The Sickness unto Death* (1849), Kierkegaard further refines his stark description of despair: "If, in the strictest sense, there is to be any question of a sickness unto death, it must be one where the end is death and where death is the end. And thinking that is precisely to despair."[157] Kierkegaard, who considered doubt a proof of true faith, hypothesized the horror of nothingness, identified the denial of personal immortality as the devastating consequence of unbelief, and chose to seek solace in God.[158]

Despair plays a central role throughout existentialism. It is not always occasioned directly by the contemplation of death, but can also result from the feeling of absurdity, which, according to Albert Camus

---

153 Reginster, *The Affirmation of Life*, 34.
154 Nietzsche, *Beyond Good and Evil*, 84.
155 See Prideaux, *I am Dynamite!*, 351: "The Norwegian artist Edvard Munch was part of the circle and Strindberg introduced him to Nietzsche's writings with such profound effect that Munch painted *The Scream*. It captured the zeitgeist as nothing else: Munch had produced the definitive icon of existential terror on contemplating the consequences of the death of God, and the subsequent responsibility of man to find meaning and significance to life."
156 Kierkegaard, *Fear and Trembling*, 14.
157 Kierkegaard, *The Sickness unto Death*, 47.
158 The irony has not gone unnoticed that Kierkegaard's name means churchyard in Danish, "usually in the sense of 'cemetery.'" See Garff, *Søren Kierkegaard*, 3.

(1913–1960), is the product of the "divorce between man and his life."[159] However much one might try to ignore it, behind the spirit of absurdity, he observes, lies the specter of "the cruel mathematics that command our condition."[160] Jean-Paul Sartre (1905–1980) writes that "existentialism is nothing else but an attempt to draw the full conclusions from a consistently atheistic position."[161] Just as the death of God is the catalyst for Nietzsche's tragic age of nihilism, so the absence of God lies behind existentialism's concern with how to live in a world devoid of eternal truth, absolute values, and irrefragable meaning. Existentialism confronts a similar set of problems to Nietzsche in his struggle with self-defined nihilism, but approaches them in a different way and with different emphases, thereby putting its own slant on the term and adding a new, visceral dimension, which is embodied in the concept of angst.

The term angst, in its existential sense, derives from Kierkegaard's 1844 book, *The Concept of Dread* (the Danish title, *Begrebet Angest*, is also rendered in English as *The Concept of Anxiety*), where it is depicted as a "consequence of original sin," defined as "the dizziness of freedom," and associated with the recurrent theme of nothingness:[162] "If then we ask further what is the object of dread, the answer as usual must be that it is nothing. Dread and nothing regularly correspond to one another."[163] Martin Heidegger (1889–1976), who, in Noreen Khawaja's words, "was clearly less forthcoming about his debt to Kierkegaard than he ought to have been," and whose book *Sein und Zeit* (Being and Time, 1927) "transposes entire paragraphs from the German translation of Kierkegaard's *Concept of Anxiety*," developed the idea further:[164] "*But the state-of-mind which can hold open the utter and constant threat to itself arising from Dasein's ownmost individualized Being, is anxiety.* In this state-of-mind, Dasein finds itself *face to face* with the 'nothing' of the possible impossibility of its existence. . . . Being-towards-death is essentially anxiety."[165] This insight can be viewed as existentialism's most important addition to the modern definition of nihilism. Needless to say, the concept of angst plays as insignificant a role in the writings of Nietzsche as does despair; neither are explicitly developed concepts in his philosophy.

As *horror vacui* (according to Thielicke's interpretation of the term as opposed to Mario Praz's), nihilistic angst can be considered to have reached a sort of poetic consummation in Philip Larkin's (1922–1985)

---

159 Camus, *The Myth of Sisyphus*, 13.
160 Camus, *The Myth of Sisyphus*, 21.
161 Sartre, *Existentialism and Humanism*, 56.
162 Kierkegaard, *The Concept of Dread*, 47, 54.
163 Kierkegaard, *The Concept of Dread*, 86.
164 Khawaja, "Heidegger's Kierkegaard," 299, 296.
165 Heidegger, *Being and Time*, 310.

"Aubade" (1977), described by Christopher Hitchens as "a waking meditation on extinction that unstrenuously contrives a tense, brilliant counterpoise between the stoic philosophy of Lucretius and David Hume, and his own frank terror of oblivion."[166] In it, Larkin confronts "the dread of dying, and being dead" with unmitigated honesty, describing his view of mortality as:

> The sure extinction that we travel to
> And shall be lost in always. Not to be here,
> Not to be anywhere,
> And soon; nothing more terrible, nothing more true.[167]

Its prosaic counterpart can be found in Thomas Ligotti's (b. 1953) *The Conspiracy against the Human Race* (2010):

> There will come a day for each of us . . . when the future will be done with. Until then, humanity will acclimate itself to every new horror that comes knocking, as it has done from the very beginning. . . . And the horror will go on, with generations falling into the future like so many bodies into open graves. The horror handed down to us will be handed down to others like a scandalous heirloom.[168]

Ligotti and Larkin, along with a host of others, are the literary heirs of Nietzsche's haunting prediction of the tragic age for Europe. They are part of the existentialist update of nihilism, which has taken the confrontation with nothingness to new levels of subjectivity. If Stirner is to be accounted a nihilist in this sense, one would expect him to articulate interests and concerns that are similar to theirs.

The existential manifestations of nihilism show just how much the meaning of the word has changed over time. The history of nihilism, from its inception towards the end of the eighteenth century to the present day, reveals a remarkable metamorphosis, from a specialized, polemical term expressing the most extreme form of censure, via the watchword of a political movement fixated on the destruction of the established order, to the description of a pervasive sociocultural malaise that has infiltrated post-religious human consciousness. The only constants in this process of rapid diversification of meaning are the etymological root in the idea of nothingness and the assumption of godlessness. Otherwise, there have been no constraints on nihilism's peregrinations through the tangled processes of human thought, which, together with the horrified fascination that the word induces, account for both the large number of definitions and the confusion that surrounds them.

166 Hitchens, *Arguably*, 331.
167 Larkin, *Collected Poems*, 208.
168 Ligotti, *The Conspiracy against the Human Race*, 220.

Having presented a detailed etymological overview of this widely used, much maligned, and often misunderstood word, the present investigation can now turn to the actual accusations of nihilism against Stirner. As there is no incontrovertible proof of Stirner having directly influenced Nietzsche, who is unquestionably the decisive figure in the word's conceptual development, and especially of Stirner's ideas having contributed to Nietzsche's notion of nihilism—which, had it been the case, might have offered a shortcut to a positive evaluation of Stirner's status as a nihilist—the allegations against Stirner must be judged solely on their individual merits. For a thinker as neglected as Stirner, the accusations of nihilism made against him have been surprisingly frequent, although the neglect may, of course, be causally connected to the level of vitriol involved. The voices to the contrary have been few and far between, but are, at times, possessed of similar conviction. Opinions often vary, but in the case of Stirner and nihilism, they are split, as the next chapter will chronicle.

CHAPTER 4

The Use and Abuse of Nihilism: Stirner under Fire

Allegations and Denials: The First Hundred Years

Since the first examples of the polemical use of the term nihilism in reference to Stirner following the publication of *Der Einzige*—namely by Karl Rosenkranz in late 1844 or early 1845, and by an anonymous journalist in 1847—the echoing voices have been both numerous and at times venomous, at least once the hiatus of almost half a century of Stirner's near total obscurity had passed. From the time of the first Stirner renaissance in the 1890s until the present day, the accusations of nihilism have been relentless, to the point where the alleged connection has arguably become a self-perpetuating truism. In this period, there have been at least half a dozen published examples in German alone per decade of Stirner and his ideas being linked to nihilism, and sometimes more than double that. It is not only the prevalence of the accusations of nihilism against Stirner that is remarkable but also the changing usage of the term over time in the relevant books, dissertations, and articles.

That Stirner did not disappear entirely from intellectual memory in the aftermath of the 1848 revolutions is evidenced by his brief appearance in two important philosophical works of the 1860s, Lange's *Geschichte des Materialismus* and Hartmann's *Philosophie des Unbewussten*. However, as Laska remarks, the few references to Stirner in this period are terse and evasive.[1] One such mention can be found in Karl Grün's 1874 edition of Feuerbach's correspondence and posthumous writings. In his introduction, Grün puts the word nihilism into Feuerbach's mouth: "Thus Max Stirner called him a 'pious atheist' and claimed: 'Feuerbach fled from faith into love.' . . . Feuerbach's initial response to Stirner was that his nihilism was also dogmatic."[2] Feuerbach does use the word *Nihilismus* in 1860 to describe the ideas of Schopenhauer, but neither in the essay by Feuerbach to which Grün is alluding, which was written fifteen years earlier in 1845,

---

1 See Laska, *Ein heimlicher Hit*, 15.
2 Grün, ed., *Ludwig Feuerbach in seinem Briefwechsel*, 1:119.

nor elsewhere in his published writings does Feuerbach connect Stirner with nihilism. One can only assume that Grün (1817–1887), who was a Young Hegelian journalist, political theorist, and socialist politician, was applying the increasingly popular term with a combination of poetic license and the benefits of hindsight. Both Grün's attribution of the word to the response of Feuerbach to Stirner's criticism and Feuerbach's own use in 1860 referring to Schopenhauer reflect the broader definition of nihilism that was evolving in the middle of the nineteenth century, which went beyond the one-dimensional, polemical sense associated with German idealism, and was starting to embrace broader ethical and ideological concepts of denial.

A similar understanding of nihilism can be found in a reference to Stirner in a work of 1881 by the liberal politician, Karl Biedermann (1812–1901):

> A certain radicalism in a religious context . . . had merged to some extent with a similar radicalism in the political, moral, and social spheres, finally reaching the point where it entirely called into question everything in the existing order including the church, the state, society, public morals, etc. In Berlin, a small circle of followers of this doctrine formed, mostly still very young writers, who . . . gave themselves the name of nihilists. A kind of literary manifesto of this school of thought . . . was the work: *Der Einzige und sein Eigenthum* by Max Stirner.[3]

The identity of the young Berlin writers, whom Biedermann labels self-styled nihilists, is not clear. If he means *Die Freien*, there is no other source which claims that they baptized themselves in this manner, and nor is the epithet particularly applicable to the liberal, humanist, and socialist ideologies of most of its members. The nihilists of Gutzkow's novella, *Die Nihilisten*, are neither writers, nor real, nor located in Berlin. The group of rebellious, young authors around Heinrich and Julius Hart, Hermann Conradi, Karl Henckell, and Wilhelm Arent called themselves *Das jüngste Deutschland* (Youngest Germany), were later subsumed under German Naturalism, and, in any case, their main activities took place after Biedermann's book was published.[4] Whoever they are, Biedermann's nihilists sound like a literary version of the Russian nihilists, with their rejection of all political and moral norms, and this is the sense he seems to apply to Stirner. Ernst Laas (1837–1885), the positivist philosopher, writing one year later and in the same vein, speaks

---

3   Biedermann, *1840–1870*, 1:138–39.
4   See Hamann and Hermand, *Naturalismus*, 12–13. Hermann Wendel does, however, describe the Conradi generation as "pure nihilists, as nothings" (*Nichtser*). Wendel, "Die Generation um Conradi," 420.

of "this nihilistic-Promethean turning away from all that is moral."[5] Comparing Stirner to Callicles, he vilifies *Der Einzige* as: "the most reckless and demented denigration of all moral ideas and sentiments ever."[6] One thing that many of Stirner's detractors over the years have shared is the excessive use of invariably negative hyperbole, apparently fighting the perceived fire with fire.

These early associations of Stirner with nihilism took place just prior to the publication of Nietzsche's writings on nihilism, at a time when the term was undergoing exponential growth in its prevalence. As the first Stirner renaissance gained pace in the 1890s, spurred on by the mounting *fin-de-siècle* fascination with Nietzsche, so the identification of Stirner with nihilism grew more widespread and more complex. In 1891, the social-democratic political scientist and politician, Eduard Bernstein (1850–1932), in the process of expressing his disdain for Stirner's alleged philosophical idealization of bourgeois individualism, argued that Stirner's uncompromising version of nihilism should be distinguished from Russian nihilism: "The nihilism, in which Stirner's theory ends, has a different face to that which bears the same name in Russia. He has 'made nothing his concern.' But nothing comes from nothing. After that, there is no way forward."[7] Georg Keben (1859–1921) declared shortly before this that Stirner's philosophy ends in the sense of its own impotence, "in a sort of nihilistic crapulence."[8] A similar conclusion was reached by Schellwien in his book on Stirner and Nietzsche (the first but not the last of its kind): "Here there is some spook in Stirner, it spooks out at one, nihilism. The 'Unique One' is 'the mortal creator, who consumes himself.' All striving is rejected."[9] A few years later, the socialist politician, Heinrich Ströbel (1869–1944), was even more forthright in his denunciation: "Where Stirner's moral nihilism leads may be demonstrated by the following quotation: 'But I am entitled by myself to murder if I myself do not forbid it to myself.'"[10]

A new element that entered the discourse on Stirner and nihilism at this time was the connection to anarchism. Keben had already brought up the question of Stirner's relationship to anarchism in his article of 1890, but had dismissed any serious link: "The Stirnerian world is the realm of unrestricted hedonism and irresponsibility; anarchism, at least ideally,

---

5   Laas, *Idealismus und Positivismus*, 2:19.
6   Laas, *Idealismus und Positivismus*, 2:18.
7   Bernstein, "Die Soziale Doktrin des Anarchismus," 428. Nothing comes from nothing (*Aus nichts wird nichts*) is a phrase deriving ultimately from Parmenides, via Lucretius, as *ex nihilo nihil fit*, and the early Christian theologians. Shakespeare uses a variation of it in *King Lear*, 1.1.
8   Keben, "John Henry Mackay und sein Philosoph," 174.
9   Schellwien, *Max Stirner und Friedrich Nietzsche*, 21.
10 Ströbel, "Stirners 'Einziger und sein Eigentum,'" 86.

restricts enjoyment through the feeling of solidarity."[11] Bernstein, on the other hand, calls Stirner "the most consequential of all the anarchists," and his views are echoed by the French journalist and adventurer, Félix Dubois (1862–1945), who describes Stirner's philosophy as nihilistic-anarchistic and *Der Einzige* as "the first anarchist work."[12] Similarly, Leo Berg (1862–1908), writer, journalist, and supporter of German Naturalism, remarked on the similarities between Stirner and the "French nihilist," Pierre-Joseph Proudhon (1809–1865).[13] The lack of consensus between these various commentators can, at least partially, be put down to their diverse interpretations and sometimes imprecise usage of the terminology. What they all generally have in common is a sense of revulsion at Stirner's perceived ethical impropriety, which takes on a political dimension through the reference to anarchism.

In what Kast identifies as the first academic dissertation on Stirner, an 1897 doctoral thesis entitled *Die Individualitätsphilosophie Max Stirners* (Max Stirner's Philosophy of Individuality), Matteo Johannes Paul Lucchesi (1869–?) reaffirms the relationship between Stirner and anarchism, though his definition of anarchism is a loose one and seems not to be restricted to the sociopolitical arena: "The egoist must show himself to be an *anarchist*. He is supposed to identify himself as the creator and owner of the spiritual world."[14] Like Berg, Lucchesi seems to employ nihilism and anarchism interchangeably, dividing his theological analysis of Stirner's "annihilation of the spirit" into three sub-headings, logical, ethical, and social "anarchism or nihilism," which, in terms of the categories discussed in chapter 2 above, correspond to alethiological, moral, and political nihilism respectively.

In a number of fragments from 1887 and 1888, Nietzsche also grouped anarchism and nihilism together as symptoms of pessimism or consequences of degeneration, though without, of course, any reference to Stirner.[15] Lucchesi would not previously have read these fragments, as they were published only later in *Der Wille zur Macht*, but at this time of simultaneous popularity of, and comparison between, Stirner and Nietzsche, both were being linked to anarchism, if only because of their shared animosity towards the state and its institutions. Lucchesi acknowledges the connection between the two thinkers: "Both worldviews stand in irreconcilable opposition to Christianity as well as to prevailing trends

---

11 Keben, "John Henry Mackay und sein Philosoph," 189.
12 Bernstein, "Die Soziale Doktrin des Anarchismus," 422. Dubois, *Die Anarchistische Gefahr*, 9.
13 Berg, *Der Übermensch in der modernen Litteratur*, 14.
14 Lucchesi, *Die Individualitätsphilosophie Max Stirners*, 31.
15 See Nietzsche, *The Will to Power*, 33.

in general, both are representatives of absolute individualism."[16] He goes on to describe Stirner as a Nietzsche before Nietzsche and to define his nihilism in terms of anthropocentrism, before opposing it with a declaration of faith: "Only when our thinking and willing is theocentric does our life have the right substance and purpose."[17] Like many of Stirner's critics, Lucchesi, who was elected third deacon of the Dresden Trinity Church in 1896, had an overtly theological agenda that underpinned his condemnation of Stirner as a nihilist.

In 1898, a journalist by the name of Arthur Goldschmidt adopted a less conventional standpoint by stating that Stirner's negation of morality was *not* representative of nihilism, but rather of subjectivism, defined as a perspective based on the uniqueness of the individual.[18] Nonetheless, he does not shy away from calling Stirner an individualist anarchist, leaving his denial of the connection to nihilism as little more than an anomaly amidst the otherwise steady flow of assertions to the contrary in the last quarter of the nineteenth century.[19] There were three further indictments in the by now customary vein before the century ended: the ethnologist Thomas Achelis (1850–1909) described Stirner as a philosophical nihilist in an article of 1898; a year later, Tomáš Garrigue Masaryk (1850–1937), the future liberator-president of Czechoslovakia, called him a political nihilist; and Julius Hart (1859–1930), the Naturalist author, employed more imaginative terminology in characterizing Stirner's *Einziger* (unique one) rather incongruously as a nihilistic Torquemada.[20]

1906, the centenary of Stirner's birth and the fiftieth anniversary of his death, was, relatively speaking, a prolific year for publications about Stirner. Lucchesi chose, understandably, to mark only the latter, in an article in the *Dresdner Anzeiger* (Dresden Gazette), where he repeats the slogan, a Nietzsche before Nietzsche, and once again delineates the purported threefold thrust of Stirner's nihilistic anarchism. The message is largely the same as in his doctoral dissertation, although the articulation is rather more sophisticated, as he tries, with rhetoric that is both sanctimonious and derisive, to mobilize the German people against the Stirnerian-Nietzschean philosophy: "One would think that the people would have

16   Lucchesi, *Die Individualitätsphilosophie Max Stirners*, 3.
17   Lucchesi, *Die Individualitätsphilosophie Max Stirners*, 96. Although Lucchesi connects Stirner's ideas with Nietzsche's, he does not enter into the Stirner-Nietzsche debate, remarking simply that Nietzsche need not necessarily have known about Stirner.
18   See Goldschmidt, "Max Stirner, sein Leben und sein Werk," 233.
19   See Goldschmidt, "Max Stirner, sein Leben und sein Werk," 230.
20   See Achelis, "Ethische Probleme," 151; Masaryk, *Masaryk on Marx*, 261–62; Hart, *Der neue Gott*, 247.

gradually become disgusted by such fare. . . . How can it be countered and remedied? Our schools and churches have a great task here."[21]

A number of the centenary publications four months later, while undoubtedly kinder about Stirner and his legacy, were equally convinced about which isms best applied to him. Alexander von Gleichen-Rußwurm (1865–1947), the great-grandson of Schiller, described Stirner as a precursor of the nihilists; for Hugo Nathanson, he was "the most radical of radicals, . . . the spiritual father of anarchism and nihilism"; while the evangelical theologian Friedrich Heman (1839–1919), in a reference to the Russian nihilists, declared that: "Stirner's anarchism and nihilism developed into a party secretly subverting the whole of Europe, whose followers want, with dagger, revolver, and bombs, to make themselves owners of the whole world and prove that they have made nothing their cause."[22] At this time when the era of Russian nihilism was gradually drawing to a close, to be succeeded by the even more ruthless ideology of Bolshevism, some of the criticism of Stirner became increasingly political in nature.

The one dissenting voice in the publications of 1906 was that of the writer and publisher, Anselm Ruest, whose sympathetic monograph on Stirner appeared in the same year, and who dismissed the condemnation of Stirner as a nihilist as the product of ignorance and misunderstanding:

> Stirner . . . was a philosopher, a thinker; and the philosopher has to deal solely with the truth, the naked, undisguised truth. . . . And so he has become, as is now the general verdict, and not infrequently the condemnation, the worst skeptic and even nihilist; he is said to have left us nothing unscathed, to have attacked law, state, and property—indeed to have called into question the magic of disinterested love and compassion. Those who speak in this way and claim to prove something with single sentences and phrases, which gain an entirely different light within the context of a great and complex intellectual narrative, do not understand how to trace a river back to its source.[23]

Ruest's positive assessment of Stirner's individualism and his rejection of nihilism as an appropriate epithet are echoed in Max Messer's (1875–1930) monograph, which was published in the following year, asserting

---

21 Matteo Johannes Paul Lucchesi, "Max Stirner: ein Nietzsche vor Nietzsche," *Dresdner Anzeiger, Sonntagsbeilage*, June 24, 1906: 98–100 (100).

22 See Gleichen-Rußwurm, "Der Einzige und sein Eigentum," 41; Nathanson, "Max Stirner," 1636; Heman, "Der Philosph des Anarchismus und Nihilismus," 74.

23 Anselm Ruest, "Max Stirner. Zum hundertsten Geburtstag," *Die Gartenlaube: Illustriertes Familienblatt* 43 (1906): 918–19 (919).

"how fundamentally wrong it is to stigmatize Stirner as a nihilist."[24] Messer's incisive analysis is based on the observation that although, inevitably, there are destructive elements in Stirner's thought, his ultimate aim is a constructive one, namely the liberation of the individuals who comprise humanity by fundamentally changing their perspective on the supposedly apodictic principles of established dogma. He thus concludes that Stirner's philosophy "is not a nihilistic one, but an optimistic, life-affirming one, in the Nietzschean sense."[25]

Messer's and Ruest's opinions nonetheless remained the exceptions; otherwise, the accusations of nihilism continued unabated. In 1908, Ludwig Stein (1859–1930), a political journalist and pacifist, characterized Stirner's philosophy as a declaration of the urban lumpenproletariat and asserted the inevitability of extreme individualism ending in bottomless nihilism.[26] The nationalist and royalist, Franz Ludwig (1868–1927), in his trenchant attack on communism, anarchism, and socialism, called Stirner a preacher of mortal enmity towards morality and an agitator for the revolutionary politics of violence, declaring: "Stirner's anarchist theory thus built the bridge to nihilism."[27] Wally Zepler (1865–1940), the social-democratic politician and campaigner for women's rights, wrote that "Stirner had dug most systematically and deeply and dissolved all apparently indissoluble social and moral concepts until nothing remained for him but the inviolable sovereignty of the ego and a system of economic anarchism that sprang from this philosophical nihilism."[28] And the theology professor and future Bishop of Danzig, Franz Sawicki (1877–1952), who seems to have read and been positively impressed by Lucchesi's work, pronounced with studied emphasis: "Stirner's philosophy is . . . a radical nihilism, a logical, ethical, religious, social nihilism."[29] The attacks on Stirner came from all points of the sociopolitical compass, converging on the focal point of nihilism, variously understood.

This pattern of denunciation from all sides, interrupted intermittently by voices more favorably inclined to Stirner, continued into the second decade of the twentieth century, with the term nihilism, which was by then quite commonly associated with Stirner, being bandied about often without due care and attention. Salomo Friedlaender (1871–1946), philosopher and writer of the Expressionist and Dadaist avantgarde and, in 1919, co-editor with Ruest of the individualist anarchist periodical, *Der Einzige*, calls Stirner the self-proclaimed nihilist, defining nihilism as a

---

24   Messer, *Max Stirner*, 53.
25   Messer, *Max Stirner*, 53–54.
26   See Stein, *Philosophische Strömungen*, 239.
27   Ludwig, *Kommunismus, Anarchismus, Sozialismus*, 47.
28   Zepler, "Individualismus," 892.
29   Sawicki, *Das Problem der Persönlichkeit*, 112.

synonym for atheism and, perhaps for this reason, giving no source for the assertion of self-appellation.[30] The philosophy professor and follower of Hartmann, Arthur Drews (1865–1935), writes of Stirner's "personalistic anarchism and nihilism," while the conservative Austrian philosophy professor, Othmar Spann (1878–1950), calls Stirner a preacher of "social nihilism."[31] Hugo Ball (1886–1927), one of the founders of Dadaism and author of the Dada Manifesto, commenting on Stirner's failure to man the barricades in 1848, writes: "Stirner's cynical nihilism remained seated in the wine tavern."[32]

The exception in this decade, with regard to Stirner and nihilism, was Aurélie Polturak (1892–1943), whose dissertation on Stirner, submitted in Vienna in 1917, begins with a sober appraisal of Stirner research hitherto, which concludes: "Since the publication of his book until the present day, Stirner has been portrayed in all his monographs as a nihilist in the fields of knowledge, morality, and society, who preaches the law of the jungle and calls for self-gratifying indulgence."[33] This indictment of Stirner as a nihilist is, she asserts, based on a fundamental failure to understand his philosophy. Polturak's message, it seems, was largely ignored. In the period of the Weimar Republic that followed shortly thereafter, Hermann Graf Keyserling (1880–1946), the Baltic German philosopher, fresh from the loss of his ancestral estate in Livonia following the Estonian Land Reform of 1919, speaks of the inevitability of individualistic immoralism like Stirner's descending into bottomless nihilism; W. Stockgänger, writing in *Der freie Arbeiter* (The Free Worker), calls Stirner "the most consequential nihilist," while highlighting his significance for the working class in identifying the state as depending on the slavery of labor; the Protestant theologian Wilhelm Lütgert (1867–1938) concurs to some extent, describing Stirner's nihilism as the necessary conclusion of a logical development, which prepared the way for communism; Jakob Baxa (1895–1979), the Austrian sociologist and cultural historian, denounces *Der Einzige* as "the lunatic hymn to anarchism in philosophical nihilism";

---

30 See Friedlaender, *Friedrich Nietzsche*, 44. Friedlaender edited the periodical, *Der Einzige*, under the pseudonymic semordnilap, "Mynona."

31 Drews, *Geschichte der Philosophie*, 25; Spann, *Kurz gefaßtes System der Gesellschaftslehre*, 236.

32 Ball, *Die Folgen der Reformation*, 262.

33 Polturak, "Die Philosophie Max Stirners," 5. Aurélie Polturak later became an art and literary critic in Paris, the wife of the modernist painter Leopold Gottlieb (1883–1934), a member of the Jewish resistance in Klaus Barbie's Lyon, and, finally, a deportee to Auschwitz. See Marx [Marc] Fineltin, "Gottlieb née Polturak Aurélie 'dite Relia,'" in *Les Amis de la Fondation de la Résistance: Memoirs et Espoirs de la Resistance*, accessed June 30, 2023, http://www.memoresist.org/resistant/gottlieb-nee-polturak-aurelie/.

and even a philosophical historian of the stature of Löwith writes perfunctorily about Stirner's nihilistic philosophy as if it were a given.[34]

Löwith's assumption that Stirner was a nihilist reappeared in his magnum opus, *Von Hegel zu Nietzsche* (From Hegel to Nietzsche), first published in 1941, where he writes: "Bauer and Stirner brought all philosophy to an end in radical criticism and nihilism."[35] In a later passage Löwith puts a little more meat on the bone, but the word is nonetheless used in a way that seems to assume the reader's prior knowledge of its meaning: "The problem of their [Stirner's and Kierkegaard's] common radicalism is the nihilism which arises from extreme isolation. For Stirner it is the careless nihilism of 'I entrust my cause to nothing'—namely, to nothing other than myself. For Kierkegaard, it is the melancholy nihilism of irony and boredom, of anxiety and despair."[36] As with many of Stirner's other detractors, one may assume Löwith saw no reason to give a detailed definition of nihilism, because its general post-Nietzschean meaning had, by this time, become sufficiently well-established.

Throughout the 1930s and 1940s, the printed references to Stirner and nihilism continued, even if their frequency was affected by the general decline in the quality and quantity of cultural journals and scholarly publications in Nazi Germany. In the section about Stirner in his history of philosophy, Joël writes: "Pure egoism ends in pure indifference; pure individualism ends in nihilism"; Kurt Adolf Mautz (1911–2000), in his 1936 doctoral dissertation on Stirner, declares: "The initial, negative tendency, the 'nihilism' of Stirner's thought, emerges at once from the whole conception of *Der Einzige und sein Eigentum*"; and Ludwig Binswanger (1881–1966), the pioneer of existential psychology, describes Stirner as "a very skilled stylist and dialectician, a passionate revolutionary and fighter, but in the guise of a dictator, an intellectual nihilist, but with the weapons of the mind."[37] The connotations and insinuations evident here, in the absence of actual definitions of nihilism, are that Stirner's thought involves negation, destruction, and the complete absence of a moral compass.

---

34   Keyserling, *Unsterblichkeit*, 154; W. Stockgänger, "Max Stirner," *Der freie Arbeiter. Wissen und Wollen. Publikations-Organ der Föderation der kommunistischen Anarchisten Deutschlands* 15, no. 44 (1922): 2. See Lütgert, "Die Religion des deutschen Idealismus und ihr Ende," 220; Baxa, *Gesellschaftslehre*, 106. See Löwith, *Das Individuum*, 177.
35   Löwith, *From Hegel to Nietzsche*, 71.
36   Löwith, *From Hegel to Nietzsche*, 359.
37   Joël, *Wandlungen der Weltanschauung*, 2:649; Mautz, *Die Philosophie Max Stirners*, 78; Binswanger, *Grundformen und Erkenntnis menschlichen Daseins*, 458.

Allegations and Denials: After World War II

There can be little doubt that the discourse surrounding Stirner and nihilism in the period around World War II was heavily influenced by historical events, which appeared to confirm Nietzsche's diagnosis of Western decadence. Despite the optimism that accompanied the end of the war, there was inevitably a strong sense of the breakdown of traditional values, a scenario into which Stirner's rampant iconoclasm seemed easily to fit. The rare exceptions to the orthodox view of Stirner's status as a nihilist expressed at this time only serve to prove the enduring rule. The one such occurrence in the 1940s is Rudolf Schröder's article in *Die freie Welt* (The Free World), where he writes:

> It is pointless to argue about whether Stirner, with his formula, "I have made nothing my cause," is to be counted among the nihilists. He is not a nihilist, despite his statement that his cause is neither the divine nor the human, but his own. The accusation of nihilism is already refuted by the reference to the fact that for him the "individual" exists, admittedly as the "Unique One," but to whom everything else is "property."[38]

For Schröder, nihilism seems to exist mainly in the sense of ontological nihilism, or denial of being, which is a narrow definition on which to base one's judgment. Yet however firm his refutation of Stirner's connection to nihilism, his opinion is otherwise largely a conventional one, concurring with the usual assessment of Stirner's anarchism, which he posits unquestioningly.

Otherwise, in the post-war period, the familiar depictions of Stirner as a nihilist soon resumed. The Marxist historian Auguste Cornu (1888–1981) wrote dismissively: "Stirner . . . recognized only one reality, the ego, and only one principle, the cult of the ego; he made absolute egoism the sole motive of human activity, ending up with nihilism and anarchism."[39] This is not the place to elucidate the obvious reasons for Marxist enmity towards individualism, nor is it within the scope of this book to examine in detail Marx and Engels's comprehensive character assassination of Stirner in *Die deutsche Ideologie*, especially as they accuse Stirner of many things, but not nihilism, explicitly at least. It is telling though that writers and commentators of all political and philosophical persuasions, including Marxists like Cornu, make use of the epithet "nihilist" to describe—and invariably to discredit—Stirner, even though it is a term Stirner never

---

38 Rudolf Schröder, "Max Stirner," *Die freie Welt* 1, no. 1 (1949): 25.
39 Cornu, *Karl Marx*, 77.

used himself. The Japanese scholar, Keiji Nishitani (1900–1990), who had studied under Heidegger, identifies "the outlines of nihilism" in *Der Einzige*, while the Protestant theologian Walter Künneth (1901–1997) imagines the form of Stirner's free individual taking shape in a no-man's land, "on the border of nihilism, anarchism, and atheism."[40] Camus had used a similar image in *L'Homme révolté* (The Rebel, 1951) to delineate the realm of Stirner's *Einziger*: "Stirner, and with him, all the nihilist rebels, run to the borders, drunk with destruction."[41]

Among the few articles written in 1956 to mark the centenary of Stirner's death and the sesquicentennial of his birth, there are two that mention Stirner in connection with nihilism: Hans Heinz Holz (1927–2011), a Marxist philosopher, called Stirner "a harbinger of modern nihilistic trends," while Wilhelm Klutentreter (1908–1986), a Catholic journalist, described him as "a radical outsider as a trendsetter for nihilism."[42] Holz was more expansive in a later publication, in which he helpfully gives a definition of nihilism, as well as showing his true Marxist colors:

> What is to be understood by nihilism . . . [is] the negation of any objective obligations and values that could provide man with a framework and guideline for his actions. . . . In an extreme form, the attempt to create a nihilistic system of thought was once undertaken in the nineteenth century; namely by Max Stirner. . . . This attempt was an utter failure. . . . The ideology of a petty-bourgeois megalomania, which Stirner's work reflects, was not up to the problem of nihilism.[43]

In the 1950s and 1960s, one also finds the Jesuit theologian Jean-Yves Calvez (1927–2010) calling Stirner "the father of nihilism"; the eminent professor of history at the Sorbonne Jacques Droz (1909–1998) referring to Stirner in relation to "extreme individualism and nihilist anarchy"; and the post-structuralist philosopher Gilles Deleuze writing of "Stirner's extreme nihilism" and how he is "*the dialectician who reveals nihilism as*

---

40 Nishitani, *The Self-Overcoming of Nihilism*, 101; Künneth, *Politik zwischen Dämon und Gott*, 234.

41 Camus, *L'Homme révolté*, 87–88.

42 Hans Heinz Holz, "Das entfesselte Ich. Zum 100. Todestag Max Stirners am 26. Juni," *Frankfurter Allgemeine Zeitung*, June 26, 1956: 10; W. Klutentreter, "'Mir geht nichts über mich.' Zum 150. Geburtstag von Max Stirner—Ein radikaler Außenseiter als Schrittmacher des Nihilismus," *Düsseldorfer Nachrichten*, October 20, 1956: 246.

43 Holz, *Der französische Existentialismus*, 12–13.

the truth of the dialectic."⁴⁴ A lone voice of dissent, at least on the issue of nihilism, was provided by the Dutch sociologist Johan Goudsblom (1932–2020), who declared: "Outright denial of the existence of truth and values is already a step beyond the complex of the nihilist problem. It is often called nihilism because of its provocative denial of all ethical norms. However, the nihilist problematic is more clearly present in the doubts of Kleist or Kierkegaard than in the fanaticism of Stirner."⁴⁵ Here Goudsblom raises an important question to be taken up in chapter 7, namely whether Stirner's untormented outlook can be squared with the modern, existential definition of nihilism.

Laska identifies the second Stirner renaissance as starting in 1968, coinciding with Helms's edition of Stirner's writings.⁴⁶ There is certainly a proliferation of scholarly works on, or involving, Stirner that starts around this time, in which the charge of nihilism is as prevalent as ever. The Feuerbach scholar Werner Schuffenhauer (1930–2012) speaks of "his nihilistic-anarchistic tendency"; David McLellan (b. 1940) writes that "Stirner was indeed a solipsist and a nihilist"; the political philosopher Friedrich Berber (1898–1984) calls Stirner's union of egoists "purely negative, destructive, nihilistic"; and Dieter Arendt, in his anthology of nihilist texts, states that: "Stirner's self-absorbed philosophical thinking based on negation is not explicitly nihilism, but to all intents and purposes it is."⁴⁷ Giorgio Penzo, in a work first published in 1971, condenses many of the previous denunciations, damning Stirner with very faint praise in a few lines of nihilism-filled prose:

> Stirner's current relevance lies . . . above all in his particular conception of nihilism, which, in its radicalism, is unique in the history of ideas. Stirner illuminates in it a nihilism devoid not only of metaphysical but also of existential transcendence, a nihilism that means the end of all philosophizing. In the conclusion of his work, *Der Einzige*, Stirner writes explicitly not that he wants to make his concern "nothingness," but "nothing." . . . No thinker has succeeded in surpassing Stirner's nihilism in its profound radicalism.⁴⁸

In the history of Stirner criticism, the most prolific repetition of the accusation of nihilism can be found in Paterson's canonical work, *The Nihilistic Egoist: Max Stirner*, which was also published in 1971. In the

---

44   Calvez, *Karl Marx*, 108; Droz, *Europe between Revolutions*, 155; Deleuze, *Nietzsche and Philosophy*, 162, 161.
45   Goudsblom, *Nihilism and Culture*, 137.
46   See Laska, *Ein heimlicher Hit*, 6–7.
47   Schuffenhauer, *Feuerbach und der junge Marx*, 137; McLellan, *The Young Hegelians*, 119; Berber, *Das Staatsziel*, 407; Arendt, "Introduction," 72.
48   Penzo, *Die existentielle Empörung*, 11–12.

last six sentences of the final chapter alone (before the conclusion), the words nihilism, nihilist, and nihilistic are mentioned no less than sixteen times. It is a book that will be considered in more detail later in this chapter, but a foretaste of its forthright, if repetitive, condemnation can be found in the introduction: "His one great book, *Der Einzige und sein Eigenthum*, must be the only sustained attempt to present a philosophy of unsparing nihilism systematically and without reserve.... He intends ... to stand as the avowed representative of the most extreme dimension of nihilism to which logic can carry him. For Stirner, this is the nihilism of the nihilistic *egoist*."[49] As Paterson's book was, for a long time, the only full-length monograph on Stirner written in English, it has exerted considerable influence in the world of anglophone Stirner scholarship. David Holbrook was one of those sufficiently convinced by Paterson's argument to place Stirner within an apocalyptic vision of Nietzschean-existential nihilism: "I believe that the underlying philosophy of our culture has become nihilistic. If we pursue the implications of nihilism to their ultimate conclusions, where do we arrive? Very few have dared to do this: Max Stirner ... was one who dared.... He is the unacknowledged prophet of today's fashionable culture."[50]

John P. Clark (b. 1928), commenting on Paterson's ideas from a social anarchist perspective, challenges this orthodoxy: "He [Stirner] believes that the values which are created by the ego are worthwhile, and thus it seems invalid to call him a nihilist, in the sense of one who lives in a world without value."[51] Lawrence Stepelevich (b. 1930) does likewise: "But Stirner is no more the nihilist than Hegel or Sartre, who speaks of consciousness as 'the worm of nothingness.' Paterson's misinterpretation of Stirner as a nihilist commits a common error based upon ignoring the phenomenology of consciousness."[52] Stepelevich accuses Paterson of misconstruing Stirner's message as being of exclusively negative import, thus pointing, if only implicitly, to the oxymoronic nature of Paterson's formulation of nihilistic egoism. The heterodox opinions of Clark and Stepelevich in the 1970s and 1980s, respectively, continued the loose tradition throughout the twentieth century of one dissenting voice every decade or so on the subject of Stirner and nihilism. In the 1990s, the consensus was reasserted by Schmitz's immortal phrase (even if it is borrowed from Nietzsche), describing Stirner as "the only perfect nihilist in the history of modern philosophy."[53]

49 Paterson, *The Nihilistic Egoist*, ix.
50 Holbrook, "A Philosopher for Today?," 382.
51 Clark, *Max Stirner's Egoism*, 53.
52 Stepelevich, "Max Stirner as Hegelian," 610.
53 Schmitz, *Selbstdarstellung als Philosophie*, 309. The only "consummate nihilist" is perhaps a better translation, but I am following the examples of various

The steady increase in the number of references to Stirner as a nihilist, and the relative scarcity of declarations to the contrary, has largely resulted in the label sticking. In current general works of reference, one frequently finds Stirner standing "nearer . . . to . . . the nihilists," being placed "among the first philosophical nihilists," and ranking "as one of the literary grandfathers of nihilism."[54] This is also true for books on nihilism, where Stirner is often cited as one of its many representatives. Carr writes with unconvincing vagueness: "The only possible supporter of nihilism during this period [of the earliest discussion of nihilism] was a left-wing Hegelian, Max Stirner. . . . Stirner offered a view that seemed to embrace everything denounced as nihilistic by these critics. He never, however, explicitly described himself as a nihilist, which perhaps suggests that he also saw the term negatively."[55] The self-evident limits of Carr's knowledge about Stirner seem to have led her to fill in the lacunae using little more than the prodigious power of her imagination. She thus places Stirner within the discussion of nihilism in relation to Fichtean subjective idealism and makes Stirner an advocate of the nihilistic standpoint. This is misleading, both conceptually and chronologically. It also drives her to explain why Stirner failed to confess to being a nihilist and to speculate that it was because he was concerned about the stigma associated with the term. One can only describe this as pure fantasy; Stirner was the last person to worry about opprobrium. The reason he did not describe himself as a nihilist was because the word was hardly used at the time; and, in any event, on the occasions when it was used, it was as a term of polemical abuse rather than as the description of a philosophical outlook. None of those accused of nihilism within the framework of this historical discussion, like Moses Mendelssohn or Fichte himself, would have considered wearing this derogatory term as a badge of honor. Carr goes on to compound her error by misnaming Stirner's magnum opus *Das Ich und Sein Eigenes*, apparently a poor retranslation back into German of the already unsatisfactory English title, *The Ego and Its Own*, calling

---

translators of Nietzsche's *The Will to Power*, from which the phrase is borrowed, including Walter Kaufmann and R. J. Hollingdale and R. Kevin Hill and Michael A. Scarpitti, all of whom translate the corresponding phrase of Nietzsche's using the adjective "perfect."

54   *Encyclopedia.com*, "Stirner, Max (1806–1856)," by George Woodcock, accessed June 30, 2023, https://www.encyclopedia.com/humanities/encyclopedias-almanacs-transcripts-and-maps/stirner-max-1806-1856; *Internet Encyclopedia of Philosophy*, "Nihilism," by Alan Pratt, accessed June 30, 2023, https://www.iep.utm.edu/nihilism/; *New World Encyclopedia*, s.v. "Max Stirner," accessed June 30, 2023, http://www.newworldencyclopedia.org/entry/Max_Stirner.

55   Carr, *The Banalization of Nihilism*, 147–48.

it "probably the most frankly nihilistic work ever written."[56] It is hard to believe that her overall appraisal of Stirner is anything more than a fanciful regurgitation of prevailing opinions.

Vercellone also includes Stirner conclusively and superlatively in the inventory of nihilists: "On a philosophical level, there is probably no text that presents the dissolution of Hegelianism into nihilism in a more paradigmatic way than *Der Einzige und sein Eigentum* (1852) [*sic*] by Max Stirner."[57] Winfried Schröder speaks of Stirner's "outspoken moral nihilism," and Will Slocombe repeats the same mantra as Paterson, informing us that "the conflation of 'nihilism' and 'egoism' is implied throughout *The Ego and Its Own*."[58] Even Ludger Lütkehaus, in his monumental attempt at a constructive reevaluation of nothingness, describes the motto with which Stirner begins and ends his magnum opus, "Ich hab' Mein Sach' auf Nichts gestellt" (All things are nothing to me), as "the new nihilistic hymn."[59] Jörg Ulrich refers extensively to Lütkehaus's ideas concerning both nihilism and Stirner in his 2002 social-scientific analysis of modern individuality, and reaches the following assessment: "And indeed, Stirner sides with perfect [consummate] nihilism, precisely by consistently and unreservedly standing on the ground of nothingness."[60]

A novel position on Stirner's relationship to nihilism is taken by John Marmysz in his 2003 book, *Laughing at Nothing: Humor as a Response to Nihilism*. According to Marmysz's reading, Stirner, like the Pyrrhonists, "confronted the themes . . . in the basic premises of nihilism" and found his own solution in the concept of egoism and its realization in self-enjoyment, which represents Stirner's version of ataraxia.[61] Such a view is controversial insofar as it claims that Stirner engages with the problem of nihilism by giving "attention to the personal frustration involved in striving toward the unattainable."[62] This seems, at the very least, to involve the superimposition of the modern conception of nihilism onto Stirner's ideas, suggesting that he saw atheism as a problem to be overcome rather than a liberation from spurious dogma, or life as an experience in search of a meaning rather than an opportunity for individual self-realization. The impression thus made of conceptual and chronological confusion is reinforced by the statement: "Nihilists, as both Kant and Stirner have quite correctly pointed out, must always fail in their desire to realize the ideal."[63] Marmysz here contradicts his earlier remark that Stirner does

56 Carr, *The Banalization of Nihilism*, 164.
57 Vercellone, *Einführung in den Nihilismus*, 34–35.
58 Schröder, *Moralischer Nihilismus*, 56; Slocombe, *Nihilism*, 11.
59 Lütkehaus, *Nichts*, 661.
60 Ulrich, *Individualität als politische Religion*, 265–66.
61 Marmysz, *Laughing at Nothing*, 79.
62 Marmysz, *Laughing at Nothing*, 81.
63 Marmysz, *Laughing at Nothing*, 104.

not discuss nihilism explicitly, and posits an interplay between Stirner and nihilism for which it is hard to find any concrete evidence.

Returning to a more orthodox view, Gillespie, in a 2011 essay on nihilism in the nineteenth century, continues the tradition of dismissing Stirner (often in very few words and without making any attempt to demonstrate an understanding of his ideas) as the odious voice of unconscionable nihilism: "We also see this nihilistic impulse in its extremity in the thought of Max Stirner, . . . who sought to free the individual not only from God but also from society and indeed from humanity as such. . . . Here the connection to the earlier Fichtean and Romantic nihilists and to later nihilism is especially apparent. This is equally true of Stirner's moral stance, for he was willing to countenance incest, infanticide and murder."[64] Although Jon Stewart, in his 2023 history of nihilism in the nineteenth century, avoids repeating this common litany of charges, he nonetheless observes that "Stirner's work *The Ego and Its Own* . . . has often been associated with nihilism."[65] If nothing else, this demonstrates that the truism of Stirner's nihilistic tendencies persists to this day. Another recent, though more general, textbook on nihilism, Elmar Dod's *Der unheimlichste Gast wird heimisch* (The Uncanniest Guest Returns Home, 2019), also briefly mentions Stirner, "whose work, *Der Einzige und sein Eigentum*, sketched out, even before Nietzsche, the elements of a consistent nihilism."[66] It is, once again, a claim that relies heavily on *Der Einzige*'s opening and closing line, which is the title Dod uses for the relevant sub-section, and that (perhaps understandably in a wide-ranging work where Stirner plays only a minute role) offers nothing more substantial than a concise recapitulation of the consensus view.

The last quarter of a century, however, has also seen the first concerted efforts to challenge the accusations of nihilism leveled against Stirner. The chief catalyst for this loosely coordinated endeavor was the establishment of the Max Stirner Society in 2002, which acted as a forum for the exchange of ideas between its members and associates, who were, naturally enough, favorably disposed towards Stirner. Laska, in his 1996 work, *Ein dauerhafter Dissident*, had already included the nihilist as one of the labels used to undermine Stirner's standing, along with the unperson, the anarchist, and the proto-fascist, among many others.[67] The essence of Laska's intriguing but speculative argument is that it was the shared interest of the two antithetical philosophical colossi of the nineteenth century, Marx and Nietzsche, along with their numerous followers and acolytes, to deprecate Stirner and deny the significance of his contribution to the

---

64 Gillespie, "Nihilism in the Nineteenth Century," 284.
65 Stewart, *A History of Nihilism in the Nineteenth Century*, 280–81.
66 Dod, *Der unheimlichste Gast wird heimisch*, 20.
67 See Laska, *Ein dauerhafter Dissident*, 5.

history of ideas, fundamentally because Stirner offered a viable philosophical alternative which threatened to subvert their ideologies. The charge of nihilism is therefore, in Laska's opinion, just another manifestation of the intrinsically hostile reception of Stirner, which is characterized by clandestine suppression rather than serious, intellectual engagement.[68]

After Laska's bold statement in defense of Stirner, a number of other writers publicly questioned the orthodox association of Stirner with nihilism. Halil Ibrahim Türkdogan, a founder member of the Max Stirner Society, wrote: "Camus contents himself . . . with pointing out that Stirner can be classified as nihilistic. As part of his revolt, Stirner pronounces his disgust for words and ideas, but that is far from making him nihilistic."[69] Another founder member, Herbert Scheit, in his speech delivered at the 2002 Stirner conference in Hummeltal, cast further doubt on the standard view: "The only duty that Stirner would to some extent consider valid, would be: be yourself! Or also: be an egoist, i.e., live your own life, for you only have this one, and pursue only your real interests. . . . Is that really supposed to be the whole Stirner? The prophet of self-realization and enjoyment of life through self-denial? . . . But where is the nihilist and violent cynic in this almost sympathetic picture of Stirner?"[70] Another founder member of the society, Kurt W. Fleming, in an unpublished speech to commemorate the two hundredth anniversary of Stirner's birth, also challenges the labeling of Stirner as, among other things, a nihilist.[71] In the anglophone world, Newman echoes these opinions in the introduction to his anthology of essays on Stirner. Like Fleming, he criticizes the application of unsatisfactory labels to Stirner and, like Scheit, he rejects the hackneyed reproach of nihilism in favor of a positive interpretation of his philosophy, declaring: "far from leading to nihilism, I contend that Stirner provides us with a new ethics of freedom and autonomy."[72]

With his three short books on Stirner, Laska attempted to liberate him from the stigma of the previous hundred and fifty years, an endeavor which stimulated an increasingly open-minded debate among his colleagues and in the wider scholarly community. At any rate, there has been a noticeable softening in the critical approach to Stirner since the appearance of Laska's publications on Stirner in the 1990s. One example of this is to be found in Reschika's chapter on Stirner in his book, *Philosophische*

---

68 See Laska, *Ein dauerhafter Dissident*, 105–7.
69 Türkdogan, "Fragmentarisches über die Revolte," 46.
70 Scheit, "Max Stirner—ein antipädagogischer Pädagoge," 13–14.
71 Kurt Fleming, "Max Stirner—ein Prä-Anarchist," unpublished speech marking the two-hundredth anniversary of Max Stirner's birth, delivered on November 28, 2006, at the Rosa-Luxemburg-Stiftung Sachsen in Leipzig.
72 Newman, "Introduction: Re-encountering Stirner's Ghosts," 16.

Abenteurer (Philosophical Adventurers, 2001), in which he states: "Most people consider Stirner to be the epitome of a pathological solipsist, a relentless, megalomaniacal egoist, and ethical nihilist. . . . Despite these unanimously damning verdicts, it is an . . . undeniable fact that philosophers of very different provenances engage intensively . . . with this archenemy of all religion, morality, and traditional political order."[73] In his conclusion, Reschika does not fully endorse Laska's opinion, but nor does he reject it, opting instead to leave it up to the reader to decide whether to accept Laska's claim "that Stirner had already opened up 'ways beyond nihilism.'"[74] Bernd Kast, who was the chairman of the Max Stirner Society and editor of the *Stirner-Jahrbuch* for a number of years, is less equivocal. He makes a vehement refutation of the characterization of Stirner as a nihilist, describing the association as an eradicable misunderstanding and insisting that Stirner is anything but a nihilist if nihilism is defined as the absence of meaning.[75]

Despite the considerable efforts of Laska and Kast, their view of Stirner with regard to nihilism remains a minority one in the history of Stirner's reception. The chronological record of the discussion of Stirner and nihilism throws up a recognizable pattern, which, as one might expect, follows the word's etymological development. It starts with Rosenkranz's polemical attack on Stirner's subjectivism, atheism, and social radicalism, which can be seen as an extension of usage of the term nihilism within the context of the atheism dispute, having spilled over into post-Hegelian philosophy. The next phase begins in the final quarter of the nineteenth century with such critics as Grün, Biedermann, and Laas identifying elements of moral and political nihilism in Stirner, to which anarchism was added by the likes of Bernstein and Dubois. In the first half of the twentieth century, the moral nihilism of which Stirner had frequently been accused becomes increasingly Nietzschean, especially in the hands of Löwith. Finally, with Camus and Arvon, the existentialist element starts to play a more significant role, a trend that has continued to the present day. In the following chapters, each of these distinct forms of nihilism will undergo specific investigation in relation to Stirner's thought.

73   Reschika, *Philosophische Abenteurer*, 70.
74   Reschika, *Philosophische Abenteurer*, 100. He is referring to Laska's article in *Die Zeit* in 2000, where he wrote: "No one wanted to follow Stirner's step beyond the New Enlightenment. His 'nihilism' simply could not be the result of enlightened thought. Greatly alarmed, all were blind to the fact that Stirner had already opened up ways 'beyond nihilism.'" Bernd A. Laska, "Dissident geblieben," *Die Zeit*, January 27, 2000: 49.
75   See Kast, "Afterword," in *EE*, 380.

Nothingness in *Der Einzige und sein Eigentum*

One common theme throughout the evolution of the debate surrounding Stirner and nihilism, at least from the time of the first Stirner renaissance, is the importance given to the heading of the prologue of *Der Einzige*, which is also the book's last line: "Ich hab' Mein' Sach' auf Nichts gestellt" (All things are nothing to me.)[76] Even in an era that celebrates countercultural rebellion, the impression generally made by this statement is a thoroughly negative one; it resonates for many like a Faustian incantation. It is understood not as the opening line of a drinking song (as in Goethe's original poem, "Vanitas! vanitatum vanitas!", from which Stirner borrowed it and which will be discussed in more detail in chapter 7 below) and thus as an expression of gay abandon, but rather as a hymn to the diabolical force of the void. Löwith writes in an endnote: "The inspiration for Stirner's motto probably was Goethe's poem 'Vanitas vanitatum vanitas.' Kierkegaard, too, was acquainted with it. In his *Journals* (edited Ulrich, p. 145), he describes it as being 'very interesting,' because it is the nihilistic 'summation of life' of a very great individuality."[77] The alleged nihilistic import of the short but pregnant line that bookends Stirner's magnum opus is a recurrent theme in the criticisms of Stirner by his many detractors, examples of which can be found in the comments of Bernstein, Heman, Penzo, Lütkehaus, Ulrich, and Dod, all mentioned above. Lucchesi sums up the argument as follows: "The Stirnerian ego is the nothing from which the entire content of consciousness emerges. . . . In order to end as nothing, this ego must consume itself, destroy itself, dissolve itself. . . . Stirner's individualism ends in nihilism."[78]

Nishitani is another commentator who endows this short sentence with great significance, thus leading him to infer: "Here we have Stirner's basic standpoint *in nuce*: the negation of any and all standpoints. . . . It means a lack of interest in anything . . . and a feeling of general apathy."[79] Like so many others before and after him, Nishitani places a disproportionate emphasis on this one, once-repeated, line. Assuming it does not reflect a drastically abridged reading of the book, the reason for this hyperfocus can perhaps be found in the striking nature of the statement, which is reinforced by its two conspicuous locations. Added to this is the problematic nature of the concept of nothingness: the scourge of the ancient Greeks, the absence in Neoplatonism's *privatio boni* theory of evil, the void of Christian pre-creation, and the absolute antithesis in

---

76 *EE*, 13, 370; *EO*, 5, 324.
77 Löwith, *From Hegel to Nietzsche*, 411.
78 Lucchesi, *Die Individualitätsphilosophie Max Stirners*, 96.
79 Nishitani, *The Self-Overcoming of Nihilism*, 103.

Hegelian dialectics. Rooted subliminally in the idea of the undiscovered country of death, the concept of nothingness both fascinates and horrifies the human mind, but it is horror that dominates. Stirner's highlighting of this epigrammatic line exploits an elemental insecurity, thereby grabbing the reader's attention and underlining the radical nature of his message. The fact that the Goethean original is a parody of a Christian hymn, "Ich hab' mein Sach Gott heimgestellt" (I have entrusted my affairs to God), which Stirner is very likely to have known, would have made it seem all the more appropriate for his subversive purposes.[80] Stirner is notorious for having reveled in the provocation of his readers, seemingly enjoying the alienating effect it had on his conservative opponents while no doubt believing that the enlightened observer would see the funny side. In view of the overwhelmingly hostile reception his ideas have received, it might be argued that this was a serious miscalculation.

In ending his book with *Nichts*, Stirner was emulating not only Klingemann in *Nachtwachen* and Jean Paul in *Clavis Fichtiana*, but also Schopenhauer, who concludes his 1819 magnum opus, *Die Welt als Wille und Vorstellung* (The World as Will and Representation), with the following solemn lines:

> Before us there is certainly left only nothing; but that which struggles against this flowing away into nothing, namely our nature, is indeed just the will-to-live which we ourselves are.... That we abhor nothingness so much is simply another way of saying that we will life so much, and that we are nothing but this will.... What remains after the complete abolition of the will is, for all who are still full of the will, assuredly nothing. But also conversely, to those in whom the will has turned and denied itself, this very real world of ours with all its suns and galaxies, is—nothing.[81]

Nothingness plays a central role in Schopenhauer's *Weltanschauung*; it is the essential pre- and post-condition of human existence: "Of course in *that* sense in which he arises out of nothing when he is begotten, man becomes nothing through death."[82] This is a fundamental axiom to which all of Schopenhauer's main philosophical propositions relate, and its negative import predetermines his pessimistic outlook. In *Parerga und Paralipomena* (1851), he writes: "Time is that by virtue of which everything becomes nothingness in our hands and loses all real value."[83]

---

80 "Ich hab' mein Sach Gott heimgestellt" is a chorale cantata by Bach (BWV 351) with words by Johann Leon (1531–1597).
81 Schopenhauer, *The World as Will and Representation*, 1:411–12.
82 Schopenhauer, *The World as Will and Representation*, 2:481.
83 Schopenhauer, *Essays and Aphorisms*, 51.

If Stirner's thought involves negation, as many of his detractors have claimed, it is of a different order of magnitude to Schopenhauer's.

Stirner's intention is quite dissimilar to Schopenhauer's, or Klingemann's, or Jean Paul's for that matter, whose concepts of nothingness were born out of the subject-object dichotomy of German idealism. For Stirner, the real import of the word *Nichts* in his opening and closing lines is to describe the rejection of all alien, externally imposed causes. This is made much clearer in another line borrowed from Goethe, which concludes *Der Einzige*'s short prologue: "Mir geht nichts über Mich!" (Nothing is more to me than myself!).[84] There can be no question, at least in the German original, that *nichts* in this sentence, unlike in the book's opening and closing motto, is an indefinite pronoun, that it is used, in other words, to apotheosize the individual self, not to burden it under the weight of nothingness. As for the motto, *Nichts* is capitalized, as it is in Goethe's poem, presumably to emphasize the rejection of all external causes. It also functions as a parody of the German Romantics' use of the word and indicates Stirner's naturalist credentials, later made plain by such lines as: "If I concern myself for myself, the unique one, then my concern rests on its transitory, mortal creator, who consumes himself."[85] Stirner clearly harbors no illusions regarding the immortality of the soul.

The finitude of human existence and the fact of personal extinction are givens throughout *Der Einzige*, though they do not elicit deep reflection, or worse, despair. Strauss, Feuerbach, and Bruno Bauer had done a thorough job of—figuratively speaking—incinerating the scriptures of Christianity, and religion in general, and with them the belief in an afterlife; Stirner plays in the ashes that are left behind. When Stirner writes of "the creative nothing, the nothing out of which I myself as creator create everything," it is a joke at God's expense, mimicking the early Christian theologians' concept of *creatio ex nihilo*, and declaring that God has been replaced, not by what Stirner considered to be Feuerbach's fiction of mankind, but by the unique reality of the individual self.[86] Clearly, such profanity is highly offensive to those who choose to ignore or disbelieve

---

84   EE, 15; EO, 7. Stirner took the line from Johann Wolfgang von Goethe, *Satyros oder der vergötterte Waldteufel* (Satyros or the Deified Forest Devil, 1773/1817), 2: "Mir geht in der Welt nichts über mich; Denn Gott ist Gott, und Ich bin Ich" (Naught in the world is more to me than I; For God, he is God, and I, I am I).

85   EO, 324; EE, 370: "Stell' Ich auf Mich, den Einzigen, meine Sache, dann steht sie auf dem Vergänglichen, dem sterblichen Schöpfer seiner, der sich selbst verzehrt."

86   EO, 7; EE, 15: "das schöpferische Nichts, das Nichts, aus welchem Ich selbst als Schöpfer Alles schaffe." For the Christian concept, see May, *Creatio Ex Nihilo*.

Strauss, Feuerbach, and Bauer's accounts of religion as a human invention, which helps to explain some of the extreme theological reactions Stirner's work has provoked. Kast, in the footnotes of his study edition of *Der Einzige*, identifies more than seventy references to biblical verses, many of them mischievous, all of them, without doubt, blasphemous in the eyes of most believers.[87]

In view of the actual role of the word *Nichts* in Stirner's thought, Deleuze seems to be overstating the case when he identifies Stirner's ideas as fundamentally nihilistic: "The unique ego turns everything but itself into nothingness, and this nothingness is precisely its own nothingness, the ego's own nothingness. Stirner is too much of a dialectician to think in any other terms but those of property, alienation and reappropriation—but too exacting not to see where this thought leads: to the ego which is nothing, to nihilism."[88] Stirner does indeed affirm the nothingness of the ego, in terms of the impermanence of individual human consciousness, but the judgment of nihilism is entirely Deleuze's. Although his opinion may lean on received wisdom, it is Deleuze who overlays Stirner's observation of the ephemerality of life with Macbeth's assumption of life signifying nothing, which is a sentiment that is completely absent from Stirner's writings. As we have seen, however, Deleuze is far from being alone in labeling Stirner as nihilistic. He is not even the most extreme of Stirner's accusers: this accolade unquestionably belongs to Paterson, whose monograph on Stirner therefore deserves particular attention in the context of this study.

Paterson's book is an exercise in excoriation, combining a moralizing tone with repetitive and intemperate language and a pedantic style of writing. His assertions of Stirner's nihilism are legion, often availing themselves of the familiar superlatives commonly encountered in the condemnations penned by many of Stirner's other detractors. Thus, he writes: "*Der Einzige und sein Eigenthum* must be the most uncompromising of atheistic manifestos."[89] Just sixty pages later, it is "arguably the most complete and uncompromising of all nihilist manifestos."[90] Atheism and nihilism possess, for Paterson, virtual synonymity, though he does not express this simply as his own opinion, but suggests it was also Stirner's view: "a genuinely total atheism, according to Stirner, will find itself to be indistinguishable from the nihilism of the nihilistic egoist."[91] As there is no record in Stirner's writings of his ever having used the words nihilism

---

87   See Camus, *L'Homme révolté*, 85: "Stirner goes as far as he can with blasphemy."
88   Deleuze, *Nietzsche and Philosophy*, 161–62.
89   Paterson, *The Nihilistic Egoist*, 192.
90   Paterson, *The Nihilistic Egoist*, 252.
91   Paterson, *The Nihilistic Egoist*, xii.

or nihilist, one wonders on what basis Paterson makes this extravagant assertion. It is not, in any case, a slip of the pen on Paterson's part, for Stirner the incorrigible, self-confessed, ultimate nihilist ("the avowed representative of the most extreme dimension of nihilism"), is a recurrent theme of his monograph.[92] The epithet nihilist is, again, Paterson's interpretation, but he presents it as if it were Stirner's own self-confession.

Paterson's understanding of nihilism becomes clear from such phrases as the "systematic refusal to ascribe virtue or meaning to experience" and the "vision of a world without God, . . . of a meaningless world, . . . which is strictly no 'world' but rather a moral and metaphysical chaos."[93] It is essentially Nietzsche's definition based on the disorientation that follows the death of God as a credible concept, which is not to say, however, that Paterson agrees with Nietzsche concerning either God's demise or Christianity's contribution to the rise of nihilism. Paterson elevates Stirner, whom he compares to Mephistopheles, to a symbolic apotheosis of the nihilist.[94] He denounces him with such immoderate statements as: "The monster of nihilism assuredly found in Stirner its most complete avatar."[95] One overused word in this process of demonization is "total": Stirner represents "total egoism," "total atheism," and, of course, "total nihilism."[96] Paterson identifies "in Stirner's Unique One the one finished, historic instance of that total encounter with nothingness."[97] What distinguishes the total atheist from the common or garden existentialist variety, according to Paterson's assessment at least, is that the former "actively wills and lives it," whereas, for the existentialists, "their atheism is a reluctant atheism."[98]

It is here that Paterson's underlying agenda becomes apparent, for, having meticulously explained the meaning of belief in a transcendent God, he proceeds to accuse Stirner of rejecting God as a "deliberate and perpetual choice."[99] Stirner is presented as the most sinful of sinners, or, as Herbert Read ironically expresses the general opinion of Stirner's detractors, "a lost soul condemned to the lowest regions of limbo."[100] When Paterson writes that Stirner's "metaphysical construction" is a "project of self-gratification," it conjures up images of Stirner in a darkened room willfully condemning himself to eternal blindness.[101] Schiereck has called

---

92 Paterson, *The Nihilistic Egoist*, ix.
93 Paterson, *The Nihilistic Egoist*, 45, 226.
94 See Paterson, *The Nihilistic Egoist*, 191.
95 Paterson, *The Nihilistic Egoist*, xii.
96 See Paterson, *The Nihilistic Egoist*, ix, 191, 51.
97 Paterson, *The Nihilistic Egoist*, 171.
98 Paterson, *The Nihilistic Egoist*, 225.
99 Paterson, *The Nihilistic Egoist*, 224.
100 Read, *The Tenth Muse*, 75.
101 Paterson, *The Nihilistic Egoist*, 293.

Paterson's monograph "a shambles through and through";[102] what is certainly true is that, aside from the historical and biographical information it contains, the book is of little use to anyone but the devout religious believer, as an instrument either of self-correction or of self-vindication, based on a fictitious recreation of the man and his philosophy. Paterson's Presbyterian interpretation intentionally misconstrues Stirner's meaning in the service of religion, and, to this end, "nihilist" represents the perfect epithet to express his utter condemnation. In this way, at least, the accusation of nihilism against Stirner in the modern, existentialist sense, is closely related to that of the very first indictment of this kind made by Rosenkranz soon after the publication of *Der Einzige*.

Egoism in Stirner's Thought

The other epithet that Paterson employs polemically, not only in the title of his monograph on Stirner but throughout the work, is that of egoist. It is a term that must also be considered because of its correspondence with nihilism and its repeated use by Stirner's accusers. Unlike nihilist, egoist is a word Stirner uses frequently and more or less interchangeably with the subject of his book, *der Einzige*. Egoism, seen not in terms of callous selfishness, but as the exaltation of the autonomous, subjective individual, is demonstrated throughout the work by the habitual (though inconsistent) capitalization of first-person pronouns. But, as Kast has observed, Stirner's concept of egoism has been one of the root causes of the misunderstanding of his philosophy.[103] Kast lists numerous, colorful examples of this, including: Hartmann's assertion that Stirner's *Eigner* (owner) would inevitably strive to be "a bloodthirsty, cruel, cunning, treacherous, perfidious and conquest-mad tyrant"; the economist (and coiner of the phrase "Arbeit macht frei") Heinrich Beta (1813–1876) calling Stirner "the inventor of a philosophy for sharks"; and Drews referring to "the bestiality of radical egoism."[104] Inevitably, Paterson's voice can be added to this litany, calling Stirner "rapacious, serpentine, evasive, ruthlessly self-centered and self-destructive" and "the brutally frank exponent of the most extreme form of ruthless egoism."[105] The aim of all these allegations is clearly to present Stirner's notion of egoism as directly analogous to—if not indeed identical with—mean-spirited selfishness, with all its assorted connotations of vanity, greed, and egomania, thus reinforcing the claim of Stirner's nihilistic credentials.

102 Schiereck, *Max Stirner's Egoism and Nihilism*, 54.
103 See Kast, *Max Stirners Destruktion der spekulativen Philosophie*, 215.
104 Hartmann, *Ethische Studien*, 85; Heinrich Beta (Bettziech), "Ein deutscher Freihandelsapostel," *Die Gartenlaube. Illustriertes Familienblatt* 17 (1863): 266–70 (267); Drews, *Die deutsche Spekulation seit Kant*, 1:251.
105 Paterson, *The Nihilistic Egoist*, 306, 252.

The debate about the motivation behind human actions, and indeed the concept of egoism itself, have undergone great change as a result of the coining of the word altruism, a term "created by Auguste Comte [1798–1857] in his *Cours de philosophie positive* 1830–1842."[106] Prior to that, less harsh terminology was used to represent the dichotomy: "self-love/benevolence, private affection/public affection, selfishness/kindness, selfish/social, etc."[107] In ancient Greece, long before the arrival of monotheism, this duality was defined in far less categorical and judgmental terms than in modern times. Homer's *Odyssey* provides a good example of the ancient Greek outlook: "The story becomes a way of working through the question of what kinds of self-interested behaviour are to be rewarded and what kinds punished."[108] Centuries later, in classical Greece, the discussion of the ethics of human conduct continued along similar lines: "In neither Plato nor Aristotle does altruistic benevolence appear in the list of the virtues, and consequently the problem of how human nature, constituted as it is, can possibly exhibit this virtue cannot arise."[109]

As one might expect, Nietzsche tended towards the pre-Christian view on this issue, and thus he merrily poked fun at Comte's increasingly popular neologism: "From France, Comte's superficial juxtaposition of altruism and egoism—but there is no such thing as altruism!—has reached England. . . . In Germany . . . H<artmann> has recently brought Comte's idea to wide attention; . . . and . . . ceremoniously and formally thrown egoism out of the front door, in order, in the name of 'altruism,' to force it back in through the back door."[110] While Nietzsche's opinion of altruism ranges within his oeuvre from it being a fiction to a valid description of certain types of action which nonetheless involve self-interest, in the final analysis his position appears to be, as Reginster states, that "there is no (necessary) opposition in value between egoism and altruism."[111] In a fragment written in 1888, he writes: "In short: the worship of altruism is a specific form of egoism, which occurs regularly under certain physiological conditions."[112] The

---

106 *The Penguin Dictionary of Philosophy*, 2nd ed. (2005), s.v. "altruism."

107 *The Penguin Dictionary of Philosophy*, 2nd ed. (2005), s.v. "altruism." See Nietzsche, *On the Genealogy of Morals*, 26: "It was only when aristocratic value judgments *declined* that the whole antithesis 'egoistic' 'unegoistic' obtruded itself more and more on the human conscience."

108 Whitmarsh, *Battling the Gods*, 41.

109 *Encyclopedia.com*, "Egoism and Altruism," by Alasdair MacIntyre, accessed June 30, 2023, https://www.encyclopedia.com/humanities/encyclopedias-almanacs-transcripts-and-maps/egoism-and-altruism.

110 Nietzsche, *Werke*, 7.3:246.

111 Reginster, "Nietzsche on Selflessness," 197.

112 Nietzsche, *The Will to Power*, 218.

result of this cult of altruism, Nietzsche goes on to say, is, quite simply, "*hatred of egoism.*"

The arrival on the scene, therefore, of altruism, as a word to describe what is (or should be) considered the gold standard of human behavior, has led to the discrediting of its supposed antithesis, egoism, to the extent where the latter carries, in common usage, connotations of despicable selfishness and immorality. Even the best efforts of Richard Dawkins in *The Selfish Gene* (1976) and elsewhere, to explain apparent instances of biological altruism in terms of genetic selfishness, have not helped to rehabilitate egoism's battered reputation.[113] Indeed, the sociobiological (not to say empirical) evidence that humans are programmed to feel empathy, compassion, and love, quite plausibly in the interests of social cohesion and therefore gene survival, has largely been ignored in the discussion of egoism in general, and of psychological egoism in particular.[114]

Psychological egoism is the claim that a person's ultimate aim is her or his own welfare. It is the form of egoism, as opposed to ethical or rational egoism, that seems to correspond most closely to Stirner's outlook, not least because it is descriptive, unlike the others which are normative. Like most categorizations, however, it is subject to the shortcomings of a one size fits all approach, as is indicated by Leopold's doubts about its pertinency to various examples of egoism described by Stirner in *Der Einzige*.[115] Nonetheless, it corresponds adequately enough to Stirner's view that people act ultimately in their own interests, even if they are deluded about what their own interests are, and even though their interests may sometimes coincide with the interests of others. Stirner's detractors, inspired by the egoism-altruism dichotomy, have willingly assumed that psychological egoism's denial of the existence of true altruism simultaneously discounts the possibility of kindness, an assumption expressed by George Santayana in his short chapter on Stirner (whom he freely admits to finding tiresome), where he writes: "To deny that a man is capable of generosity because his generosity must be his own, is insufferable quibbling."[116]

---

113 See Dawkins, *The Selfish Gene*, 2: "I shall argue that a predominant quality to be expected in a successful gene is ruthless selfishness. This gene selfishness will usually give rise to selfishness in individual behaviour. However, as we shall see, there are special circumstances in which a gene can achieve its own selfish goals best by fostering a limited form of altruism at the level of individual animals."

114 For a scientific view of the sociobiological origins of cooperative behavior, see Ridley, *The Origins of Virtue*.

115 See Leopold "Introduction," xxiv–xxv. Elsewhere, Leopold also questions the association of Stirnerian egoism with ethical egoism. See Leopold, "The State and I," 182–85.

116 Santayana, *Egotism in German Philosophy*, 101. For a typically negative description of psychological egoism, see Shafer-Landau, *The Fundamentals of Ethics*, 102: "The truth of psychological egoism would spell the defeat of morality as

Stirner, in fact, does nothing of the sort. The point, for Stirner, is not to disbelieve the ample evidence of experience with regard to feelings such as kindness and generosity in oneself and others, but more accurately to understand the underlying motivations of human behavior, as well as to subvert the sanctimonious myth of behavior entirely devoid of self-interest. Egoism for Stirner is an inevitable quality of the self-centered nature of human experience and is therefore a fact of life: "I and the egoistic are the really general, since every one is an egoist and of paramount importance to himself."[117] Such a claim is not dissimilar in meaning to the famous dictum of the economist and moral philosopher, Adam Smith (1723?–1790), concerning self-interest as the basis of socioeconomic order: "It is not from the benevolence of the butcher, the brewer, or the baker, that we expect our dinner, but from their regard to their own interest. We address ourselves, not to their humanity but to their self-love."[118] This understanding of human behavior seemed obvious both to Smith and Stirner, although it was almost certainly a minority view during their lifetimes, and, arguably, remains so today.

In view of their similar outlooks concerning self-interest, it is hardly surprising that Stirner chose to translate Smith's magnum opus, *An Inquiry into the Nature and Causes of the Wealth of Nations* (1776), into German, despite the fact that two published German translations already existed, the first by J. F. Schiller, cousin of the famous poet, and the other by the late-Enlightenment philosopher, Christian Garve (1742–1798). Along with a translation of *A Treatise on Political Economy* by the liberal French economist, Jean-Baptiste Say (1767–1832), the Smith translation was the first work that Stirner undertook after the publication of *Der Einzige*.[119] As clues to understanding Stirner's thought, these translations should not be ignored, or, as in Paterson's case, passed over without comment as if completely insignificant.[120] Herbert Read, at least, had the perspicacity to observe that "some of Stirner's statements can be construed as a defence of the competitive spirit, and therefore as a defence of capitalism."[121] It is certainly hard to deny the existence of some degree of

---

we know it. If altruism is impossible, then morality cannot reasonably ask us to sacrifice self-interest for the sake of others. The central moral virtues of benevolence, kindness, and compassion would have no place in morality."

117 *EO*, 162; *EE*, 187: "Ich und das Egoistische ist das wirklich Allgemeine, da Jeder ein Egoist ist und sich über alles geht."

118 Smith, *The Wealth of Nations*, 14. Cf. *EO*, 275: "I would prefer to be referred to men's selfishness than to their kindnesses, their mercy, pity, etc."; *EE*, 315: "Ich will aber lieber auf den Eigennutz der Menschen angewiesen sein, als auf ihre 'Liebesdienste', ihre Barmherzigkeit, Erbarmen usw."

119 See Mackay, *Max Stirner*, 201–2.

120 See Paterson, *The Nihilistic Egoist*, 13.

121 Read, *The Tenth Muse*, 80.

affinity between Stirner and the thinkers of the Scottish Enlightenment, not only with Smith, but also with Hume with regard to his empiricism, skepticism, and moral relativism. As far as egoism is concerned, one of Stirner's principal aims is to discard the illusions created by millennia of accumulated dogma, including the moralistic belief in the existence and excellence of human conduct that disregards the individual's own inclinations. Instead, Stirner contends that all positive human actions, even those that manifestly benefit others, are motivated by self-interest, which the Stirnerian egoist identifies with self-enjoyment (*Selbstgenuss*). Thus, he writes:

> Consequently my relation to the world is this: I no longer do anything for it "for God's sake." I do nothing "for man's sake," but what I do I do "for my sake." . . . My intercourse with the world consists in my enjoying it, and so consuming it for my self-enjoyment.

> [Somit ist denn mein Verhältnis zur Welt dieses: Ich tue für sie nichts mehr "um Gottes willen," Ich tue nichts "um des Menschen willen," sondern, was Ich tue, das tue Ich "um Meinetwillen." . . . Mein Verkehr mit der Welt besteht darin, dass Ich sie genieße und so sie zu meinem Selbstgenuss verbrauche.][122]

Such a statement is, of course, anathema to Paterson, who takes full advantage of the invention of altruism to express his self-righteous indignation, using egoism, a term so marked with negative connotations, as a stick with which to chastise Stirner: "The conscious egoist is constantly mindful that the other is the object of his love purely and entirely because he happens to evince certain qualities which directly gratify the wishes and desires of the egoist himself."[123] To ram home his point, Paterson quotes the following typically immoderate statement from *Der Einzige*:

> To the egoist nothing is high enough for him to humble himself before it, nothing so independent that he would live for love of it, nothing so sacred that he would sacrifice himself to it. The egoist's love rises in selfishness, flows in the bed of selfishness, and empties into selfishness again.

> [Dem Egoisten ist nichts hoch genug, dass er sich davor demütigte, nichts so selbständig, dass er ihm zu Liebe lebte, nichts so heilig, dass er sich ihm opferte. Die Liebe des Egoisten quillt aus dem

---

122 *EO*, 282; *EE*, 322–23.
123 Paterson, *The Nihilistic Egoist*, 259. Cf. *Poems of William Blake*, 141: "What is it men in women do require? / The lineaments of gratified desire. / What is it women in men do require? / The lineaments of gratified desire."

Eigennutz, flutet im Bette des Eigennutzes und mündet wieder in den Eigennutz.]124

Paterson chooses to ignore the possibility of this being an accurate assessment of the motivation behind love, preferring instead to adjudge it an annihilation of the very idea of love. He is therefore able to conclude, disregarding in the process the concept of self-love, that Stirner is callously heartless: "The Unique One, then, is an egoist because ultimately he cares for no one. But if he is distinctively a *nihilistic* egoist, this is because ultimately he may be said to care for nothing."[125] Stirner's adoption of the word egoist as a self-appellation, once egoism is misdefined as the antithesis of altruism, gives Paterson the excuse to condemn Stirner as nihilistic. It is a simple but effective misrepresentation that completely ignores Stirner's own acknowledgment of a sense of compassion: "If I see the loved one suffer, I suffer with him, and I know no rest until I have tried everything to comfort and cheer him; if I see him glad, I too become glad over his joy."[126]

Moreover, Stirner is openly critical of those who are "egoists in the usual sense, selfish people, looking out for their own advantage, sober, calculating."[127] He is equally disapproving of those who egoistically devote themselves to one ruling passion: "Their entire activity is egoistic, but it is a one-sided, unopened, narrow egoism; it is possessedness."[128] Instead, Stirner envisages an authentic form of egoism based on enlightened and autonomous self-possession, which he personifies in the concept of the *Eigner* (owner). The speciousness of Paterson's interpretation of Stirnerian egoism is demonstrated by Stirner's understanding of love and empathy, which are not diminished by the admission of self-interest:

> I love men too, not merely individuals, but every one. But I love them with the consciousness of egoism; I love them because love makes *me* happy, I love because loving is natural to me, because it pleases me. I know no "commandment of love." I have a *fellow-feeling* with every feeling being, and their torment torments, their refreshment refreshes me too.

---

124 *EO*, 260–61; *EE*, 297. *Eigennutz* actually means self-interest rather than selfishness—another example of how Byington's translation is at times unhelpful.

125 Paterson, *The Nihilistic Egoist*, 285.

126 *EO*, 258; *EE*, 295: "Sehe Ich den Geliebten leiden, so leide ich mit, und es lässt mir keine Ruhe, bis Ich alles versucht habe, um ihn zu trösten und aufzuheitern; sehe Ich ihn froh, so werde auch Ich über seine Freude froh."

127 *EO*, 70; *EE*, 85: "im gewöhnlichen Verstande Egoisten, Eigennützige, auf ihren Vorteil bedacht, nüchtern, berechnend."

128 *EO*, 70; *EE*, 85: "Egoistisch ist ihr ganzes Tun und Treiben, aber es ist ein einseitiger, unaufgeschlossener, borniter Egoismus: es ist Besessenheit."

> [Ich liebe die Menschen auch, nicht bloß einzelne, sondern jeden. Aber Ich liebe sie mit dem Bewußtsein des Egoismus; Ich liebe sie, weil die Liebe *Mich* glücklich macht, Ich liebe, weil Mir das Lieben natürlich ist, weil Mir's gefällt. Ich kenne kein "Gebot der Liebe." Ich habe *Mitgefühl* mit jedem fühlenden Wesen, und ihre Qual quält, ihre Erquickung erquickt auch mich.][129]

Once again, there is a clear similarity with Adam Smith, who wrote in his first published work, *The Theory of Moral Sentiments* (1759): "How selfish soever man may be supposed, there are evidently some principles in his nature, which interest him in the fortune of others, and render their happiness necessary to him, though he derives nothing from it except the pleasure of seeing it. Of this kind is pity or compassion, the emotion which we feel for the misery of others."[130] Stirner's affinity with thinkers who would never normally be associated with nihilism is a recurrent theme of the present study, an observation which plainly runs counter to the orthodox view of Stirner's place in the history of ideas.

Stirner takes pains to explain how his egoistic conception of love is fully compatible with self-sacrifice (or altruism, as it would become known after Comte), not through an act of sublime inconsequence, as Friedell falsely interprets it, but through the egoistic acknowledgment and appreciation of the rewards inherent in self-sacrifice itself:[131]

> Am I perchance to have no lively interest in the person of another, are *his* joy and *his* weal not to lie at my heart, is the enjoyment that I furnish him not to be more to me than other enjoyments of my own? On the contrary, I can with joy sacrifice to him numberless enjoyments, I can deny myself numberless things for the enhancement of *his* pleasure, and I can risk for him what without him was the dearest to me, my life, my welfare, my freedom. Why, it constitutes my pleasure and my happiness to refresh myself with his happiness and his pleasure. But *myself, my own self*, I do not sacrifice to him, but remain an egoist and—enjoy him.

---

129   *EO*, 258; *EE*, 294. Cf. Nietzsche, *Ecce Homo*, 75: "The Circe of mankind, morality, has falsified all *psychologica* to its very foundations—has *moralized* it—to the point of the frightful absurdity that love is supposed to be something 'unegoistic.'"

130   Smith, *The Theory of Moral Sentiments*, 1.

131   See Friedell, *A Cultural History of the Modern Age*, 3:114: "This clever fancy, for it is no more, is then applied in the most ingenious, boldest and most logical fashion to all fields of life and knowledge, only to emerge—and herein lies its splendid inconsequence—in a new altruism."

[Soll Ich etwa an der Person des anderen keine lebendige Teilnahme haben, soll *seine* Freude und *sein* Wohl Mir nicht am Herzen liegen, soll der Genuss, den Ich ihm bereite, Mir nicht über andere eigene Genüsse gehen? Im Gegenteil, unzählige Genüsse kann ich ihm mit Freuden opfern, Unzähliges kann Ich Mir zur Erhöhung *seiner* Lust versagen, und was Mir ohne ihn das Teuerste wäre, das kann Ich für ihn in die Schanze schlagen, mein Leben, meine Wohlfahrt, meine Freiheit. Es macht ja meine Lust und mein Glück aus, Mich an seinem Glück und seiner Lust zu laben. Aber *Mich, Mich selbst* opfere Ich ihm nicht, sondern bleibe Egoist und—genieße ihn.][132]

Such an explanation of the motivation for benevolent (or apparently altruistic) behavior is nothing substantially new. It is the same reciprocity which Portia, in *The Merchant of Venice*, extols in the quality of mercy;[133] it is very similar to Hobbes's renowned reason for his act of charity in the Strand;[134] it is even compatible with Dostoevsky's skillful use of compersion (in its broadest sense, as enjoyment of another's happiness), for instance in the story of Kolya and the dog, Perezvon, in *The Brothers Karamazov*, where an almost overwhelming emotion is felt by the reader, the friends and family around Ilusha's bed, and, of course, by Kolya himself.[135] Bearing in mind Nietzsche's disdain for pity referred to in chapter 3 above, Stirner's discussion of egoistic love and compassion shows as great a gulf between him and Nietzsche as it does an affinity with Smith,

---

132 *EO*, 257–58; *EE*, 293–94. See *EO*, 148: "But how about that 'doing the good for the good's sake' without prospect of reward? As if here too the pay was not contained in the satisfaction that it is to afford"; *EE*, 172: "Aber jenes 'das Gute um des Guten willen tun' ohne Aussicht auf Belohnung? Als ob nicht auch hier in der Befriedigung, die es gewähren soll, der Lohn enthalten wäre."

133 See Shakespeare, *The Merchant of Venice*, 4.1: "The quality of mercy is not strain'd, / . . . / . . . It is twice blest; / It blesseth him that gives, and him that takes."

134 See Aubrey, *"Brief Lives,"* 352: "One time, I remember, goeing in the Strand, a poor and infirme old man craved his almes. He, beholding him with eies of pitty and compassion, putt his hand in his pocket, and gave him 6*d*. Say a divine . . . that stood by—'Would you have donne this, if it had not been Christ's command?'—'Yea,' sayd he.—'Why?' quoth the other.—'Because,' sayd he, 'I was in paine to consider the miserable condition of the old man; and now my almes, giving him some reliefe, doth also ease me.'"

135 See Dostoevsky, *The Brothers Karamazov* (2003), 693–98. For a definition of compersion, see Marie Thouin, "Compersion: A radical love phenomenon," accessed June 30, 2023, https://www.whatiscompersion.com/: "Compersion is our wholehearted participation in the happiness of others. It is the sympathetic joy we feel for somebody else, even when their positive experience does not involve or benefit us directly."

a fact that must surely have some relevance to the question of Stirner's relationship to nihilism.[136]

The Reception and Repercussions of Stirner's Egoism

However perceptive Stirner's analysis of human behavior may be, his concept of egoism was, and has remained, largely misunderstood. Ironically, of all his contemporary critics, Engels seems to have appreciated it most. In a letter to Marx largely about Stirner and his book, he writes: "But we must also adopt such truth as there is in the principle [of egoism]. And it is certainly true that we must first make a cause our own, egoistic cause, before we can do anything to further it—and hence that in this sense . . . we are communists out of egoism also."[137] Other Young Hegelians, in their published reviews of *Der Einzige*, were less understanding. Thus, in Stirner's article entitled "Recensenten Stirners" (Stirner's Critics, 1845), where he responds to the specific criticisms of Szeliga, Feuerbach, and Hess, egoism plays a significant role in the discussion. Writing in the third person, Stirner bemoans his critics' preconceived notions of egoism and their subsequent inability to appreciate his meaning:

> The critics display even more irritation against the "egoist" than against the unique. Instead of delving into egoism as Stirner meant it, they stop at their usual childish depiction of it and roll out to everyone the well-known catalogue of sins.
>
> [Mehr Aergerniss noch als an dem Einzigen nehmen die Recensenten an dem "Egoisten." Statt auf den Egoismus, wie er von Stirner aufgefasst wird, näher einzugehen, bleiben sie bei ihrer von Kindesbeinen an gewohnten Vorstellung von demselben stehen und rollen sein allem Volke so wohlbekanntes Sündenregister auf.][138]

The infantile list of transgressions, Stirner continues ironically, includes "how stupid, vulgar and predatorily murderous egoism is."[139]

---

136 See Nietzsche, *Human, All Too Human*, 180: "Friend.—Fellow rejoicing, not fellow suffering makes the friend."
137 Marx and Engels, *Collected Works*, 38:12.
138 Stirner, *Stirner's Critics*, 60; Stirner, *Max Stirner's Kleinere Schriften*, 119. The article appeared in the third volume of *Wigand's Vierteljahrschrift* in 1845 (147–94). Despite it being written in the third person, it is signed M. St., and Mackay was therefore convinced of Stirner's authorship. His assessment is not generally disputed.
139 Stirner, *Stirner's Critics*, 62; Stirner, *Max Stirner's Kleinere Schriften*, 121: "wie einfältig, wie gemein und wie raubmörderisch der Egoismus sei."

The link between egoism and sin is, according to Stirner, wholly dependent on an imagined external, higher cause, which designates behavior not dedicated to the higher cause as sinful. In itself, he declares, no such relationship exists; nor is there a necessary connection between egoism, as he understands it, and only caring for oneself, as that would depend on being unaware of the joys of sympathy and community.[140] Stirner concludes by elaborating on the meaning of his concept of egoism:

> Egoism . . . is not opposed to love nor to thought; it is no enemy of the sweet life of love, nor of devotion and sacrifice; it is no enemy of intimate warmth, but it is also no enemy of critique, nor of socialism, nor, in short, of any *actual interest*. It doesn't exclude any interest. It is directed against only disinterestedness and the uninteresting; not against love, but against sacred love, not against thought, but against sacred thought, not against socialists, but against sacred socialists, etc.
>
> [Der Egoismus . . . ist kein Gegensatz zur Liebe, kein Gegensatz zum Denken, kein Feind eines süssen Liebeslebens, kein Feind der Hingebung und Aufopferung, kein Feind der innigsten Herzlichkeit, aber auch kein Feind der Kritik, kein Feind des Socialismus, kurz, kein Feind eines *wirklichen Interesses*: er schliesst kein Interesse aus. Nur gegen die Uninteressirtheit und das Uninteressante ist er gerichtet: nicht gegen die Liebe, sondern gegen die heilige Liebe, nicht gegen das Denken, sondern gegen das heilige Denken, nicht gegen die Socialisten, sondern gegen die heiligen Socialisten u. s. w.][141]

Paterson had, of course, read Stirner's *Kleinere Schriften* (minor works), and he quotes extensively from them. Nonetheless, he appears either not to have understood, or consciously to have disregarded, Stirner's explication. It is indeed generally the case that it has fallen on deaf ears. Kast has observed that the spectrum of Stirner's reception was "large, contradictory, and fraught with numerous misunderstandings."[142] This, Kast believes, can be attributed not only to the nature of Stirner's message but also to the way it was communicated. He considers Stirner's

---

140 See Stirner, *Stirner's Critics*, 80; Stirner, *Max Stirner's Kleinere Schriften*, 142.

141 Stirner, *Stirner's Critics*, 81; Stirner, *Max Stirner's Kleinere Schriften*, 144. Stirner here makes clear that he is not opposed to myths *per se*, but only myths that become heteronomous abstractions, i.e., sacred myths. He does not, however, spell out what this means in practical terms, nor does he discuss the viability of mythopoeia without the quality of sacredness.

142 Kast, "Afterword," in *EE*, 371.

parading of egoism as a virtue to be a provocation in itself, and an ill-advised one at that.[143] For Stirner, though, provocation seems to have been a conscious instrument in his campaign to sweep away sacred abstractions in all their manifestations, as a means of rousing his readers from their dogmatic slumber. The man who appeared so shy and retiring at the meetings of *Die Freien* at times used something akin to shock tactics in his writing, thus risking, and indeed creating, serious misunderstanding in the process.[144]

Those readers who have not been immediately repelled by the radical nature of his ideas have been able to reach a more balanced judgment than those, like Paterson and Helms, whose ideological beliefs place them automatically in a position of antagonism. Read, while recognizing that Stirner is "usually dismissed as the most extreme representative of the philosophy of egoism known to history," concludes that "Stirner's doctrine is, in fact, a plea for the integration of the personality, and on that basis the charge of 'selfishness' becomes somewhat naïve."[145] Kast holds a similar view. He summarizes the essence of Stirner's concept of egoism as follows: "What Stirner calls egoism is not the trite egoism of his critics' understanding, but an appeal to everyone not to advocate externally imposed interests, but to stand up for their own interests."[146] Peter Sloterdijk (b. 1947) views Stirner's egoism as an attempt to overcome alienation at the level of the private individual: "Stirner's idea is simply to expel all foreign programming from his mind. After this total self-purification of the mind, a naked, in a sense empty, reflective egoism should remain."[147]

Stirner's concept of egoism can be understood in one sense as the culmination of the Enlightenment's focus on subjective self-consciousness from Descartes to Fichte, combined with Kant's pursuit of man's liberation from his "self-incurred minority." Schröder writes: "Thus Stirner saw himself as completing the project of 'self-emancipation' set in motion by the Enlightenment, which had been driven forward by Feuerbach's critique of religion but had not yet reached its goal."[148] Egoism, as a principle, is, however, equally a discontinuity, as it distinguishes Stirner from the universalism of Hegel, from the humanism of Feuerbach, and

143 See Kast, "Afterword," in *EE*, 374–75.
144 See Mackay, *Max Stirner*, 91: "As loud and noisy as it usually was at Hippel's, just as quietly did Stirner keep a low profile. . . . One never heard from him a vehement, raw, or even vulgar word, such as were no rarity at Hippel's. . . . Most people . . . held the 'contented,' simple, painfully modest man to be a harmless man of little importance."
145 Read, *The Tenth Muse*, 75, 80.
146 Kast, "Afterword," in *EE*, 375.
147 Sloterdijk, *Kritik der zynischen Vernunft*, 1:192.
148 Schröder, *Moralischer Nihilismus*, 161.

of course from the theism of Christianity. Stirner was effectively trying to inaugurate a new, third way of thinking distinct from the religious-metaphysical and the humanist-materialist doctrines which had dominated the intellectual landscape of the first half of the nineteenth century in Germany.

One reason for Stirner's failure to establish this as some form of popular movement may be the naïvety of his thought on the sociopolitical level, or the refusal to take the sociopolitical dimension sufficiently seriously in the first place, a charge that has of course also been directed against Nietzsche.[149] However psychologically astute Stirner's analysis of egoism may be, he seems largely to have ignored the full range of potential human behavior—from gentle to brutal, compassionate to cruel, social to sociopathic—in his seemingly utopian egosystem that he calls the *Verein der Egoisten* (union of egoists). Whether this is because of a lingering belief in the Enlightenment tenet of the perfectibility of man is unclear, but, especially with hindsight, his social theory seems naïvely optimistic in its loose arrangement of unregulated human interaction. As Sloterdijk points out, naïvety is essentially what Marx was accusing Stirner of in *Die deutsche Ideologie*.[150] Hartmann, in *Ethische Studien*, speaks of "Stirner's infantile anarchism," and even Kast concedes that Stirner's philosophy reaches the limits of its effectiveness in the concept of the "union of potentially equal owners as the materialization of the forms of association of these owners."[151] Kast also notes critically in Stirner's philosophy "the exclusion, by and large, of socioeconomic factors within a philosophy that makes a claim to ubiquity."[152] In his answer to his critics, the best examples of unions of egoists that Stirner is able to furnish are children playing games, two lovers uniting their hearts as one, and three friends drinking wine together in a tavern.[153] Although he admits to these examples being trivial, they nonetheless demonstrate the unsophistication of his sociopolitical thought, which has opened him up to stinging criticism, most notably from Marx.[154]

---

149 See Stern, *A Study of Nietzsche*, 133: "[Nietzsche's] explicit aim . . . is to make men self-reliant and self-determining, content with their earthly lot and free from all need of gods, yet the arrangements of social and political life that would be required to institute such an autonomous humanity do not interest him."

150 See Sloterdijk, *Kritik der zynischen Vernunft*, 1:192.

151 Hartmann, *Ethische Studien*, 86; Kast, *Max Stirners Destruktion der spekulativen Philosophie*, 330.

152 Kast, *Max Stirners Destruktion der spekulativen Philosophie*, 330. For further analysis of Stirner's union of egoists, see Clark, *Max Stirner's Egoism*, 78–86.

153 See Stirner, "Recensenten Stirners," 164–65.

154 There is a parallel with what Stern calls Nietzsche's "innocence of politics": "One's criticism is not that he fails to provide what he never attempted—a systematic sociology—but that the view of society and of the individual entailed

In a way, Stirner was born and died too early. His major work, *Der Einzige und sein Eigentum*, was published four years before Marx and Engels's *Manifest der Kommunistischen Partei* (The Communist Manifesto, 1848). He missed the Darwinian revolution (*On the Origin of Species* was published three years after his death, *The Descent of Man* a further twelve years later), as well as the Freudian revolution (Freud was born six weeks before Stirner's death). Without the pieces of the puzzle that these thinkers added to man's collective knowledge, he was ill-placed to understand and explore the full social, biological, and psychological implications of his model for the existence and co-existence of unique individuals based on enlightened egoism. His perspective, in other words, was too focused on the intellectual debate of his time for him to develop a realistic, comprehensive social theory applicable to modern industrial society. In this sense, Marx and Engels's criticism of Stirner is both predictable and justified.

Although Stirner represents, supports, and champions the interests of the individual, he is apparently oblivious to the fact that the history of mankind has never been about the individual in isolation, but always about interest groups bound together by a powerful myth. Complex societies, according to Jared Diamond's analysis of human history, "can exist only if they develop centralized authority to monopolize force and resolve conflicts."[155] In contrast, Stirner's union of egoists seems to be a blueprint for a society of outsiders, a model as unviable as Nietzsche's proposed elitist society of *Übermenschen*. As outsiders are always by definition a minority, its only at least semi-practical social application would be in a remote and extremely loose commune of like-minded, self-aware, well-balanced, non-conformist individuals, the success and indeed survival of which would nonetheless be subject to the vagaries of human behavior. It might be a serviceable arrangement for a solitary animal like an ocelot but is of little use for humans.

Carroll hits the nail on the head when he writes that "the Stirnerian egoist is most fully embodied in artists like Max Ernst, isolated men whose extreme lives are sustained by the force of their imaginations, and an inviolable confidence in their own capacity for revolutionizing human consciousness."[156] Another such example is Marcel Duchamp (1887–1968), the creator, in 1917, of *Fountain* (a porcelain urinal since lost

---

by his reflections on social morality issue in an almost absolute individualism which does not provide an account of the way things are in the world." Stern, *A Study of Nietzsche*, 105, 132.

155 Diamond, *Guns, Germs and Steel*, 313.

156 Carroll, *Break-Out from the Crystal Palace*, 57. See the cover image of the present book, Max Ernst's homage to Stirner, *L'Unique et sa propriété*, 1925, frottage and pencil on paper, 26 x 19.8 cm. Photograph courtesy of Sotheby's.

without trace, but nonetheless voted the most influential work of modern art in a 2004 poll of leading figures in the art world), of whom Molderings writes: "In Duchamp's weltanschauung, . . . where there were no longer any absolute certainties or truths, the only remaining fixed point of reference was the individual himself; hence Duchamp's lifelong fascination for the radically original theses of the German philosopher Max Stirner."[157] Of course, Stirner made no claim to universality; *Der Einzige* is best viewed not as a systematic, sociopolitical manifesto but as a handbook for optimistic, subversive outsiders.

Nevertheless, regardless of his inherently narrow appeal (at least unless and until outsiders paradoxically become the rule) and the apparent naïvety of his social philosophy, Stirner took the anti-dogmatic principles of the Enlightenment to their ultimate pre-Darwinian and pre-Freudian conclusion. But in so doing, he aroused the antagonism, not to say contempt, of a host of enemies. Thus, since Stirner let the ocelot out of the bag, to use Theodor Adorno's (translated and slightly modified) metaphor, everyone imaginable (the state, the censor, Marx, Engels, other Young Hegelians, Rosenkranz, perhaps Nietzsche, certainly Förster-Nietzsche, Hartmann, Lauterbach, Buber, Löwith, Helms, Paterson, et al.) has done his, her, and its absolute best to thrust it back in and tie up the sack once and for all.[158] The few voices in support of Stirner have scarcely been audible above the cacophony of condemnation.

The terms of disparagement most regularly hurled at Stirner throughout the history of his largely unfavorable reception are "egoist" and "nihilist," which have been appended to his name by countless critics, irrespective of their political, philosophical, or theological persuasions. In the case of the former, a clear reason for doing so can be found in Stirner's frequent use of the word, although it must be noted that his various attempts at clarifying what he means by egoism have been routinely ignored by his accusers. As for the latter, it has been applied to Stirner without any such immediate justification, in several, invariably negative ways, but most commonly, as the above chronology has shown, in the sense of political, moral, or existential nihilism. In the following three chapters, each of these types of nihilism will be analyzed in relation to Stirner's ideas, in order to assess their usefulness for a proper understanding of his thought.

---

157 Molderings, *Duchamp*, xvi. Duchamp's "Stirner work" was *3 stoppages étalon* (*3 Standard Stoppages*), 1913–14. See Molderings, *Duchamp*, xii.

158 See Helms, *Die Ideologie der anonymen Gesellschaft*, 200: "Stirner, as Adorno put it, 'let the cat out of the bag.'" The German idiom is, literally, let the hare out of the sack.

CHAPTER 5

The State of Denial: Stirner and Political Nihilism

The Meaning and History of Political Nihilism

THERE IS LITTLE DISPUTE about the meaning of political nihilism. Although the term can be, and has been, used in other contexts, in the history of ideas it is generally considered synonymous with the nineteenth-century phenomenon of Russian nihilism. In other words, political nihilism is the generalized form of Russian nihilism, from which it derives its essential properties. This is evidently the sense in which it is meant by Biedermann when he speaks of Stirner's *Der Einzige* as a literary version of nihilism, "which . . . allowed none but the sovereign ego to celebrate its triumphs on the ruins of society."[1] Likewise for Masaryk when he declares that, in *Der Einzige*, he "was already advocating political nihilism; . . . for Stirner, a republic was no longer enough: the state as such is to be abolished."[2] Perhaps the most colorful instance of Stirner's association with political nihilism is Heman's description of Stirner as an anarchist and nihilist "whose followers want, with dagger, revolver, and bombs, to make themselves owners of the whole world."[3]

It is significant that all of these comments were written in the quarter century following the assassination of Tsar Alexander II in 1881 when the memory of this and other acts of violence committed by Russian nihilists was still fresh in the mind. Nonetheless, however negative Stirner's critics meant the association to be, these crimes, shocking though they were, especially in an age where monarchical government was the rule, were

---

1   Biedermann, *1840–1870*, 1:139. Biedermann is probably borrowing from Hartmann, who wrote two years earlier: "This [arbitrary] viewpoint is almost realized . . . in Max Stirner, who left but one illusion standing on the ruins of all destroyed illusions: the reality of the ego." Hartmann, *Phänomenologie des sittlichen Bewusstseins*, 403. Later in the same work, Hartmann compares Stirner and the Russian nihilists (768).
2   Masaryk, *Masaryk on Marx*, 261–62.
3   Heman, "Der Philosoph des Anarchismus und Nihilismus," 74.

carried out as part of an escalating response to the brutal repressiveness of the Russian imperial regime, which was characterized by countless atrocities in the form of indiscriminate massacres, public executions, and mass deportations to Siberia of perceived enemies of the state, be they rebellious Poles or revolting peasants. The Russian nihilists were not, as a rule, unprincipled thugs who practiced violence for its own sake. As the eminent Russianist, Eugene Lampert, writes: "They were rebels because they felt man's inhumanity to man. . . . They were the conscience of Russia."[4]

The effective equivalence of political and Russian nihilism is borne out in general usage. In the *Routledge Encyclopedia of Philosophy*, one finds the following definition: "Political nihilism calls for the complete destruction of existing political institutions, along with their supporting outlooks and social structures, but has no positive message of what should be put in their place."[5] In the same publication, Russian nihilism is described as a doctrine that "negated not the normative significance of the world or the general meaning of human existence, but rather a particular social, political and aesthetic order." Moreover, "it is . . . the vagueness of their positive programmes that distinguishes the [Russian] Nihilists from the revolutionary socialists who followed them."[6] The similarity between the two definitions is obvious: both describe the general outlook of Turgenev's embodiment of nihilism, Bazarov, who recognizes no authority, repudiates everything, and believes only in destruction. Bazarov represents the spirit of radical youth in Russia during the period spanning the promising start and catastrophic end of the reign of Alexander II, which lasted from his coronation following the death of his autocratic father, Nicholas I, in 1855, until his assassination in 1881. Fisher sets the scene concisely in his history of Europe:

> It was a reign of stern domestic tyranny . . . and of protesting nihilism, a reign in which no suspect was safe from the secret police, . . . while conversely every member of the government from the Tzar downward was the mark for the dagger or the bomb. This was the time when the young intellectuals of Russia, impatient of the tardiness of reform and intoxicated with the new wine of physical science, began to assail the whole fabric of society with a savage recklessness, and, having nothing to suggest in place of all that they were resolved to destroy, earned for themselves the name of nihilist.[7]

---

4 Lampert, *Sons against Fathers*, 91.
5 *Concise Routledge Encyclopedia of Philosophy*, 1st ed. (2000), "NIHILISM," by Donald A. Crosby.
6 *Concise Routledge Encyclopedia of Philosophy*, 1st ed. (2000), "NIHILISM, RUSSIAN," by Stephen Lovell.
7 Fisher, *A History of Europe*, 2:1132–33.

In order to reach an objective judgment concerning the link between Stirner and this particular type of nihilism, the nature and meaning of Russian nihilism as a historical phenomenon must be considered in more detail. The most significant dates in its chronology were: 1861, which saw the emancipation of the serfs, with its unintended consequences that included the first major student riots in Russia; 1866, when Karakozov carried out the first unsuccessful assassination attempt on the life of the Tsar, for which he was duly hanged; the period immediately thereafter of the counter-revolutionary White Terror, from 1866 to 1870, led by the notoriously ruthless Count Mikhail Muravyov, which brought the first, foundational phase of nihilism to a close; and 1878–1881, the conclusion of the second, revolutionary phase of nihilism, which saw a series of attempted and occasionally successful political murders, culminating in the assassination of Alexander II and the subsequent elimination of the nihilist movement following the state's brutal crackdown.[8]

Russian nihilists, who were also known at the time as New People, generally came from the lower middle class; they were "mostly sons and daughters of poor gentry, of minor officials and of priests or lower clergy."[9] They were predominantly youths, students for part or all of their nihilist careers, and one or (usually) more of atheist, materialist, and positivist in their philosophical outlooks. Many were teachers (as, of course, was Stirner), including Karakozov, Alexander Solovyov, another would-be assassin of the Tsar, Chernyshevsky, the editor-in-chief of the literary and political journal, *Sovremennik*, and Nechaev, who, in the memorable words of Hingley, turned "from moulding younger brains to blowing out older ones."[10] In the course of the movement's formation, they developed a radical, anti-establishment uniform, that made them instantly recognizable: "They had quirks of dress and manner, the men going about with huge beards and long hair flopping over their shoulders, while girls had their hair bobbed and renounced such frivolities as combs, crinolines and allowing men to kiss their hands. Both sexes favoured blue-tinted spectacles and high boots. Other common features were a heavy walking-stick and a rug flung over the shoulders in cold weather."[11] Diverse

---

8   See Lampert, *Sons against Fathers*, 85: "It is one of the most bitter ironies of Russian history that the 19th of February 1861, which should have been the climax of the nineteenth century, the day awaited by conscience-stricken Russia . . .—'the great day of reconciliation', as Dostoevsky called it, between the Tsar and 'the people'—in fact opened an impassable gulf between them and was the signal for the final rupture between the Government and the intelligentsia. Faced with the substitution of one kind of bondage for another, the intelligentsia resumed its militant role on a more serious scale."
9   Hingley, *Nihilists*, 16.
10   Hingley, *Nihilists*, 26.
11   Hingley, *Nihilists*, 16.

fictional manifestations of progressive and revolutionary nihilists abound in Russian literature of the 1860s, 1870s, and 1880s, from Turgenev's ambivalent hero, Bazarov, through Chernyshevsky's saintly Rakhmetov, to Dostoevsky's sundry skeptics and malefactors, like Stavrogin, Verkhovensky, Raskolnikov, and Ivan Karamazov, and elaborate caricatures, such as Kirillov and Lebezyatnikov.

Stirner and the Fathers of Russian Populism

Although the term nihilism was not popularized in Russia until the publication of Turgenev's *Fathers and Sons* in 1862, the origins of the negative political ideology, which is its hallmark and most fundamental principle, can be traced back to Mikhail Bakunin (1814–1876), who wrote twenty years earlier: "Revolutionary propaganda is in its deepest sense the NEGATION of the existing conditions of the State, for . . . it has no other program than the destruction of whatever order prevails at the time. . . . Let us then trust the eternal Spirit which destroys and annihilates only because it is the unfathomable and eternal source of all life. The passion for destruction is a creative passion, too!"[12] In emphasizing the paradoxically creative effect of sublation (*Aufhebung*) within the dialectical process, this passage shows that Bakunin was profoundly influenced by Hegel, as were many Russian intellectuals at the time, including his erstwhile friends and colleagues, Vissarion Belinsky (1811–1848) and Alexander Herzen (1812–1870), who, together, made up the triumvirate of revolutionary, socialist, and populist (or pre-populist) Russian thinkers in the period that followed the Decembrist uprising of 1825.[13] "The Reaction in Germany," the essay from which the above quotation is taken, is a product of Bakunin's encounter with the Young Hegelians in Berlin, where he lived from 1840 to 1842. It was written for Arnold Ruge's *Deutsche Jahrbücher für Wissenschaft und Kunst* (German Yearbooks for Science and Art), the group's most important mouthpiece. It was through his acquaintance with the Young Hegelians that Bakunin came to understand the revolutionary potential of Hegelianism. His exposure to the ideas of Strauss, Feuerbach, et al. precipitated a profound intellectual crisis, which, in the words of Lampert, "carried him . . . through

---

12   Bakunin, "The Reaction in Germany," 56–57.
13   For Hegel's influence on Bakunin, see Venturi, *Roots of Revolution*, 38–43. For a definition of Russian populism, see Berlin, "Introduction," in Venturi, *Roots of Revolution*, vii–viii. Venturi, among others, has pointed out that populism was a relatively late development in the history of nineteenth-century revolutionary Russian thought, although the term is generally used to cover the pre-populist phase as well. See Venturi, *Roots of Revolution*, xxxii–xxxiii.

all imaginable and unimaginable nihilisms in regard to society, culture, morality and religion."[14]

As discussed in chapter 1 above, it was within the context of Young Hegelianism, and specifically of the Berlin branch, *Die Freien*, that Stirner's philosophy emerged. Inevitably, Bakunin came to know about Stirner during his time in the city, though the extent to which he was aware of and influenced by Stirner's ideas is a matter of debate. There is no incontrovertible evidence that the two ever met or that Bakunin read *Der Einzige*. Engels (who was no friend of either of them) seems to have been convinced of Stirner's effect on Bakunin, but he gives no details to support this, simply declaring tersely: "Finally came Stirner, the prophet of contemporary anarchism—Bakunin has taken a great deal from him."[15] Mikhail Kurtschinsky (1876–1939), writing about Stirner soon after the Russian Revolution, repeats Engels's assertion: "With regard to Stirner's influence on the development of anarchist doctrine, it must be noted . . . that Stirner's theory undoubtedly exerted an influence on the worldview of the creator of communist anarchism, M. Bakunin."[16] In the absence of any proof, however, it is difficult to judge whether this claim is merited or, as seems more likely, is just a reflection of what Paul McLaughlin, in his study of Bakunin's anarchism, calls the "tendency among Marxists (and others) to conflate different anarchisms, whether closely related (as in the case of Proudhon and Bakunin) or not (as in the case of Stirner and Bakunin)."[17]

McLaughlin does nonetheless acknowledge that Bakunin knew of Stirner, insisting, however, that he would have rejected Stirner's ideas in the main. It is certainly true that there is an essential incongruity between Bakunin's view of the primarily social function of the individual, and

---

14   Lampert, *Studies in Rebellion*, 128.
15   Marx and Engels, *Collected Works*, 26:364. In his letter to Max Hildebrand of October 22, 1889, Engels gives a little more detail: "Stirner enjoyed a revival thanks to Bakunin who, by the way, was also in Berlin at the time and, during Werder's course of lectures on logic (1841–42), sat on the bench in front of me along with four or five other Russians. Proudhon's harmless, purely etymological anarchy (i.e. absence of government) would never have resulted in the present anarchist doctrines had not Bakunin laced it with a good measure of Stirnerian 'rebellion.' As a result the anarchists have themselves become nothing but a collection of '*Unique Ones*,' so much so that no two of them can abide one another's company." Marx and Engels, *Collected Works*, 48:394.
16   Kurtschinsky, *Der Apostel des Egoismus*, 142. This work was first published in Russian in 1920.
17   McLaughlin, *Mikhail Bakunin*, 184.

Stirner's focus on the individual egoist, for whom society is a coercive abstraction.[18] As Lampert explains:

> All the operations in the life of an individual had for Bakunin a social meaning, and any separation of individual and social acts was for him a way of objectifying society into a separate entity, and hence a way of subjecting man to the tyranny of abstractions. He differed fundamentally in this respect from the most radical, solipsistic anarchist, Max Stirner, who regarded man as a dissociated body, and society as a collection of dissociated, extraneous bodies.[19]

Lampert fails to acknowledge that Stirner dismissed all known manifestations of society as themselves tyrannical abstractions, but his analysis is nonetheless sound, even if the designation of Stirner as a solipsist remains controversial though perhaps not entirely without justification.

Paterson, too, points to the dissimilarity between Bakunin's and Stirner's social visions: "While Stirner's philosophy may have some tenuous affinities with the revolutionary destructiveness of Bakunin, the latter's passionate zeal for social justice and his lifelong commitment to popular emancipation could hardly be further removed from Stirner's self-preoccupation."[20] It is certainly true that Stirner's individualistic egoism implies a negative opinion of society, at least as Stirner understood it:

> But the dissolution of *society* is *intercourse* or *union*. A society does assuredly arise by union too, but only as a fixed idea arises by a thought. . . . If a union has crystallized into a society, it has ceased to be a coalition; for coalition is an incessant self-uniting; it has become a unitedness, come to a standstill, degenerated into a fixity; it is—*dead* as a union, it is the corpse of the union or the coalition, it is—society, community.

> [Die Auflösung der *Gesellschaft* aber ist der *Verkehr* oder *Verein*. Allerdings entsteht auch durch Verein eine Gesellschaft, aber nur wie durch einen Gedanken eine fixe Idee entsteht. . . . Hat sich ein Verein zur Gesellschaft kristallisiert, so hat er aufgehört, eine Vereinigung zu sein; denn Vereinigung ist ein unaufhörliches Sich-Vereinigen; er ist zu einem Vereinigtsein geworden, zum Stillstand gekommen, zur

---

18   See, e.g., *EO*, 111: "Society . . . is a new master, a new spook, a new 'supreme being', which 'takes us into its service and allegiance!'"; *EE*, 131: "Die Gesellschaft . . . ist eine neue Herrin, ein neuer Spuk, ein neues 'höchstes Wesen', das Uns 'in Dienst und Pflicht nimmt!'"
19   Lampert, *Studies in Rebellion*, 160.
20   Paterson, *The Nihilistic Egoist*, 128.

Fixheit ausgeartet, er ist—*tot* als Verein, ist der Leichnam des Vereins oder der Vereinigung, d. h. er ist—Gesellschaft, Gemeinschaft.]²¹

For Stirner, the problem is not, as it was for Bakunin, man's alienation from his social essence, but rather the alienating nature of society itself for the individual. His solution is to eradicate society (in an ill-defined, but non-revolutionary way) and replace it with the dynamic concept of the union of egoists.

Despite his otherwise assiduous impartiality on the question of Stirner's influence on Bakunin, McLaughlin includes Bakunin, quite bizarrely, in the long list of those who have accused Stirner of nihilism: "The influence of Stirner may have contributed to the libertarian aspect of Bakunin's mature socialism. Nevertheless, Stirner's egocentric philosophy represents a quasi-Kierkegaardian corruption of Left-Hegelian logic—the twisting of either-or into an absurd personalistic logic—that Bakunin would never endorse. On one of the few occasions that Bakunin mentions Stirner in his writings, he refers to the 'cynical logic' of this 'nihilist.'"²² The three words of Bakunin's that McLaughlin quotes here as if they referred to Stirner, are from the 1873 work *Statism and Anarchy*, where Bakunin writes: "[Marx] was the soul and center of the notable circle of progressive Hegelians with whom he began to publish an opposition journal. . . . This circle also included the brothers Bruno and Edgar Bauer, Max Stirner, and later, in Berlin, the first circle of German nihilists, who far surpassed the most frenzied Russian nihilists with their cynical logic."²³

The translator of the English edition, Shatz, clarifies in a footnote that the Young Hegelian circle to which Bakunin is referring is the "Doctors' Club" (*Doktorenklub*), while the German nihilists are "the Freemen" (*Die Freien*).²⁴ In his remarks, however, Bakunin seems to imply some sort of separation between the members of the former, including the Bauer brothers and Stirner, and those of the latter. In fact, *Die Freien* were the successors of the *Doktorenklub*, and many of the Young Hegelians were therefore members of both, including the Bauers, Rutenberg, and Köppen, but while he was certainly a member of *Die Freien*, there is no record of Stirner ever having attended the *Doktorenklub*.²⁵ McLaughlin's assertion that Bakunin's words are meant as a direct attack on Stirner is therefore misleading at best and disingenuous at worst. It is not impossible

---

21   *EO*, 271; *EE*, 310.
22   McLaughlin, *Mikhail Bakunin*, 68.
23   Bakunin, *Statism and Anarchy*, 141–42.
24   Bakunin, *Statism and Anarchy*, 232–33.
25   Concerning the relationship between the Doctors' Club and the Freemen, see McLellan, *Karl Marx*, 32, 52.

that this speculative interpretation is, once again, inspired by the received wisdom of Stirner being an archetypal nihilist. Throughout the history of his reception, Stirner's dismal reputation has invariably preceded him, distorting his image and undermining the exercise of independent and objective critical analysis.

Nonetheless, traces, however faint, of Stirner's impact can undoubtedly be found throughout the evolution of Russian nihilism, and indeed the anti-nihilism with which it went hand in hand, starting as far back as its post-Decembrist antecedents. Tangible evidence of Stirner's connection with another member of the revolutionary triumvirate, Herzen, may be even harder to discover than with Bakunin, but Isaiah Berlin, in his introduction to the English edition of Herzen's memoirs, still sees fit to mention their intellectual kinship: "Like the more extreme of the left wing disciples of Hegel, in particular like the anarchist Max Stirner, Herzen saw danger in the great magnificent abstractions the mere sound of which precipitated men into violent and meaningless slaughter."[26] Elsewhere, Berlin writes of Herzen's belief "that a minimum area of free action is a moral necessity for all men, not to be suppressed in the name of abstractions or general principles . . . such as eternal salvation, or history, or humanity, or progress, still less the State or the Church or the proletariat."[27] He makes particular note of Herzen's declaration in a letter to Giuseppe Mazzini (1805–1872) of September 13, 1850: "I have served one idea . . .—war against all imposed authority—against every kind of deprivation of freedom, in the name of the absolute independence of the individual."[28] The similarity with Stirner's anti-heteronomous, anti-authoritarian egoism is self-evident.

Likewise, Martin Malia, in his book on Herzen, identifies a telling connection between them: "In some way Herzen never made explicit—save for his vague vision of the fraternal commune—the absolute egoism of each was entirely compatible with the absolute egoism of all. In contemporary thought there was no individualism so extreme except the very similar egoism of Max Stirner."[29] Masaryk also recognizes a fundamental affinity between the two thinkers: "Herzen's disillusionment and Herzen's interpretation of nihilism harmonise perfectly with Stirner's nihilistic iconoclasm. Herzen, like Stirner, deduces the ultimate logical conclusions from the teachings of Feuerbach."[30] Such references demonstrate at the very least the extent to which Stirner's thought is perceived

---

26   Berlin, "Introduction," in Herzen, *My Past and Thoughts*, xxvii.
27   Berlin, *Russian Thinkers*, 98–99.
28   Berlin, *Russian Thinkers*, 93.
29   Malia, *Alexander Herzen*, 277.
30   Masaryk, *The Spirit of Russia*, 2:482.

by many to have permeated the intellectual discourse of mid-nineteenth-century Russian radicalism.[31]

Identifying a link between Stirner and the third member of the triumvirate, Belinsky, is less difficult thanks to the memoirist, Pavel Annenkov (1813–1887), who writes of the dramatic effect Stirner had on Belinsky in 1847, a year before his death, at a time when *Der Einzige* was, in Annenkov's words, "creating a sensation."[32] Belinsky, described by Berlin as "the most passionate and influential voice of his generation," had a profound impact on his friends Turgenev and Dostoevsky, as well as on contemporary Russian radical opinion, through his articles for *Sovremennik*, the journal that was to become the organ of one of the two branches of Russian nihilism during its foundational period, first under Chernyshevsky and then his successor Nikolai Dobrolyubov (1836–1861).[33] According to Annenkov—who reconstructed his conversations with Belinsky from memory—Belinsky, speaking about Stirner and *Der Einzige*, said something along these lines:

> It has been proved that a man feels and thinks and acts invariably according to the laws of egotistical urges, and indeed, he cannot have any others. The unfortunate thing is that mystical doctrines have brought the term into disgrace, giving it the meaning of the caterer to all the base passions and instincts in man.... The word was dishonored for no good reason, since it denotes a completely natural ... phenomenon, and, moreover, includes ... the possibility of a moral inference. But what I see in this case is an author who retains the word's pejorative connotation, the connotation given it by mystics, and merely converts it into a beacon to illuminate mankind's way by claiming to have discovered in all the pejorative ideas attributed to the word new and different qualities of it and new rights of it to universal respect.[34]

It must be assumed that Belinsky, like so many others, was deceived by Stirner's provocative language into believing that his version of egoism was equivalent to sinfully self-centered behavior. For Stirner, sin is no more than a figment of the imagination; he categorically rejects the

---

31   See, e.g., Helms, *Die Ideologie der anonymen Gesellschaft*, 346: "Stirner first had a comprehensive, powerful effect in the country to which he had denied culture and which he had accused of barbarism and Hunnish lust for the subjugation of Europe, in Russia.... Long before Marx inspired Russian revolutionaries, ever since the publication of the first edition of *Der Einzige*, Russian philosophers had dealt extensively with Stirner."
32   Annenkov, *The Extraordinary Decade*, 211.
33   See Berlin, "Fathers and Children," 12.
34   Annenkov, *The Extraordinary Decade*, 211–12.

concept: "There is no sinner and no sinful egoism!"[35] Instead, he conceives of egoism as the expression of *Eigenheit*, which may be translated variously as ownness, autonomy, or self-mastery, thus making, as Leopold points out, heteronomy, rather than altruism, its antonym.[36] Strangely, Belinsky seems to have arrived at a similar understanding of egoism to Stirner's, but, apparently oblivious to this, accuses him of precisely the negative definition that Stirner decries as "one-sided, unopened, narrow egoism."[37] Once again, Stirner's odious reputation, for which he largely has himself to blame owing to his seemingly mischievous desire to scandalize his readers, has resulted in a serious misinterpretation of his message.

The radicalism of Stirner's thought, amplified over time by his sensationalist approach, has certainly brought him notoriety and led to much critical opprobrium. It has been noted in the previous chapter that some of the outspoken views expressed in *Der Einzige* seem to contrast starkly with the placid, reserved impression Stirner made at the meetings of *Die Freien*, but of course, it is not a given that the contents of a book must necessarily reflect a writer's public behavior. It is conceivable that Stirner, having quietly witnessed the explosive opinions of his radical colleagues, felt compelled in his magnum opus to rise to the challenge of shocking even them, reveling in the opportunity to expose all vestiges of sanctimony by transgressing the conventional boundaries of good taste and propriety. One by one, therefore, he demolishes the most sacred precepts of Western civilization, starting with arguably the most prominent of the Ten Commandments, which he attempts to obliterate with his infamous phrase, so often quoted in subsequent assassinations of his character: "But I am entitled by myself to murder if I myself do not forbid it to myself."[38]

But Stirner's heterodoxy does not stop at apparently condoning homicide. He takes his iconoclastic, anti-Christian mission a step further by supporting, like Schopenhauer, the right to commit suicide:

> To await death is what the moral commandment postulates as the good; to give it to oneself is immoral and bad: *suicide* finds no excuse before the judgement-seat of morality. . . . Only when I am under obligation to no being is the maintaining of life—my affair.
>
> [Den Tod abzuwarten, heischt das sittliche Gebot als das Gute; ihn sich selbst zu geben, ist unsittlich und böse: der *Selbstmord* findet

---

35 EO, 317; EE, 364: "Es gibt keinen Sünder und keinen sündigen Egoismus!"
36 See Leopold, "Introduction," xxiii.
37 EO, 70; EE, 85: "einseitiger, unaufgeschlossener, bornierter Egoismus."
38 EO, 169; EE, 195: "Ich bin aber durch Mich berechtigt zu morden, wenn Ich Mir's nicht verbiete."

keine Entschuldigung vor dem Richterstuhl der Sittlichkeit. . . . Nur wenn ich keinem Wesen verpflichtet bin, ist die Erhaltung des Lebens—meine Sache.][39]

In the same vein, though further still beyond the pale of conventional morality, Stirner unashamedly offers an apparent justification of the normally unthinkable act of infanticide:

> Denounce that officer's widow who, in the flight in Russia, after her leg has been shot away, takes the garter from it, strangles her child with it, and then bleeds to death alongside the corpse—denounce the memory of the—infanticide. . . . The mother murdered it because she wanted to die *satisfied* and at rest.

> [Brandmarkt jene Offiziers-Witwe, die auf der Flucht in Russland, nachdem ihr das Bein weggeschossen, das Strumpfband von diesem abzieht, ihr Kind damit erdrosselt und dann neben der Leiche verblutet,—brandmarkt das Andenken der—Kindesmörderin. . . . Die Mutter ermordete es, weil sie *befriedigt* und beruhigt sterben wollte.][40]

Nor is it just different types of killing that seem to win his tacit approval. Incest and polygamy also receive implicit endorsement:

> If you ask him [a "moral man"] whether he has ever doubted that the copulation of brother and sister is incest, that monogamy is the truth of marriage, . . . then a moral shudder will come over him at the conception of one's being allowed to touch his sister as wife also. And whence this shudder? Because he *believes* in those moral commandments.

> [Wenn man ihn (den "Sittlichen") fragt, ob er je daran gezweifelt habe, dass die Vermischung der Geschwister eine Blutschande sei, dass die Monogamie die Wahrheit der Ehe sei, . . . so wird ein sittlicher Schauder ihn bei der Vorstellung überfallen, dass man seine Schwester auch als Weib berühren dürfe usw. Und woher dieser Schauder? Weil er an jene sittlichen Gebote *glaubt*.][41]

---

39   EO, 286; EE, 327–28. Cf. Schopenhauer, *Essays and Aphorisms*, 77: "Thus we hear that suicide is the most cowardly of acts, that only a madman would commit it, and similar insipidities; or the senseless assertion that suicide is 'wrong', though it is obvious there is nothing in the world a man has a more incontestable *right* to than his own life and person."
40   EO, 281; EE, 322.
41   EO, 45; EE, 55.

If, however, one takes these remarks in context, one finds, not a defense or advocacy of murder, suicide, infanticide, incest, and polygamy, but rather a critique of the assumptions of religion and morality, and of the enslavement of the individual to their extraneous demands. He is, in other words, engaged in the breaking of taboos, rather than the encouragement of violence or interbreeding. His intention is to challenge all forms of heteronomy and to assert the inability of the individual to attain self-fulfillment when under the control of external moral or political authority, on the basis that: "*Everything sacred is a tie, a fetter.*"[42] In the process, he uses the most extreme examples, of the kind already mentioned, to try to ram home his point in the most challenging and provocative way. Unfortunately (although to some extent understandably in light of Stirner's apparent endorsement of unthinkable acts), his readers have often failed to grasp his meaning, and what remains instead is the impression of satanic amorality. His colleagues among them turned out to be easier to scandalize than he had perhaps expected, and the result was reactions just as extreme as Stirner's views appeared to be.

Like so many of these commentators, Belinsky was unable to see past the blasphemies and provocations. He therefore takes the opportunity of condemning Stirner's version of egoism as he erroneously understood it, while offering his own benevolent alternative, which arrives at a similar conclusion to Stirner at least regarding fellow feeling:

> Crude animal egoism . . . cannot be advanced not only to an ideal, as the German author [Stirner] would have liked, but even to a simple rule of communal life. . . . The feeling of egoism, which governs the whole living world on earth, is exactly equally the source of all the horrors that occur on earth and the source of all the good it has seen! Therefore, if it is impossible to rid oneself of that feeling, . . . then it stands to reason that there is an obligation to make sense of it and to give it moral content. . . . But egoism will become a moral principle only when each individual person is able to join to his own private interests and needs also the interests of persons outside himself.[43]

Stirner would have rejected the designation of egoism as a moral principle, but he nonetheless repeatedly emphasizes the importance of reciprocity and shared interests between individuals: "And if I can use him [the fellow man], I doubtless come to an understanding and make myself at one with him, in order, by the agreement, to strengthen *my power*, and by

---

42 EO, 192; EE, 221: "*Alles Heilige ist ein Band, eine Fessel.*"
43 Annenkov, *The Extraordinary Decade*, 212–13.

combined force to accomplish more than individual force could effect."[44] Stirner rejects the idea of subordinating the interests of the individual to those of the community, but he evidently understands that a union can only function if it benefits all of its members.[45]

Even if the relationship of Stirner's ideas to those of the first generation of the Russian socialist and populist movements involves more differences than similarities, it is nonetheless clear from the above examples that the overwhelming influence of Hegelian and Young Hegelian thought on the progressive Russian intelligentsia of the time inevitably resulted in some scrutiny of Stirner's work, which subsequently provoked a discussion of the concept of egoism. Of course, none of the three intellectual figureheads of this generation—Herzen, Bakunin, or Belinsky—can properly be called a proto-nihilist, let alone a nihilist in the Russian sense, but in their revolutionary opposition to the Russian state (or, in Bakunin's case, the very concept of the state) and its mechanisms of political repression, they laid the groundwork for the later, more radical, doctrines of Russian nihilism. Moreover, all three placed considerable emphasis on the power of negation: Belinsky, the westernizing writer and critic, was called by Goncharov "the apostle of negation";[46] "The Reaction in Germany" by Bakunin, the collectivist anarchist, has been dubbed a "manifesto of negation";[47] and of Herzen, the father of Russian socialism, Lampert writes: "The emphasis on negation in Herzen's interpretation of Hegel owes a great deal to the influence of Bakunin. . . . Philosophy . . . is defined as a 'perpetual revolutionary tribunal', as 'the guillotine within man'. . . . 'It abhors canonized truths' and 'turns all that is religious and political into that which is simple and human, and subject to negation.'"[48] It is this spirit of negation which the fathers of Russian populism bequeathed to the next generation of radicals, and which is the meaning behind the epithet that Turgenev applied to them. It is conceivable that, over time, Stirner has, by association, been implicated in this conspiracy of negativity.

---

44   *EO*, 276; *EE*, 315: "Und wenn Ich ihn [den Mitmenschen] gebrauchen kann, so verständige Ich wohl und einige Mich mit ihm, um durch die Übereinkunft *meine Macht* zu verstärken und durch gemeinsame Gewalt mehr zu leisten, als die einzelne bewirken könnte."
45   See Onfray, *A Hedonist Manifesto*, 135: "Of course [Max Stirner] celebrated the absolute freedom of the individual, but he also knew how important it is for that individual not to remain alone."
46   Lampert, *Studies in Rebellion*, 107.
47   Lampert, *Studies in Rebellion*, 130.
48   Lampert, *Studies in Rebellion*, 202.

Stirner's Influence on Dostoevsky and Turgenev

From a historical perspective, the best-known group of radical intellectuals in nineteenth-century Russia was the so-called Petrashevsky Circle, which was a discussion group that met on Fridays in St. Petersburg during the 1840s to converse about Western philosophy and literature. The Circle's subsequent prominence can be put down largely to the involvement of Dostoevsky, whose membership resulted in his being arrested, sentenced to death, subjected to mock execution, and imprisoned in Siberia, all of which were defining events both for his life and for his literary career. Petrashevsky, who was essentially an atheistic devotee of the utopian socialist Charles Fourier (1772–1837), had an extensive private library of forbidden books, which included many foreign titles "by French socialists as well as French philosophes and German Left Hegelians."[49] As the circle was not broken up by the authorities until April 1849, four and a half years after the publication of *Der Einzige*, it is certainly possible that Stirner's book was on Petrashevsky's shelves and was thus accessible to his many visitors, who included Belinsky.[50]

As Frank notes in his monumental work on Dostoevsky, "it was Belinsky who first acquainted Dostoevsky with the new . . . arguments of Strauss, Feuerbach, and probably Stirner. And though his religious faith ultimately emerged unshaken—even strengthened—from the encounter, these doctrines did present him with an acute spiritual dilemma. Traces of this inner crisis can certainly be found in the wrestlings of Dostoevsky's own characters with the problems of faith and Christ."[51] As for Petrashevsky himself, the Austrian journalist and politician Ernst Viktor Zenker (1865–1946) was evidently convinced of Stirner's influence on him: "Petraschewski himself, in a satirical *Dictionary* which he published under the pseudonym of Kirilow, praised as one of the merits of early Christianity the abolition of private property and so on. We can easily recognise here the elements of Proudhon's and Stirner's Anarchism."[52]

Within the Petrashevsky Circle, there were various separate subgroups, including Nikolay Speshnev's secret society, to which Dostoevsky also belonged. Speshnev (1821–1882), whom Lampert acknowledges as, "apart from Dostoevsky, . . . perhaps the most remarkable figure among the Petrashevkists," was an aristocrat, communist, and revolutionary.[53]

---

49 Frede, *Doubt*, 114.
50 See Scheibert, *Von Bakunin zu Lenin*, 203: "A few years later, the Petrashevskyites read him [Stirner]."
51 Frank, *Dostoevsky*, 127.
52 Zenker, *Anarchism*, 118.
53 Lampert, *Sons against Fathers*, 207.

Before joining the Petrashevsky Circle, Speshnev had traveled in Europe from 1842 to 1847, during which time he is said to have been influenced "by the egoism and amoralism of Max Stirner."[54] Frank declares that Speshnev "sided with Max Stirner's totally subjective egoism," and assesses the sparse documentary evidence for Stirner's impact on Speshnev as follows: "The most important remarks are those that show how strongly he had come under the influence of Max Stirner. Rejecting all attempts to establish any sort of metaphysical system, Speshnev writes: . . . 'Is the difference between a God-man and a Man-god really so great?' Both, he says, are abstractions, which do not concern the existing individual of flesh-and-blood."[55] Frank goes on to speculate that Dostoevsky "may well have been present" at Petrashevsky's in 1848 when Speshnev delivered a lecture "on religion from a 'philosophical' point of view," and intimates that Stirner's ideas may thus have found their way (twenty-five years later) into the make-up of Stavrogin's character in *Demons*.[56] Without identifying Stavrogin directly with either Speshnev or Stirner, the implication is that Stavrogin is nonetheless a construct based on their perceived amorality, decadence, and atheism.[57] A minor corroboration of this theory can possibly be found in the fact that the young Dostoevsky is said to have had a copy of Stirner's book in his own library.[58]

The infiltration of Stirner's extremist philosophy into nineteenth-century Russian literature is a common charge, and Dostoevsky is the author who is most often cited to corroborate this. Drawing on Masaryk, the Marxist writer Helms states: "Through Dostoevsky, Stirner's ideas were disseminated across the world in literary form, and the figure of Ivan Karamazov has since become part of the consciousness of millions."[59] Similarly, the Polish anti-Marxist philosopher, Kołakowski, writes that "Raskolnikov, in Dostoevsky's *Crime and Punishment*, may be taken as an embodiment of the Ego as conceived by Stirner."[60] This rare example of consensus between those normally separated by an ideological divide

---

54   Lantz, *The Dostoevsky Encyclopedia*, 409.
55   Frank, *Dostoevsky*, 147.
56   Frank, *Dostoevsky*, 148.
57   See Frank, *Dostoevsky*, 646.
58   See Scheibert, *Von Bakunin zu Lenin*, 203. Scheibert cites N. Belʹčikov in *Venok Belinskomu*, 279.
59   Helms, *Die Ideologie der anonymen Gesellschaft*, 347. See Masaryk, *The Spirit of Russia*, 2:392–93: "Especially influential . . . have been . . . Nietzsche, Stirner. . . . I may refer to F. Sologub with his solipsist paroxysms; and to L. Šestov, an imitator of Stirner and Nietzsche. . . . / Dostoevskii must be mentioned in this connection, in so far as the conceptions of individualistic anarchism incorporated by him in the figure of Ivan Karamazov are given a positive turn by the anarchists and are accepted by them."
60   Kołakowski, *Main Currents of Marxism*, 1:166.

demonstrates just how widespread the conviction has been that Stirner played a significant role in the intellectual discourse of Russia at this time. Carroll, for instance, writes: "in the latter half of the nineteenth century it was in the hotbed of revolutionary thought and action, Russia, that Stirner's ideas were seized upon with the greatest enthusiasm. There they formed an important component of the egoist-nihilist-anarchist complex of doctrines."[61]

Laska, in keeping with his self-appointed role as Stirner's defender, begs to differ; he sees in the oft-repeated association of Stirner with Russian nihilism just another attempt to discredit him, based on completely unsubstantiated claims: "Even those Russian authors of the nineteenth century who described themselves as nihilists (such as Pisarev, Dobrolyubov, Chernyshevsky) did not refer to Stirner at all. In secondary literature, however, one occasionally finds . . . the assertion (not substantiated in a single case) that in them, as in other Russian authors (such as Belinsky, Herzen, Dostoevsky), positive influences of Stirner can be recognized."[62] Apart from the fact that Dobrolyubov and Chernyshevsky did not call themselves nihilists, by apparently questioning the veracity of so many reports of Stirner's influence on nineteenth-century Russian intellectuals, Laska would seem to be overstating his case.

One such report involves a letter purportedly written by Turgenev in Berlin in 1847, and published in *Sovremennik* in the same year, which indicates that Turgenev certainly knew of Stirner and was most probably personally acquainted with him:

> In a witty account of another visit to Berlin in 1847, Turgenev spoke poignantly about the end of the "literary, theoretical, philosophical, mythical epoch of German life." . . . The visitor saw the youth of the day turn away from philosophy for good, no students at Stahl's, Schelling forgotten, Steffens dead, only "the good Werder with three students as eager as ever." Bruno Bauer seemed to be lost without trace—at a concert he met the completely depressed Stirner.[63]

Turgenev studied philosophy and history at the University of Berlin from 1838 to 1841, at the height of Young Hegelian activity in Germany.[64] Stirner had left the university in 1834, but became, according to Mackay,

---

61   Carroll, "Introduction," 28.
62   Laska, *Ein dauerhafter Dissident*, 156.
63   Scheibert, *Von Bakunin zu Lenin*, 88, quoting from Turgenev's letter in *Sovremennik* (March 1847) reproduced in *Russkie Propilei. Materialy po istorii russkoi mysli i literatury*, 3 (1916): 110. See Schapiro, *Turgenev*, 56.
64   Strauss published *Das Leben Jesu* just before Turgenev's arrival in Berlin, in 1835, while Feuerbach's *Das Wesen des Christentums* appeared before he left, in the spring of 1841.

a member of *Die Freien* in 1841, the same year that Schelling started his lectures in Berlin, which were attended by, among many others, Bakunin and Turgenev.[65] There is certainly nothing in the chronology that rules out Turgenev's having known, or at least known of, Stirner, with all the potential implications this could have for the genesis of his best-known character, Bazarov.

Laska may have a point in his assertion that numerous claims concerning Stirner's relationship to nineteenth-century Russian thinkers are unsubstantiated, but that is not to say that no evidence exists at all, or that none of the assumptions made in this regard is based on sound reasoning. Only rarely does an account strain credulity, as with James Billington's colorful description of Stirner's influence on the controversial political writer, V. S. Pecherin (1807–1885), where he seems to be confusing Stirner's thought with elements from Hegel and Mainländer: "[Pecherin] had in his student days been driven to 'the Hamlet question' by Max Stirner, whose lectures at Berlin inspired him to embark on one of the many unfinished trilogies of the Russian nineteenth century. The first part of this untitled drama is a weird apotheosis of Stirner's idea that man can achieve divinity through his own uncaused act of self-assertion: suicide."[66]

As touched on above, Stirner is certainly unconventional in his attitude towards suicide: he does not rule it out as a potentially reasonable response to human existence, and he roundly condemns its demonization in Christian ethics. However, he is not in the least concerned with the idea of achieving divinity, either by taking one's own life or indeed in any other way. As for him lecturing in Berlin, there is no record of that in Mackay or elsewhere and, in the unlikely event that he did, it is improbable that he would have lectured to a student just eight months his junior. Notwithstanding his confusion in this instance, Billington was an influential academic, and he thus provides a further example of how a false image of Stirner has entered, and been perpetuated in, the mainstream, through the use and reuse of inaccurate testimony.[67]

Stirner and Russian Nihilism

Regarding the protagonists in the historical period of Russian nihilism, which started in the 1860s, the connections with Stirner are, if anything,

---

[65] See Mackay, *Max Stirner*, 90. See also Pinkard, "The Social Conditions of Philosophy in the Nineteenth Century," 57.
[66] Billington, *The Icon and the Axe*, 356–57.
[67] Billington was however correct concerning the influence of Stirner on the Russian writer and playwright, Mikhail Petrovich Artsybashev (1878–1927). See Billington, *The Icon and the Axe*, 764; and Artzibashef, "Introduction," 9.

even less easy to trace than in the pre-nihilist era. As already observed in chapter 2 above, there were two main branches of Russian nihilism, whose principal ideologists were Chernyshevsky and Pisarev. Chernyshevsky has been dubbed by Hingley "the chief inspiration of Nihilism," although he actually disowned the term as a self-appellation.[68] Yet so central was he, as the editor of *Sovremennik*, to the landscape of radical debate in Russia around the time of the publication of *Fathers and Sons* in 1862 and so many were his detractors who used the term to describe him in their polemical attacks, that the label stuck; and anyway, despite his disavowal, the fact is that he contributed significantly to the evolving image of the nihilist, not least in his advocacy of communal living and his championing of an extreme version of female emancipation, which raised uxorial promiscuity to the status of a solemn family duty. Chernyshevsky's only novel, *What Is to Be Done?* (1863), which has earned itself the title of "the Nihilist Bible" and been called "a sermon on rational egoism," was a highly successful vehicle for propagating his views.[69] As Hingley explains: "[*What Is to Be Done?*] has been described with reason as the worst novel ever written, but to many Russians of the 1860s it was a sacred text. . . . It did more to mould the Nihilists' beliefs and influence their actions than any other single document."[70] Rakhmetov, who is generally considered to be the real hero of the book (even though he only has a relatively minor role), with his saintly devotion to the popular cause, acted as perhaps the most potent inspiration for the throng of disaffected and rebellious Russian youths who gravitated towards the nihilist movement.

Nonetheless, ideologically speaking, Chernyshevsky can best be described as a democratic socialist; he was a follower of Belinsky and Herzen, but Feuerbach was "his first and enduring philosophical love."[71] As for Stirner's influence on Chernyshevsky, the absence of any acknowledgment to that effect by Chernyshevsky himself means that it can only be speculated about. Chernyshevsky's principle of rational egoism (that rational action must maximize self-interest) is conceivably relevant in this regard, as it throws up certain similarities with Stirner's concept of egoism, as well as with his ideas on social organization. Chernyshevsky, like Stirner, maintained that the values governing human actions are predicated on self-interest. Thus, he writes: "On closer scrutiny, we shall discover that an action or sentiment which appears to us disinterested has,

---

68 Hingley, *Nihilists*, 33.
69 Hingley, *Nihilists*, 36, 48.
70 Hingley, *Nihilists*, 35.
71 Lampert, *Sons against Fathers*, 141.

nonetheless, its origin in the consideration of personal advantage, personal pleasure, personal welfare, i.e., in the sentiment known as egoism."[72]

One of the main characters in Chernyshevsky's novel, Dmitry Lopukhov (who, like Turgenev's Bazarov, is a medical student), expresses the tenets of Chernyshevsky's rational egoism in the following internal monologue: "I hadn't been planning to make sacrifices. I haven't been foolish enough to make any so far, and I hope I never will. I did what was best for me. I'm not the sort of person who makes sacrifices. No one is. It's a fallacious concept. Sacrifice is all stuff and nonsense. One does what's most pleasurable."[73] There is a parallel here with Stirner's scorn for sacrifice as a principle of human behavior, which is a recurrent theme in *Der Einzige*: "Egoism does not think of sacrificing anything, giving away anything that it wants."[74] Moreover, like Chernyshevsky, Stirner questions the very credibility and authenticity of the concept of self-sacrifice: "And are these self-sacrificing people perchance not selfish, not egoist? . . . Their entire activity is egoistic."[75] In Stirner, we also find the same connection between human motivation and personal pleasure, as evidenced in his mature egoist, "who deals with things and thoughts according to his heart's pleasure, and sets his personal pleasure above everything."[76]

There are, however, plenty of differences as well. Lopukhov, like the author who created him, considers one product of enlightened self-interest in a man to be the obligation to redress historical gender inequality by condoning, or even encouraging, his wife's adultery. Chernyshevsky explains: "To straighten a stick which has been bent for too long in one direction, it is necessary to bend it the other way. . . . Woman is put below man, and, in my view, every decent man is duty bound to put his wife above himself. Such temporary disparity is essential for the sake of the equality to come."[77] For such a position to be self-evidently compatible with egoism, one might need to delve into the realms of sexual frigidity or Freudian masochism: it is hard, at any rate, to imagine it eliciting any enthusiasm from Stirner.

---

72   Chernyshevsky, *Polnoe sobranie sochinenii*, 7:291. Translation from Lampert, *Sons against Fathers*, 150.

73   Chernyshevsky, *What Is to Be Done?* 149.

74   EO, 228; EE, 262: "Der Egoismus denkt nicht daran etwas aufzuopfern, sich etwas zu vergeben."

75   EO, 70; EE, 85: "Und sind diese Aufopfernden etwa nicht eigennützig, nicht Egoisten? . . . Egoistisch ist ihr ganzes Tun und Treiben."

76   EO, 18; EE, 24: "der mit den Dingen und Gedanken nach Herzenslust gebahrt und sein persönliches Interesse über alles setzt."

77   Pypina, *Lyubov' v zhizni Chernyshevskogo*, 32. Translation from Lampert, *Sons against Fathers*, 104–5.

More importantly, Chernyshevsky's theory of rational egoism led him to a utilitarian conclusion, whereby the enlightened individual recognizes that his own interests are well served by the maximization of the interests of the greatest number, because this results in the best possible social environment, which is characterized by communal happiness and prosperity. The individual is therefore encouraged, for his own good, to put all his efforts into the establishment of a new system of cooperative socialism. The divergence from Stirner's understanding of egoism could hardly be greater. Thus, it is unsurprising that Chernyshevsky, despite being an intellectual name-dropper, never once mentions Stirner in his writings.[78] If he did know of Stirner, he saw no reason to acknowledge him, unless his repetition in a notebook of Goethe's line, of which Stirner had availed himself, is a heavily veiled reference: "Whoever has learned to apply this [continuous rejection of existing forms] to every manifestation of life will boldly hail the forces of chance which alarm the fainthearted. He will echo the poet [Goethe] who said: / Ich hab' mein Sach' auf nichts gestellt / Und mir gehört die ganze Welt."[79] Once again, the question can be asked whether the apostrophe after *Sach*, as Stirner had misspelled it, might be a clue to the source, but, especially in the absence of any conclusive evidence that Chernyshevsky knew of Stirner, there can be no useful answer.

Chernyshevsky's adversary, Pisarev, the chief ideologue of the revolutionary journal *Russkoe Slovo*, has been called "the most prominent of the Russian 'nihilists.'"[80] Unlike Chernyshevsky, he did not reject the label nihilist, which makes perfect sense when one observes how, in his essay "Bazarov," he elevates his fictional, intellectual forebear's concept of negation to a new level of exaltation: "In a word, here is the ultimatum of our camp: what can be smashed must be smashed; whatever is able to withstand, let it stand; whatever flies into pieces is rubbish; in any case, hit right, hit left, from that no evil can nor will come."[81] Pisarev's endorsement of the annihilation of the status quo expresses the essence of the meaning of Russian nihilism, in the words of the one prominent nihilist of that period who unequivocally accepted, and even welcomed,

---

78   See Chernyshevsky, *What Is to Be Done?*, where the following appear in the text: Hume, Gibbon, Ranke, and Thierry, 75–76; Dickens, George Sand, 103; Gogol, 154, 233, 283; Fourier and Considérant, 191; Comte, 204; Voltaire, 210; Beecher Stowe; 231; Robert Owen, 247; John Stuart Mill, Adam Smith, Thomas Robert Malthus, David Ricardo, Thackeray, 283; Feuerbach, 292; Rousseau, 365; Turgenev, 380; and Kant, Fichte, and Hegel, 405.

79   Chernyshevsky, *Polnoe sobranie sochinenii*, 10:745. Translation from Lampert, *Sons against Fathers*, 177.

80   Lampert, *Sons against Fathers*, 272.

81   Pisarev, *Collected Works*, 1:66. Translation from Gillespie, *Nihilism before Nietzsche*, 143.

the soubriquet. It is the raising of negation to the status of a first principle that gives Russian nihilism its specific definition. As such, Slocombe seems to be missing the point when he writes: "Russian Nihilism was social Darwinism: if an institution was strong enough to survive, then it would; if it was not, then it would fall. Such radicals were not interested in the *nihil*, but in revolution, and therefore Russian Nihilism was nihilistic only inasmuch as it relied upon certain aspects of Western philosophy that were *themselves* only tangentially nihilistic."[82]

Hingley also frames Russian nihilism within a more general definition of the term, which, to some extent, calls into question its nomenclature: "the name Nihilist seems to imply a belief either in nothing at all or in destruction for its own sake. In fact, . . . [Russian] Nihilists were not men of little or no faith. Far from it: they mostly believed passionately in something, if only in a hotch-potch involving revolution, the Russian peasant, Chernyshevsky, some kind of Socialism, the idea of progress, science, materialism and so on."[83] Russian nihilism may indeed have acquired the term from the philosophical debate in Germany which focused on the denial of God and religion, but its theorists and adherents adapted it for the most pressing issues in Tsarist Russia, namely political repression and social inequality. The focus thus shifted to the denial, and therefore the destruction, of the state in all its political and social manifestations, as Masaryk observed: "The nihilists have by no means thought out their doctrine metaphysically; their nihilism is social and political; they aim at destroying Old Russia, the Russia of Nicholas. (That is their 'nihil')."[84] It is the vagueness of the word nihilism which has allowed it, over the last two hundred and fifty years, to adopt so many guises and, indeed, to be applied so freely to Stirner.

Venturi, in his definitive work on revolutionary thought in nineteenth-century Russia, views Russian nihilism as just another occurrence of a dynamic, but essentially enduring phenomenon. He traces the term nihilism from its eighteenth-century origins and concludes that the conservative Russian journalist, Mikhail Katkov's, use of the term in 1840 in an undisguised attack both on the Young Hegelians and on Belinsky and Herzen, is evidence that "the word as used in the Hegelian Left by Bruno Bauer and Stirner was beginning to assume a philosophical and polemical significance."[85] Apart from the fact that Bauer and Stirner are

82 Slocombe, *Nihilism*, 15.
83 Hingley, *Nihilists*, 57.
84 Masaryk, *The Spirit of Russia*, 2:73.
85 Venturi, *Roots of Revolution*, 326. Katkov, who, like Turgenev, was studying in Berlin at the time, had written: "If one looks at the universe, and has to choose one of two extreme attitudes, it is easier to become a mystic than a nihilist. We are everywhere surrounded by miracles." Katkov, "Sochineniia," 17. Translation from Katz, *Mikhail N. Katkov*, 31.

not known ever to have employed the term, and also disregarding the fact that the word certainly had a philosophical and polemical significance well before 1840, for instance in the writings of Obereit, Jenisch, and Jacobi in the eighteenth century, such a reading fundamentally underestimates the separate development of all the specific types of nihilism in general, and of Russian nihilism in particular.

Gillespie, in his attempt to force all manifestations of nihilism (before Nietzsche) into a single Promethean narrative, reaches the same conclusion as Venturi does from the evidence of Katkov's lone use of the word, and proclaims: "The Russian debate over nihilism is thus an extension of the German controversy."[86] This is an oversimplification. Katkov's use of the word is certainly an example of how the word was transmitted into the realm of Russian intellectual debate as a result of the encounter of Russian students and thinkers with Left-Hegelianism. However, although Katkov clearly does use it in a similar way, for instance, to Rosenkranz in his attack on Stirner, more than twenty years were to elapse before the concept of Russian nihilism was to mature fully. Once Turgenev had given it its definitive application in *Fathers and Sons*, it very much developed a life of its own. Venturi's failure to recognize this is illustrated by the following assertion: "It was at once obvious that the word had been badly chosen. The 'Nihilists', more than anyone else, believed—blindly and violently—in their own ideas. Their positivist and materialist faith could be accused of fanaticism, of a youthful lack of a sense of criticism, but not of apathy."[87]

Venturi, writing here at the beginning of the 1950s, seems to be guilty of an anachronism by inferring that the choice of the epithet nihilist for the Russian nihilists failed to take into account their lack of apathy, given that the explicit connection between nihilism and apathy is a more modern assumption generally associated with the existentialism of Sartre and Camus. Slocombe demonstrates a sounder appreciation of the development of Russian nihilism as a particular phenomenon with his acknowledgment of a fundamental shift in the meaning of the word nihilism from a religious to a political context, coinciding with its geographical shift from Western Europe to Russia in the mid-nineteenth century. Even though he lumps Stirner together with the Russian nihilists in one subsection under the heading of anti-authoritarian nihilism, he recognizes Stirner's role as a link in the chain of nihilism's evolution rather than an instigator of Russian nihilism:

> [Marx and Engels] fail to do justice to the central component of *The Ego and Its Own*: anti-authoritarianism. . . . Stirner's desire to free

---

86 Gillespie, *Nihilism before Nietzsche*, 138.
87 Venturi, *Roots of Revolution*, 326.

individuals from all forms of control, whether religious or secular, links him with the movement that was developing in Russia at the time. As such, Stirner's radical perspective is one of the links between the decline in religious orthodoxy (nihilism-as-atheism) and the rise of political extremism (nihilism-as-anarchism), a movement from the atheistic origins of nihilism towards Russian Nihilism.[88]

Like all movements, Russian nihilism certainly had its antecedents, but it must be understood nonetheless on its own terms and not confused with earlier or later manifestations of the diverse and malleable term, nihilism. There is, therefore, no internal contradiction in the fact that Russian nihilists passionately believed in progress or that they did not (generally) consider human life to be meaningless. As with all types of nihilism, it is what the *nihil* refers to that matters. Herzen offers the following interpretation:

> "Nihilism" is the force of logic without restraint; it is science without dogma; it is unconditional allegiance to experience and a ready acceptance of all consequences, wherever they may lead. . . . Nihilism doesn't turn "something" into "nothing," but shows that "nothing" that has been taken for "something" is an optical illusion, and that every truth, however it contradicts our comfortable notions, is more wholesome than they are. Whether the name be appropriate or not does not matter. We are accustomed to it.[89]

If one takes Russian nihilism as the self-contained historical event that it clearly was, it is easy to understand why Pisarev is its most complete representative, both because of his unique self-identification with the name, and because of his dedication to the concept of annihilation. Moreover, he held the typical nihilist beliefs in materialism, positivism, and anti-establishmentarianism. Where he differed from Chernyshevsky and the other so-called nihilists was in his conviction that social transformation should be the task of an elite consisting of enlightened realists, rather than of the broad masses. This focus on the individual led Pisarev to refine the notion of egoism, which had already featured in the ideas of his radical colleagues and predecessors, making it an even more central element of his ideology. Lampert describes Pisarev's position as follows:

> The self or "ego," . . . was the ultimate measure of moral as of any other experience. And when he analysed the actual motives which made men take a certain course of action he usually discovered—*à*

---

88 Slocombe, *Nihilism*, 12.
89 Herzen, *Sobranie sochinenii*, 20:349. Translation from Lampert, *Sons against Fathers*, 310–11.

la Bazarov—self-interest and ambition; he did not discover a desire to promote principles and ideals, in which, in any case, he did not believe. Coquart explains Pisarev's moral solipsism as "l'égotisme éternel de la vingtième année." This may account for declarations such as Pisarev made to his mother: "For me," he wrote, "each person exists only to the extent to which he causes satisfaction in me"; ... or for saying about his mother that he "would not hesitate to kill her if that should serve his purpose."[90]

The correlation between Pisarev's comment on matricide and Stirner's on infanticide, both demonstrations of egoistic amorality at its most provocative, could hardly go unnoticed for long. Masaryk, in a detailed analysis of Pisarev's thought, makes repeated reference to the apparent influence of Stirner: "Freely following Stirner and Feuerbach, Pisarev negates all principles, all ethical aims, the concept of duty, ideals in general. . . . Pisarev, like Stirner, denies the existence of crime."[91] Masaryk finds not only ideological but also terminological similarities between the two: "with the reference to spooks, [Pisarev] recalls Feuerbach and Stirner."[92] However, in the final analysis, Masaryk's conviction of Stirner's influence on Pisarev remains speculative in nature: "He knew of Stirner's work, but I believe at second hand. . . . He preached radical individualism, understanding by this term the struggle for the emancipation of the individuality."[93] It is true that, at least in his most revolutionary period, Pisarev combined an individualism like Stirner's with a concept of negation like Bakunin's to produce his own radical form of political nihilism, but this, in itself, does not prove knowledge of Stirner.

Nechaev's Revolution versus Stirner's Insurrection

More radical still than Pisarev, though not a self-confessed nihilist, was Nechaev, communist revolutionary, advocate of merciless destruction, assassin of Ivanov, and author of "The Revolutionary Catechism," which inspired Narodnaya Volya, the revolutionary terrorist organization responsible for the assassination of Tsar Alexander II in 1881. Nechaev has been described by Hingley variously—but consistently—as "satanic," "most Nihilist of Nihilists," "a ruthless murderer, blackmailer, extortioner and confidence trickster," and "chief ogre of the Nihilist

---

90 Lampert, *Sons against Fathers*, 304.
91 Masaryk, *The Spirit of Russia*, 2:54.
92 Masaryk, *The Spirit of Russia*, 2:55.
93 Masaryk, *The Spirit of Russia*, 2:53.

movement."[94] It was the excesses of what Gillespie calls Nechaev's "terroristic religion of negation," especially the cold-blooded murder of Ivanov, which captured the imagination of Dostoevsky; his horror and disgust gain full expression in his retelling of the miracle of the Gadarene swine in *Demons*, where the nihilists, and those complicit with them, are envisioned entering the swine and drowning, and thus healing the beloved motherland.[95]

Remarkably, Stirner and Nechaev are rarely associated with each other. When they are, the connection is not usually seen as being of any great depth or import, as in Cedric Robinson's casual assessment: "Though Stirner . . . failed to act out any of his asocial dictums, . . . Sergei Nechayev, several decades later, was the egoist incarnate."[96] It is significant, though, that the comparison between the two is based on the amorality of their common egoism, which Robinson develops into a more sinister complicity: "Stirner, Nechayev and . . . Joseph Dejacque, anticipated, and perhaps gave some impetus to, the violence in assassinations and bombings which would characterize the anarchist movement."[97] Robinson thus echoes Camus, who discerns in Stirner's rejection of the very notion of crime, and his championing of might is right, the seeds of the violent terrorism of the future: "Revolt leads . . . to the justification of crime. Stirner not only attempted this justification (in this respect his direct heirs can be found in the terroristic forms of anarchy), but he was visibly exhilarated by the possibilities he was thus opening up."[98]

However, even Paterson refrains from drawing too close a parallel between Stirner and Nechaev, despite the obvious similarity of their reputations as *enfants terribles*. Instead, he argues that "it is excessively fanciful to relate the purely metaphysical, inward-looking nihilism of Stirner to the only too fiercely active, socially revolutionary nihilism of the Nechayevs and Bakunins."[99] The distinction is an important one, even if it ignores the social implications of Stirner's philosophy as expressed in the concept of the union of egoists. The fact is that Russian nihilism involves a primary, and at times monomaniacal, focus on the revolutionary destruction of the state for the sake of the people as a whole, while Stirner's primary focus is on the liberation of the individual from external coercion and control. That they are both therefore hostile to the state is almost coincidental, as they arrive at this conclusion from entirely different premises.

---

94   Hingley, *Nihilists*, 26, 57, 59.
95   Gillespie, *Nihilism before Nietzsche*, 164. See Dostoevsky, *Demons*, 724.
96   Robinson, *The Terms of Order*, 182.
97   Robinson, *The Terms of Order*, 182.
98   Camus, *L'Homme révolté*, 86–87.
99   Paterson, *The Nihilistic Egoist*, 314.

Paterson's point is that Stirner is calling for a revolution in the way we think, whereas the Russian nihilists were conspiring to bring about a political revolution leading to the overthrow of the Tsarist state. It was Hartmann who first alluded to this distinction in 1879, in his reference to Stirner and the Russian nihilists as the theoretical and practical representatives, respectively, of the belief in the futility of existence:

> Ultimately, everything is so ridiculous that it comes down to one thing; life and death are equally senseless and are therefore a matter of indifference to me. . . . Only here is the standpoint of absolute indifference to all and every purpose reached, the most horrific state imaginable, for in its total burn-out it is as far removed from positive interest as negative despair—like the emptiness of the abyss of nothingness. . . . Practically, this point of view is shown in Russian nihilism, formally it is developed by Max Stirner, who did not even require pessimism for it, as the sovereignty of the ego sufficed for him.[100]

While recognizing that Stirner cannot be called a pessimist, Hartmann tries, contrarily, to force both Stirner and Russian nihilism into a negative worldview. His argument holds little water: unlike Hartmann himself (along with Bahnsen and Mainländer), Stirner does not fit into the Schopenhauerian tradition, while Russian nihilism's primary issue was with the tyranny of the Tsarist state, not with the (lack of) meaning of life. Nonetheless, Hartmann does correctly identify a fundamental difference of approach between the two, even if he appears to misrepresent the nature of their affinity.

Their disparity is rooted in the fact that Stirner's focus is on *zoon logikon*, while the Russian nihilists are concerned with *zoon politikon*. This is most evident in the distinction Stirner makes between revolution and insurrection (*Empörung*).[101] Speaking of the French Revolution, he writes:

> If the revolution ended in a reaction, this only showed what the revolution *really was*. . . . The revolution was not directed against *the established*, but against the *establishment in question*, against a *particular* establishment. It did away with *this* ruler, not with *the* ruler.
>
> [Verlief sich die Revolution in eine Reaktion, so kam dadurch nur zu Tage, was die Revolution *eigentlich* war. . . . Die Revolution war

---

100 Hartmann, *Phänomenologie des sittlichen Bewusstseins*, 767–68.
101 Byington translates *Empörung* with "insurrection." Other possible translations include revolt and rebellion. Apart from the connotation of resisting authority, control, or convention, the word can also express outrage and disgust.

> nicht gegen *das Bestehende* gerichtet, sondern gegen *dieses Bestehende*, gegen einen *bestimmten* Bestand. Sie schaffte *diesen* Herrscher ab, nicht *den* Herrscher.]¹⁰²

The history of France after the French Revolution had clearly taught Stirner all he needed to know about the nature of revolution. Far from being synonymous with liberation, revolution is, for Stirner, an obligation in the form of a fixed idea, which, in dialectical fashion, replaces one hegemony with another. He therefore has the prescience to declare: "Communism rightly revolts against the pressure that I experience from individual proprietors; but still more horrible is the might that it puts in the hands of the collectivity."¹⁰³ Moreover, revolution involves for Stirner, as Camus observes, a form of belief: "To be revolutionary, one must still believe in something where there is nothing to believe in."¹⁰⁴ Instead, Stirner advocates the principle of permanent insurrection:

> Revolution and insurrection must not be looked upon as synonymous. . . . The revolution aimed at new *arrangements*; insurrection leads us no longer to *let* ourselves be arranged, but to arrange ourselves, and set no glittering hopes on "institutions." . . . Now, as my object is not the overthrow of an established order but my elevation above it, my purpose and deed are not a political or social but (as directed toward myself and my ownness alone) an *egoistic* purpose and deed.

> [Revolution und Empörung dürfen nicht für gleichbedeutend angesehen werden. . . . Die Revolution zielte auf neue *Einrichtungen*, die Empörung führt dahin, Uns nicht mehr einrichten zu *lassen*, sondern Uns selbst einzurichten, und setzt auf "Institutionen" keine glänzende Hoffnung. . . . Da nun nicht der Umsturz eines Bestehenden mein Zweck ist, sondern meine Erhebung darüber, so ist meine Absicht und Tat keine politische oder soziale, sondern, als allein auf Mich und meine Eigenheit gerichtet, eine *egoistische*.]¹⁰⁵

Stirner advocates rebellion against all man-made myths in the interests of the emancipation of the self from heteronomous tyranny; the Russian nihilists' aim, on the other hand, was to end Tsarist repression in the interests of the emancipation of the Russian people from political tyranny.

102 *EO*, 99–100; *EE*, 119.
103 *EO*, 228; *EE*, 262: "Gegen den Druck, welchen Ich von den einzelnen Eigentümern erfahre, lehnt sich der Kommunismus mit Recht auf; aber grauenvoller noch ist die Gewalt, die er der Gesamtheit einhändigt."
104 Camus, *L'Homme révolté*, 86.
105 *EO*, 279–80; *EE*, 320.

While the rebellious, emancipatory impetus may be similar, the former represents a general approach, which is acted out first and foremost in the mind, while the latter is a response to a specific set of circumstances, which is acted out on the sociopolitical stage.[106]

There is a social dimension to Stirner's philosophy, as manifested in the union of egoists, but it is a corollary to his prime objective of demythologizing human thought. Thus, the Russian nihilists may have borrowed certain elements of Stirner's atheism, egoism, and iconoclasm, but they completely ignored his sociopolitical ideas. The very different plans for society proposed by Stirner and the Russian nihilists nonetheless have one thing in common, namely, an astonishing naïvety. In Stirner's case, it is the apparent belief that the social interaction of sovereign individuals, free from the political and judicial framework of the state, will necessarily lead to a form of equilibrium, however protean. Such a state of affairs would necessitate an excessively high level of enlightenment, especially with regard to self-interest, which would seem unattainable and utopian, at least in the context of industrial and post-industrial mass society. As Kołakowski notes, paraphrasing Marx:

> It is a pious illusion . . . to expect individuals to live together without the aid of the community and its institutions. It is not in the power of the individual to decide whether his relations with others are to be personal or institutional; the division of labour means that personal relations are bound to transform themselves into class relations, and the superiority of one individual over another is expressed in the social relationship of privilege. Whatever individuals may intend, the nature and level of needs and productive forces determine the social character of their mutual relations.[107]

The Russian nihilists, for their part, had an equally utopian outlook in their belief that an equitable society would necessarily emerge following the annihilation of the old order. Isaiah Berlin articulates this outlook as follows: "All these [populist] thinkers share one vast apocalyptic assumption: that once the reign of evil—autocracy, exploitation, inequality—is consumed in the fire of the revolution, there will arise naturally and spontaneously out of its ashes a natural, harmonious, just order, needing

---

106 See Masaryk, *The Spirit of Russia*, 2:73: "Stirner, . . . refraining in 1848 from participating in the revolution, incorporated into his life the true significance of his book *The Ego and his Own*, whereas the Russian 'ego' is a theoretical and practical revolutionist guided by the teaching of Bakunin, his aim is socio-political destruction, pandestruction." See also Mackay, *Max Stirner*, 197: "It hardly needs to be expressly mentioned that Stirner had taken not the slightest outward part in the March days of 1848 or in the whole movement."

107 Kołakowski, *Main Currents of Marxism*, 1:169.

only the gentle guidance of the enlightened revolutionaries to attain to its proper perfection."[108] History, of course, has not been kind to either point of view. Just societies have not sprung up following revolutions, and individualist anarchism has not proved to be a workable social model.

In conclusion therefore, their many differences notwithstanding, there is at least sufficient evidence to confirm a limited connection between Stirner and Russian nihilism, as Masaryk has recognized: "The positivism of the [Russian] nihilists was derived from Feuerbach and Stirner, and in part from Hegel."[109] Despite Laska's protestations, it is clear that Stirner's ideas, most notably his concept of egoism, did play a role in the evolution of Russian nihilism from the 1840s onwards, when Young Hegelianism became popular among the Russian intelligentsia. Furthermore, as Frank points out, Stirner very probably had a significant influence on Speshnev, above all with regard to moral relativism. But just because Stirner unwittingly contributed some radical elements to the development of Russian nihilism does not make him a political nihilist himself. He does not encourage either clandestine terrorism or violent revolution; annihilation of the state is far from being his primary concern; and he is not lacking in ideas concerning his vision of a new social order, however naïve, impracticable, or inconsequential they may be. Despite his rebellious advocacy of liberation from authority, Stirner's paramount aim is not political at all: it is, first and foremost, to complete the Enlightenment task of eradicating the dogmatic, hegemonic myths that enslave the individual's mind, as he implies in the preface to the second part of *Der Einzige*: "The *other world outside us* is . . . brushed away, and the great undertaking of the men of the Enlightenment completed; but the *other world in us* has become a new heaven and calls us forth to renewed heaven-storming."[110] The sociopolitical dimension, however unavoidable, is incidental in this endeavor.

What we are left with from the analysis of the relationship between Stirner and Russian or political nihilism are many coincidental connections, a few striking similarities, some evidence of influence, but a fundamental discrepancy in terms of aims and objectives, and no reasonable grounds for describing Stirner as a political nihilist. Nonetheless, what the current chapter's investigation does demonstrate is that there is enough of a link between Stirner and the development of political radicalism in nineteenth-century Russia to explain, at least to some extent, the assumption that Stirner shares the principal characteristics of the Russian

---

108 Berlin, "Introduction," in Venturi, *Roots of Revolution*, xiii.
109 Masaryk, *The Spirit of Russia*, 2:72.
110 *EO*, 139; *EE*, 162: "Das *Jenseits außer Uns* ist . . . weggefegt, und das große Unternehmen der Aufklärer vollbracht; allein *das Jenseits in Uns* ist ein neuer Himmel geworden und ruft Uns zu erneutem Himmelsstürmen auf."

nihilists, even if this opinion is based on incomplete knowledge or even unsound reasoning. Such an assumption, indeed, feeds into the argument that Stirner's lasting significance is a political one, as one of the original theoreticians of individualist anarchism, an idea put forward by Mackay and enthusiastically supported by Victor Basch.[111] But the discussion of Stirner's anarchist credentials lies outside the remit of the present study; instead, attention now turns to the question of Stirner's relationship to the second type of nihilism of which he is most commonly accused, namely moral nihilism. While sociopolitical issues may not be central to Stirner's project, morality is at the core of his concerns, thus perhaps offering more scope for the aptness of moral nihilism as a characterization of his thought.[112]

---

111 See Mackay, *Max Stirner*, 21: "The legacy of Stirner, however, rests in the faithful and strong hands of the individualist anarchists." See also Basch, *L'Individualisme anarchiste*, 281.

112 Morality is the first of the abstractions that Stirner challenges in the preface to *Der Einzige*. See *EO*, 5: "What is not supposed to be my concern! First and foremost the good cause, then God's cause, the cause of mankind . . ."; *EE*, 13: "Was soll nicht alles Meine Sache sein! Vor allem die gute Sache, dann die Sache Gottes, die Sache der Menschheit. . . ."

CHAPTER 6

The Absence of Absolutes: Stirner and Moral Nihilism

The Definition of Moral Nihilism

MORAL NIHILISM IS DEFINED, simply, as the denial of absolute values and is the type of nihilism which, since the first publication of *Der Einzige*, has been most frequently used by Stirner's critics to discredit him. Laska goes so far as to view it as the fulcrum of Stirner defamation and demonization: "Whoever labeled Stirner the most extreme, radical, systematic advocate of atheism, immoralism, subjectivism, individualism, egoism, solipsism or the like, meant, even if he did not say so explicitly, that vague concept of ethical nihilism, to which belongs essentially, as already with Jacobi, Hegel, and Rosenkranz, the horror vision of the destructive and apocalyptic, the evil, demonic and satanic."[1] The justification for the accusation of moral nihilism is to be sought, naturally enough, in Stirner's numerous pronouncements on morality, ethicality, and good and evil (*Moral, Sittlichkeit, gut und böse*), but before proceeding with their evaluation, it is necessary, once again, to address the familiar issue of terminological ambiguity. Unlike with Russian nihilism, there are no historical figures who readily confess to being moral nihilists, which makes it all the more difficult to identify the term's full range of meanings and connotations.

There is both the implicit and explicit imputation of moral nihilism in much of the censure of Stirner described in chapter 4 above. It is implicit in Bernstein's distinguishing of Stirner's nihilism from Russian nihilism and in Keben's concept of the nihilistic hangover that Stirner's philosophy allegedly engenders.[2] A more recent reference to Stirner's moral decadence (though without mention of the word nihilism), can be found in Helms's Marxist critique of Stirner as a petty-bourgeois proto-fascist.[3]

---

1 Laska, *Ein dauerhafter Dissident*, 106.
2 See Bernstein, "Die Soziale Doktrin des Anarchismus," 428; and Keben, "John Henry Mackay und sein Philosoph," 174.
3 See Helms, *Die Ideologie der anonymen Gesellschaft*, 500: "The doctrine of the Unique One justifies capitalism and administratively organized chaos, it

The explicit association of Stirner with ethical nihilism first appeared in Karl Rosenkranz's diary entry concerning the recently published *Der Einzige*, which included the line: "Theoretically, such nihilism in relation to all ethical pathos cannot develop into anything."[4] Similar declarations have appeared ever since, as in Laas's description of Stirner's thought as "this nihilistic-Promethean abandonment of all that is moral"; Ströbel's assessment of "Stirner's moral nihilism"; and Schröder's remark about Stirner's "outspoken moral nihilism."[5]

What these critics mean by moral nihilism, however, often seems to be little more than the common polemical connotation of the word nihilism applied to Stirner's perceived immorality, evidenced by his apparent willingness to spurn the Ten Commandments and condone acts that are proscribed by conventional morality, including incest, polygamy, murder, suicide, and infanticide. Stirner appears to have no use for conventional morality, and he rides roughshod over common moral sensibilities. But, as shall become apparent, moral nihilism is not synonymous with an attitude that is antagonistic towards traditional moral practice or with an open-minded consequentialism so permissive as to contemplate the advantages of even the most unspeakable acts under certain exceptional circumstances. In order properly to answer the question about Stirner's link to moral nihilism, one must first drill down into the details of the term's definition.

The relevant entry in the *Stanford Encyclopedia of Philosophy* offers the following explanation: "Moral Nihilism = Nothing is morally wrong." The author, Walter Sinnott-Armstrong, goes on to clarify: "Moral nihilism here is not about what is semantically or metaphysically possible. It is just a substantive, negative, existential claim that there does not exist anything that is morally wrong."[6] The claim, he continues, is justified by such arguments as the ubiquity of moral disagreement and the capacity to explain moral belief without recourse to moral fact. Carr, however, in her account of the different forms of nihilism, offers a slightly different interpretation: "*Ethical or moral nihilism* is the denial of the reality of moral or ethical values, expressed in the claim 'There is no good' or 'All ethical claims are equally valid.' An ethical or moral nihilist does not deny that people use moral or ethical terms; the claim is rather that these terms refer

---

justifies falsehood and injustice, having and not having, its ideal is an asocial and anonymous existence, it even justifies murder."

4 Rosenkranz, *Aus einem Tagebuch*, 133.
5 Laas, *Idealismus und Positivismus*, 2:19; Ströbel, "Stirners 'Einziger und sein Eigentum,'" 86; Schröder, *Moralischer Nihilismus*, 56.
6 *Stanford Encyclopedia of Philosophy*, "Moral Skepticism," by Walter Sinnott-Armstrong, accessed June 30, 2023, https://plato.stanford.edu/archives/sum2019/entries/skepticism-moral/.

to nothing more than the bias or taste of the assertor."[7] Carr seems to be confusing two related, and indeed overlapping, meta-ethical theories, moral nihilism and moral relativism. Her first example, namely of there being no such thing as "good," could be an expression of either—moral nihilism's denial of moral facts, or moral relativism's rejection of objective moral values. But the second example, which acknowledges the validity of moral values, is incompatible with moral nihilism's assertion of the general falseness of all ethical claims, while being fully consistent with moral relativism's acceptance of subjective value judgments.

Nonetheless, the inaccuracy of Carr's description is, to some extent, understandable, as both theories have much in common. There is no fundamental disagreement between moral nihilism and moral relativism on an ontological level; both are characterized by a thoroughgoing skepticism towards statements of moral fact, and both reject completely the idea of moral objectivism. Moreover, moral nihilism relies on many of the assertions of moral relativism to arrive at its position. What differentiates them is that nihilism argues that nothing can be considered right or wrong, while relativism contends that the values of right and wrong are only applicable in relation to a particular frame of reference. Moral nihilism is therefore the more radical of the two. As Dreier explains: "Nihilism is the view that there are no moral facts. It says that nothing is right or wrong, or morally good or bad. Nihilists believe that moral language is infected by a massive false presupposition, much as atheists understand religious talk."[8]

A. J. Ayer (1910–1989) was among the first philosophers openly to discuss the correspondence between the meaninglessness of theological and moral concepts, identifying them as similarly fallacious pseudo-concepts. Building on two of Wittgenstein's dicta, "there can be no ethical propositions" and "God does not reveal himself *in* the world," Ayer presents the arguments for so-called theological and moral knowledge to be viewed as declarations of emotional attitudes, rather than as statements of fact:[9]

> The fact that people have religious experiences is interesting from the psychological point of view, but it does not in any way imply that there is such a thing as religious knowledge, any more than our having moral experiences implies that there is such a thing as moral knowledge.... It follows that those philosophers who fill their books with assertions that they intuitively "know" this or that

---

7   Carr, *The Banalization of Nihilism*, 18.
8   Dreier, "Moral Relativism and Moral Nihilism," 240.
9   Wittgenstein, *Tractatus Logico-Philosophicus*, 182, 186.

moral or religious "truth" are merely providing material for the psychoanalyst.[10]

Ayer's so-called emotivism, whereby moral judgments express feelings rather than facts, is a form of moral skepticism which includes elements of moral relativism, in that such feelings are relative to the locus of the individual, and moral nihilism, in that it considers ethical statements to be unverifiable and without validity. Gilbert Harman has characterized the intermediate nature of emotivism as moderate nihilism.[11]

The distinction between moral nihilism and moral relativism is an important one, precisely because the two positions are so frequently confused. In order to make a proper evaluation of Stirner's ethics, one must identify which of the two theories best describes his point of view. Stirner is undoubtedly a moral skeptic; the question is whether his moral skepticism culminates in nihilism. For a comprehensive description of moral nihilism with which to compare Stirner's ethical outlook, there is, as Dreier states, one standard and definitive source in John Mackie's *Ethics: Inventing Right and Wrong* (1977).[12] Mackie (1917–1981) sets out his stall early in the preface to his book, where he writes: "But perhaps the truest teachers of moral philosophy are the outlaws and thieves who, as Locke says, keep faith and rules of justice with one another, but practice these as rules of convenience without which they cannot hold together, with no pretence of receiving them as innate laws of nature."[13] Although he does not use the term in *Ethics*, Mackie is commonly acknowledged as the first, and most persuasive, academic philosopher to propose a comprehensive theory of moral nihilism.[14] The first sentence of the first chapter states bluntly: "There are no objective values."[15] Mackie does not simply endorse moral skepticism by passing doubt on the claims of moral statements but goes significantly beyond this to put the case for the denial of the possibility of moral facts.

Mackie bases his argument on an error theory of ethics, which states that moral claims presuppose nonexistent objective moral values: "The claim to objectivity, however ingrained in our language and thought, is not self-validating. It can and should be questioned. But the denial of objective values will have to be put forward not as the result of an analytic approach, but as an 'error theory', a theory that although most people in making moral judgments implicitly claim . . . to be pointing to something

10   Ayer, *Language, Truth and Logic*, 158.
11   See Harman, *The Nature of Morality*, 27–40.
12   See Dreier, "Moral Relativism and Moral Nihilism," 245.
13   Mackie, *Ethics*, 10–11.
14   See Dreier, "Moral Relativism and Moral Nihilism," 245.
15   Mackie, *Ethics*, 15.

objectively prescriptive, these claims are all false."[16] He supports his error theory with two arguments. The first is the argument from relativity, which states that the diversity of moral codes, depending on both their social location and historical period, makes it more likely that values "reflect ways of life" than that they "express perceptions . . . of objective values."[17] The second is the argument from queerness, to which he gives greater importance, and which he subdivides into metaphysical and epistemological parts. He sums up his two-pronged assault as follows: "If there were objective values, then they would be entities or qualities or relations of a very strange sort, utterly different from anything else in the universe. Correspondingly, if we were aware of them, it would have to be by some special faculty of moral perception or intuition, utterly different from our ordinary ways of knowing everything else."[18] For Mackie, historical examples of moral values are too varied and too contrasting to be considered emanations of objective moral fact, while objective values, and the unique ability to perceive them, are both unverifiable and deeply implausible. What is credible, however, according to Mackie, is that there has been a gradual, false objectification of social attitudes as a consequence of the important role morals play in the regulation of interpersonal relations. This tendency is reinforced, he claims, by a deep-seated need for authority, combined with the gradual externalization of human desires; as evolution by natural selection has favored social cohesion, so the erroneous notion of absolute, objective, and universal moral values has prospered.[19]

Having challenged the idea of objective moral values, Mackie goes on to discuss the application of moral skepticism to the principles of ethical conduct. While it is beyond the scope of this book to enter into a detailed analysis of his suggestions for a practical moral system, there are two points he raises which are of relevance to the inquiry into Stirner's ethical position. The first of these is that he broadly endorses egoism as a valid description of normal human behavior:

> We can . . . say firmly that for any individual a good life will be made up largely of the effective pursuit of activities that he finds worthwhile, either intrinsically, or because they are directly beneficial to others about whom he cares. . . . Egoism and self-referential altruism will together characterize, to a large extent, both his actions and his motives. The happiness with which I am, inevitably, most

---

16 Mackie, *Ethics*, 35.
17 Mackie, *Ethics*, 37.
18 Mackie, *Ethics*, 38.
19 See Mackie, *Ethics*, 42–43.

concerned is my own, and next that of those who are in some way closely related to me.[20]

This assessment is clearly consistent with Stirner's identification of egoism as the immutable essence of human conduct, whether or not it is consciously recognized as such. Furthermore, Mackie's emphasis on the importance of human relationships for the realization of human happiness is remarkably close to Stirner's conviction of the intimate connection between egoism and love, i.e., that loving is motivated by the happiness it induces in the lover.[21]

The second point relevant to Stirner's attitude to morality is that, although Mackie emphasizes that the "right to life [is] only a claim-right" and therefore "cannot be absolute," he nonetheless rejects the death penalty specifically, and killing generally, but concedes that there are circumstances under which it is reasonable to permit suicide, euthanasia, and abortion.[22] While his views on practical morality are far from conservative, Mackie is clearly not prepared to adopt so radical and permissive a position as Stirner's with regard to murder. The reason for this is that Mackie essentially follows Geoffrey Warnock in thinking that "the function of morality is primarily to counteract the limitation of men's sympathies," and, while he may reject morality's claims to being objective or absolute, Mackie nonetheless accepts the importance of social cohesion.[23] Murder, therefore, cannot, in his opinion, be condoned under any circumstances, as it would defeat the social purpose of morality. This standpoint represents an implicit rejection of the excesses of Machiavelli, whose political philosophy has become synonymous with murderous duplicity.

Moral Nihilists: Machiavelli and Nietzsche?

Niccolò Machiavelli (1469–1527) is one of the few figures in history to have been considered an archetype of moral nihilism; his perceived infamy has resulted in, and been enhanced by, his being likened to the Devil by his English translator, George Bull, and dubbed "the murderous Machiavel" by Shakespeare.[24] Even Macaulay, who saw in

---

20 Mackie, *Ethics*, 170.
21 See *EO*, 258: "I love . . . because love makes *me* happy"; *EE*, 294: "Ich liebe, . . . weil die Liebe mich glücklich macht." Cf. Nietzsche, *Beyond Good and Evil*, 88: "Ultimately one loves one's desires and not that which is desired."
22 Mackie, *Ethics*, 195–99.
23 Mackie, *Ethics*, 108.
24 See Bull, "Introduction," 9–10; Shakespeare, *Henry VI*, 3.2.

Machiavelli a great mind, nonetheless accuses him of "obliquity of moral principle," while doubting "whether any name in literary history be so generally odious."[25] Had Macaulay known about Stirner (Macaulay's essay on Machiavelli was published in 1827), he might have revised this opinion; Stirner is much less well known than Machiavelli, but his standing among those who do know him is hardly any better.[26] A brief comparison of their views of morality may therefore help to shed some light on the question of whether Stirner can reasonably be described as a moral nihilist.

Machiavelli's notoriety is based on his defense of the principle that the end justifies the means, to the extent where he advocates parsimony, cruelty, wickedness, and dishonesty, as well as war, devastation, violence, and murder.[27] As he declares in his *Discourses*: "For although the act condemn the doer, the end may justify him; and when, as in the case of Romulus, the end is good, it will always excuse the means."[28] His praise for the founder of Rome includes an appeal for his absolution for the killing of Remus, thus openly condoning fratricide.[29] The parallels with Stirner's attitude towards murder, suicide, and infanticide are, superficially at least, conspicuous.

The chief reason for Machiavelli's cavalier attitude towards conventional morality is that his principal concern is politics rather than ethics; his aim is not to prescribe moral conduct but to describe the attributes and actions required of a political ruler to enable the formation and perpetuation of a strong, stable state. He creates what he calls an "original set of rules" to govern behavior because "the gulf between how one should live and how one does live is so wide that a man who neglects what is actually done for what should be done learns the way to self-destruction rather than self-preservation."[30] Thus, far from proposing moral precepts for the attainment of salvation in the hereafter, Machiavelli puts forward practical guidelines to help achieve political success in the

---

25 Macaulay, *Readings*, 60. Cf. Russell, *A History of Western Philosophy*, 491: "Much of the conventional obloquy that attaches to his [Machiavelli's] name is due to the indignation of hypocrites who hate the frank avowal of evil-doing."

26 See Martin, "Introduction," xx: "*The Ego and His Own* . . . deserves to be read in the same spirit and in the same way one reads *The Prince*."

27 See Machiavelli, *The Prince*, for the following: parsimony, 92; cruelty, 95; wickedness, 92; dishonesty, 99; war, 87; devastation, 47; violence, 66; and murder, 36.

28 Machiavelli, *Discourses*, 42.

29 See Machiavelli, *Discourses*, 45; and Machiavelli, *The Prince*, 50–52.

30 Machiavelli, *The Prince*, 90, 91.

here and now.[31] This is not completely dissimilar to Stirner, whose focus, however, is on the welfare of the individual rather than that of the state.

To a large extent in Machiavelli's work, morality in its prevailing, traditional form is not challenged in itself, but rather its status as an eternal, absolute, and all-pervading truth is impugned. Machiavelli accepts that an act of cruelty, for instance, is reprehensible, but is convinced that any moral stain is expunged if the result of that act is good for the strength and stability of the state. Morality, in other words, is portrayed as subject to man and not vice-versa. This may, or may not, be seen as a form of moral relativism, but, however scandalous such a position may have appeared in sixteenth-century Italy, it essentially leaves conventional morality intact, even if its application is subject to human volition. Stirner shows no such deference towards morality, nor does he, like Machiavelli, identify Christianity as "our religion."[32] Stirner's outlook with regard to morality is clearly more extreme than Machiavelli's, and, while Stirner's status in this respect remains to be fully examined in the course of this chapter, it is clear that Machiavelli cannot actually, in any meaningful way, be considered a moral nihilist. He does not, as a nihilist would, state that moral judgments are necessarily false in themselves (e.g., that murder is neither right nor wrong), but only that there are circumstances under which it is better not to apply them. Contrary to the common understanding of Machiavellianism, one finds in Machiavelli's thought only a selective indifference to morality, not a conscious antimoral impulse of the kind that characterizes Stirner's thought.

A truer reflection of moral nihilism can be found in Nietzsche, despite his ultimate championing of the anti-nihilist cause. Harman's definition of moral nihilism as "the doctrine that there are no moral facts, no moral truths, and no moral knowledge" is exemplified by a passage from *Götzen-Dämmerung*, which is typical of Nietzsche's reflections on morality:[33] "One knows my demand of philosophers that they place themselves *beyond* good and evil. . . . This demand follows from an insight first formulated by me: *that there are no moral facts whatever*. Moral judgment has this in common with religious judgment that it believes in realities which do not exist. Morality is only an interpretation of certain phenomena, more precisely, a *mis*interpretation."[34] Nietzsche's description of the unbridgeable gap between morality and reality contrasts with the logical

---

31 See Machiavelli, *The Prince*, 90: "Since my intention is to say something that will prove of practical use to the inquirer, I have thought it proper to present things as they are in real truth, rather than as they are imagined." Russell notes the irony of Machiavelli's "intellectual honesty about political dishonesty." Russell, *A History of Western Philosophy*, 491.
32 See, e.g., Machiavelli, *Discourses*, 201.
33 Harman, *The Nature of Morality*, 11.
34 Nietzsche, *Twilight of the Idols and The Anti-Christ*, 55.

positivist view, expressed by Ayer, that "since the expression of a value judgment is not a proposition, the question of truth or falsehood does not here arise."[35] For Nietzsche, morality, rather than being unverifiable, is necessarily false: "The beast in us wants to be lied to; morality is an official lie told so that it shall not tear us to pieces. Without the errors that repose in the assumptions of morality man would have remained animal."[36] As such, Nietzsche's position must be considered much closer to the more radical moral nihilism of Mackie's error theory. Although Stirner does not provide such a carbon copy of Harman's definition of moral nihilism in his writings, he is certainly no less dismissive of morality.

Stirner and Morality

Harman distinguishes between various types of moral nihilism, dividing them between extreme and moderate forms, and describing examples of each as follows:

> An extreme version of nihilism holds that morality is simply an illusion: nothing is ever right or wrong, just or unjust, good or bad. . . . Such extreme nihilism is hard to accept. It implies that there are no moral constraints—that everything is permitted. As Dostoevsky observes, it implies that there is nothing wrong with murdering your father. . . . A more moderate nihilism holds that the purpose of moral judgments is not to describe the world but to express our moral feelings. . . . Moderate nihilism is easier to accept than extreme nihilism. It allows us to keep morality and continue to make moral judgments. It does not imply that there is nothing wrong with murdering your father.[37]

It is somewhere between these two distinct positions—extreme and moderate nihilism—that we must seek to place Stirner's ethical standpoint if he is to be rightly adjudged a moral nihilist. Of course, the question may arise as to whether Stirner's detractors, such as Rosenkranz, Helms, or Paterson, have this relatively modern definition (or range of definitions) in mind when accusing him of moral nihilism, especially as it originates from a specialist discussion within the discipline of ethical philosophy. However, the denial of absolute, objective moral values lies at the bottom of all the different shades of meaning of moral nihilism, and this is the fundamental issue to be addressed as far as Stirner's thought is concerned.

---

35   Ayer, *Language, Truth and Logic*, 29.
36   Nietzsche, *Human, All Too Human*, 35.
37   Harman, *The Nature of Morality*, 11–12.

Although Paterson, the critic who has most consistently accused Stirner of nihilism, does not describe Stirner's nihilism specifically as moral nihilism, he does include morality as an element within its framework. He states that "it is precisely 'absolute values' which excite The Unique One's most implacable hostility."[38] This antipathy towards morality, Paterson suggests, is uncompromising. Its aim is to remove, not to improve, morality: "although Stirner, like Nietzsche, intends to accomplish a 'transvaluation of all values', unlike Nietzsche he has no intention of replacing Christian and humanist values by a new set of moral values."[39] Paterson bases his assessment on Stirner's rejection of all externally imposed obligations, which necessarily includes the imperatives and constraints of morality. He dismisses the view that Stirner creates a moral value system of his own, an opinion expressed by the pragmatist philosopher, Sidney Hook, who writes: "Despite his avowals of complete ethical antinomianism, Stirner does seek to formulate his moral code. It turns out to be a variant of Hobbes' doctrine."[40] Instead, Paterson argues that Stirner's aim is to "expose all moral imperatives as essentially verbal figments," concluding that: "The Unique One . . . is not an immoralist, but an amoralist. His text is not 'Evil, be thou my good', but 'Let me be beyond good and evil.'"[41]

Leaving aside the apparent contradiction in citing Nietzsche as a moralist (of sorts), while applying a Nietzschean phrase to Stirner as an illustration of amoralism, the issue here revolves around how one defines the difference between moral and non-moral values. It goes without saying that Stirner unavoidably expresses choices, preferences, and values, unavoidably because evaluation is inherent in human thought. However rudimentary his social theory may be, Stirner nonetheless presents a picture of human co-existence that rests on the intrinsic values of ownness, self-determination, and the sovereignty of the individual. It is equally true, though, that he rejects conventional morality, which he considers to be extrinsic to the individual self. The dichotomy between internally constructed and externally imposed values is made explicit in the concept of ownness: "Ownness has not any alien standard, . . . as it is not in any sense an *idea* like freedom, morality, humanity, and the like: it is only a description of the—*owner*."[42] For Stirner, ownness has a descriptive function, placing it in opposition to the normative principles of prescribed

---

38 Paterson, *The Nihilistic Egoist*, 315.
39 Paterson, *The Nihilistic Egoist*, 157.
40 Hook, *From Hegel to Marx*, 170.
41 Paterson, *The Nihilistic Egoist*, 264.
42 *EO*, 154; *EE*, 178: "Die Eigenheit hat . . . keinen fremden Maßstab, wie sie denn überhaupt keine *Idee* ist, gleich der Freiheit, Sittlichkeit, Menschlichkeit u. dgl.: sie ist nur eine Beschreibung des—*Eigners*."

dogma. As an individual is unique, there is a further opposition between the relative values of each individual and the absolute values of any given external cause. Thus, he writes: "It is egoistic to ascribe to no thing a value of its own, an 'absolute' value, but to seek its value in me."[43]

The dispute between Paterson and Hook is thus essentially a matter of semantics. Hook's position is based on a standard definition of ethics as "a body of doctrine concerning what is right and wrong, good and bad, in respect of character and conduct."[44] For Hook, Stirner is proposing something of this nature, even though the values he upholds are both relative and subjective. Paterson, on the other hand, from his theistic point of view, is unable to equate Stirner's values with what he understands as morality:

> Stirner's whole argument is surely that moral obligations of *any* kind are no more than hollow verbal devices for dividing a man from his own best interests.... If ... Stirner deliberately cites those moral obligations which have been widely held to be among the most sacred and binding—piety and truthfulness, for example—this is not because he is adumbrating a specific new moral code in which blasphemy and lying are to be obligatory but because he is concerned to reaffirm that *nothing, not even* those primordial "obligations," can induce the self-possessed egoist to take any step that is not in the fullest accord with his own distinct interests.[45]

The disagreement between this assessment and Hook's rests on the question of when a system of values can be considered a moral code, and when not. The fact that Stirner proposes a theory of autonomous human behavior suffices for Hook, whereas Paterson is prevented from concurring by his much narrower understanding of the definition of morality.

The answer to this question is important for the present discussion, because if Stirner, as Hook proposes, does devise a moral code, then it can hardly be claimed that he fulfills the primary condition of moral nihilism, in its broadest sense, of describing all moral statements as false. But if, on the other hand, one accepts the general thrust of Paterson's view that Stirner's aim was to annihilate morality and replace it with the unprincipled behavior of (sinful) egoism, then this rejection of morality could very well be equated with moral nihilism. Stirner certainly does reject traditional morality entirely; unlike Machiavelli, he does not leave Christian moral values largely intact. In fact, in *Der Einzige*, morality is treated throughout as an extraneous myth. As Carroll writes: "Stirner

---

43   EO, 152; EE, 176: "Egoistisch ist es, keiner Sache einen eigenen oder 'absoluten' Wert beizulegen, sondern ihren Wert in Mir zu suchen."
44   *The Penguin Dictionary of Philosophy*, 2nd ed. (2005), s.v. "ethics."
45   Paterson, *The Nihilistic Egoist*, 263–64.

views 'good' and 'evil' as artificial indices taken up by individuals to save them making the difficult choices of life; they neatly divide the activities of man into the positive and the negative."[46] Stirner's term for such fictions is fixed ideas (*fixe Ideen*):

> Man, your head is haunted.... You have a fixed idea! ... What is it, then, that is called a "fixed idea"? An idea that has subjected the man to itself.... Is not all the stupid chatter ... the babble of fools who suffer from the fixed idea of morality, legality, Christianity, and so forth, and only seem to go about free because the madhouse in which they walk takes in so broad a space?

> [Mensch, es spukt in Deinem Kopfe; ... Du hast eine fixe Idee! ... Was nennt man denn eine "fixe Idee"? Eine Idee, die den Menschen sich unterworfen hat.... Ist nicht alles dumme Geschwätz, ... das Geplapper von Narren, die an der fixen Idee der Sittlichkeit, Gesetzlichkeit, Christlichkeit usw. leiden, und nur frei herumzugehen scheinen, weil das Narrenhaus, worin sie wandeln, einen so weiten Raum einnimmt?][47]

The association of morality (and other alien causes) with obsession and possessedness is a recurrent theme in Stirner's writing. Virtue is called "a madman's delusion"; moral faith is "as fanatical as religious faith!"[48] This pathological dimension was to reappear in Nietzsche, who wrote of "morality as consequence, as symptom, as mask, as tartufferie, as illness, as misunderstanding."[49] For Nietzsche, morality as a form of sickness, consumed by its own principle of truth, is at the root of nihilism.[50] But Stirner's perspective is slightly different: his concern is not for the nature of morality itself but for the autonomy of the individual, which, he believes, depends, among other things, on liberation from moral constraints. Stirner's objection to morality is not that it has become decadent, but that it is, by definition as a code of conduct, an imposition. The process of moral inculcation, he contends, starts in childhood:

---

46   Carroll, *Break-Out from the Crystal Palace*, 28.
47   EO, 43; EE, 53.
48   EO, 44; EE, 54: "der Irrwahn eines Tollen." EO, 45. EE, 56. "so fanatisch als der religiöse!"
49   Nietzsche, *On the Genealogy of Morals*, 20.
50   See Nietzsche, *The Will to Power*, 16: "But among the virtues cultivated by morality was *truthfulness*: in the end, it is this which turns us against morality, and discovers its *function*, its *partiality*. At this point, our *insight* (into this long ingrained mendacity that one despairs of putting off) acts as a stimulant to nihilism."

> Who is there that has never ... noticed that our whole education is calculated to produce *feelings* in us, ... instead of leaving their production to ourselves.... If we hear the name of God, we are to feel veneration; ... if we hear that of morality, we are to think that we hear something inviolable; if we hear of the Evil One or evil ones, we are to shudder. The intention is directed to these *feelings*, and he who should hear with pleasure the deeds of the "bad" would have to be "taught what's what" with the rod of discipline.
>
> [Wer hätte es niemals ... gemerkt, dass Unsere ganze Erziehung darauf ausgeht, *Gefühle* in Uns zu erzeugen, ... statt die Erzeugung derselben Uns zu überlassen.... Hören Wir den Namen Gottes, so sollen Wir Gottesfurcht empfinden, ... hören Wir den der Moral, so sollen Wir etwas Unverletzliches zu hören meinen, hören Wir von dem und den Bösen, so sollen Wir schaudern usw. Auf diese *Gefühle* ist's abgesehen, und wer z. B. die Taten der "Bösen" mit Wohlgefallen vernähme, der müsste durch die Zuchtrute "gezüchtigt und erzogen" werden.][51]

In his essay entitled "Das unwahre Prinzip unserer Erziehung oder Humanismus und Realismus" (The False Principle of Our Education or Humanism and Realism), which appeared in the *Rheinische Zeitung* in 1842, Stirner had expressed his fundamental objections to an education system that fills children's brains with preconceived concepts and does not allow individual students to develop their own sovereign identities. The germ of Stirner's rebellious anti-authoritarianism can be found in this short work:

> Truth itself consists in nothing other than man's revelation of himself, ... the liberation from all that is alien, the uttermost abstraction or release from all authority, the re-won naturalness. Such thoroughly *true* men are not supplied by school; if they are nevertheless there, they are there *in spite* of school.
>
> [Die Wahrheit selbst besteht in nichts anderem als in dem Offenbaren seiner selbst, ... die Befreiung von allem Fremden, die äusserste Abstraktion oder Entledigung von aller Autorität, die wiedergewonnene Naivität. Solche durchaus *wahre* Menschen liefert die Schule nicht; wenn sie dennoch da sind, so sind sie es *trotz* der Schule.][52]

---

51 *EO*, 62; *EE*, 75.
52 Stirner, *The False Principle of Our Education*, 21; Stirner, *Max Stirner's Kleinere Schriften*, 21.

It is from this earnestly expounded pedagogical theory in support of independent thinking and against educational indoctrination that Stirner, the schoolmaster, came to develop his idea of the rejection of externally imposed principles, especially those that are inculcated with the aid of violence and humiliation, which is given full expression in *Der Einzige*:

> Moral influence takes its start where *humiliation* begins; yes, it is nothing else than this humiliation itself, the breaking and bending of the temper down to *humility*. . . . Children must early be *made* to practice piety, godliness, and propriety; a person of good breeding is one into whom "good maxims" have been *instilled* and *impressed*, poured in through a funnel, thrashed in and preached in.

> [Der moralische Einfluss nimmt da seinen Anfang, wo die *Demütigung* beginnt, ja er ist nichts anderes, als die Demütigung selbst, die Brechung und Beugung des Mutes zur *Demut* herab. . . . Die Kinder müssen bei Zeiten zur Frömmigkeit, Gottseligkeit und Ehrbarkeit *angehalten* werden; ein Mensch von guter Erziehung ist einer, dem "gute Grundsätze" *beigebracht* und *eingeprägt*, eingetrichtert, eingebläut und eingepredigt worden sind.][53]

In his earlier essay, the emphasis is on freedom of thought versus the aridity of mental servitude: "The universal education of school is to be an education for freedom, not for subservience: to be free, that is true *life*."[54] Stirner identifies the purpose of the educator as the empowerment of each student to develop her or his personal potential: "Now if the idea and impulse of modern times is free will, then pedagogy must hover in front as the beginning and aim of the education of the *free personality*."[55] This message is underlined in the conclusion with a rhetorical flourish that anticipates the bold assertiveness (and biblical parody) of *Der Einzige*:

> If my conclusion is to express in a few words which goal our time has to steer toward, then the necessary decline of non-voluntary learning and rise of the self-assured will which perfects itself in the glorious sunlight of the free person may be expressed somewhat as follows:

---

53   *EO*, 75; *EE*, 90–91.
54   Stirner, *The False Principle of Our Education*, 26; Stirner, *Max Stirner's Kleinere Schriften*, 27–28: "Die universelle Bildung der Schule sei Bildung zur Freiheit, nicht zur Unterwürfigkeit: Freisein, das ist das wahre *Leben*."
55   Stirner, *The False Principle of Our Education*, 27; Stirner, *Max Stirner's Kleinere Schriften*, 28: "Ist nun die Idee und der Trieb der neuen Zeit die *Willensfreiheit*, so muss der Pädagogik als Anfang und Ziel die Ausbildung der *freien Persönlichkeit* vorschweben."

knowledge must die and rise again as will and create itself anew each day as a free *person*.

[Soll daher am Schluss mit kurzen Worten ausgedrückt werden, nach welchem Ziel unsere Zeit zu steuern hat, so liesse sich der notwendige Untergang der willenlosen Wissenschaft und der Aufgang des selbstbewussten Willens, welcher sich im Sonnenglanz der freien Person vollendet, etwa folgendermassen fassen: das *Wissen* muss sterben, um als *Wille* wieder aufzuerstehen und als freie *Person* sich täglich neu zu schaffen.][56]

Soon afterwards, Stirner started work on his magnum opus, in which the tone alters from a plea for liberal (and liberating) education to an uncompromising attack on all heteronomous abstractions. In *Der Einzige*, the constructive criticism of educational methods is transformed into the condemnation of the evils of indoctrination; the focus shifts from the method of pedagogy to its content, with morality becoming one of the chief targets: "He on whom the principles of morality have been duly inculcated never becomes free again from moralizing thoughts."[57] Morality is now presented as a false, extraneous imposition that must be combatted and eradicated. Its negative connotation permeates *Der Einzige*; there is no explicit mention of replacing it with a new morality more fit for the purposes of the egoist.

Nietzsche famously—and (even if he hadn't read Stirner) immodestly—awarded himself the accolade of being the first immoralist.[58] Carroll thinks that Stirner has a stronger claim to the title, but one should not forget that Nietzsche's proud assertion appears in his last original book, *Ecce Homo*, where his writing was at its most hyperbolic.[59] Nietzsche identifies two negations implicit in his meaning of the term immoralist, the negation of the benevolent moralist, and the negation of decadent Christian morality.[60] Stirner is also scathing in his criticism of various contemporary examples of the moral character which he encounters, perhaps most notably, and certainly shockingly for all but his most radical readers, in his condemnation of chastity. Having related the story of a young girl who has sacrificed her concupiscence on the altar of self-renunciation, he exclaims: "O Lais, O Ninon, how well you did to scorn

---

56 Stirner, *The False Principle of Our Education*, 28; Stirner, *Max Stirner's Kleinere Schriften*, 30.
57 *EO*, 302; *EE*, 345: "Wem die Grundsätze der Moral gehörig eingeprägt wurden, der wird von moralischen Gedanken niemals wieder frei."
58 See Nietzsche, *Ecce Homo*, 127: "I am the first immoralist. I am therewith the *destroyer par excellence*."
59 See Carroll, "Introduction," 66.
60 See Nietzsche, *Ecce Homo*, 131.

this pale virtue! One free grisette against a thousand virgins grown grey in virtue!"[61]

Stirner's description of the girl's struggle in an almost touching, unquestionably erotic, but ultimately tongue-in-cheek vignette, reveals three important elements of his thought: his unconventional sexual liberality, his opposition to established morality, and his antagonism to any form of external obligation that restricts and constrains the individual's ability or desire to follow her or his egoistic aims. The resultant rejection of morality is absolute: "Unchastity can never become a moral act."[62] He cannot, in other words, envisage a morality that would uphold the principle of promiscuity which he is advocating. Stirner's criticism of morality largely concerns the Christian-humanist variety, and so he also preempts Nietzsche's second immoralist negation (of decadent Christian morality), although, as already mentioned, Stirner's issue with conventional morality is not its decadence, but the fact that it is inimical to the principles of egoism. Nonetheless, as Carroll observes, Stirner's and Nietzsche's versions of immoralism have many features in common: "Stirner and Nietzsche demonstrate the relativity of all moral judgments: there is no absolute *good*, there is no Kantian categorical imperative. They seek to defuse morality: to reduce obligations to preferences."[63]

Just as Paterson does with Stirner, Carroll points out that what Nietzsche really means with the term immoralist is anti-moralist.[64] Even if in his later works there is a shift to the revaluation of values, Nietzsche's initial objective was to transcend morality, to propel philosophy into a new dimension beyond good and evil. He talks of morality as something that needs to be overcome, which, as we have seen, is very similar to Stirner's position, even if Stirner presents his case more prosaically:[65]

> Away, then, with every concern that is not altogether my concern! You think at least the "good cause" must be my concern? What's good, what's bad? Why, I myself am my concern, and I am neither good nor bad. Neither has meaning for me.

---

61 EO, 59; EE, 72; "O Lais, o Ninon, wie tatet Ihr wohl, diese bleiche Tugend zu verschmähen. Eine freie Grisette gegen tausend in der Tugend grau gewordene Jungfern!"

62 EO, 53; EE, 66: "Unkeuschheit kann nie zu einer sittlichen Tat werden."

63 Carroll, *Break-Out from the Crystal Palace*, 38.

64 See Carroll, *Break-Out from the Crystal Palace*, 28; Paterson, *The Nihilistic Egoist*, 264.

65 See Nietzsche, *Beyond Good and Evil*, 45–46: "In brief, we believe . . . that morality in the sense in which it has been understood hitherto, . . . has been a prejudice, a precipitancy, perhaps something provisional and precursory, perhaps something of the order of astronomy and alchemy, but in any event something that must be overcome."

[Fort denn mit jeder Sache, die nicht ganz und gar Meine Sache ist! Ihr meint, Meine Sache müsse wenigstens die "gute Sache" sein? Was gut, was böse! Ich bin ja selber Meine Sache, und Ich bin weder gut noch böse. Beides hat für Mich keinen Sinn.][66]

The concepts of good and evil are meaningless, Stirner suggests, because they are antiquated, obsolescent, and externally imposed: he complains, for instance, that moralists (who condemn egoism) are drifting "in the antediluvian opposition of good and evil."[67] Morality has no more value for Stirner than ancient superstition. Unsurprisingly, therefore, he is scathingly critical of Proudhon for asserting that *la loi morale* is eternal and absolute, and for asking who today would dare to attack morality.[68] Stirner accuses him, along with the modern ideologues of humanism, of uncritically accepting and indeed adopting Christian moral values: "Moral people skimmed off the best fat from religion, ate it themselves, and are now having a tough job to get rid of the resulting scrofula."[69] He abhors what he sees as the pusillanimous failure to question morality's authenticity:

> Morality . . . is such a sacred conception; one must be moral, and must look only for the right "how," the right way to be so. One dares not go at morality itself with the question whether it is not itself an illusion.
>
> [Sittlichkeit ist . . . eine heilige Vorstellung: sittlich müsse man sein, und müsse nur . . . die rechte Art es zu sein, aufsuchen. An die Sittlichkeit selbst wagt man sich nicht mit der Frage, ob sie nicht selbst ein Truggebilde sei.][70]

As one would expect of a moral skeptic, Stirner applies to morality the argument from relativity. He quotes the dictum of the Pyrrhonist philosopher, Timon of Phlius: "in itself nothing is either good or bad, but man only *thinks* of it thus or thus."[71] He illustrates this axiom by observing:

---

66   *EO*, 7; *EE*, 15.
67   *EO*, 317; *EE*, 363: "zwischen dem altfränkischen Gegensatz von Gut und Böse."
68   See *EO*, 46; *EE*, 57.
69   *EO*, 46; *EE*, 57: "Die Sittlichen schöpften das beste Fett von der Religion ab, genossen es selbst und haben nun ihre liebe Not, die daraus entstandene Drüsenkrankheit loszuwerden."
70   *EO*, 68; *EE*, 83.
71   *EO*, 26; *EE*, 34: "An sich sei weder etwas gut noch sei es schlecht, sondern der Mensch denke sich's nur so oder so." Cf. Shakespeare, *Hamlet*, 2.2: "There is nothing either good or bad, but thinking makes it so."

"A Nero is a 'bad' man only in the eyes of the 'good.'"[72] Furthermore, Stirner points to the moral ambiguity posed by the assassination of August Friedrich Ferdinand von Kotzebue (1761–1819), a middle-aged, political conservative and dramatist, by Karl-Ludwig Sand (1795–1820), a young, militant student, and member of a liberal *Burschenschaft* (student fraternity). Sand's action, Stirner claims, could be judged moral from the point of view of its noble self-sacrifice and its good intention to serve the welfare of the people, but immoral from the point of view of murder always being morally reprehensible:

> According to the principle of morality, which commands us to serve the good, you could really ask only whether murder could never in any case be a realization of the good, and would have to endorse that murder which realized the good.
>
> [Ihr könntet dem Prinzip der Sittlichkeit nach, welches befiehlt, dem Guten zu dienen, doch nur fragen, ob der Mord nie und nimmer eine Verwirklichung des Guten sein könne, und müsstet denjenigen Mord anerkennen, der das Gute realisierte.][73]

Predictably enough, Stirner comes down on the side of Sand, but what the story demonstrates is, firstly, that good and evil are relative to the standpoint of the observer and, secondly, as Machiavelli had argued, that the means and ends of a particular act may conceivably be moral antitheses.

Stirner accepts, perhaps simplistically, that the end is generally taken to justify the means, in other words, that ethical consequentialism is the dominant principle of conventional morality:

> The moral man wants the good, the right; and if he takes to the means that lead to this goal, . . . then these means are not his means, but those of the good, right, etc., itself. These means are never immoral, because the good end itself mediates itself through them: the end sanctifies the means.
>
> [Der Sittliche will das Gute, das Rechte, und wenn er die Mittel ergreift, welche zu diesem Ziele führen, . . . so sind diese Mittel nicht *seine* Mittel, sondern die des Guten, Rechten usw. selbst. Unsittlich sind diese Mittel niemals, weil der gute Zweck selbst sich durch sie vermittelt: der Zweck heiligt die Mittel.][74]

---

72   EO, 51; EE, 63: "Ein Nero ist nur in den Augen der 'Guten' ein 'böser' Mensch."
73   EO, 49; EE, 61.
74   EO, 285–86; EE, 327.

He poses the question of whether Emilia Galotti's death (stabbed by her father at her own request in order to protect her virtue) can be considered moral, pointing out not only the potential contradiction between the values of chastity and the sanctity of human life but also the moral cowardice implicit in her failure to take personal responsibility (by committing suicide) for the deed she deemed unavoidable. Finally, though, he dismisses the bourgeois moral dilemma thus presented with a yawn of disdain: "Such contradictions form the tragic conflict universally in the moral drama; and one must think and feel morally to be able to take an interest in it."[75] Stirner finds the problems of bourgeois morality odd to the point of tedium, anticipating, to some extent, Mackie's argument from queerness. He writes elsewhere about "the measureless hypocrisy of devotion, love, etc., from whose repulsiveness one may daily get the most thorough nausea."[76]

Egoism and Moral Nihilism

The hypocrisy of morality is a recurrent theme in *Der Einzige*. Stirner identifies morality's falsehood in its denial of the true motivation of man's actions, or, in other words, in the denial of egoism. He seems to envisage a version of Hegelian historical teleology that leads from the darkness of moral prejudice to the promised land of enlightened egoism. The time he lives in is, in his view, an age of transition, where man is vacillating between two extremes: "No longer vigorous enough to serve *morality* without doubt or weakening, not yet reckless enough to live wholly to egoism."[77] For Stirner, morality and egoism are entirely antithetical; there is no room for morality in the worldview of the true egoist, just as the true moralist can only feel enmity towards the egoist. The relationship between the two is mutually exclusive: "The moral man is necessarily narrow in that he knows no other enemy than the 'immoral' man. 'He who is not moral is immoral!' and accordingly reprobate, despicable, etc. Therefore the moral man can never comprehend the egoist."[78] The

---

75 *EO*, 286; *EE*, 328: "Solche Widersprüche bilden in dem sittlichen Trauerspiele den tragischen Konflikt überhaupt, und man muss sittlich denken und fühlen, um daran Interesse nehmen zu können."
76 *EO*, 50; *EE*, 62: "die maßlose Heuchelei von Ergebenheit, Liebe usw., an deren Widerwärtigkeit man sich täglich den gründlichsten Ekel . . . holen kann."
77 *EO*, 51; *EE*, 63: "Nicht mehr kräftig genug, um zweifellos und ungeschwächt der *Sittlichkeit* zu dienen, noch nicht rücksichtslos genug, um ganz dem Egoismus zu leben."
78 *EO*, 53; *EE*, 65: "Der Sittliche ist notwendig darin borniert, dass er keinen andern Feind kennt als den 'Unsittlichen'. 'Wer nicht sittlich ist der ist unsittlich!', mithin verworfen, verächtlich usw. Darum kann der Sittliche niemals den Egoisten verstehen."

reverse is equally true; one should understand, Stirner says, that "one must commit *immoral* actions in order to commit his own."[79]

The picture thus presented of Stirner's ethical outlook is one that is best described as anti-moralistic. As Kast observes: "Stirner's 'owner' breaks . . . with all traditional norms, and the psychoanalyst and philosopher Ludwig Binswanger therefore calls Stirner an 'opponent of all ethical traditions,' I would rather say Stirner is an annihilator of all conventional ethics."[80] It is nonetheless prudent to ask what exactly Stirner means when he refers to ethics: is it the concept of morality itself in all its manifestations that he is criticizing, or just a conventional type of morality? After a lengthy diatribe against the ethical life (*Sittlichkeit*), culminating in the discussion of the Galotti question, Stirner informs us: "Yet all this applies, more or less, only to 'civic morality.'"[81] Elsewhere he exposes the origin and essence of the prevailing moral customs in the mercantile practices of the bourgeoisie: "The commonalty professes a morality which is most closely connected with its essence. The first demand of this morality is to the effect that one should carry on a solid business, an honourable trade, lead a moral life."[82]

However, Stirner does not entirely ignore other forms of morality. He imagines, for instance, a prototypical version of morality, which garners no more approbation from him than the bourgeois variety: "In its first and most unintelligible form morality shows itself as *habit*. To act according to the custom and habit of one's country is to be moral there."[83] This differentiated approach suggests that Stirner admits of a multiplicity of moralities, which would leave open the possibility of his position being one of moral relativism, rather than moral nihilism. Such a view also seems to be supported by Stirner's apparently relativistic discussion of the topical issue of avoidance of censorship, where he asks:

> If someone let his moral judgment go, and set up a secret press, one would have to call him immoral; . . . but will such a man lay claim to

---

79   EO, 210; EE, 242: "dass man *unsittlich* handeln müsse, um eigen zu handeln."
80   Kast, "Rechtfertigt Stirner Mord, Selbstmord, Inzest und Prostitution?," 32.
81   EO, 53; EE, 66: "Mehr oder weniger trifft jedoch dies alles nur die 'bürgerliche Sittlichkeit.'"
82   EO, 101; EE, 121: "Das Bürgertum bekennt sich zu einer Moral, welche aufs Engste mit seinem Wesen zusammenhängt. Ihre erste Forderung geht darauf hin, dass man ein solides Geschäft, ein ehrliches Gewerbe betreibe, einen moralischen Wandel führe."
83   EO, 63; EE, 78: "In ihrer ersten und unverständlichsten Form gibt sich die Sittlichkeit als *Gewohnheit*. Nach seines Landes Sitte und Gewohnheit handeln—heißt da sittlich sein."

a value in the eyes of the "moral"? Perhaps!—That is, if he fancied he was serving a "higher morality."

[Quittierte einer sein sittliches Urteil und errichtete z. B. eine geheime Presse, so müsste man ihn unsittlich nennen; . . . aber wird ein solcher Anspruch darauf machen, in den Augen der "Sittlichen" einen Wert zu haben? Vielleicht!—Wenn er sich nämlich einbildete, einer "höheren Sittlichkeit" zu dienen.][84]

Even so, the lawbreaker's belief in a higher morality is characterized as a delusion (*Einbildung*). It would appear therefore that, at bottom, Stirner considers morality a chameleon concept with many guises, all of which are false.

Despite this, Hook is not alone in seeing Stirner as the architect of a new moral code. Messer makes a similar assertion, albeit combined with its opposite: "Long before Nietzsche, Stirner triumphantly waged war against morality. . . . Stirner is . . . the great anti-moralist and moralist."[85] Whether or not this contradiction is tenable in itself, it is difficult to make the case that Stirner is a moralist. While he inevitably expresses values and preferences, as well as outlining certain elements of behavior within the union of egoists, it is stretching semantic boundaries to describe this as the creation of a system of morals. Messer seems to be a victim of his own enthusiasm; inspired by his veneration for Stirner he declares him a moralist, rejects the suitability of the epithet nihilist, and even suggests there would be room for religion in the Stirnerian world: "His philosophy is not the end of philosophy, his doctrine of egoism not the end of ethics, not even the end of religion, it is only the end of *sacred* philosophy, *sacred* ethics, *sacred* religion, and it puts in the place of these concepts a living, autonomous, individual philosophy—*my* ethics, *my* religion."[86] While the sentiment expressed here has some basis in fact, extrapolating from Stirner's statement in *Stirner's Critics* that egoism is not the enemy of any real interest, it is questionable whether Stirner himself would have extended it to religion, or to morality as he understood it, both of which demand, in his view, the subjugation of the individual.[87]

The debate about whether Stirner created a new code of morality revolves around the old question of when does a value become a moral value. Leopold has this to say on the subject:

---

84   *EO*, 51; *EE*, 62.
85   Messer, *Max Stirner*, 50.
86   Messer, *Max Stirner*, 53.
87   See Stirner, *Stirner's Critics*, 81–82; Stirner, *Max Stirner's Kleinere Schriften*, 144.

Although egoism is opposed to, rather than a form of, morality, it does not follow that the egoist is immoral—Stirner rejects the idea of an exclusive opposition between morality and immorality as "antediluvian." ... Stirner's rejection of morality is grounded not, as is often suggested, in a rejection of values as such, but in the affirmation of what might be called *non-moral goods*, that is, he allows a realm of actions and desires, which, although not moral (because they involve no obligations to others), are still to be assessed positively. Stirner's conception of morality is in this sense a narrow one, and his rejection of its claims is in no way coextensive with a rejection of the validity of all evaluative judgment.[88]

While Leopold makes the valid point that Stirner's concept of egoism rests on a framework of values, the suggestion that the egoist is not immoral is less tenable. It is not so much the opposition of morality and immorality that Stirner rejects, but rather the concept of an opposition between good and evil, which, of course, is the building block of morality.[89] This, therefore, is no argument against Stirner's egoist being (regarded as) immoral. Furthermore, if egoism is diametrically opposed to morality, as Leopold acknowledges, then Stirner's egoism must be immoral from the point of view of a moralist, as Stirner indeed states. And if Stirner nonetheless employs values in his ideas, albeit non-moral ones, as Leopold also recognizes, this has no bearing on his immorality in the eyes of a moralist. In fact, complex thought is hardly possible without evaluating, in which case, according to Leopold's criteria, all men are necessarily moralists, or at least are not immoralists, which would seem to amount to something very similar. However blurred the boundary between moral and non-moral values may be, it should remain clear that the espousal of non-moral values does not, in itself, preclude immorality.

Conclusive confirmation of Stirner's immorality is to be found precisely in the incompatibility of morality and egoism. If morality is defined as a system of moral conduct proposed by and for a society, or, as Leopold says, as the placing of obligations on others, then how can it apply to Stirner, the champion of the egoism of the unique individual, for whom it is anathema to impose any form of obligation on anyone, and for whom the values of each egoist are sacrosanct and cannot therefore be compromised by being conjoined with others to form a code of conduct? Thus, Stirner writes:

88   Leopold, "Introduction," xxiv.
89   Leopold is referring to Stirner's phrase "in the antediluvian opposition of good and evil" (zwischen dem altfränkischen Gegensatz von Gut und Böse). *EO*, 317; *EE*, 363.

> Morality is incompatible with egoism, because the former does not allow validity to *me*, but only to the man in me. But if the state is a *society of men*, not a union of egos each of whom has only himself before his eyes, then it cannot last without morality.
>
> [Die Sittlichkeit verträgt sich nicht mit dem Egoismus, weil sie nicht *Mich*, sondern nur den Menschen an Mir gelten lässt. Ist aber der Staat eine *Gesellschaft der Menschen*, nicht ein Verein von Ichen, deren jedes nur sich im Auge hat, so kann er ohne Sittlichkeit nicht bestehen.]⁹⁰

Morality, for Stirner, is a tool of the state and a function of its ideology, and is thus clearly irreconcilable with his union of egoists, which is supposed to be the natural manifestation of the interaction of autonomous, enlightened individuals seeking their advantage in relationships with other members of the species, rather than an externally enforced template for the ethics of social behavior. The fact that an association of this nature would require an organic balance to arise (whether through negotiation or extermination), in a community devoid of rules of conduct, need not concern us here. What is important for the purposes of this study is not the viability of the unregulated coexistence of human beings in a social setting, but that a system of morality is incompatible with Stirner's prime objective of unrestricted self-determination, and it is thus one of the targets of his war on heteronomy, even if he usually means it in the relatively limited sense of its prevailing nineteenth-century European manifestation. He makes no attempt to reinvent morality in an egoistic form, as this would defeat his purpose of emancipating the individual so she or he can choose autonomously, free from external influence and coercion. Stirner naturally extends this freedom of choice to the individual's evaluation of right and wrong: "Whether I am in the right or not there is no judge but myself."⁹¹

Crosby offers yet another point of view that lies somewhere between those of Leopold, Paterson, Messer, and Hook. For Crosby, Stirner is one of the prime examples of a moral nihilist by virtue of his doctrine of egoism, which, he claims, is itself a form of morality: "The third form of moral nihilism [along with amoralism and moral subjectivism], *egoism*, differs from amoralism mainly in that it purports to be a moral position in its own right, not a denial of all moral positions. One is morally obligated to realize or to fulfil *oneself* at whatever price to others."⁹² Egoism, Crosby contends, is nihilistic because it "rejects what is commonly regarded as

---

90 *EO*, 160–61; *EE*, 185.
91 *EO*, 167; *EE*, 193: "Ob Ich Recht habe oder nicht, darüber gibt es keinen andern Richter, als Mich selbst."
92 Crosby, *The Specter of the Absurd*, 14.

the moral point of view," namely "to look at the world from the perspective of *anyone*, not just of oneself."[93] According to this analysis, egoism is a deviant form of morality that is simultaneously immoral and nihilistic. This is a strangely paradoxical formulation, which completes the set of opinions concerning Stirner's relationship to moral nihilism. Stirner is thus immoral and nihilistic (Paterson), moral and non-nihilistic (Hook), not necessarily immoral and non-nihilistic (Leopold), both moral and immoral as well as non-nihilistic (Messer), and both moral and immoral as well as nihilistic (Crosby).

Stirner actually leaves little room for doubt regarding his views on morality. One of his principal aims is to encourage independent thinking, and this depends on the individual being freed from the is-ought problem of Hume's law: "Christianity's magic circle would be broken if the strained relation between existence and calling, that is, between me as I am and me as I should be, ceased."[94] Despite such declarations, supporters of individual anarchism, like Ruest and Lachmann at the beginning of the twentieth century, have suggested that Stirner was a moral reformer rather than a moral nihilist, but however much one admires Stirner's philosophy, it makes little sense to suggest that he replaces the discarded concept of morality with a new version precisely of morality.[95] Ruest's and Lachmann's arguments can, perhaps, be best viewed as well-meaning but ill-conceived attempts to contradict the more jaundiced accusations of Stirner's detractors who endeavor to portray him as the devil incarnate.

Stulpe presents the counterargument that Stirner's concept of anarchistic co-existence, devoid of prescriptive controls on the individual, is bound to culminate in "a moral-ethical nihilism that normatively allows everything that individuals want or do on the basis of their respective individuality: even then ... when other individuals do not want this on the basis of their respective individuality."[96] While such a viewpoint correctly exposes the impracticality of Stirner's social theory, it arguably misuses the term "moral nihilism"; social chaos would be a more accurate description of what one might reasonably expect to ensue. One can envisage the practical result of its implementation being as dystopian as the concept itself is utopian. This does not however detract in any way from the applicability of the term moral nihilism as a description of Stirner's ethical outlook.

---

93   Crosby, *The Specter of the Absurd*, 14, 15.

94   *EO*, 323; *EE*, 369: "Der Zauberkreis der Christlichkeit wäre gebrochen, wenn die Spannung zwischen Existenz und Beruf, d. h. zwischen Mir, wie Ich bin, und Mir, wie Ich sein soll, aufhörte."

95   Sartre also expressed the opinion that Stirner was "seeking to substitute one ethic for another." Sartre, *Saint Genet*, 244.

96   Stulpe, *Gesichter des Einzigen*, 658.

Stirner and the Label of Moral Nihilist

For the dispassionate observer, it is hard to avoid the conclusion that Stirner's philosophy does fulfill the requirements of moral nihilism, even the extreme version identified by Harman. He presents morality as a fiction, dismisses the conventional concepts of good and evil, and implies there is nothing wrong with murder under certain circumstances. He is uninterested in the notion of justice and accords right and wrong significance only with respect to each individual's self-interested preferences. He rejects moral facts, moral truths, and moral knowledge, and he explicitly states that morality, along with religion, should be discarded.

The deep connection between moral nihilism and atheism, which runs like a thread from the polemical origins of the word nihilism in the eighteenth century, through Nietzsche's "Gott ist todt!" to the thoroughgoing skepticism of Ayer and Mackie, is manifestly evident in Stirner's writings. There would even be sufficient reason to consider Stirner a theological nihilist, were it not for its definition being associated with the godly nothingness in the mysticism of certain medieval theologians; or, more compellingly, though more obscurely, an alethiological nihilist (a denier of truth), so damning are his pronouncements on truth and truthfulness.[97] According to Stirner, truth is "only a—*thought*," "a—ghost," "valueless," "is dead," "exists only—in your head."[98] He praises the "courage for a lie," and, ultimately, he denies truth's very existence: "For me there is no truth, for nothing is more than I!"[99] For Stirner, the iconoclastic demythologizer, religion, truth, and morality are all human fabrications imposed upon the individual, and all are equally deserving of annihilation.

Stirner's position regarding morality differs from that of Mackie, who does not go so far as to condone murder under any circumstances, and Machiavelli, who does, but still leaves room for conventional morality. Mackie rejects murder despite his moral nihilism, while Machiavelli only

---

97   See Thacker, *Starry Speculative Corpse*, 21–30. Thacker lists Dionysius the Areopagite, Meister Eckhart, and Angela of Foligno as theological nihilists.

98   *EO*, 311, 312, 313, 313, 312, 311; *EE*, 356, 357, 358, 358, 358, 357: "nur ein—Gedanke," "ein—Gespenst," "wertlos," "eitel und nichtig," "ist tot," "existiert nur in—deinem Kopf."

99   *EO*, 267; *EE*, 306: "Mut zur Lüge"; *EO*, 313; *EE*, 358: "Für Mich gibt es keine Wahrheit, denn über Mich geht nichts!" Stirner means this in the sense of absolute truth. Truth exists for him in the sense of verifiability but remains, nonetheless, relative to the observer. See *EO*, 313: "Objects are to me only material that I use up. Wherever I put my hand I grasp a truth, which I trim for myself"; *EE*, 358: "Mir sind die Gegenstände nur Material, das Ich verbrauche. Wo Ich hin greife, fasse Ich eine Wahrheit, die Ich Mir zurichte."

justifies murder within the context of political pragmatism, but not in itself. As far as breaking with conventional morality is concerned, Stirner can be considered more extreme than either Mackie or Machiavelli. He makes no bones about following in the realist tradition of Machiavelli and Hobbes: indeed, he gives a nod to them both by repeating their best-known maxims, "the end sanctifies the means," and "the war of all against all."[100] There is perhaps also a hint of admiration for Thrasymachus when Stirner writes, quoting a German proverb: "Might is a fine thing, and useful for many purposes; for 'one goes further with a handful of might than with a bagful of right.'"[101] But Carroll makes an important distinction between Stirner and these forebears: "Stirner follows the realist theory, that of Machiavelli and Hobbes, in extracting one principle from politics—might is right. However, instead of completing his social picture with a dour pessimistic view of man as a violent warmonger by nature, he shares with Rousseau a passionate optimism for the creative potentiality of life."[102]

Carroll thus points to the paradox that, although Stirner's disdain for morality is compatible with moral nihilism, to regard him as a moral nihilist runs the risk of fundamentally misunderstanding his underlying positive philosophical message. It is this that Leopold, along with those others who have denied Stirner's moral nihilism, are really driving at. Stirner's concern is for human emancipation at the most basic level, namely the level of the individual, and not for the nature of moral values. Morality is a purely secondary or contingent issue; he does not set out to be a moral nihilist, as Pisarev, for instance, does to be a political nihilist. Moral nihilism is not fundamental to Stirner's philosophy, it is instead an incidental consequence of the liberation from authority which he is advocating.

The essential aim of Stirner's philosophy is to sweep away once and for all the fixed ideas of dogma and thus to release the individual from all external constraints. The process of jettisoning all extraneous causes inevitably appears negative in its destructiveness, especially to those who hold those causes dear, but Stirner himself views the result as an affirmative act of emancipation, as well as an opportunity for man finally to come to terms with his undisguised and unadorned reality:

> Thousands of years of civilization have obscured to you what you are, have made you believe you are not egoists but are *called* to be

---

100   *EO*, 286; *EE*, 327: "der Zweck heiligt die Mittel"; *EO*, 229, 230; *EE*, 262, 264: "Krieg aller gegen alle."

101   *EO*, 151; *EE*, 174: "Die Gewalt ist eine schöne Sache, und zu vielen Dingen nütze, denn 'man kommt mit einer Handvoll Gewalt weiter, als mit einem Sack voll Recht.'" For Thrasymachus on power and justice, see Plato, *The Republic*, 72–73.

102   Carroll, *Break-Out from the Crystal Palace*, 49.

idealists ("good men"). Shake that off! . . . Just recognize yourselves again, . . . and let go your hypocritical endeavours, your foolish mania to be something else than you are. Hypocritical I call them because you have yet remained egoists all these thousands of years, but sleeping, self-deceiving, crazy egoists, . . . for man is *mercenary* and does nothing "gratis." But how about "doing the good for the good's sake" without prospect of reward? As if here too the pay was not contained in the satisfaction that it is to afford.

[Jahrtausende der Kultur haben Euch verdunkelt, was Ihr seid, haben Euch glauben gemacht, Ihr seiet keine Egoisten, sondern zu Idealisten ("guten Menschen") *berufen*. Schüttelt das ab! . . . Erkennt Euch nur wieder, . . . und lasst eure heuchlerischen Bestrebungen fahren, eure törichte Sucht, etwas anderes zu sein, als Ihr seid. Heuchlerisch nenne Ich jene, weil Ihr doch alle diese Jahrtausende Egoisten geblieben seid, aber schlafende, sich selbst betrügende, verrückte Egoisten, . . . denn *lohnsüchtig* ist der Mensch, und "umsonst" tut er nichts. Aber jenes "das Gute um des Guten willen tun" ohne Aussicht auf Belohnung? Als ob nicht auch hier in der Befriedigung, die es gewähren soll, der Lohn enthalten wäre.][103]

Like Machiavelli, Stirner is intent on dealing with "things as they are in real truth, rather than as they are imagined."[104] His approach is descriptive rather than normative, exploring the actuality and effect of human behavior, rather than trying to bend it to conform to certain ideological principles. What needs to be changed, he argues, is not simply our beliefs but our awareness of their wider implications, for if we yield to the power of dogma, "the lack of *consciousness* . . . alone bears the blame."[105]

Stirner's vision, therefore, is of enlightened consciousness bringing about the end of abstraction and mythologization. However, he seems seriously to underestimate the power of myth; he imagines that the awareness alone of the fictitious nature of an institution or belief would be enough to make it disappear. Extrapolating from the recurring theme of state censorship, he writes:

---

103 *EO*, 149; *EE*, 172. See *EO*, 147: "But the habit of the religious way of thinking has biased our mind so grievously that we are—terrified at *ourselves* in our nakedness and naturalness"; *EE*, 169: "Allein die Gewohnheit religiöser Denkungsart hat unsern Geist so arg befangen, dass Wir vor *Uns* in unserer Nacktheit und Natürlichkeit—erschrecken."

104 Machiavelli, *The Prince*, 90.

105 *EO*, 229; *EE*, 263: "der Mangel an *Bewusstsein* . . . trägt allein die Schuld."

The press is my *property* from the moment when nothing is more to me than myself; for from this moment state, church, people, society, and the like, cease, because they have to thank for their existence only the disrespect that I have for myself, and with the vanishing of this undervaluation they themselves are extinguished. . . . Or can you imagine a state whose citizens one and all think nothing of it? It would be as certainly a dream . . . as "united Germany."

[Mein *Eigentum* ist die Presse von dem Augenblicke an, wo Mir nichts mehr über Mich geht: denn von diesem Moment an hört Staat, Kirche, Volk, Gesellschaft u. dgl. auf, weil sie nur der Missachtung, welche Ich vor Mir habe, ihre Existenz verdanken, und mit dem Verschwinden dieser Geringschätzung selbst erlöschen. . . . Oder könnt Ihr Euch einen Staat denken, dessen Einwohner allesamt sich nichts aus ihm machen? der wäre so gewiss ein Traum . . . als das "einige Deutschland."][106]

Even if it is clear that the relevant myth's disappearance would depend on unanimity of disbelief, Stirner's idea nonetheless seems remarkably naïve in its failure to grasp the general dynamics of both sociopolitical practice and human psychology. It ignores the fact that sacred myths exist for a reason, that they are fundamental to the way human society functions. In recent times, this observation has been expressed most vigorously by Harari: "Any large-scale human cooperation—whether a modern state, a medieval church, an ancient city or an archaic tribe—is rooted in common myths that exist only in people's collective imagination."[107] Myth is an essential element of human bonding and social cohesion: it enables power structures to be formed, complex societies to develop, empires to be built, and, ultimately, human civilization to flourish. According to Harari, it is the single most important factor in *Homo sapiens*' domination, transformation, and, in all probability, destruction, of the Earth. Myth makes the weak strong, pain bearable, distress tolerable, suffering worthwhile, hardship desirable, the absurd meaningful, chaos intelligible, and death even glorious. Moreover, the power of myth to achieve all this depends on its being believed, often to the point of fanaticism; basing one's philosophy, therefore, on the abandonment of all sacred myths is a perilous—and perhaps unrealizable—enterprise. In contrast, Nietzsche sought not to eliminate all myths, but to choose or create new ones that, unlike Christianity, remain inherently believable in the modern world, not that he was any more successful in this endeavor than Stirner was in his.

---

106 *EO*, 252; *EE*, 287. Stirner, like Nietzsche, was opposed to German nationalism.
107 Harari, *Sapiens*, 30.

Despite the apparent shortcomings in Stirner's conceptual thinking, his central, life-affirming message remains, contained in his notion of egoism and the liberation of the individual which it entails. It is this that has led his supporters, like Sveistrup, in 1928, to place his philosophy in direct opposition to nihilism: "It is life itself that defends itself in the 'Unique One' against the nihilism of the ideal."[108] Leopold, too, is moved to write: "Stirnerian egoism is perhaps best thought of, not in terms of the pursuit of self-interest, but rather as a variety of individual self-rule or autonomy. . . . Judged against this account of egoism, characterisations of Stirner as a 'nihilist'—in the sense that he rejects all normative judgement—would . . . appear to be mistaken."[109]

There is, however, no simple answer to the question of the relationship between Stirner's thought and moral nihilism. It is hardly surprising that his unconcealed contempt for morality has led to Stirner being branded a moral nihilist, especially according to the looser definition of moral nihilism prevalent before the horrors of the twentieth century forced ethicists to question and reevaluate conventional moral norms. At the very least, any conservative commentator would be bound to consider Stirner's annihilation of traditional morality shockingly negative. And in actual fact, although almost ironically because it is a contingent consequence rather than a key concern, Stirner's philosophy does include the salient features of moral nihilism, and a version thereof, moreover, that goes beyond Mackie's error theory to the extremes of moral eliminativism.

Whether the term moral nihilist is a useful or appropriate epithet for Stirner, however, is another matter entirely, not least because terminological precision has rarely been one of the principal objectives of Stirner's accusers. It can be argued that, rather than being an apt description of Stirner the philosopher, it is, more often than not, used simply as a conveniently pejorative classification for a perceived moral pariah. There is therefore a strong case for rejecting the label of moral nihilist for Stirner (while acknowledging the elements of moral nihilism in his ideas) because it gives such a misleading impression of both the tone and focus of his philosophy. Stirner is a champion of individual autonomy, not a prophet of the moral void. Demythologization in the interests of the liberty of the individual is what he promotes, and morality is simply one of the victims of this process.

Stirner reveals his principal objective implicitly, but nonetheless quite clearly, in the preface to the second part of *Der Einzige*:

---

108 Sveistrup, "Stirner als Soziologe," 24.
109 *Stanford Encyclopedia of Philosophy*, "Max Stirner," by David Leopold, accessed June 30, 2023, https://plato.stanford.edu/entries/max-stirner/.

At the entrance of the modern time stands the "God-man." At its exit will only the God in the God-man evaporate? And can the God-man really die if only the God in him dies? They did not think of this question, and thought they were finished when in our days they brought to a victorious end the work of the Enlightenment, the vanquishing of God. . . . How can you believe that the God-man is dead before the man in him, besides the God, is dead?

[An dem Eingang der neuen Zeit steht der "Gottmensch." Wird sich an ihrem Ausgange nur der Gott am Gottmenschen verflüchtigen, und kann der Gottmensch wirklich sterben, wenn nur der Gott an ihm stirbt? Man hat an diese Frage nicht gedacht und fertig zu sein gemeint, als man das Werk der Aufklärung, die Überwindung des Gottes, in unsern Tagen zu einem siegreichen Ende führte. . . . Wie mögt Ihr glauben, dass der Gottmensch gestorben sei, ehe an ihm außer dem Gott auch der Mensch gestorben ist?][110]

Stirner thus positions himself as a consummator of the Enlightenment, an essentially constructive role aimed at creating the conditions for individual human beings to flourish free of the tyranny of hegemonic control, even if the process of achieving this goal involves the destruction of traditional values.

It would be remiss not to point out that the issue of Stirner's relationship to the Enlightenment is contentious. There is certainly some justification for the argument that his anti-humanist tendencies are profoundly antagonistic towards the Enlightenment, as is his non-essentialist interpretation of human identity, although such a view focuses on a narrow definition of humanism that is relevant to Stirner's historical context, rather than Steven Pinker's notion of the maximization of human flourishing.[111] On the other hand, there is no apparent contradiction between Stirner's philosophy and Horkheimer and Adorno's opening statement in *Dialectic of Enlightenment*, that "the Enlightenment has always aimed at liberating men from fear and establishing their sovereignty."[112] Having said that though, Horkheimer and Adorno then proceed, as Pinker points out, to demonize the Enlightenment in a way that foreshadows Helms's comprehensive attack on Stirner in *Die Ideologie der anonymen Gesellschaft*.[113] The victims, in both cases, are blamed for a multitude of sins including fascism and Nazism. It need come as no surprise that Helms was a private student of Adorno.

110 *EO*, 139; *EE*, 162.
111 See Pinker, *Enlightenment Now*, 410.
112 See Horkheimer and Adorno, *Dialectic of Enlightenment*, 3.
113 For Pinker on Horkheimer, Adorno, and the Enlightenment, see Pinker, *Enlightenment Now*, 396–97.

Despite such controversies, Bernd Laska feels justified in calling Stirner "a key figure in . . . the history of the 'Enlightenment.'"[114] There certainly appears to be a significant amount of overlap between Stirner's philosophy as a whole and the fundamental principles of the Enlightenment according to Onfray, namely: "condemnation of superstition, rejection of intolerance, abolition of censorship, resistance to tyranny, opposition to political absolutism, an end to state religion, proscription of magical thinking, extension of freedom of thought and expression, promulgation of equal rights, the notion that all law arises from contractual immanence, the wish for social happiness here and now, the aspiration toward the universal reign of reason."[115] Moreover, Stirner's hostility to humanism derived from his critique of its dogmatic deification of man, meaning that, in his opinion, it was his Young Hegelian colleagues who were betraying the Enlightenment, not him.

It was Stirner's conviction that the reports of the death of the divine had been greatly exaggerated. He argued that Strauss, Feuerbach, Bauer, Hess, et al. had not gone far enough; they had replaced dogmata with different, and often not dissimilar, dogmata. Stirner's intention was to bring the Enlightenment's war on dogma to a successful conclusion through the reduction of interests to the one and only sovereign, indivisible, unhypocritical, and non-heteronomous type: self-interest. He probably imagined that the result of his explanatory efforts would be a series of light-bulb moments, as the minds of his radical colleagues woke up to the possibilities of egoism. What, after all, could be more liberating than the rejection of all forms of heteronomy? In fact, he did not even manage to guide most of his readers beyond the questionable dichotomy of egoism and altruism. Nietzsche might have understood him: he even used one of Stirner's favorite terms to describe the dubious conflation of egoism and immorality: "the prejudice that takes 'moral,' 'unegoistic,' '*désintéressé*' as concepts of equivalent value already rules today with the force of a 'fixed idea' and brain sickness."[116]

As observed in chapter 3 above, the parallels between Nietzsche and Stirner are undeniable, regardless of how they arose. It is conceivable that Stirner's affinity with Nietzsche, who is often considered to be the principal founder of atheist existentialism, may hold the key to the final question

---

114 Laska, *Ein dauerhafter Dissident*, 120.
115 Onfray, *Atheist Manifesto*, 209–10.
116 Nietzsche, *On the Genealogy of Morals*, 26. Cf. *EO*, 69: "Spiritual men . . . want to set up a kingdom of love on earth, in which no one any longer acts from selfishness, but each one 'from love.' . . . What they have taken into their head, what shall we call it but—*fixed idea*?"; *EE*, 84. "Die geistlichen Menschen . . . wollen . . . ein Reich der Liebe auf Erden errichten, worin keiner mehr aus Eigennutz, sondern jeder "aus Liebe" handelt. . . . Was sie sich in den Kopf gesetzt haben, wie soll man das anders nennen, als—fixe Idee?"

to be addressed in this study: whether Stirner's thought can reasonably be linked to existential nihilism. Having ascertained that Stirner influenced the Russian nihilist movement, but that he can hardly be adjudged a political nihilist himself, and that Stirner's philosophy contains the basic, and indeed most extreme, principles of moral nihilism, although the aptness of the term moral nihilist to describe Stirner is highly questionable, it now remains to be seen whether Stirner's relationship to existential nihilism is able to supply a less equivocal conclusion.

CHAPTER 7

The Fear of Nothing: Stirner and Existential Nihilism

The Existential Question

IF THE EXAMINATION OF the relationship between Stirner and political and moral nihilism has thrown up little more than inconclusive answers, the current chapter, which looks at the most familiar form of nihilism in modern parlance, existential nihilism, offers the opportunity to come down decisively on one side of the argument or the other. Although Stirner has rarely been accused explicitly of being an existential nihilist, it is the sense behind most of the examples of his association with nihilism since World War II. During this time, Stirner has been described as an existentialist far more frequently than as an existential nihilist, but the link between his supposed existentialist characteristics and his nihilistic tendencies is often at least implied.

Carr defines existential nihilism as "the feeling of emptiness and pointlessness that follows from the judgment, 'Life has no meaning.'"[1] This understanding of nihilism has become so prevalent that Gertz, in his recent book on the subject, barely discusses it in any other sense. Although he recognizes nihilism's complexity and diversity, all definitions, in his analysis, ultimately revolve around the absence of meaning: "Nihilism is not merely the denial that life is inherently meaningful, as nihilism can instead be seen as a particular way of responding to the anxiety caused by the discovery of life's inherent meaninglessness."[2] The predominance of existential nihilism over all other types of nihilism has been attested to by numerous modern commentators. Crosby attributes its primacy to its widespread use, its ability to subsume other forms, such as moral, epistemological, and cosmic nihilism, and its broad relevance to life in general rather than to a specific discipline. Thus, he concludes that "existential nihilism is the most basic and inclusive, and therefore the most important, form of nihilism."[3] Carr likewise recognizes existential

---

1   Carr, *The Banalization of Nihilism*, 18.
2   Gertz, *Nihilism*, 109.
3   Crosby, *The Specter of the Absurd*, 8.

nihilism as "probably the most commonplace sense of the word," noting its significance in modern literature (citing Dostoevsky and Camus) and observing that Nietzsche was "preoccupied with this form," although it might be more accurate to say he invented it.[4]

Existential nihilism can be considered not just the heir to, but also the fulfillment of Nietzsche's infamous prophecy: "What I relate is the history of the next two centuries. I describe what is coming, what is inevitable: *the rise of nihilism*."[5] It is no surprise that existentialism, as a philosophical movement, emerged in the 1940s, towards the end of a thirty-year period of turmoil, horror, and global conflict, that shattered hitherto well-established concepts and values, and affirmed the myth of Nietzsche's supposed clairvoyance. Nietzsche's posthumous notes and fragments, popularized in the unauthorized compilation, *Der Wille zur Macht*, are strewn with references to nihilism as the consequence of the feeling of senseless futility, some examples of which include: "nihilism[,] . . . 'Everything is meaningless';"[6] "the futility, the pointlessness[,] nihilism";[7] and "the most extreme form of nihilism: nothingness (that is: 'meaninglessness') for ever!"[8]

In a well-known fragment of 1887, Nietzsche explained the psychology behind the appearance of this overwhelming sense of meaninglessness: "Nihilism appears, . . . because the idea that evil, or for that matter existence itself, has a 'meaning' is regarded with the utmost suspicion. *One* interpretation has failed, but since it was considered *the* interpretation, it now seems as if there is no meaning in existence at all, as if all is *in vain*."[9] The modern existentialists may have assimilated this relativization of nihilism, at least insofar as they share Nietzsche's opinion of it as a state that must be overcome, but they focus largely on its disconcerting effects on human consciousness, made manifest by a pervasive sense of disquiet, alienation, and despair.[10]

Crosby considers there to be a striking similarity between Stirner, Nietzsche, and Sartre in this regard: "We are brought . . . to the view of Stirner, Nietzsche, and Sartre, i.e., to their concept of absurd, normless volition as the ultimate basis of the beliefs and actions of individuals. . . . Meaning, truth, and value are not in any sense discovered, therefore, but can only be blindly posited or sheerly invented. This thesis was earlier [in the book] associated with various types of nihilism, especially with

---

4   Carr, *The Banalization of Nihilism*, 18, 19.
5   Nietzsche, *The Will to Power*, 7.
6   Nietzsche, *The Will to Power*, 11.
7   Nietzsche, *Werke*, 8.3:222.
8   Nietzsche, *The Will to Power*, 43.
9   Nietzsche, *The Will to Power*, 43.
10 See Macquarrie, *Existentialism*, 17–18.

existential nihilism."[11] This seems a curious assertion, firstly because absurdity is hardly a theme which is common to all three thinkers, and secondly because one does not have to be a nihilist to believe that values are not preordained. Such a belief could apply equally well to an atheist or a freethinker or a moral relativist. There is also the question of why values would necessarily have to be posited blindly. Could the refusal to accept the existence of unchanging and unverifiable universal values not be considered, on the contrary, to be evidence of clear-sightedness? Crosby appears to be confusing the attributes of faith with those of enlightenment, despite the fact that they are, in many ways, diametrically opposed to each other. Nonetheless, he is one of the few authors who directly associate Stirner with existential nihilism, so his claim deserves to be mentioned as part of this inquiry.

In order to understand the relationship between Stirner and existential nihilism, it is important first to examine the fundamental characteristics of existentialism itself, for, as Macquarrie observes: "even the most extreme among the existentialists seem to stop short of a doctrine of sheer absurdity and of nihilism."[12] As there is no self-confessed existential nihilist with whom to compare Stirner, it is necessary instead to consider the link between Stirner and existentialism, and to extrapolate from that to the viability of Stirner as a model for existential nihilism. Macquarrie, along with many others, has pointed to the elusiveness of existentialism as a term, both because of the breadth of its application and the looseness of its usage, but there is a general consensus about the themes common to existentialism in all its guises.[13] If Stirner is to be classified as an existential nihilist, as Crosby maintains, it would be important, if not essential, for there to be a broad affinity between Stirner and the existentialists regarding their respective outlooks and methods.

The most basic property of existentialism is that it "begins from man rather than from nature. It is a philosophy of the subject rather than of the object."[14] Sartre expresses this in his famous dictum that "*existence* comes before *essence*," which he elucidates as follows:[15] "What do we mean by saying that existence precedes essence? We mean that man first of all exists, encounters himself, surges up in the world—and defines himself afterwards. If man as the existentialist sees him is not definable, it is because to begin with he is nothing. . . . Man is nothing else but that which he makes of himself. That is the first principle of existentialism."[16]

11   Crosby, *The Specter of the Absurd*, 328–29.
12   Macquarrie, *Existentialism*, 215.
13   See Macquarrie, *Existentialism*, 13.
14   Macquarrie, *Existentialism*, 14.
15   Sartre, *Existentialism and Humanism*, 26.
16   Sartre, *Existentialism and Humanism*, 28.

The parallels with Stirner's *Einziger*—who is a self-defining individual, originating from nothing and with the sole purpose of realizing himself through the exercise of his own will—are unmistakable. In Stirner's magnum opus one can find the assertion of self-definition: "I myself am my concern";[17] the concept of creative nothingness: "In the *unique one* the owner himself returns into his creative nothing, of which he is born";[18] the exaltation of the will: "One does look at things rightly when one makes of them what one *will*. . . . And therefore the things and the looking at them are not first, but I am, my will is";[19] and the exhortation to self-realization: "*Get the value out of thyself!*"[20] Stirner's outlook seems completely compatible with the avowed first principle of existentialism.

It is precisely the dichotomy of existence and essence which is the basis of the first known description of Stirner as an existential philosopher. Rudolf Gottschall (1823–1909), poet, dramatist, and literary critic, writing nearly a century before Sartre, states: "Stirner is also an existential philosopher who, with Schelling, asserts the quod of existence against the quid? of essence."[21] Gottschall is referring to Stirner's declaration in the concluding remarks of *Der Einzige*:

> The ideal "man" is *realized* when the Christian apprehension turns about and becomes the proposition, "I, this unique one, am man." The conceptual question, "what is man?"—has then changed into the personal question, "who is man?"
>
> [Das Ideal "der Mensch" ist *realisiert*, wenn die christliche Anschauung umschlägt in den Satz: "Ich, dieser Einzige, bin der Mensch." Die Begriffsfrage "was ist der Mensch?"—hat sich dann in die persönliche umgesetzt: "wer ist der Mensch?"][22]

Macquarrie refers to the same distinction, or shift of focus, asserting its centrality to existentialism and thereby (inadvertently) confirming an

---

17 EO, 7; EE, 15: "Ich bin ja selber Meine Sache."

18 EO, 324; EE, 370: "Im *Einzigen* kehrt selbst der Eigner in sein schöpferisches Nichts zurück, aus welchem er geboren wird."

19 EO, 297–98; EE, 340: "Die Dinge schaut man eben recht an, wenn man aus ihnen macht, was man *will*. . . . Und darum sind die Dinge und ihre Anschauung nicht das Erste, sondern Ich bin's, mein Wille ist's."

20 EO, 278; EE, 319: "*Verwerte Dich!*"

21 Gottschall, "Die deutsche Philosophie seit Hegel's Tode," 310.

22 EO, 323; EE, 370. The question "what is man?" is repeated several times in the Bible. See: Job 7:17, "What is man, that thou shouldest magnify him?"; Psalms 8:4, "What is man, that thou art mindful of him?"; Psalms 144:3, "Lord, what is man, that thou takest knowledge of man!"; Hebrews 2:6 repeats the above line from Psalms 8:4.

affinity with Stirner concerning the understanding of human existence: "The existentialist philosopher claims that man must always be understood as a 'who' and not as a 'what', and further that, because existence implies with it the understanding of existence, there is open to man the possibility of a knowledge of the 'who' more certain and more fundamental than any knowledge that he can reach of the 'what.'"[23]

Gottschall clarifies what he means by *Existenzialphilosophie* in an earlier comment about Feuerbach: "It is the true existential philosophy which recognizes the actual not abstractly, as in Hegel, but concretely, the real in its reality, as true, therefore, in a way that corresponds to the essence of the real and elevates it to the principle and object of philosophy."[24] Gottschall sees Stirner's thought as a continuation rather than a refutation of Feuerbach's, and, thus, he associates both thinkers with existential philosophy, a term Gottschall may have borrowed from Kierkegaard.[25] The debate around existence and essence can be traced back through Hegel, Aquinas, Avicenna, and Aristotle to Plato, and although two and a half millennia of deliberation have given rise to numerous shifts of interpretation, it is substantially the same duality to which Sartre refers.[26] What is important for the purposes of this study is that Stirner certainly agrees with Sartre concerning the precedence of existence over essence, from which derives an undeniable commonality between Stirner and existentialism. The problem with Gottschall's definition, however, is that it is so broad that Marx, for instance, would have to be included among the existential philosophers.

Positive and Negative Themes of Existentialism

Overlaying what Macquarrie identifies as its first principle, namely that it begins from man, one finds in the existentialist outlook a number of recurrent themes. These can be divided into positive and negative groups, the former being smaller in size than the latter, which is a fair indication of the balance between the different types of issues that existentialism sets out to tackle. The positive group includes, as Macquarrie notes, the themes of freedom, decision, and responsibility, the exercise of which constitutes man's authenticity.[27] Here the links to Stirner start to become

---

23   Macquarrie, *An Existentialist Theology*, 37.
24   Gottschall, "Die deutsche Philosophie seit Hegel's Tode," 308.
25   See Kierkegaard, *Philosophical Fragments*, 90–107.
26   See *Encyclopedia.com*, "Essence and Existence," by J. C. Taylor, accessed June 30, 2023, https://www.encyclopedia.com/religion/encyclopedias-almanacs-transcripts-and-maps/essence-and-existence.
27   See Macquarrie, *Existentialism*, 16.

a little more tenuous, although Copleston, even in the broad brushstrokes of his *History of Philosophy*, is able to identify the outlines of similitude: "some may wish to see in it [Stirner's philosophy of egoism] some spiritual affinity with existentialism. And there is at least some ground for this. It can hardly be said that emphasis on the theme of property is a characteristic of existentialism, but the theme of the unique free individual certainly is."[28]

That Stirner's *Einziger* shares the subjectivist orientation of the unique free individual, who forms the basis for the existentialist perspective, is self-evident. Macquarrie, in his discussion of existential authenticity, speaks of each individual's existence being "characterized by a unique 'mineness,'" which could be considered an adequate definition for Stirner's *Einziger*.[29] Macquarrie explains: "'Mineness' is a term that has sometimes been used to express the awareness that my existence is unique and distinct from the existence of everyone else. I am not just a specimen of a class. I am I."[30] Compare this with Stirner's description of the "I," or the ego, and the overlap is almost total: "But I am not an ego along with other egos, but the sole ego: I am unique."[31]

This similarity in the outlooks of Stirner and the existentialists is not, however, particularly remarkable, bearing in mind the prominence of subjectivism in modern Western thought, starting with Descartes and proceeding through Fichtean idealism and German Romanticism to twentieth-century movements like existentialism and postmodernism. The question is whether this resemblance extends beyond a general outlook to more specific themes that both Stirner and the existentialists address. As far as the idea of freedom is concerned, Crosby writes of "the insistence of thinkers such as Stirner, Nietzsche, and Sartre on the reality and critical importance of human freedom."[32] Indeed, he further underscores a purported close resemblance between Stirner and Sartre in this regard with the assertion that "Stirner pushes this theme [the reality and importance of human freedom] to a ridiculous extreme, of course, as does Sartre."[33] However, a more detailed analysis of Stirner's and Sartre's respective concepts of freedom is required in order to evaluate the claim of a close intellectual kinship, which Crosby and, to a lesser extent, Copleston suggest.

As Macquarrie observes, the significance of freedom for existentialism can hardly be overstated: "there can be few themes, if any, nearer

---

28   Copleston, *A History of Philosophy*, 7.2:71.
29   Macquarrie, *Existentialism*, 206.
30   Macquarrie, *Existentialism*, 72–73.
31   *EO*, 318–19; *EE*, 365: "Ich bin aber nicht ein Ich neben andern Ichen, sondern das alleinige Ich: Ich bin einzig."
32   Crosby, *The Specter of the Absurd*, 368.
33   Crosby, *The Specter of the Absurd*, 368.

to the heart of existentialism.... It is prominent in Kierkegaard, for whom to exist and to be free are almost synonymous expressions. The interest in freedom, or rather the passion for freedom, is not confined to any particular variety of existentialist. Surely two of the greatest apostles of freedom in the twentieth century have been the atheists Sartre and Camus."[34] An example of the overwhelming importance of freedom for Sartre can be found in the existential hero of *La Nausée* (Nausea, 1938), Antoine Roquentin, who declares: "all I have ever wanted was to be free."[35] Stirner, however, takes a quite different view; while recognizing the universal appeal of freedom, he immediately dismisses it as qualitatively inferior to ownness:

> You do not want the freedom to have all these fine things, for with this freedom you still do not have them; you want really to have them.... And, if you became free from everything, you would no longer have anything; for freedom is empty of substance.
>
> [Du willst ... nicht die Freiheit, alle diese schönen Sachen zu haben, denn mit der Freiheit dazu hast Du sie noch nicht; Du willst sie wirklich haben.... Und würdest Du von allem frei, so hättest Du eben nichts mehr; denn die Freiheit ist inhaltsleer.][36]

Stirner describes freedom variously as an ideal, a spook, and an empty word.[37] He declares dismissively: "Freedom lives only in the realm of dreams!"[38] Indeed, in the prologue to *Der Einzige*, he lists it as one of the extraneous causes that are foisted upon the human mind, along with truth, humanity, justice, and various other sacred abstractions.[39] Whether in its positive or negative form (although Stirner's attention is more often than not directed towards the latter, as in liberation from hegemony), freedom is seen as a useless attribute unless it is subsumed under ownership and combined with power:[40] "My freedom becomes complete only when it is my—*might*; but by this I cease to be a merely free man, and become an own man."[41] Stirner, in other words, while acknowledging

---

34 Macquarrie, *Existentialism*, 177.
35 Sartre, *Nausea*, 97.
36 EO, 141; EE, 163.
37 See EO, 141, 142; EE, 163, 165.
38 EO, 143; EE, 165: "Freiheit lebt nur in dem Reich der Träume!"
39 See EO, 5; EE, 13.
40 For a detailed discussion of positive and negative freedom, see Berlin, *Two Concepts of Liberty*.
41 EO, 151; EE, 174: "Meine Freiheit wird erst vollkommen, wenn sie meine—*Gewalt* ist; durch diese aber höre ich auf, ein bloß Freier zu sein, und werde ein Eigener." Stirner's belittling of the *Freier*, a word which means

the urge to be free, rejects as a diversion the abstract concept of freedom. As Clark explains: "While Stirner seems tempted at times to strongly emphasize the importance of individual freedom, it must ultimately take a subordinate place in his thought, in view of his psychological and ethical egoism. Since all one does is ultimately for the sake of the ego, . . . freedom must be kept in its place as a value subordinate to the ego. If not, it becomes another enslaving idea."[42] Stirner's concept of freedom is therefore far from the idealized, and at times almost romanticized, version envisaged by the existentialists, expressed, for example, in Camus' dramatic statement: "Men are never really willing to die except for the sake of freedom."[43] The idea of dying for any cause is, of course, anathema to Stirner, which helps to explain his lack of participation in the 1848 revolutions.[44] Stirner does not view freedom from the perspective of the ontological matrix of existentialism, but rather as a practical function of the power of the individual.

In Sartrean existentialism, freedom entails responsibility. One of Sartre's best-known philosophical maxims is: "I am condemned to be free," from which he develops the idea that man is responsible for the world and for himself.[45] Responsibility is not a quality that immediately springs to mind when one thinks of Stirner; indeed, as already observed, there are many who have considered him an example of the exact opposite, foremost of whom is Paterson, who writes with all the disapprobation he can muster that "the philosophy of the Unique One . . . is above all a philosophy of irresponsibility."[46] Nonetheless, in considering the ethical implications of existential ontology, Sartre outlines a concept of selfhood that, although he distinguishes it from egoism, could be interpreted as having some similarities with the psychological egoism of Stirner:

> Existential psychoanalysis is *moral description*, for it releases to us the ethical meaning of various human projects. It indicates to us the necessity of abandoning the psychology of interest along with any utilitarian interpretations of human conduct—by revealing to us the *ideal* meaning of all human attitudes. These meanings are beyond egoism and altruism, beyond also any behavior which is

---

whoremonger as well as freeman, is almost certainly an ironic comment on his brethren in *Die Freien*.
   42   Clark, *Max Stirner's Egoism*, 64.
   43   Camus, *The Rebel*, 255.
   44   See Mackay, *Max Stirner*, 197.
   45   Sartre, *Being and Nothingness*, 439, 553–56.
   46   Paterson, *The Nihilistic Egoist*, 186. See Paterson, *The Nihilistic Egoist*, 295: "His relationship to his philosophical ideas . . . is strictly irresponsible."

called *disinterested*. Man makes himself man in order to be God, and selfness considered from this point of view can appear to be an egoism.[47]

Sartre's comment on man becoming God at least reveals a shared point of departure with Stirner, who, in his attack on humanism, declared "that man has killed God in order to become now—'*sole* God on high'"[48] However, as far as the positive themes of existentialism are concerned, although there are clearly a few points of intersection with Stirner's thought, these are outweighed by the differences, most notably with respect to the key concept of freedom.

The recurrent negative themes of existentialism include finitude, guilt, alienation, death, anxiety, despair, boredom, and nausea.[49] Macquarrie is careful to point out that this prevalence of negative motifs does not mean existentialism can or should be equated with pessimism, but he observes, nonetheless, that existentialists are united in their awareness of "the tragic elements in human existence."[50] This awareness can be seen as a direct result of the questioning of religious belief. In other words, it is, as Nietzsche observed in "The Parable of the Madman" and elsewhere, intricately connected to the phenomenon of the death of God and all the uncertainties that that engenders. Atheistic existentialism examines the wider significance of this momentous event through the eyes of the individual, thereby flirting with, though generally not embracing, the possibility of nihilism. Perhaps foremost of the existentialists in this regard is Heidegger, of whom Macquarrie says: "The prominence of such themes as care, anxiety, guilt, finitude, and above all death, in Heidegger's account might be taken as indications of a trend towards a kind of nihilism. This impression might be further strengthened by his famous inaugural lecture, . . . 'What is Metaphysics?' . . . [where] we learn that metaphysics has to do with nothing."[51] He sums up Heidegger's position as follows: "The self becomes aware of its finitude and nothingness through the ontological experience of anxiety in the face of death."[52] Or, as Sartre puts it, anxiety (*Angst*) is, for Heidegger, "the apprehension of nothingness."[53] The concept of nothingness had, for obvious reasons,

---

47   Sartre, *Being and Nothingness*, 626.
48   *EO*, 139; *EE*, 162: "daß der Mensch den Gott getötet hat, um nun—'alleiniger Gott in der Höhe' zu werden." Cf. Nietzsche, *The Gay Science*, 181: "Must we ourselves not become gods simply to appear worthy of it [the greatness of this deed]?"
49   See Macquarrie, *Existentialism*, 17–18.
50   Macquarrie, *Existentialism*, 17.
51   Macquarrie, *Existentialism*, 57.
52   Macquarrie, *Existentialism*, 247.
53   Sartre, *Being and Nothingness*, 29.

always been associated with nihilism, but the existentialists, and especially Heidegger, drew attention to this relationship as never before.

The most fundamental of all the negative themes of existentialism is death. Death plays a prominent role throughout French existentialist literature, as, for instance, in Camus' first two published novels, *L'Étranger* (The Outsider, 1942) and *La Peste* (The Plague, 1947). The former begins with the death of Meursault's mother and climaxes with him shooting the Arab. The latter opens with the death of a rat, followed by the death of some of the major characters in the novel (Jean Tarrou, Father Paneloux) as well as some minor ones (M. Michel, M. Othon's son) and, finally, of numerous townsfolk of the plague-stricken city of Oran. In Sartre's first novel, *La Nausée*, death is not part of the action, but is like a ghost that haunts Roquentin's world, suffusing it with meaninglessness, as illustrated by his meditation on suicide:

> And I—weak, languid, obscene, digesting, tossing about dismal thoughts—*I too was superfluous.* . . . I dreamed vaguely of killing myself, to destroy at least one of these superfluous existences. But my death itself would have been superfluous. Superfluous, my corpse, my blood on these pebbles, between these plants, in the depths of this charming park. And the decomposed flesh would have been superfluous in the earth which would have received it, and my bones, finally, cleaned, stripped, neat and clean as teeth, would also have been superfluous; I was superfluous for all time.[54]

Stirner defends suicide as a matter of individual choice;[55] Sartre's hero considers it a valid response to existence but ultimately rejects it because, like everything else, it is superfluous. The sense of meaninglessness, embodied in the feeling of nausea to which the title refers, seeps through the entire narrative of Sartre's novel, and the concept with which this senselessness is most associated is nothingness. Nothingness lurks behind reality, echoing the imagery and terminology of German Romanticism: "Things are entirely what they appear to be and *behind them* . . . there is nothing."[56] It also gives existence its flavor, or lack of one: "If anybody had asked me what existence was, I should have replied in good faith that it was nothing, just an empty form which added itself to external things, without changing anything in their nature."[57] There is no doubt a vague parallel here with Stirner as far as the awareness of man's ephemerality is concerned, which Stirner acknowledges for instance in the concepts of the "mortal creator" and "creative nothing," but on

---

54 Sartre, *Nausea*, 184–85.
55 See *EO*, 286; *EE*, 327–28.
56 Sartre, *Nausea*, 140.
57 Sartre, *Nausea*, 183.

which he never explicitly dwells.[58] Roquentin, in contrast, considers this inescapable result of godlessness with something close to despair: "And all those existents . . . came from nowhere and were going nowhere. All of a sudden they existed and then, all of a sudden, they no longer existed."[59] He sees life as pointless and arbitrary: "Every existent is born without reason, prolongs itself out of weakness and dies by chance."[60] And so he tells the autodidact only half in jest: "there's nothing, nothing, absolutely no reason for existing."[61] This is a train of thought that is completely alien to Stirner's egoist, who never seems to doubt that life has meaning.

Giorgio Penzo, nonetheless, supports the surprisingly common view that Stirner shares existentialism's tragic awareness: "Stirner's nihilism presents us exactly with the finitude of man in its basic conditions of suffering and death."[62] The suggestion would seem to be that Stirner is the elusive archetype of the existential nihilist. Existential nihilism is essentially the negative face of existentialism; what, after all, is existential nihilism without the despair, the alienation, the emptiness, and the *horror vacui* that follow the death of God? Read sums up these tendencies as follows:

> The philosopher who calls himself an existentialist begins with an acute attack of self-consciousness. . . . There he is, a finite and insignificant speck of protoplasm pitched against the infinite extent of the universe. . . . Modern physicists may have succeeded in proving that the universe itself is also finite, but that only makes matters worse, for now the universe shrinks to littleness and is pitched against the still more mysterious concept of *Nothingness*. . . . So there we have the Little Man gaping into the abyss, and feeling . . . not only very small, but terrified. That feeling is the original *Angst*, the dread or anguish, and if you do not feel *Angst* you cannot be an existentialist.[63]

If one accepts Read's interpretation, then Stirner, based on his writings, is not, and cannot be, an existentialist. He does not express a feeling of angst in this or any similar sense of the term. The word itself is only mentioned in *Der Einzige* with regard to Christianity's self-tortured effort to reify God; Stirner does not use it in relation to the feelings of the individual.[64] It is similar with the concepts of alienation, despair, and death. Death is simply treated as a sober fact, dissociated from the self

---

58   *EO*, 324; *EE*, 370: "sterblicher Schöpfer," "schöpferisches Nichts."
59   Sartre, *Nausea*, 190.
60   Sartre, *Nausea*, 191.
61   Sartre, *Nausea*, 162.
62   Penzo, *Die existentielle Empörung*, 13.
63   Read, *Existentialism, Marxism and Anarchism*, 5–6.
64   See *EO*, 312; *EE*, 357.

except insofar as one administers it by one's own choice. Stirner infamously declares "that I do not renounce, from any fit of humility, even the power over life and death."[65] There is no sense of anxiety, let alone horror; on the contrary, Stirner seems to revel in his ability to unsettle the reader with his insouciant attitude towards murder and suicide. Finitude is proudly, and without any hint of apprehension, presented as a fundamental axiom of his philosophy, distinguishing the egoism of his unique individual from the idealism of Fichte's abstract "I": "only the . . . *finite* ego is really I. Fichte speaks of the 'absolute' ego, but I speak of me, the transitory ego."[66] The exaltation of the ego is not diminished in any way by the fact of its impermanence, which is simply accepted as a reality, though not a grim one. For Stirner, who was in his late thirties when he was writing *Der Einzige*, transience and death appear to have been distant concerns, as already observed in his nonchalant comment on old age: "Finally, the old man? When I become one, there will be time enough to speak of that."[67] Such a remark would be thoroughly out of place in existentialist thought.

The negative imagery employed by Read to describe the existential outlook bears little relation to what is found in Stirner's writings. Stirner is untroubled by existential abandonment, ethical uncertainty, contingency, futility, the ephemerality of existence, or personal extinction, and likewise by the states of mind expressed by Kierkegaard's *angst*, Heidegger's *Geworfenheit*, Camus' *absurdité*, and Sartre's *nausée*.[68] Indeed, this goes some way to explaining Stirner's lack of allure. Confessions of self-torment and the agony of despair inevitably make for more sensational reading than a sober analysis of the mendacity of man's dogmatic mythological creations; no one could claim that *Der Einzige* is as compelling a read as *L'Étranger*. Stirner's philosophical perspective is far closer to the calm serenity of Epicurus than the agitated disquiet of Camus, Sartre, or Dostoevsky. He concerns himself with how best to live this life rather than how to prepare for, or live in the absence of, the next one:

> My intercourse with the world, what does it aim at? I want to have the enjoyment of it. . . . I do not want the liberty of men, nor their equality; I want only *my* power over them. I want to make them my property, *material for enjoyment*.

---

65   EO, 282; EE, 322: "dass Ich auch der Macht über Leben und Tod aus keiner Anwandlung von Demut entsage."
66   EO, 163; EE, 188: "nur das . . . *endliche* Ich ist wirklich Ich. Fichte spricht vom 'absoluten' Ich, Ich aber spreche von Mir, dem vergänglichen Ich."
67   EO, 18; EE, 24: "Endlich der Greis? Wenn Ich einer werde, so ist noch Zeit genug, davon zu sprechen."
68   Respectively: anxiety, thrownness, absurdity, and nausea.

[Mein Verkehr mit der Welt, worauf geht er hinaus? Genießen will Ich sie. . . . Ich will nicht die Freiheit, nicht die Gleichheit der Menschen; Ich will nur *meine* Macht über sie, will sie zu meinem Eigentum, d. h. *genießbar* machen.][69]

Stirner and Existentialism: Commonalities and Contrasts

Despite the numerous dissimilarities, there are some general traits that Stirner and the existentialists have in common apart from the "unique mineness" discussed above. Firstly, there is the element of rebellion: "Existentialists are usually rebels against the establishment. In many fields—theology, politics, morals, literature—they struggle against the accepted authorities and the traditional canons."[70] Such a characterization could, of course, also be applied to Stirner (although to many others besides). Thus, Camus, in his philosophical study of rebellion, includes a short section about Stirner, portraying him as the ultimate prophet of nihilistic rebellion and contrasting him unsympathetically with Nietzsche.[71]

Camus, like many others, seems to have based his negative opinion on Stirner's sensational utterances, which can appear to justify murder and suicide, two of Camus' chief *bêtes noires*. His condemnation of Stirner is therefore suitably abrupt: "But to decree the legitimacy of murder is to decree the mobilization and war of the unique individuals. Murder will thus coincide with a kind of collective suicide. Stirner, who neither admits it nor recognizes it, does not, however, shrink from any act of destruction."[72] One can question the negativity of Camus' reading of Stirner, but not his emphasis on Stirner's spirit of rebellion, as manifested in his relentless war on dogma: "Nothing can stop this bitter and imperious logic any more, nothing but an ego that stands up against all abstractions."[73] Indeed, antagonism towards abstractions is another general characteristic that Stirner shares with the existentialist, who, according to Macquarrie, "sees his task as that of fighting against every distorting abstraction. The notion of the corporate personality of the state is such an abstraction."[74] This applies equally well to Stirner, as is borne out by his reputation as an individualist anarchist.[75]

69   EO, 281; EE, 322.
70   Macquarrie, *Existentialism*, 31.
71   See Camus, *L'Homme révolté*, 84.
72   Camus, *L'Homme révolté*, 87.
73   Camus, *L'Homme révolté*, 87.
74   Macquarrie, *Existentialism*, 239.
75   See Mackay, *Max Stirner*, 21: "The legacy of Stirner . . . rests in the faithful . . . hands of the individualist anarchists."

It would also be possible to make the case for the quality of own-ness, as demonstrated in Stirner's enlightened egoist, being to some extent aligned with the existentialist concept of authenticity; and, conversely, for the egoist's adversary, the dogmatist, be he of the Christian or humanist variety, exemplifying the existentialist idea of bad faith, insofar at least as myths, in claiming to be true, inevitably engender hypocrisy. Macquarrie's description of the existentialist notion of authentic and inauthentic existence could be superimposed on Stirner's philosophy without giving rise to any significant contradiction: "Existence is authentic to the extent that the existent has taken possession of himself and . . . has moulded himself in his own image. Inauthentic existence, on the other hand, is moulded by external influences, whether these be circumstances, moral codes, political or ecclesiastical authorities, or whatever."[76] However, Widukind De Ridder argues persuasively that the existentialist notion of authenticity is "yet another form of subject-object thinking" and would thus fall under Stirner's negative category of possessedness. Stirner's position, he claims, "is far more radical than a merely atheist form of existentialism."[77]

Indeed, once one looks beyond the general features to more specific elements of existentialism, the discrepancies with Stirner's thought become increasingly obvious. Concerning bad faith, Carroll points out that: "Stirner's . . . egoist critique of hypocrisy, or *mauvaise foi*, is not backed by any moral affirmation of truth or honesty. . . . What he rejects . . . is the brand of nihilistic existentialism which when articulated states: 'in this meaningless world at least I must display before others my honesty in the face of despair, my integrity.'"[78] What Carroll does not make clear is that Stirner probably did not reject this standpoint explicitly, because it was not one with which he was ever confronted. Ontological despair is not a conspicuous feature of his thought, indeed, Stirner and the existentialists generally inhabit very different mental universes. Psychology, though not unimportant, does not play the same role in Stirner's work as it does in Kierkegaard, Dostoevsky, or Nietzsche, all of whom, in their different ways, have been characterized as psychologists of the soul. Stirner's is instead a very rational, dispassionate worldview, concerned primarily with material rather than spiritual problems of human existence. Carroll nonetheless speaks of "Stirner's existentialist leanings" and "the strong existentialist themes in Stirner's philosophy."[79] Like many post-war writers caught up in the spirit of the times, Carroll seems to have been eager to discover parallels between Stirner's thought

---

76 Macquarrie, *Existentialism*, 206.
77 De Ridder, "Max Stirner: The End of Philosophy," 156.
78 Carroll, *Break-Out from the Crystal Palace*, 43.
79 Carroll, *Break-Out from the Crystal Palace*, 43, 40.

and existentialism and to squeeze him retroactively into an existentialist, or at least proto-existentialist, mold. This is just another example of the way in which Stirner's supposed nihilism has changed as the notion itself has evolved.

A further example can be found in Clark, who, despite his principal focus on Stirner and anarchism, endorses the orthodox view concerning Stirner's link to existentialism: "A related aspect of Stirner's historical importance is his connection with existentialism. . . . An examination of Stirner's thought verifies Paterson's contention that 'just as Kierkegaard is acknowledged to be the founder of Christian existentialism, . . . it would seem that Stirner has some claim to be considered the earliest definite precursor of atheistic existentialism.'"[80] Stirner, as a contemporary of Kierkegaard, is of course a convenient candidate for the originator of the atheistic version of existentialism, in that he provides an appealing historical symmetry to the rise of existentialism's two distinct, theistic and atheistic, strands, planting them firmly in the intellectually fertile ground of post-Hegelianism. Stirner's life (1806–1856) and Kierkegaard's (1813–1855) largely overlap chronologically, and their most important works were published within a few years of each other in the 1840s. This beguiling but misleading parallelism has proven irresistible to numerous observers.

One of the most prominent of these is Löwith, whose 1928 postdoctoral dissertation compares Kierkegaard's single one (*der Einzelne*) with Stirner's unique one (*der Einzige*), arguably marking the beginning of the existentialization of Stirner, alluded to in chapter 4 above.[81] Unsurprisingly, Löwith's sympathies lie with Kierkegaard, rather than with Stirner's allegedly nihilistic philosophy, a preference he reiterates in his magnum opus, *Von Hegel zu Nietzsche*, where the two philosophers are once again juxtaposed, and Stirner is presented as being both marginal and disreputable: "His thought, as well as his actual life, stood at the extreme limit of his world, which had lost its substance and become disillusioned."[82] Although he does not use the term existential nihilist, Löwith does assert Stirner's connection both to nihilism and existentialism. The former rests above all on the familiar insinuations regarding nothingness: "Stirner's 'I,' having freed itself completely from everything, has nothing else to do than turn back to its own nothingness."[83] The

---

80 Clark, *Max Stirner's Egoism*, 14–15. The quotation is from Paterson, *The Nihilistic Egoist*, 184.
81 For more detail on Stirner's existentialization, see Laska, *Ein dauerhafter Dissident*, 78–81.
82 Löwith, *From Hegel to Nietzsche*, 248–49.
83 Löwith, *From Hegel to Nietzsche*, 105. See 71 and 111, where Löwith mentions Stirner's nihilism.

latter is seen as the product of subjective egoism, or as Löwith describes it, "the existential concentration of the entire world upon the particular, individual 'I.'"[84] Finally, he posits the theory of the origins of the two strands of existentialism, which has remained so influential: "Stirner's cliché of the 'unique individual' and Kierkegaard's concept of the 'individual' both illustrate the same question, asked in religious and profane terms."[85]

In the period between the publication of Löwith's dissertation in 1928 and his best-known book, *Von Hegel zu Nietzsche*, in 1941, the relationship between Kierkegaard's and Stirner's thought was also considered by one of the foremost twentieth-century theistic existentialists, Martin Buber (1878–1965), namely in *Die Frage an den Einzelnen* (The Question to the Single One, 1936), in the first chapter of which, Kierkegaard's single one and Stirner's unique one are once again contrasted and compared. As with Löwith, there is no doubt about where the author's sympathies lie; he dismisses Stirner straight away as "a pathetic nominalist and unmasker of ideas."[86] The essay starts with an epigraph in the form of Buber's wife Paula's apothegm, "Responsibility is the navel-string of creation."[87] It is immediately clear that Stirner is not going to make the grade, as, indeed, he does not. In the contest between the two thinkers' attitudes towards responsibility and truth, Stirner comes a distant second: "For Stirner both are bound to be false questions. But it is important to see that intending to destroy both basic ideas he has destroyed only their routine forms and thus, contrary to his whole intention, has prepared for their purification and renewal."[88] At least Buber accords Stirner a useful role as an accidental purifier; this is not, however, enough to save him from further censure: "This reality of responsibility is not what is questioned by Stirner; it is unknown to him."[89] The unambiguous message is that Stirner has no idea what he is talking about: "He wishes to show the nothingness of the word which has decayed into a phrase; he has never known the living word."[90]

One should not be misled by Buber's apparently conciliatory comments about Stirner's cathartic usefulness. His final verdict is damning: "And yet . . . the two, primally different, primally strange to one another, . . . work together, . . . the one announcing decay as decay, the other proving the eternal structure to be inviolable."[91] For the remainder of

---

84 Löwith, *From Hegel to Nietzsche*, 299.
85 Löwith, *From Hegel to Nietzsche*, 359.
86 Buber, *Between Man and Man*, 41.
87 Buber, *Between Man and Man*, 40.
88 Buber, *Between Man and Man*, 44.
89 Buber, *Between Man and Man*, 45.
90 Buber, *Between Man and Man*, 45.
91 Buber, *Between Man and Man*, 49.

the book, Buber concentrates on Kierkegaard; Stirner has served his purpose, to act as a negative contrast and to reduce old dogma to ashes, from which the truth of Kierkegaard's single one can rise like a phoenix. But the damage done to Stirner was not only in terms of his good name (if he ever had one). Being subject matter for Buber and being compared with Kierkegaard, together with the explicit accusation that he concerned himself with "the tearing apart of his existential bindings and bonds," combined to make the subsequent association of Stirner with existentialism all but inevitable.[92]

As Kast points out, Buber, whose chief concern in the book is the nature of interpersonal relationships, fails to acknowledge, or perhaps to recognize, the role that these play in Stirner's thought, but this issue has more of a bearing on Stirner's connection to individualist anarchism than to existentialism, and is therefore outside the scope of this study.[93] What is of much greater relevance is that, paradoxically, although he underscores Stirner's detachment from the existentialist values of freedom and responsibility, the theistic existentialist's—Buber's—comparison of Stirner with the Christian existentialist, Kierkegaard, has served to reinforce the perception of Stirner's atheist existentialist credentials, whether or not this was Buber's intention. Together with Löwith, Buber succeeded in including Stirner in the existentialist narrative, and in a period of some twenty-five years from 1952 to 1976, at the height of existentialism's influence, there was a series of largely unchallenged references to the allegedly self-evident connection between Stirner and existentialism.

In the anglophone world, it was Herbert Read who initially took the lead in calling attention to this supposed affinity. Writing in 1952, he observes: "[Existentialism] is saying that man is the reality—not even man in the abstract, but the human person, you and I; and that everything else—freedom, love, reason, God—is a contingency depending on the will of the individual. In this respect existentialism has much in common with Max Stirner's egoism."[94] Apparently basing his argument solely on Stirner and the existentialists' shared focus on the individual's perspective, Read goes so far as to declare: "Stirner is one of the most existentialist of all past philosophers, and whole pages of *The Ego and His Own* read like anticipations of Sartre."[95] Influenced, perhaps, once again, by a desire to fit Stirner into the existentialist mood of his time, Read appears to have been blind to the fact that Stirner does not fulfill his own definition of an existentialist according to the litmus test of angst referred to above. Thus, five years later, Read repeated his claim: "I would like to suggest that the

---

92   Buber, *Between Man and Man*, 44.
93   See Kast, "Afterword," in Arvon, *Max Stirner*, 216.
94   Read, *Existentialism, Marxism and Anarchism*, 10.
95   Read, *Existentialism, Marxism and Anarchism*, 24.

fashionable doctrine of existentialism must owe something to Stirner—the resemblances are too many and too close to be accidental. . . . The characters in Sartre's plays and novels are constructed round a philosophy which seems to me to be identical with Stirner's."[96] This is, at the very least, an exaggeration. Stirner and Sartre do concur on *ex nihilo/ad nihilum* subjectivism, self-realization, and existence preceding essence, as Leopold correctly recognizes: "In the 1960s Stirner was rediscovered again, this time as a thinker with conceptual affinities—for example in his anti-essentialist conception of the self as a 'creative nothing' . . .—with existentialist thought."[97] But on specific existentialist themes, especially the negative ones, there is little or no consensus.

Around the same time, in the francophone world, Henri Arvon (1914–1992) advanced a similar theory about existentialism's debt to Stirner in his aptly titled book, *Aux sources de l'existentialisme: Max Stirner* (At the Roots of Existentialism: Max Stirner, 1954). Despite the title, however, the issue of Stirner's connection to existentialism is only raised in the four-page conclusion, where Arvon bemoans Mackay's influence on Stirner's legacy in creating what he considers to be a false association with anarchism. Like Buber before him, to whom he gives a nod of approval, Arvon sees Stirner's true place in the history of philosophy alongside Kierkegaard:[98] "The two philosophers . . . were ignorant of each other; the atheist Stirner and Kierkegaard the believer are apparently separated by an impassable gulf. And yet, what an astonishing encounter between them. It is with the same dialectical vigor that they combat the system of Hegel; it is with the same violence that they attack impersonal reason. Both define the existential 'I' and infinitely expand its field of action."[99] Arvon, like his predecessors, offers no better, or more conclusive, evidence than Kierkegaard's and Stirner's shared subjectivism. As for the fact that they were both reacting to the monolithic figure of Hegel, this was something of an inevitability for any European thinker living in the first half of the nineteenth century, so dominant was Hegelianism in the philosophical discourse of that period. Nonetheless, Arvon finishes his book with a confident challenge: "Stirner and Kierkegaard have accomplished the same work of liberation: they have restored the preeminent value of the Ego to its true primacy. . . . Christian existentialism recognizes itself in Kierkegaard; will atheist existentialism continue to ignore Stirner?"[100]

---

96 Read, *The Tenth Muse*, 81.
97 Leopold, "Introduction," xii.
98 See Arvon, *Aux sources de l'existentialisme*, 178.
99 Arvon, *Aux sources de l'existentialisme*, 177.
100 Arvon, *Aux sources de l'existentialisme*, 178.

Support for the idea of Stirner's connection to existentialism came from all around Europe. The German Marxist, Holz, reaffirmed the link, claiming that Stirner and the existentialists share in the counter-revolutionary isolation of the individual, a theme that is expanded on by another Marxist, Helms, who lumps Stirner together with existentialism and other forms of (lower-)middle-class fascistic ideology:[101]

> Stirner is the first prophet of "authenticity," which has since become, via Heidegger, Jaspers, and existentialism, the most primitive, vacuous banality of middle-class ideology. In contrast, Marx: "The real human being is recognized only in the figure of the egoistic individual, the true human being only in the figure of the abstract citizen." To emancipate both dialectically into ζῶον πολιτικόν is Marx's idea. To beat the one to death with the other is the ideal of Stirner and fascism.[102]

Penzo, writing in 1971, followed Arvon's example by including the identification of Stirner with existentialism in the title of his book, *Max Stirner: La rivolta esistenziale* (Max Stirner: the Existential Revolt), in which he repeatedly affirms Stirner's existential qualities: "In my opinion, Stirner must be regarded as the proponent of a new existential philosophy of being, which represents the most nominalistic position that the history of Western thought has ever known."[103] As well as explicitly agreeing with Paterson's assessment of Stirner's existentialist credentials, Penzo also follows Paterson in labeling Stirner a nihilist.[104] It is only a short step to branding Stirner an existential nihilist, although this is anyway implied by such inaccurate statements as: "Stirner's point of departure was the terrible experience of the meaninglessness of everything."[105] Such assertions reveal a manifestly false assumption, namely that, because a theist views Stirner's godless world devoid of absolutes as horrifying and

---

101 See Holz, *Der französische Existentialismus*, 106–11.

102 Helms, *Die Ideologie der anonymen Gesellschaft*, 95. ζῶον πολιτικόν (*zoon politikon*/political animal) was a phrase used by Aristotle to describe human beings.

103 Penzo, *Die existentielle Empörung*, 24.

104 See Penzo, *Die existentielle Empörung*, 297: "Naturally, I share Paterson's view that the core of Stirner's subject matter should not be seen in his relations to anarchism and Marxism, but lies instead, as Buber has already established, in the field of existentialism." 298: "At the end of this brief elucidation, it should be pointed out that the merit of Paterson's study lies in having shown English-speaking readers the figure of Stirner as a precursor of existentialism." 15: "Stirner's nihilism is nothing more than thought carried with relentless logic to its ultimate consequences."

105 Penzo, *Die existentielle Empörung*, 298.

meaningless, so Stirner must have felt the same. There is no evidence of this being the case.

The tenuous nature of Penzo's conclusions about Stirner is demonstrated by the following extract:

> Paterson writes that Stirner essentially remains a child of his time. On the one hand, he was influenced by the nihilistic literature of the nineteenth century. His work reflects the world of despair and satanism that is typical of Leopardi, Poe, Schopenhauer, [Hartmann,] Ibsen, and Baudelaire. On the other hand, Stirner's work belongs to the literature that emerged from the activity of political terrorists and was defended by them. This explains the dark, nihilistic elements that already appeared in the writings of Baudelaire, Rimbaud, and Strindberg.[106]

Even allowing for the inaccuracies that can creep into translations (my translation is from the German version), the mere suggestion of influence by authors where no record exists that Stirner knew them (Leopardi, Poe, Schopenhauer), or worse still that had not been published (Ibsen, Baudelaire, Hartmann) or even born (Rimbaud, Strindberg) before the first edition of *Der Einzige*, smacks, at the very least, of confusion on Penzo's (or his translator's) part.[107]

Another questionable contribution to the discussion of Stirner and existentialism in the anglophone world of scholarship has come from Isaiah Berlin. In a lecture on the roots of Romanticism, he firstly establishes a relationship of dependency between existentialism and Romanticism: "The central sermon of existentialism is essentially a Romantic one, namely that there is in the world nothing to lean on."[108] He then proceeds to identify Stirner as a thinker who took this logic too far, by denying not only institutions and doctrines but also theories and general propositions, culminating in the rejection of the established meanings of words themselves:

> Why should words be uniform? Why cannot I make up my own universe each time I begin? But if I do that, if there is no systematic symbolism, then I cannot think. If I cannot think, I go mad.

---

106 Penzo, *Die existentielle Empörung*, 297. For some reason, Hartmann is omitted from the first list of authors in the authorized German translation.
107 For the Italian original, see Penzo, *Max Stirner: La rivolta esistenziale*, 364. Paterson writes that *Der Einzige* "belongs with the nihilistic literature of the nineteenth century," and lists the authors mentioned by Penzo. He does not speak of influence. See Paterson, *The Nihilistic Egoist*, 313.
108 Berlin, *The Roots of Romanticism*, 142.

> To do him justice, Stirner did duly go mad. He ended his life very honourably and very consistently in a lunatic asylum as a perfectly peaceful harmless lunatic, in 1856.[109]

In fact, Stirner neither went mad, nor did he die in a lunatic asylum (although his mother did), and nor, as Berlin claimed in the original lecture (the above quotation is taken from a redacted transcript), did his death occur in the 1860s.[110] More importantly, Stirner did not propose the arbitrary implementation of words, but only that language should be emptied of its ideological content. He rejected the abstract, universal meanings of words like man (*Mensch*) or spirit (*Geist*) and criticized the unquestioning acceptance of such words' established content. Far from denying that language has any meaning at all, Stirner was trying to free language from its inherent bias, in order to allow the self-creating individual to start from the status of a blank slate rather than being the victim of conceptual expectations and preconceptions.[111] Hidden away amongst the numerous bizarre falsehoods of Berlin's assessment is at least the grain of truth that Stirner was a radical iconoclast.

Paterson's Indictment of the Nihilistic Egoist: Max Stirner

Berlin's jocular inexactitudes are in sharp contrast to the earnest pronouncements of the high priest of Stirner scholarship, Ronald Paterson. Unlike Arvon and Penzo, Paterson avoided using the word existential(ism) in the title of his book on Stirner, perhaps because it was such a fashionable term at the time of writing in the early 1970s; nihilist and egoist were much more appropriately negative labels for the heading of a polemical work. Paterson's war was with Stirner in the first instance, and he probably saw no reason to open a second front against so popular an opponent as existentialism or, indeed, to dignify Stirner with such a glamorous label. He is nonetheless at pains to point out throughout the book that the origin of Stirner's alleged nihilistic egoism is the very same sense of meaninglessness which underlies existentialism: "In the present book I have tried to locate and define the main resemblances between

---

109 Berlin, *The Roots of Romanticism*, 144.

110 In the original lecture, Berlin declared that Stirner "ended his life . . . somewhere in the middle sixties." See Isaiah Berlin, "Existentialism, Stirner, & When Romanticism Goes Too Far," YouTube, accessed June 30, 2023, https://www.youtube.com/watch?v=EC_eC32RAyc. In his defense, Berlin was speaking extemporaneously. Concerning Stirner's mother, see Mackay, *Max Stirner*, 207.

111 See Stirner, *Stirner's Critics*, 54–59; Stirner, *Max Stirner's Kleinere Schriften*, 113–18.

existentialist philosophy and the philosophy of *Der Einzige*, . . . and in doing so I have suggested that the point of departure for both Stirner and the existentialists is this crucial experience of the meaninglessness of all things."[112] Paterson falls squarely into that group of post-war critics whose anachronistic readings of Stirner rely heavily on the prevailing spirit of existentialism.

It becomes clear though, in the course of Paterson's diatribe, that the root of his grievance against Stirner is his lack of religious belief: "The vision which Stirner unfolds is the vision of a world without God and hence without any unifying or directive value; it is the vision of a meaningless world, in which there are no inscribed purposes or true values; it is the vision of a world which is strictly no 'world' but rather a moral and metaphysical chaos."[113] The inference that godlessness necessarily means purposelessness is, however, entirely Paterson's. Stirner does not reach such a conclusion; it is rather Paterson, as a man of God contemplating what Stirner's annihilation of absolutes and abstractions would mean for his own world, who arrives at this result. This misplaced reasoning, like Penzo's mentioned above, allows Paterson to adjudge Stirner a nihilist because the feelings that Stirner's godlessness inspire in Paterson are compatible with the common definition of existential nihilism: "His atheism is the denial that reality has any fixed and necessary meaning. It is an affirmation of the ultimate insignificance of all things. The egoism of the total atheist is thus the egoism of the nihilist, and thus the total atheist, according to Stirner, is ultimately identical with the *nihilistic egoist*."[114] The phrase "according to Stirner" is particularly misleading because it could imply that this was Stirner's opinion; what Paterson really means is that "total atheism" (whatever that is) is equivalent to nihilism according to his own assessment of what life would be like in Stirner's godless world. In other words, Paterson is a kind of Nietzschean passive nihilist, who assumes that, if one interpretation of meaning collapses (namely his own), then existence can have no meaning at all.[115] He then proceeds to project his own experience of passive nihilism onto Stirner, as if Stirner considered that the removal of God created an absence rather than an opportunity.

Paterson argues that existentialism pusillanimously recoils from the consequences of its nihilistic roots:

---

112 Paterson, *The Nihilistic Egoist*, 317.
113 Paterson, *The Nihilistic Egoist*, 226.
114 Paterson, *The Nihilistic Egoist*, 217.
115 See Nietzsche, *The Will to Power*, 43: "*One* interpretation has failed, but since it was considered *the* interpretation, it now seems as if there is no meaning in existence at all, as if all is *in vain*."

> To the truly self-consistent nihilist this is existentialism's real point of failure. On the one hand, the existentialist seeks to remain true to his original vision of the meaninglessness and futility of everything; . . . on the other hand, his stark personal reality is that he finds himself *unable* to appropriate the truth of nihilism existentially: . . . it is at this point that he clutches at the artifice of commitment, hoping to save himself from nihilistic despair by a desperate leap towards a faith that will restore meaning and purpose to his shattered world.[116]

Paterson's reasoning seems to be that, although the existentialist's starting point must always be existential nihilism because existentialism relies on the assumptions of nihilism for the basis of its worldview, the existentialist must always reject nihilism, since she or he finds its consequences unacceptably desolate. According to this theory, a fully developed existentialist can never be a nihilist, which could explain why there is no historical example of a self-confessed existential nihilist. Existential nihilism, in this case, would just be a temporary precondition of existentialism. However, Paterson then somewhat confuses matters: "If an existentialist is a man who seeks to experience the encounter with nothingness inwardly and in his whole person, . . . then the refusal to make the truth of nihilism one's own and build one's life entirely within its shadow is indeed a refusal of existentialism itself. The existentialist cannot find salvation in a significant, purposeful faith without ceasing to be an existentialist."[117] This would apparently mean not only that existential nihilism is the truth of existentialism, but also that all of those whom one knows today as existentialists (Kierkegaard, Sartre, et al.) are not actually existentialists at all. It would, indeed, leave no existentialists whatsoever—unless the only one were: Max Stirner.

Equally bewildering is Paterson's assumption that the existentialist seeks to experience, encounter, appropriate, and live within nothingness. Nothingness may be what the existential nihilist discovers at the heart of existence, in a world where the myths associated with religion (God, immortality of the soul, absolute values, etc.) are no longer credible. But it is hard to argue that the encounter is sought; the narratives of existentialism show nothingness being experienced with disorientation and dismay, which accounts for the search for meaning *malgré tout*. The explanation for this distortion may lie in the fact that Paterson is playing a rather clumsy blame game. By making lack of faith a matter of volition rather than the product of enlightened reason, he puts himself in the position of being able to chastise the nihilist by asserting, "it is in . . . such a vacuum that the nihilistic egoist [i.e., Stirner] has consciously and

---

116 Paterson, *The Nihilistic Egoist*, 238.
117 Paterson, *The Nihilistic Egoist*, 238.

voluntarily taken up his abode. It is in the dimension of meaninglessness that he lives and moves and has his being."[118] The moralistic conclusion, therefore, is that "the true nihilist does not want to be saved."[119] Worse still: "The total atheist [i.e., Stirner] does not find himself abandoned by God: it is God who is abandoned by the total atheist."[120] Finally, having posited unbelief as an act of heinous free will, Paterson naturally introduces the concept of sin into the discussion: "To the religious believer, . . . Stirner's account ought to shed a grim light on the nature and implications of 'sin', conceived as estrangement from God, from the ground and goal of our being; for in his proud self-sufficiency The Unique One is the archetype of the sinful individual, basing his life on a conscious refusal of present grace or future salvation."[121] As an exercise in religious instruction, this is no doubt useful, but it sheds no light at all on the nature or meaning of Stirner's thought.

As for his insight into the nature of the existentialist, Paterson clarifies to some extent the earlier confusion by making a distinction between the theoretical and practical variety: "The existentialist is defined by his commitment to this [nihilistic] truth, which renders all other commitments impossible; although actual existentialists, in their desperate search for meaningful commitments, have . . . refused this original commitment to meaninglessness, and it has . . . been left to the nihilist to preserve the nihilistic truth which is at the heart of existentialism."[122] In other words, by nihilist Paterson means existential nihilist, by true existentialism he means existential nihilism, and by actual existentialist he means a lapsed nihilist. Again, the point of these redefinitions is to make Stirner appear the worst of a thoroughly bad bunch, in the guise of the one unique example of an existential nihilist. Thus, Paterson declares:

> Meaninglessness, for Stirner, is not just an objective feature of experienced reality which the nihilist simply discovers and passively records: meaninglessness is the household demon which he himself unleashes, it is his personal mark which he deliberately stamps upon his experience, it is a governing and universal phenomenon which he has freely chosen and wholly wills; and thus the metaphysical desert which he inhabits is ultimately a desert of his own creation; in looking into the abyss he is ultimately looking into himself.[123]

118 Paterson, *The Nihilistic Egoist*, 241.
119 Paterson, *The Nihilistic Egoist*, 233.
120 Paterson, *The Nihilistic Egoist*, 224.
121 Paterson, *The Nihilistic Egoist*, 317–18.
122 Paterson, *The Nihilistic Egoist*, 241. See 251: "To consummate the original truth of existentialism . . . is to recognize oneself as a nihilistic egoist."
123 Paterson, *The Nihilistic Egoist*, 242. The abyss image is lifted from Nietzche, *Beyond Good and Evil*, 84.

Largely ignoring Stirner's ideas, while considering only the implications of Stirner's godlessness for a devout believer, Paterson's purple prose continues, littered with inappropriate adjectives and inaccurate assertions: "Rootless, vagrant, detached; frivolous, unstable, irresponsible; squandering his fluid and transient being in a consciously promiscuous career of deliberately gratuitous acts of repudiation: in the solitary and arbitrary figure of The Unique One is personified everything that is negative and destructive. On the grim, predatory features of the ruthless egoist Stirner has etched the hollow, dissipated features of the uncaring nihilist."[124]

The allegation of nihilism, by which he unquestionably means existential nihilism, is at the core of Paterson's condemnation of Stirner. Paterson sums up the case for the prosecution as follows:

> Like the existentialists, Stirner starts from the nihilistic premise. Meaninglessness, the essential nullity of everything, is for Stirner the governing and universal phenomenon, the key feature of the individual's experience, draining it of all significance and value. To exist is to live—not under the reign of God, or of law, or of humanity—but under the reign of nothingness. "All things are nothing to me!" says Stirner in the primordial accents of the nihilist. Unlike the existentialists, however, Stirner moves from his nihilistic premise to an equally nihilistic dénouement. The existence into which he finally projects himself remains the Godless, lawless, inhuman existence of his original instinct.[125]

In Stirner's defense, this is plainly neither what he says nor means. He does not assert the nullity of everything, nor does he uphold the reign of nothingness. He proclaims the mythical nature of abstractions and external causes, which is no doubt a form of annihilation, but by no means a universal one; and he implies that an individual's consciousness is a temporary phenomenon confined to a person's lifetime, which is again a form of annihilation, but only of the dream of immortality.

Stirner describes fictional constructs like God, humanity, and fatherland as unreal; sin, as well as good and evil, as making no sense; but nowhere does he refer to life itself as meaningless. On the contrary, he makes it clear that he is untroubled by his own ephemerality while reveling in the replacement of eternal, external masters by the transient, autonomous self:

> If God, if mankind, . . . have substance enough in themselves to be all in all to themselves, then I feel that *I* shall still less lack that, and that I shall have no complaint to make of my "emptiness."

124 Paterson, *The Nihilistic Egoist*, 248.
125 Paterson, *The Nihilistic Egoist*, 242.

[Hat Gott, hat die Menschheit, . . . Gehalt genug in sich, um sich Alles in Allem zu sein: so spüre Ich, dass es *Mir* noch weit weniger daran fehlen wird, und dass Ich über meine "Leerheit" keine Klage zu führen haben werde.][126]

Stirner's exaltation of the ego is plainly incompatible with the stygian imagery of existentialism: "Every higher essence above me, be it God, be it man, weakens the feeling of my uniqueness, and pales only before the sun of this consciousness."[127] This is the language of celebration, not of disorientation or despair.

Paterson's case rests to a large extent on the significance of the concept of nothingness in *Der Einzige*, which he considers similar, if not identical, to that found in Sartre: "For both Stirner and Sartre, then, it is Nothingness which is at the heart of the world, inasmuch as the being who brings the world into being is himself a Nothingness."[128] Paterson bases his judgment on such comments by Sartre as: "If man as the existentialist sees him is not definable, it is because to begin with he is nothing."[129] There are undeniable parallels here with Stirner's view of human existence. Concerning the indefinability of the self, Stirner writes: "They say of God, 'names name thee not'. That holds good of me: no *concept* expresses me, nothing that is designated as my essence exhausts me."[130] As for the nothingness of the self, Stirner says: "I, this nothing, shall put forth my *creations* from myself."[131] However, as noted above, the positions of Stirner and the existentialists regarding the subjective perspective of the unique, transient individual are far from dissimilar. What is dissimilar, though, is the effect that these parameters of human existence have on their very different versions of the individual existent.

---

126 *EO*, 7; *EE*, 15.
127 *EO*, 324; *EE*, 370: "Jedes höhere Wesen über Mir, sei es Gott, sei es der Mensch, schwächt das Gefühl meiner Einzigkeit und erblicht erst vor der Sonne dieses Bewusstseins."
128 Paterson, *The Nihilistic Egoist*, 177.
129 Sartre, *Existentialism and Humanism*, 28.
130 *EO*, 324; *EE*, 370: "Man sagt von Gott: 'Namen nennen Dich nicht.' Das gilt von Mir: kein *Begriff* drückt Mich aus, nichts, was man als mein Wesen angibt, erschöpft Mich."
131 *EO*, 209; *EE*, 240: "Ich, dieses Nichts, werde meine *Schöpfungen* aus Mir hervor treiben."

Der Einzige und sein Eigentum: A Tale of Two Nothings

Paterson may be the most vociferous of Stirner's critics, but he is certainly not alone in associating the concept of nothingness in Stirner with what implicitly amounts to existential nihilism. As seen in chapter 4 above, Bernstein, Lucchesi, Heman, Penzo, Lütkehaus, Ulrich, and Dod all belong to this group, to which Löwith and Camus can also be added. These and other upholders of Stirner's alleged nihilism do not tire of pointing out that his magnum opus is sandwiched between two nothings, in the form of the work's opening and closing line, "Ich hab' Mein' Sach' auf Nichts gestellt," which Byington renders as "All things are nothing to me."[132] The theologian, Lucchesi, seems to have been the first to make specific reference to the significance of this dual positioning: "Stirner's one-sided individualism begins with nothing and ends in nothing."[133] Inevitably, Paterson was not able to resist making the same point: "The Unique One creates his personal universe by reproducing the Nothingness of existence, which he therefore begins and ends by affirming."[134]

It is not simply that two nothings are worse than one for those who share Parmenides's horror of nothingness, but that their placement at the entrance and exit of *Der Einzige*'s text evokes Epicurus's idea of human life being sandwiched between two nothings, which is expressed thus by Lucretius in *De rerum natura* (On the Nature of the Universe), the main source of Epicurean ideas: "Look back at the eternity that passed before we were born, and mark how utterly it counts to us as nothing. This is a mirror that Nature holds up to us, in which we may see the time that shall be after we are dead."[135] This plainly atheistic idea (atheistic, at least, in the sense of denying an afterlife and therefore a god that cares about humans), has resurfaced periodically in the modern era. Examples are numerous, and it is instructive to consider the diversity of outlooks of those that have expressed such a view. On the one hand, there are those who fall squarely into the negativist camp. These include the dark Jacobean tragedian, John Webster (c. 1578–c. 1632), who, in *The Duchess of Malfi* (1612–1613), has the unfortunate Antonio declare: "Heaven fashion'd us of nothing; and we strive / To bring ourselves to nothing."[136] The archetypal pessimist, Schopenhauer, wrote in *Parerga and Paralipomena*: "You can also look upon our life as an episode unprofitably disturbing the

---

132 *EO*, 5, 234; *EE*, 13, 370.
133 Lucchesi, *Die Individualitätsphilosophie Max Stirners*, 96.
134 Paterson, *The Nihilistic Egoist*, 250.
135 Lucretius, *On the Nature of the Universe*, 91.
136 Webster, *The Duchess of Malfi*, 3.4.

blessed calm of nothingness."[137] Bazarov, in Turgenev's *Fathers and Sons*, takes an even grimmer view: "And the period of time in which it is my lot to live is so infinitesimal compared with the eternity in which I have not been and shall not be."[138]

On the more positive side, somewhere between (or beyond?) pessimism and optimism, there is Nietzsche's verse from the *Dionysus-Dithyrambs* (1888), which marked the coining of the phrase *zwischen zwei Nichtse* in German: "Between two nothings / Huddled up, / A question-mark, / A weary riddle."[139] Michel Onfray, an advocate of hedonism, adopted Nietzsche's phrase as a sub-heading and slogan in his *Hedonist Manifesto*: "Between Two Nothings / Every existence entails an emergence from nothing, and the only prospect is to return to it someday. Life unfolds between two nothings."[140] Onfray coins his own phrase in French for this idea, the clear, but wordy, "L'entre-deux néants"; no such term exists in English, but I offer up to Hermes "mesomidenika," in the manner of Mesopotamia. Finally, perhaps the most positive reference of all to mesomidenika can be found in Eric Idle's crucifixion song, "Always Look on the Bright Side of Life": "You know, you come from nothing / You're going back to nothing / What have you lost? Nothing."[141] Even if Stirner had had the Epicurean two nothings in mind when he used the word in the first and last sentences of *Der Einzige*, the heterogeneity of the concept's users hardly permits the assumption of existential nihilism.

Moreover, Stirner's detractors, who claim to recognize his nihilistic tendencies in this supposed clue, disregard the fact that the book's title includes no negative references whatsoever, and concentrate instead on the less prominent but far more controversial line that starts and finishes the text. In so doing, they ignore the primary meaning of *Nichts* in the sentence in question, extrapolating instead from the fact of Stirner's self-confessed atheism to create an image of the existential void. His critics, to borrow the words of Unamuno's attack on atheists, "have invested

---

137 Schopenhauer, *Essays and Aphorisms*, 47. See Laforgue, *Oeuvres complètes*, i, 46: "Man between two nothings is but a day of misery." Laforgue (1860–1887) was a disciple of Schopenhauer and Hartmann.

138 Turgenev, *Fathers and Sons*, 208–9. See Sartre, *Nausea*, 190: "And all those existents ... came from nowhere and were going nowhere."

139 Nietzsche, *The Complete Works of Nietzsche*, 17:181; Nietzsche, *Werke*, 6.3:390: "zwischen zwei Nichtse / eingekrümmt, / ein Fragezeichen, / ein müdes Rätsel."

140 Onfray, *A Hedonist Manifesto*, 109. See Onfray, *Atheist Manifesto*, 66: "Each life constitutes a brief interlude between the nothingness that came before it and the nothingness that comes after it."

141 Eric Idle, "Always Look on the Bright Side of Life," *Lyrics.com*, accessed June 30, 2023, https://www.lyrics.com/lyric/1921933/Always+Look+on+the+Bright+Side+of+Life.

Nothingness with substance and personality"; with more, at any rate, than a careful reading of Stirner bears out.[142] One might describe the resultant theories of Stirner's nihilism as much ado about two nothings.

The actual context of the heading, "Ich hab' Mein' Sach' auf Nichts gestellt" (which demonstrates the inadequacy of Byington's translation), can be found in the lines of text that immediately follow it, where Stirner rejects all external obligations, which he lists thus:

> What is not supposed to be my concern! First and foremost the good cause, then God's cause, the cause of mankind, of truth, of freedom, of humanity, of justice; further, the cause of my people, my prince, my fatherland; finally, even the cause of mind and a thousand other causes.

> [Was soll nicht alles Meine Sache sein! Vor allem die gute Sache, dann die Sache Gottes, die Sache der Menschheit, der Wahrheit, der Freiheit, der Humanität, der Gerechtigkeit; ferner die Sache Meines Volkes, Meines Fürsten, Meines Vaterlandes; endlich gar die Sache des Geistes und tausend andere Sachen.][143]

Stirner instead makes his cause *nothing but* himself:

> The divine is God's concern; the human, "man's." My concern is neither the divine nor the human, not the true, good, just, free, etc., but solely what is *mine*, and it is not a general one, but is—*unique*, as I am unique.

> [Das Göttliche ist Gottes Sache, das Menschliche Sache "des Menschen." Meine Sache ist weder das Göttliche noch das Menschliche, ist nicht das Wahre, Gute, Rechte, Freie usw., sondern allein das *Meinige*, und sie ist keine allgemeine, sondern ist—*einzig*, wie Ich einzig bin.][144]

The *Nichts* in the heading, therefore, refers to all abstract, generalized, external causes; Stirner submits to none of them. This oft-misconstrued line is thus a rejection of absolutes, a confession of nominalism even, but definitely not a declaration of nihilism. Stirner makes his meaning even clearer by explaining that the same principle of rejecting all causes but one's own also applies to all general causes, which likewise are concerned

---

142 Unamuno, *The Tragic Sense of Life*, 122.
143 *EO*, 5; *EE*, 13.
144 *EO*, 7; *EE*, 15.

with *nothing but* themselves: "God and mankind have concerned themselves for nothing, for nothing but themselves."[145]

As a skilled wordsmith and self-professed atheist, Stirner may well have intended the word *Nichts* in the opening epigram and elsewhere to embrace a secondary meaning, namely the nothingness of the self, in terms of the transience of each unique individual's existence. Stirner does not, as theologians are wont to do, fill the gaps in human knowledge with God. Instead, he leaves them as gaps; where God once stood, there is nothingness, above all before birth and after death. This is not dissimilar to Roquentin's view of life: "It is I, *it is I* who pull myself from the nothingness to which I aspire."[146] However, Stirner is careful to distinguish between the empty, created nothingness of generalized, fictional causes, and the creative nothing of the self that is grounded, for a lifetime at least, in material reality: "I am not nothing in the sense of emptiness, but I am the creative nothing, the nothing out of which I myself as creator create everything."[147] Stirner, therefore, is not, as is so often assumed, presenting a doctrine of nothingness, but of autonomous self-reliance within the parameters of finite existence; as such, he should be seen as a demythologizing egoist rather than a dismal and destructive nihilist.

In the world of anglophone Stirner scholarship, which would of course include Paterson, a mitigating factor concerning the misunderstanding of Stirner's *Nichts*, is Byington's loose translation of the line in question as "All things are nothing to me."[148] Although it rolls easily off the tongue, it has quite different connotations to the original German and is much more suggestive of a pervasively nihilistic outlook. Presumably for this reason, Carroll, in the 1971 abridged translation, altered it to "I have founded my affair on nothing," which is less misleading, if also less pleasing to the ear.[149] In the original 1907 edition, "I have set my affair on nothing" is offered in a footnote as "the literal translation."[150] Neither the inaccurate original translation nor the clumsy, more literal one, even in conjunction with the ensuing phrase "nothing but

---

145 EO, 6; EE, 15: "Gott und die Menschheit haben ihre Sache auf Nichts gestellt, auf nichts als auf Sich."

146 Sartre, *Nausea*, 145.

147 EO, 7; EE, 15: "Ich bin nicht Nichts im Sinne der Leerheit, sondern das schöpferische Nichts, das Nichts, aus welchem Ich selbst als Schöpfer Alles schaffe." In the first edition of 1845 (released in October 1844), the first *nicht* is omitted, so it reads: "Ich bin Nichts im Sinne der Leerheit" (I am nothing in the sense of emptiness). The *sondern* (but rather) that follows makes it clear that this is a printing error, but one which almost certainly added fuel to the nihilism fire. See Stirner, *Der Einzige* (1845), 8.

148 EO, 3.

149 EO (1971), 39.

150 EO (1907), 3.

themselves," is conducive to a ready understanding of Stirner's meaning, and they have both almost certainly helped to encourage the already widespread perception of Stirner as a nihilist.[151] Landstreicher's recent translation of the line as "I have based my affair on nothing" has not done much to improve things.[152] A clearer translation might be "I have made nothing my cause," or, better still: "There is nothing that I have made my cause."

Nothingness does not, in fact, play a major role in Stirner's philosophy. It is a point of reference and an expression of conviction, but not a *primum mobile*. It is a counterbalance to its opposite, being, but it does not overwhelm it. Stirner does not ask the scientific question of whether the void is real, nor the metaphysical question of why there is something and not nothing, nor, unlike Hegel and Sartre, the ontological question about the relationship between being and nothingness. The word nothing has a far more limited scope in Stirner's thought. As a noun, it is used primarily to describe the unreality of abstractions, as invented phantasms with no substance, much as Harari depicts the myths of mankind.[153] Stirner, like Harari, is fixated on the problem of abstractions, but not on the idea of nothingness. The following gives an insight into the relationship between these two concepts in Stirner's outlook:

> Feuerbach . . . is always harping upon *being*. In this he too, with all his antagonism to Hegel and the absolute philosophy, is stuck fast in abstraction; for "being" is abstraction, as is even "the I." Only *I am* not abstraction alone: *I am* all in all, consequently even abstraction or nothing. I am all and nothing.
>
> [Feuerbach pocht . . . immer auf *das Sein*. Darin bleibt auch er, bei aller Gegnerschaft gegen Hegel und die absolute Philosophie, in der Abstraktion stecken; denn "das Sein" ist Abstraktion, wie selbst "das Ich." Nur *Ich bin* nicht Abstraktion allein, *Ich bin* alles in allem, folglich selbst Abstraktion oder Nichts, Ich bin alles und Nichts.][154]

For Stirner, in other words, nothingness is a descriptive quality of abstractions; it has no connotation of apprehension or disquiet. Thus, when Copleston says that "Stirner's obscure remarks about 'creative nothing' recall to mind certain aspects of Heidegger's thought," it is important to add that Heidegger's notion of nothingness differs greatly from

---

151 *EO* (1907), 5.
152 Stirner, *The Unique and Its Property*, 25.
153 See Harari, *Sapiens*, 31: "There are no gods in the universe, no nations, no money, no human rights, no laws and no justice outside the common imagination of human beings."
154 *EO*, 300; *EE*, 343–44.

Stirner's in this respect.[155] The difference is most evident in Heidegger's concept of *Angst*, which he associates with nothingness: "The 'nothing' with which anxiety brings us face to face, unveils the nullity by which Dasein, in its very *basis*, is defined; and this basis itself is as thrownness into death."[156] Nothingness in Heidegger, unlike in Stirner, is inextricably linked to a negative perception of death and personal extinction. Stirner's creative nothing is a wholly positive construct and can hardly be called obscure when viewed in the context of the intellectual environment within which Stirner was operating.

It can reasonably be assumed that Stirner's most immediate source for the idea behind the term "creative nothing" was Feuerbach, whose *Das Wesen des Christentums* includes two chapters, "The Mystery of Providence and Creation out of Nothing" and "The Significance of the Creation in Judaism," which deal with the creation myths of Christianity and Judaism respectively. The language Feuerbach uses is reminiscent of Stirner's subsequent utterances on the subject. In the former, he writes: "The culminating point of the principle of subjectivity is creation out of nothing"; and in the latter one finds: "The creation out of nothing ... had its origin only in the unfathomable depth of Hebrew egoism."[157] Feuerbach had, by demonstrating the anthropomorphic nature of religion, sought to replace God with man: "*Homo homini Deus est*:—this is the great practical principle:—this is the axis on which revolves the history of the world."[158] It is quite natural that Stirner, who set out to extend Feuerbach's method from man as a collective to man as an individual, should transfer the man-made attributes of God at the same time, especially as it afforded him the opportunity to indulge in some ironic humor at the expense of religion.

Stirner's notion of the creative nothing has far more to do with an irreverent response to the Christian theological interpretation of Genesis 1:1–2 and 2 Maccabees 7:28 than it does with the Nietzschean or existential nihilist sense of the word nothingness.[159] It signifies the finite individual's usurpation of the creative function of the uncreated, omnipotent God of Christianity. But arguably of greater importance in this respect is Hegel's concept of nothing, with which Stirner would certainly have been acquainted. The relationship between being and

---

155 Copleston, *A History of Philosophy*, 7.2:236.
156 Heidegger, *Being and Time*, 356.
157 Feuerbach, *The Essence of Christianity*, 100, 116.
158 Feuerbach, *The Essence of Christianity*, 268.
159 Genesis 1:1–2: "In the beginning God created the heaven and the earth. And the earth was without form, and void, and darkness was upon the face of the deep." 2 Maccabees 7:28: "Look upon the heaven and earth, and all that is therein, and consider that God made them of things that were not."

nothing is a fundamental topic of philosophical debate stretching back to Parmenides, and one to which Hegel naturally also turned his attention. In Hegel's deliberations on the subject, one can immediately recognize the coordinates of Stirner's interplay between creation and annihilation. Hegel writes, for instance: "This mere Being, as it is mere abstraction, is therefore the absolutely negative: which, in a similarly immediate aspect, is just Nothing."[160]

In his *Wissenschaft der Logik* (Science of Logic, 1812–1816), Hegel introduces the triad of being-nothing-becoming, where nothingness, defined as "complete emptiness, absence of all determination and content" is part of a dialectical equation, rather than an object of existential horror:[161] "It is the dialectical immanent nature of being and nothing themselves to manifest their unity, that is, becoming, as their truth."[162] Nothing is, therefore, together with being, a necessary prerequisite for becoming, which annihilates both being and nothing: "Becoming is the vanishing of being in nothing and of nothing in being and the vanishing of being and nothing generally."[163] The result is that nothing is rendered, existentially at least, a harmless part of the process of becoming: "Being and non-being are the same, therefore it is the same whether [I am or am not.]"[164] This also means, of course, that nothing is no obstacle to immortality: "The popular, especially oriental proverbs, that all that exists has the germ of death in its very birth, that death, on the other hand, is the entrance into new life, express at bottom the same union of being and nothing."[165] Although Stirner, like all so-called Left Hegelians, is critical of Hegel (and not least of his conciliatory attitude towards religion), his concept of *Nichts* is essentially based on Hegel's idea that it represents the negative impulse within the dialectical process.

It is in this Hegelian sense of *Nichts*, as the absolute of the antithesis (a word Hegel only employed to describe Kantian dialectics, but which is used, most notably by Heinrich Moritz Chalybäus [1796–1862], to signify the second step of Hegel's triadic, dialectical model), that Stirner envisages the activity of the self in relation to the state:[166]

---

160 Hegel, *The Logic of Hegel*, 161.
161 Hegel, *Hegel's Science of Logic*, 82.
162 Hegel, *Hegel's Science of Logic*, 105.
163 Hegel, *Hegel's Science of Logic*, 106.
164 Hegel, *Hegel's Science of Logic*, 82. The part in square brackets is omitted from the translation. See Lütkehaus, *Nichts*, 660–61: "As it is the declared intention of Hegelian logic to use the determinate negation as a positive element of movement, so too the indeterminate negation of the '*pure nothing*' is positivized under the cover of the identity of being and nothingness."
165 Hegel, *Hegel's Science of Logic*, 83–84.
166 See Chalybäus, *Historical Development of Speculative Philosophy*, 366.

Henceforth what is to be done is no longer about the state ... but about me. With this all questions about the prince's power, the constitution, and so on, sink into their true abyss and their true nothingness. I, this nothing, shall put forth my *creations* from myself.

[Es ist fortan nicht mehr um den *Staat* ... zu tun, sondern um Mich. Damit versinken alle Fragen über Fürstenmacht, Konstitution usw. in ihren wahren Abgrund und ihr wahres Nichts. Ich, dieses Nichts, werde meine *Schöpfungen* aus Mir hervor treiben.][167]

At the same time, Stirner also indicates the secondary meaning of nothingness associated with the transience of the individual ego, which stands in opposition to the generalized abstraction of the absolute self.[168] The primary sense in Stirner remains, however, Hegel's second or negatively rational moment, although Stirner seems to be more interested in its quality of annihilation, which he implements enthusiastically in his campaign against sacred abstractions, than in its qualities of mediation and preservation implied by Hegel's concept of sublation (*Aufhebung*). Annihilation is an important aspect of Stirner's program of self-empowerment through ownership, as is demonstrated by the following remark: "to be able to utilize it [society] completely I transform it ... into my property and my creature; that is, I annihilate it."[169] But this form of annihilation is not part of the definition of existential nihilism outlined above, nor even of political nihilism, as it takes place on the nonphysical level of ideas.

Stirner's terminology places his philosophical project firmly within the context of post-Hegelian discourse.[170] But his conceptual mimicry of Hegel disguises to some extent Stirner's ideological opposition to Hegelianism. In sharp contrast to Hegelian dialectics, all processes of development in Stirner's thought begin and end with the self:[171]

---

167   *EO*, 209; *EE*, 240.
168   See *EO*, 163; *EE*, 188.
169   *EO*, 161; *EE*, 185: "um sie [die Gesellschaft] aber vollständig benutzen zu können, verwandle Ich sie ... in mein Eigentum und mein Geschöpf, d. h. ich vernichte sie."
170   Like Hegel, though by no means so thoroughly or extensively, Stirner divides his book into sections and subsections of three. Kast considers this a trivialization of Hegel's triadic system. See Kast, *Max Stirners Destruktion der spekulativen Philosophie*, 132.
171   See Kast, *Max Stirners Destruktion der spekulativen Philosophie*, 129: "Stirner breaks with Hegel's dialectical method, dismantles it, and finally destroys it."

All predicates of objects are my statements, my judgments, my—creatures. If they want to tear themselves loose from me and be something for themselves, or actually overawe me, then I have nothing more pressing to do than to take them back into their nothing, into me the creator. God, Christ, trinity, morality, the good, etc., are such creatures, of which I must not merely allow myself to say that they are truths, but also that they are deceptions. As I once willed and decreed their existence, so I want to have license to will their non-existence too.

[Alle Prädikate von den Gegenständen sind meine Aussagen, meine Urteile, meine—Geschöpfe. Wollen sie sich losreißen von Mir, und etwas für sich sein, oder gar Mir imponieren, so habe Ich nichts Eiligeres zu tun, als sie in ihr Nichts, d.h. in Mich, den Schöpfer, zurückzunehmen. Gott, Christus, Dreieinigkeit, Sittlichkeit, das Gute usw. sind solche Geschöpfe, von denen Ich Mir nicht bloß erlauben muss, zu sagen, sie seien Wahrheiten, sondern auch, sie seien Täuschungen. Wie Ich einmal ihr Dasein gewollt und dekretiert habe, so will Ich auch ihr Nichtsein wollen dürfen.][172]

As Kast observes: "By accentuating the will of the concrete individual, . . . Stirner sets himself apart from Hegel, using Hegel's own terminology."[173]

But despite his antagonism towards Hegel, Stirner's concept of *Nichts* nonetheless derives its conceptual framework directly from Hegel. Even though there is a tenuous link between the dialectical sense of nothingness in Hegel, via Fichte's notion of being and nothingness, through European Romanticism and Kierkegaard, to existentialism, it is of no particular relevance for the understanding of Stirner's use of the term. Stirner completely avoids the element of despair which characterizes the Romantic confrontation with nothingness. Giacomo Leopardi (1798–1837), who has been described as "the supreme exponent of the Romantic malady of the soul," provides a good example of such an understanding of nothingness, which contrasts strikingly with Stirner's:[174] "All is nothingness in the world, including my despair."[175] Like Stirner, he describes the self as nothing, but what for Stirner represents the opportunity of a blank slate, is for Leopardi the torment of hopeless desolation: "I was frightened to find myself in the midst of nothingness, a nothing myself. I felt as if I were suffocating, thinking and feeling that all is nothing, solid nothing."[176]

---

172 *EO*, 298; *EE*, 341.
173 Kast, *Max Stirners Destruktion der spekulativen Philosophie*, 81.
174 Schenk, *The Mind of the European Romantics*, 49.
175 Leopardi, *Zibaldone*, 75.
176 Leopardi, *Zibaldone*, 82.

Nothing Comes from Two Nothings

It is arguably the commentator's urge to compartmentalize and, during the existentialist era, to do so while looking through an existentialist lens, which has resulted in Stirner's references to *Nichts* being so frequently misinterpreted. But another reason lies in the conceptual ambiguity of the word itself. This starts with the contradiction that, as the ancient Greeks discovered, by positing nothing, one automatically describes something, the so-called paradox of negative existentials, which has troubled philosophers, theologians, and writers ever since. Parmenides, the father of metaphysics, started off the discussion with his categorical rejection of nothingness: "What is for being and thinking must be; for it can be, and nothing can not."[177] Sartre puzzled over the paradox in *La Nausée*: "In order to imagine nothingness, you had to be there already, right in the world, with your eyes wide open and alive; nothingness was just an idea in my head, an existing idea floating in that immensity: this nothingness hadn't come *before* existence, it was an existence like any other."[178] Tom Stoppard reveals the problematic nature of the concept in all its absurdity in his existential tragicomedy *Rosencrantz and Guildenstern are Dead* (1966):

> ROSENCRANTZ: We might as well be dead. Do you think death could possibly be a boat?
> GUILDENSTERN: No, no, no. . . . Death is . . . not. Death isn't. You take my meaning. Death is the ultimate negative. Not-being. You can't not-be on a boat.
> ROSENCRANTZ: I've frequently not been on boats.
> GUILDENSTERN: No, no, no—what you've been is not on boats.[179]

Nothing is, therefore, a word that at best defies definition and at worst is self-annihilating. In Fregean terms, it can always have a sense, but only has the appearance of a reference when used to describe an absence, though only insofar as the appearance does *not* include that which is absent.[180] This obscurity of meaning acts as both a spur to the imagination and an aid to misunderstanding.

---

177 Barnes, *Early Greek Philosophy*, 132. See Green, *Nothing Matters*, x: "What is this *nothing* that we can't actually see, touch or feel? Is it absolute? Is it relative to everything else? If we are able to think about it, write and read about it, is it something, and if so wouldn't it *not* be nothing?"
178 Sartre, *Nausea*, 192–93.
179 Stoppard, *Rosencrantz & Guildenstern Are Dead*, 3.
180 See Frege, "Über Sinn und Bedeutung," 25–50.

Its ambiguity is only increased by the fact that the word *Nichts* is both a noun and an indefinite pronoun. As a noun it means nothingness, nonexistence, and the void, while as a pronoun it means not anything, as in the absence of something, and can be used together with other words (prepositions, conjunctions, and quantifiers) such as *anderes*, *außer*, and *als* (else, except, but). In the case of the infamous heading of the prologue of *Der Einzige*, the primary meaning of *Nichts* is as a pronoun, while the possible secondary meaning is as a noun. Admittedly, *Nichts* is capitalized, which would imply that it is meant as a noun, but Stirner, whose capitalization is consistently unorthodox anyway, is quoting from Goethe's poem, "Vanitas! vanitatum vanitas!" where *Nichts* is also capitalized, and where it means "nothing in particular" rather than nonexistence or the philosophical concept of nothingness.[181]

The fact that the poem's first line is a relatively well-known quotation gives Stirner license to imbue the capitalized word *Nichts* with meaning, but it is still clear that the primary sense in Stirner's reproduction is as in Goethe's original, which describes a man who has tried devoting himself to money, possessions, women, travel, fame, and war, and after a series of disasters and disappointments, has decided to dedicate himself to nothing (i.e., to none of these things), with the result that he has finally found contentment. The final stanza includes the lines: "My trust is placed in nothing now, / Hurrah! / At my command the world must bow, / Hurrah!"[182] It is clear how well the sentiments expressed here correspond to Stirner's philosophy of individual autonomy, which may help to explain the repetition of the poem's first line in Stirner's magnum opus. An added bonus for Stirner may have been the intimation of the secondary meaning of *Nichts* in the title of Goethe's poem, "Vanitas! vanitatum vanitas!" which refers to the Vulgate biblical phrase, "Vanitas vanitatum dixit Ecclesiastes vanitas vanitatum omnia vanitas," used in Christianity to remind believers of the transience of earthly life, for instance in funerary art and memento mori.[183]

On the rare occasions in *Der Einzige* where Stirner uses the word *Nichts* solely as a noun, he invariably does so in the Hegelian sense, to describe the nothingness of an abstraction or the process of ontological annihilation, for example: "Let me then . . . concern myself for *myself*, who am equally with God the nothing of all others, who am my all, who am

---

181 See Goethe, *Goethe's Gedichte*, 1:88–89.
182 Goethe, *The Poems of Goethe*, 99; Goethe, *Goethe's Gedichte*, 1:89: "Nun hab' ich mein Sach auf Nichts gestellt. / Juchhe! / Und mein gehört die ganze Welt. / Juchhe!"
183 Ecclesiastes 1:2, partially repeated at 12:8. An English translation is: "Vanity of vanities says the preacher, vanity of vanities all is vanity."

the only one."[184] He uses *nichts* far more frequently as a pronoun, which leads to a further problem in English, where nouns are not capitalized as in German, meaning that there is no recognizable difference between the noun and pronoun forms of the English word nothing. Thus, the translation of "Mir geht nichts über Mich!" is "Nothing is more to me than myself!"[185] If, in this case, "Nothing" is misread as a noun, instead of meaning "no other thing," the sentence could conceivably be considered, as indeed it often seems to have been, as evidence for the glorification of nothingness. Similarly, when the word is at the beginning of a sentence in German, it is capitalized regardless of the part of speech, as in: "Indem der Egoist sich gegen die Anmutungen und Begriffe der Gegenwart wendet, vollzieht er unbarmherzig die maßloseste—*Entheiligung*. Nichts ist ihm heilig!" (The egoist, turning against the demands and concepts of the present, executes pitilessly the most measureless—*desecration*. Nothing is holy to him!).[186] Both in German and English, this brief statement could be taken as a slogan for a religion of nothingness. It is almost certainly the same in translations into other languages. This, it would seem, is how Stirner's declaration of independence from dogma and other idealized abstractions has been misconstrued by critics such as Paterson and Penzo as the satanic worship of nothingness.[187] In short, Stirner appears to be the victim of the preconceptions, prejudices, and prudery of some of his readers. Like Nietzsche, however, he did little or nothing to forestall such misconceptions, wishing to be understood only by those who would be at pains to understand—and caring not a jot for the rest.

Stirner had a foretaste of the trouble the word *Nichts* would get him into in Feuerbach's review of and riposte to *Der Einzige*, which appeared in *Wigand's Vierteljahrsschrift* (Wigand's Quarterly) in 1845. Feuerbach fired back Stirner's own accusation that Feuerbach was a pious atheist, claiming that Stirner had retained the qualities of religion within the framework of an atheistic philosophy.[188] One finds in Feuerbach's reasoning the first historical example of an overemphasis on the significance of the word *Nichts* (understood as nothingness) in *Der Einzige*: "But isn't this nothing a predicate of God, and isn't the sentence: God is nothing, an expression of religion? So the 'Egoist' has still, despite everything,

---

184 EO, 6–7; EE, 15: "Stelle Ich denn meine Sache . . . auf *Mich*, der Ich so gut wie Gott das Nichts von allem Andern, der Ich mein Alles, der Ich der Einzige bin."
185 EE, 15; EO, 7.
186 EE, 190; EO, 165.
187 See Paterson, *The Nihilistic Egoist*, 313; Penzo, *Die existentielle Empörung*, 297. Paterson also compares Stirner to Mephistopheles. See Paterson, *The Nihilistic Egoist*, 191.
188 See EO, 166; EE, 191.

also based his affairs on God!"[189] In the edition of his complete works in which this review is included, Feuerbach adds a footnote beneath this statement by way of explanation, which confirms the trivialness of his assertion: "The sentence: God is nothing or the nothing is commonly found not only in oriental religion, but also in Christian mysticism and visionary Christianity."[190] Furthermore, the first letter of the word *nichts* to which this footnote refers is written in lowercase in the original review but is capitalized in the version in the complete works—"Gott ist nichts" thus becomes "Gott ist Nichts."[191] Feuerbach was evidently prepared to go to some lengths to make his point.

Even in a pre-existentialist world, Stirner's adversaries managed to read far more into his references to *Nichts* than, as may now reasonably be asserted, was ever envisaged by Stirner himself. Stirner's response (written in the third person) appeared in the next edition of *Wigand's Vierteljahrsschrift* and was understandably dismissive: "Where Stirner says: 'I have based my cause on nothing,' Feuerbach makes it '*the* Nothing,' and so concludes from this that the egoist is a pious atheist. However, the Nothing is a definition of God."[192] Feuerbach had apparently failed to comprehend the primary sense of *Nichts* in Stirner's infamous epigram. Stirner's answer is ironic, reaffirming God's nothingness, but in the sense of his original definition of God as a fictional abstraction. One wonders, though, if Stirner's comments led to any of his contemporaries understanding his meaning any better.

Stirner sought in his reaction to Szeliga's review of his book, contained in the same article, to explain why his *Einziger* was not just another abstraction, in the form of the sacred individual, as Szeliga had claimed. Ominously enough, the word he resorted to in order to clarify this was *Nichts*:

> The unique [one] is an expression with which, in all frankness and honesty, one recognizes that he is expressing nothing. Human being, spirit, the true individual, personality, etc. are expressions or attributes that are full to overflowing with content, phrases with the greatest wealth of ideas; compared with these sacred and noble

---

189 Feuerbach, "*The Essence of Christianity* in Relation to *The Ego and Its Own*," 81.

190 Feuerbach, "*The Essence of Christianity* in Relation to *The Ego and Its Own*," 81.

191 See Feuerbach, "Ueber das 'Wesen des Christenthums,'" 193–94; Feuerbach, *Sämmtliche Werke*, 1:343.

192 Stirner, *Stirner's Critics*, 86; Stirner, *Max Stirner's Kleinere Schriften*, 149: "Aus Stirners 'Ich hab' mein' Sach' auf Nichts gestellt' macht Feuerbach 'das Nichts' und bringt dann heraus, dass der Egoist ein frommer Atheist sei. Das Nichts ist allerdings eine Definition Gottes."

phrases, the unique is the empty, unassuming and completely common phrase. . . . Only when *nothing* is said about you and you are merely *named*, are you recognized as you.

[Der Einzige ist eine Aussage, von welcher mit aller Offenheit und Ehrlichkeit eingeräumt wird, dass sie—Nichts aussagt. Der Mensch, der Geist, das wahre Individuum, die Persönlichkeit u. s. f. sind Aussagen oder Prädicate, welche von einer Fülle des Inhalts strotzen, Phrasen mit höchstem Gedankenreichtum; der Einzige ist, gegenüber jenen heiligen und erhabenen Phrasen, die leere, anspruchslose und ganz gemeine Phrase. . . . Erst dann, wenn *Nichts* von Dir ausgesagt und Du nur genannt wirst, wirst Du anerkannt als Du.][193]

Ruge may have believed *Der Einzige* to be the first readable book of German philosophy, but his flattering opinion was perhaps largely based on his having become accustomed to the often inaccessible writings of Hegel.[194] In truth, many of Stirner's readers found their understanding of his ideas hampered by his idiosyncratic prose style, which is characterized by persistent use of quotation marks, capitalized personal and possessive pronouns, ironic biblical references, and extravagant wordplay.[195] Above all, his is the language of provocation and confrontation used indiscriminately and with complete disregard for the convictions and beliefs of others. To use Bertrand Russell's phrase about Nietzsche, Stirner liked to shock conventional readers.[196] Even some of his less conventional readers have found it difficult to look beyond their initial consternation at Stirner's shameless iconoclasm.

Nonetheless, a dispassionate analysis of Stirner's use of the word *Nichts* shows that its meaning has little to do with the existentialists' despair-ridden confrontation with the terror incognito, as it were, of nothingness. Once this misconception is eliminated, all that is left of Stirner's connection to the existentialists is their shared starting point, namely, that existence precedes essence, combined with a rebellious, subjectivist outlook and a general mistrust of abstractions.[197] While these

---

193 Stirner, *Stirner's Critics*, 57–58; Stirner, *Max Stirner's Kleinere Schriften*, 115–16.

194 See Ruge, *Briefwechsel*, 386.

195 See Leopold, "Introduction," xiii: "Almost every feature of his writing seems calculated to unnerve. The use of aphorism and metaphor, the neologisms, the mixture of self-consciously obscure terminology with colloquial language, the excessive italicization and hyperbole, all confound the received framework in which philosophical argument is conducted."

196 See Russell, *A History of Western Philosophy*, 730.

197 Because of the relatively large number of theistic existentialists, the most prominent being Kierkegaard, Buber, and Jaspers, one can hardly say that Stirner

shared aspects are not insignificant, they hardly suffice to label Stirner a proto-existentialist, let alone the original atheist existentialist: Stirner's ideas reflect the zeitgeist of the *Vormärz*, not of the *Nachkriegszeit* (postwar period). Some more recent commentators have come to a similar conclusion. Kast, having posed the question of whether one can speak of Stirner's existentialism, answers thus: "The superficial similarities do not . . . justify such a categorization, even though the owner and unique individual undoubtedly possesses existentialist qualities, and he has provided existentialists with some arguments. Stirner's philosophy refuses any categorization or labeling. What is true for the unique individual is true for it: it is unique."[198] Laska, meanwhile, mentions the solitary example of an existentialist, Nicola Abbagnano (1901–1991), who, allowing himself to be provoked by Paterson's book in 1971, vehemently denied in a newspaper article any affinity between Stirner and atheistic existentialism.[199]

Stirner's Optimism, Hedonism, Eudaemonism

Stirner's relationship to existentialism may not be nonexistent, but it is too remote to offer any solid support for the claim that he is an existential nihilist. It is above all the almost complete absence of existentialism's negative tendencies in Stirner's thought that makes the connection untenable. Existential nihilism is based on an outlook which is susceptible to the unraveling of meaning and the descent into irrefutable senselessness, purposelessness, and emptiness. As Gertz writes: "Nihilism is supposed to be something dark, something negative, something destructive."[200] Nihilistic philosophers, Crosby tells us, have a "dismal view of the world"; two examples he cites are Schopenhauer and Cioran.[201] Stirner cannot be made to fit into this mold: he does not ask despairingly what the point of life is; he suffers from neither angst nor ennui; he is not tormented by the human predicament; nor is he plagued by the problem of meaninglessness or overly concerned with the nature of evil. The death of God is, for him, a given, making theological debate entirely redundant. He is a positivist

---

has atheism in common with existentialism, despite Sartre's partisan assertion: "Existentialism is nothing else but an attempt to draw the full conclusions from a consistently atheistic position." Sartre, *Existentialism and Humanism*, 56.

198 Kast, "Afterword," in Arvon, *Max Stirner*, 219.

199 See Laska, *Ein dauerhafter Dissident*, 80. The article in question was Nicola Abbagnano, "L'apologia del nulla (Stirner e l'esistenzialismo)," *La Stampa*, April 22, 1971: 3.

200 Gertz, *Nihilism*, 5.

201 Crosby, *The Specter of the Absurd*, 376.

insofar as the world according to the data of sensory experience is his starting point. His response to it is devoid of myth, mystery, and miracle.

With regard, therefore, to Paterson's implicit accusation that Stirner is an existential nihilist, there is an essential incongruity between Stirner's philosophy and the existential nihilist's outlook defined by the belief in the meaninglessness of life. In Stirner, one can find none of the oudenophobia that runs like a red line through the tortured intellectual history of nineteenth- and twentieth-century Western culture, embodied in the works of Kierkegaard, Mahler, Munch, Beckett, Cioran, and Larkin, to name but a few. Stirner's method may involve acts of destruction, clearing the ground on a philosophical level much as the Russian nihilists aimed to do sociopolitically, but, unlike the Russian nihilists, he did offer a plan for the post-apocalyptic world. His message as a whole is therefore fundamentally constructive, as well as being entirely free of morbidity or dread.

Despite pessimism's clearly established link to nihilism, few, if any, have attempted to make the case that Stirner is a pessimist. One might argue that the reason for this lies in the fact that the word pessimism has a much more specific definition than nihilism and is therefore less susceptible to misuse. It is certainly true that Stirner's writings do not include the common themes of pessimism, like the pointlessness of existence or the malevolence of the universe. It is no oversight on Thacker's part that Stirner is missing from his "Patron Saints of Pessimism," which canonizes Chamfort, Cioran, Kierkegaard, Joubert, Leopardi, Lichtenberg, Mainländer, Nietzsche, Pascal, Schopenhauer, and Unamuno.[202] Similarly, it is no coincidence that, while most of the above thinkers have been associated with anti-natalism, a conviction which shares many of the concerns and preoccupations of both nihilism and pessimism, there is no evidence of such a view in Stirner.[203]

The logic of anti-natalism is clear: if life has no intrinsic meaning, then to create new life is not only senseless but also cruel. This opinion has a long history in Western thought stretching all the way back to Thales, who, when asked why he had no children, is said to have replied: "Because I love children."[204] A contemporary version of the same argument, from the South African philosopher, David Benatar, is more explicative: "It is curious that while good people go to great lengths to spare their children from suffering, few of them seem to notice that the one (and only) guaranteed way to prevent all the suffering of their children

---

202 Thacker, *Infinite Resignation*, 247–386.
203 See, e.g., Cioran, *The Trouble with Being Born*, 3–4; Leopardi, *Moral Fables*, 114; Mainländer, *Die Philosophie der Erlösung*, 536; Coates, *Anti-Natalism*.
204 Barnes, *Early Greek Philosophy*, 66. See Sophocles, *The Theban Plays*, 109: "The greatest boon is not to be; / But, life begun, soonest to end is best."

is not to bring those children into existence in the first place."[205] Such statements, of which there have been many notable examples, reveal the essential moral core of anti-natalism.[206] Stirner does not express any hint of such a sentiment in his written works. When he uses the word *Geburt* in *Der Einzige*, he uses it in the sense of lineage or extraction; the relevance of birth in Stirner's writings is social and juridical, not existential.[207] Stirner implicitly rejects anti-natalism not only because he does not consider life meaningless and therefore better not lived (despite his own simple and uneventful existence), but also because he is not in the habit of taking a moral standpoint on any issue. The absence in Stirner's writing of any of the features that could be considered compatible with anti-natalism illustrates both Stirner's proximity to moral nihilism and his remoteness from existential nihilism.

While Stirner may not be an optimist in the philosophical sense of Leibniz's best of all possible worlds, he is one in most other senses, arguably to the point of naïvety as far as his social theory is concerned. Stirner certainly cannot with any degree of seriousness be described as a pessimist, in view of the preponderance in his thought of life-affirming principles. Stirner's central undertaking is the emancipation of the individual through the process of self-empowerment: "Look upon yourself as more powerful than they give you out for, and you have more power. . . . You are then not merely *called* to everything divine, *entitled* to everything human, but *owner* of what is yours."[208] He specifically condemns the Christian contempt for the world and its life-negating consequences, and advocates instead the positive principle of self-love:[209]

---

205 Benatar, *Better Never to Have Been*, 6.
206 Perhaps the bluntest expression of anti-natalism is to be found in Larkin's poem, "This Be The Verse." See Larkin, *Collected Poems*, 180. It also appears in Buddhism, the Bible, and Arabic thought. See, e.g., "The Meditations of Ma'arrī," in Nicholson, *Studies in Islamic Poetry*, 74: "Better for Adam and all who issued forth from his loins / That he and they, yet unborn, created never had been!"
207 See, e.g., *EO*, 103, 107, 170, 172; *EE*, 122, 127, 196, 198.
208 *EO*, 318; *EE*, 365: "Sieh Dich als mächtiger an, als wofür man Dich ausgibt, so hast Du mehr Macht. . . . Du bist dann nicht bloß *berufen* zu allem Göttlichen, *berechtigt* zu allem Menschlichen, sondern *Eigner* des Deinigen."
209 See *EO*, 85: "'We do not fear, though the earth should perish.' In all this there is room made for the Christian proposition that the world is empty, for the Christian contempt of the world"; *EE*, 102: "'Drum fürchten wir nichts, wenn gleich die Erde sich wandelt.' In alledem ist für den christlichen Satz, dass die Welt eitel sei, für die christliche *Weltverachtung* der Raum geöffnet." This theme became central to Nietzsche's philosophy. See, e.g., Nietzsche, *Twilight of the Idols and The Anti-Christ*, 135.

Not until one has fallen in love with his *corporeal* self, and takes a pleasure in himself as a living flesh-and-blood person, . . . not until then has one a personal or *egoistic* interest, an interest not only of our spirit, for instance, but of total satisfaction, satisfaction of the whole chap, a *selfish* interest.

[Erst dann, wenn man sich *leibhaftig* liebgewonnen, und an sich, wie man leibt und lebt, eine Lust hat, . . . erst dann hat man ein persönliches oder *egoistisches* Interesse, d. h. ein Interesse nicht etwa nur Unseres Geistes, sondern totaler Befriedigung, Befriedigung des ganzen Kerls, ein *eigennütziges* Interesse.][210]

Similarly to Nietzsche with his concept of *amor fati*, Stirner proposes a worldview based on the affirmation of life; though, unlike Nietzsche, Stirner focuses on this primarily in terms of enjoyment:[211]

My intercourse with the world consists in my enjoying it, and so consuming it for my self-enjoyment. *Intercourse* is the *enjoyment of the world*, and belongs to my—self-enjoyment. . . . *Enjoyment of life* is using life up.
Now—we are in search of the *enjoyment* of life!

[Mein Verkehr mit der Welt besteht darin, dass Ich sie genieße und so sie zu meinem Selbstgenuss verbrauche. Der *Verkehr* ist *Weltgenuss* und gehört zu meinem—Selbstgenuss. . . . *Lebensgenuss* ist Verbrauch des Lebens.
Nun—den *Genuss* des Lebens suchen Wir auf!][212]

In the final sub-section of *Der Einzige* prior to the short conclusion, entitled "Mein Selbstgenuss" (My self-enjoyment), Stirner extols the virtues of a life founded on pleasure:

Henceforth, the question runs, not how one can acquire life, but how one can squander, enjoy it; or, not how one is to produce the true self in himself, but how one is to dissolve himself, to live himself out. . . . Living is quite another thing in—*enjoyment*!

210 EO, 16; EE, 23. See Nietzsche, *Thus Spoke Zarathustra*, 211: "One must learn to love oneself with a sound and healthy love."
211 See Nietzsche, *Twilight of the Idols and The Anti-Christ*, 23: "Man does *not* strive after happiness; only the Englishman does that."
212 EO, 282–83; EE, 323–24. Nietzsche's affirmation of life is far more complex and far less hedonistic than Stirner's, but no less fundamental to his philosophy. See Nietzsche, *The Complete Works of Nietzsche*, 8:50: "Noble morality, master-morality, . . . is rooted in a triumphant saying of yea to *one's self*—it is the self-affirmation and self-glorification of life."

> [Von jetzt an lautet die Frage nicht, wie man das Leben erwerben, sondern wie man's vertun, genießen könne, oder nicht, wie man das wahre Ich in sich herzustellen, sondern wie man sich aufzulösen, sich auszuleben habe. . . . Ganz anders lebt es sich im—*Genuss!*][213]

Stirner's is a reductionist view of human nature: what remains after the numerous layers of sociocultural conditioning have been stripped away is the unique, individual egoist. The point of Stirner's willful annihilation of abstractions is not to destroy for the sake of destruction, but to free the individual from external control and allow him to pursue his own pleasures, which Stirner regards as the fundamental impulse behind all human behavior. There are echoes of this in Freud's pleasure principle: "It is simply the pleasure-principle which draws up the programme of life's purpose. This principle dominates the operation of the mental apparatus from the very beginning."[214] It also bears some relation to Nietzsche's idea of *Lust* (joy) that is presented as the driving force of life in Zarathustra's roundelay:

> Joy—deeper than heart's agony:
> Woe says: Fade! Go!
> But all joy wants eternity,
> Wants deep, deep, deep eternity![215]

For Nietzsche, however, the affirmation of life is in a constant state of struggle with nihilism, whereas, for Stirner, the only apparent obstacle to uninterrupted pleasure, apart from the natural parameters of life, is the tyranny of heteronomous abstractions.

Stirner remarks approvingly on the importance of pleasure for what he loosely describes as the ancients: "What is antiquity seeking then? The true *enjoyment of life*."[216] Indeed, his thought generally shows a far closer affinity with the tradition of Democritus's eudaemonism and Epicurus's hedonism than with that of pessimism or nihilism. Hartmann hinted at this in a chapter on "Stirner's Glorification of Egoism": "All egoism can only be asserted as individual eudaemonism; individual eudaemonism is again only possible on the basis of eudaemonological optimism."[217] Although Stirner refers only briefly to Democritus and Epicurus in *Der Einzige*, and then as part of a triadic exposition of the development of human consciousness (ancients, moderns, free ones),

---

213 *EO*, 284; *EE*, 325.
214 Freud, *Civilization and Its Discontents*, 27.
215 Nietzsche, *Thus Spoke Zarathustra*, 333.
216 *EO*, 25; *EE*, 32: "Was sucht also das Altertum? Den wahren *Lebensgenuss*, Genuss des *Lebens!*"
217 Hartmann, *Ethische Studien*, 89.

they are not targets of his invective, as Christians and humanists invariably are, but are instead models of good living.[218] Stirner shares with them Democritus's materialist view of the world and Epicurus's serene indifference towards death. A less obvious, though nonetheless discernible, connection to Stirner can be found in Democritus's thoughts on the relationship between virtue and egoism: "The novelty in his [Democritus's] preaching lay largely in the fact that he urged virtuous behaviour on his fellows not because it would please or placate the gods, or ensure a satisfactory afterlife, but because such virtues paved the one reliable path to individual happiness here on earth. In other words, virtue is really a matter of self-interest."[219] This idea resurfaced most famously in Cicero's dictum, "virtue is its own reward."[220] Hobbes elaborated on the theme in *Leviathan* (1651) with the assertion that "no man giveth, but with intention of Good to himselfe; because Gift is Voluntary; and of all Voluntary Acts, the Object is to every man his own Good."[221] Spinoza, clearly influenced by Hobbes, expressed something similar in his *Ethics* (1677): "Acting from virtue is nothing else in us but acting . . . from the foundation of seeking one's own advantage."[222] Stirner is hardly out of place among this group of like-minded thinkers, with his frank description of the egoistic motivation for love and compassion: "I love men . . . because love makes *me* happy."[223]

As discussed in chapter 4 above, what Stirner means by egoism is not the narrow interpretation characterized by the egoism-altruism dichotomy, which pits the selfish desire for exclusive personal benefit against the selfless desire for the benefit of another. For Stirner, the dichotomy is instead between the prescribed holy or sacred love (*heilige Liebe*) of Christianity or humanism and the voluntary self-love (*Eigenliebe*) of egoism. The former he designates "hypocrisy, or rather self-deception"; the latter represents the ownership of love "as my feeling."[224] The former, he maintains, is a Christian invention unknown to the ancients: "Antiquity lacked love as little as do Christian times; the god of love is older than the

---

218 See *EO*, 25–26; *EE*, 32–34. Among the ancient Greeks, Stirner refers specifically to Diogenes of Sinope, Aristippus, Democritus, the Stoics, and the Epicureans.
219 Gottlieb, *The Dream of Reason*, 112. See Barnes, *Early Greek Philosophy*, 270: "Democritus: *Great joys come from contemplating noble works.*"
220 Parker, *Cicero's Five Books*, 97.
221 Hobbes, *Leviathan*, 209.
222 Spinoza, *Ethics*, 126.
223 *EO*, 258; *EE*, 294: "Ich liebe die Menschen, . . . weil die Liebe *Mich* glücklich macht."
224 *EO*, 260; *EE*, 297: "die Heuchelei oder vielmehr Selbsttäuschung." *EO*, 259; *EE*, 296: "als meine Empfindung."

God of Love. But the mystical possessedness belongs to the moderns."[225] The latter acknowledges self-interest at the heart of every action and recognizes the innate sense of fellow feeling as the source of every compassionate act.[226] Stirner had no intention of denying or diminishing the importance of human emotions like love, affection, kindness, and compassion; he aimed instead to demystify the motivation behind them and show this to be firmly rooted in the self.

The eudaemonistic themes (not in a moral sense, but in terms of the ethics of choice) of egoism and hedonism that form the framework of Stirner's philosophical project stand in clear opposition to the pessimism and despair of existential nihilism. Existentialism grapples with the issues inherent in the contradictory biological programming both to die and to resist dying in a species endowed by evolution with the epiphenomenon of consciousness. In stark contrast to this, Stirner, although he seems completely aware of his own transience, responds with unflustered indifference to the prospect of personal extinction, as if he had quietly assimilated Epicurus's advice concerning death.[227] He describes "the Christian yearning and hungering for the other world" as if it were a longing that had never touched him.[228] Stirner does not rage against the dying of the light; he accepts without protest or dismay both his personal limitations and his inevitable mortality.

Even if, therefore, Stirner might reasonably, if incongruously, be called an ethical nihilist, he is far from being an existential nihilist. In this sense, Kast, Laska, Fleming, et al. are quite correct in their assertions of his being anything but a nihilist. They may not qualify explicitly what sort of nihilist they have in mind, but what they presumably mean is a Nietzschean or existential nihilist, who, like Tartaglia, says: "There is no overall point to human life."[229] Stirner's skepticism is wide-ranging, but it never stretches to doubting the meaning of existence. Instead, he expresses life's purpose by adapting Protagoras's most famous phrase, to proclaim "that man is not the measure of all things, but I am this measure."[230] While this may reveal some affinity with the subjective perspective of existentialism, it demonstrates a far greater disparity with

---

225 *EO*, 260; *EE*, 297: "An Liebe fehlte es dem Altertum so wenig wie der christlichen Zeit; der Liebesgott ist älter als der Gott der Liebe. Aber die mystische Besessenheit gehört den neuen an."

226 See Lichtenberg, *Schriften*, 2:200: "One loves neither father, nor mother, nor wife, nor child, but the pleasant sensations they cause in us; it always flatters our pride and self-love a little."

227 See Epicurus, *The Art of Happiness*, 156: "Death means nothing to us."

228 *EO*, 34; *EE*, 43: "christliche Sehnsucht und Begierde nach dem Jenseits."

229 Tartaglia, *Philosophy in a Meaningless Life*, 21.

230 *EO*, 311; *EE*, 356: "dass nicht der Mensch das Maß von allem, sondern dass Ich dieses Maß sei."

nihilism, further proof of which can be found in another significant statement in *Der Einzige*, not in quite such a prominent position as the opening and closing line, but at the end of the penultimate section, where Stirner declares:

> People have always supposed that they must give me a destiny lying outside myself.... But I am not an ego along with other egos, but the sole ego: I am unique.... I do not develop men, nor as man, but, as I, I develop—myself.
> This is the meaning of the—*unique one*.
>
> [Man hat immer gemeint, Mir eine außerhalb Meiner liegende Bestimmung geben zu müssen.... Ich bin aber nicht ein Ich neben andern Ichen, sondern das alleinige Ich: Ich bin einzig.... Nicht als Mensch und nicht den Menschen entwickle Ich, sondern als Ich entwickle Ich—Mich.
> Dies ist der Sinn des—Einzigen.][231]

The message here is unmistakably positive; above all, in positing purpose and meaning, Stirner implicitly repudiates futility and contradicts his classification as an existential nihilist. Indeed, of the three specific types of nihilism examined in this book, it is existential nihilism that is the least applicable to Stirner's thought, even though it is, at least by implication, the type of nihilism with which he has been most frequently associated since World War II, thus raising the question about the wisdom, or motivation, of those who make such a claim.

---

231 *EO*, 319; *EE*, 365.

CONCLUSION

Stirner: The Happy Nihilist?

MAX STIRNER IS SEEN AS occupying a minor position in the history of ideas, somewhere between an *enfant terrible* and the invisible man. This book has attempted to demonstrate that, at least from an unpartisan viewpoint, his ideas constitute an original and valuable contribution to philosophical inquiry and reveal new perspectives in an age of unparalleled skepticism and uncertainty, where the search for an answer to the ancient problem of how to live well is more frenetic than ever. The issue of Stirner's relationship to nihilism is key to an appraisal of his legacy because the orthodox labeling of Stirner as a nihilist, which is so widespread as to have become almost axiomatic, exposes both the crucial themes of his philosophical project and the ideological backdrop to his polarized reception. If, as this study has sought to establish, Stirner's status as a nihilist is doubtful at worst and partial at best, it underlines, among other things, the importance of reevaluating his standing as a thinker and reassessing the substance and significance of his thought.

One of the key findings to come out of this investigation is that Nietzschean or existential nihilism occupies a prominent position in the common (mis-)understanding of Stirner as a nihilist. While Stirner had a limited effect on the development of Russian nihilism, and while moral nihilism may adequately describe Stirner's ethical outlook but not his philosophy as a whole, it is the assumption that he is expounding a doctrine of emptiness, in the sense of meaninglessness, that has continually dogged the debate about Stirner and nihilism, especially since World War II. Stirner's critics in this regard have invariably ignored the fact that his version of nothingness, insofar as the concept plays any significant role in his thought, is meonic, in the form of the "creative nothing" of a transitory individual's life.[1] The equating of Stirner's meonic nothingness with the empty void of existential nihilism is a recurrent misconception in Stirner criticism and one which must be rectified before a coherent picture of his thought can emerge.

---

1   See *EO*, 7: "the creative nothing, the nothing out of which I myself as creator create everything"; *EE*, 15: "das schöpferische Nichts, das Nichts, aus welchem Ich selbst als Schöpfer Alles schaffe."

Stirner's detractors have also tended to disregard the fact that the central themes of pessimism, like the pernicious effects of the passage of time or the absurdity of human existence, which are a fundamental part of existential nihilism, are entirely absent from Stirner's writings. One of the few commentators to acknowledge this is Carroll: "Paterson makes a central point of identifying Stirner with nihilism. His argument depends on a failure to distinguish between social values, which Stirner does reject, and personal values, to which he is more overtly committed than any other philosopher. The dark pessimism, the hesitancy of Will, and the disaffection with life symptomatic of the nihilist are not to be found in Stirner—rather the contrary."[2] Like so many other critics, Carroll does not specify what type of nihilism he is referring to, but it is apparent from the context that he means it in a Nietzschean or existential sense. The same can be said of Leopold when he writes: "Stirner is clearly committed to the 'non-nihilistic' view that a certain kind of character and mode of behaviour (namely, autonomous individuals and actions) are to be valued above all others."[3] Both Carroll and Leopold acknowledge that the largely positive nature of Stirner's philosophical message precludes his being subsumed under so negative an epithet as nihilism.

If Paterson's claim is therefore erroneous, namely that *Der Einzige* strikes a similar "despairing and satanic chord" to, and thus belongs with, the "nihilistic literature" of "Leopardi, Poe, Schopenhauer," et al., it begs the question of whether Stirner can be more easily situated within some other segment of the philosophical pantheon.[4] One possibility can be found in the atomistic-Epicurean tradition, which Onfray traces from Democritus, Diogenes, Protagoras, and Epicurus, via the gnostics, Gassendi, Cyrano de Bergerac, Meslier, La Mettrie, and d'Holbach, to Bentham, Mill, Deleuze, and Foucault. Like Stirner, each of these thinkers, whom Onfray classifies collectively as anti-Platonists, demonstrates an essentially hedonistic attitude towards existence, as Onfray explains: "They want happiness on earth, here and now, not later in some hypothetical, unattainable world."[5] Thus, along with numerous modern atheists, including Hitchens, Dawkins, Pinker, and Rovelli, these happy few display no evidence of anguish or despair at the prospect of personal extinction. Conceptually speaking, Stirner seems to fit quite comfortably into this loose band of intellectual brothers—none of whom is generally regarded as a nihilist—if only because he shares with them what

2   Carroll, *Break-Out from the Crystal Palace*, 87.
3   Leopold, "Introduction," xxiv.
4   See Paterson, *The Nihilistic Egoist*, 313. Paterson's full list comprises de Sade, Leopardi, Poe, Schopenhauer, von Hartmann, Ibsen, Baudelaire, Mallarmé, Swinburne, Rimbaud, Huysmans, Strindberg, and Nietzsche.
5   Onfray, *A Hedonist Manifesto*, 10.

Onfray calls "the aspiration of the Epicurean project," namely "the pure pleasure of existing."[6] Stirner is notoriously difficult to categorize, and, as observed in previous chapters, some, like Laska and Fleming, have bemoaned his critics' tendency to pigeonhole him, but if one nonetheless felt compelled to do so, there is good evidence that he belongs among the hedonists and optimists rather than the nihilists.

Another common feature of the members of Onfray's band of anti-Platonists, which is an equally important indicator of affinity with Stirner, is that they all "share a formidable concern with deconstructing myths and fables, rendering this world inhabitable and desirable."[7] Deleuze too noted the demythologizing tendency of anti-Platonism: "The speculative object and the practical object of philosophy as Naturalism, science and pleasure, coincide on this point: it is always a matter of denouncing the illusion, the false infinite, the infinity of religion and all of the theologico-erotic-oneiric myths in which it is expressed."[8] Ironically, Stirner's own endeavor to deconstruct the myths that, in his opinion, oppress and tyrannize the individual, plays a significant role in his reputation, and often violent rejection, as a nihilist. The absence of existential despair in his thought, which makes him unsusceptible to existential nihilism, facilitates his repudiation of mythology, which, in turn, results in accusations of nihilism. This apparent paradox shows how the indeterminate nature of the word nihilism gives it an almost universal relevance, or, at least, an ability to turn up in unexpected places.

Stirner's program of radical iconoclasm, presented in a manner that is unquestionably intended to provoke, has invariably been regarded as being beyond the pale and has resulted in countless polemical attacks on Stirner by his adversaries. Although demythologization in itself does not belong to any of nihilism's distinct meanings, Stirner's acts of desecration are so comprehensive, and his disregard for others' convictions so complete, that nihilism has become the label of choice for those who want to convey their disapproval of his methods and ideas. In characterizing Stirner as a nihilist, his critics often seem to focus entirely on their abhorrence of his iconoclasm, rather than the characteristics of any of the epithet's specific definitions. However unsuitable the term nihilist might seem from the perspective of existential nihilism, Stirner nonetheless undoubtedly deserves his place in philosophical history's long line of iconoclasts that starts with Diogenes of Sinope, who, unlike Stirner, was

6   Onfray, *A Hedonist Manifesto*, 11.
7   Onfray, *A Hedonist Manifesto*, 11. Cf. Lucretius, *On the Nature of the Universe*, 95: "This is my reward for teaching on these lofty topics, for struggling to loose men's minds from the tight knots of superstition and shedding on dark material the bright beam of my song."
8   Deleuze, *The Logic of Sense*, 278.

also a moralist, and includes Machiavelli, who left numerous idols intact if not undamaged, and Nietzsche, who ultimately erected new icons in place of the idols he had shattered.[9] Stirner occupies a privileged position within this select company owing to his uncompromising commitment to demystification and demythologization; with his skepticism, irreverence, suspicion of all ideologies, and rejection of morality, religion, and the state, Stirner's philosophical rebellion is unsurpassed.

Far from earning him plaudits from his readers and critics, however, Stirner's peerless heterodoxy has led, in the main, to his vilification. He seems to have imagined that, following the spectacular dismantling of speculative philosophy and religion by his Young Hegelian colleagues, the world was ripe for the *coup de grâce* to end dogma, absolutism, and psychological self-deception once and for all.[10] He apparently thought he was presiding over a seminal moment: the completion of the Enlightenment project regarding dogma, the final step in man's progress from self-incurred minority to self-determined autonomy.[11] This turned out to be a serious error of judgment on Stirner's part. He underestimated the strength of the negative reaction to his ruthless assault on heteronomy and its mythologies, failing to realize how deeply unpalatable—not to say offensive—his iconoclasm would be to those with a vested interest in the fashioning of icons and the perpetuation of sacred myths. It is one of the more surprising findings of this study that the backlash against Stirner's call for universal demythologization plays a far greater role in his characterization as a nihilist than any specifically nihilistic features of his thinking.

If Harari's theory is to be believed, namely that it is the ability to create myths and the willingness to believe them that distinguishes *Homo sapiens* from all other animals, then it is clear that Stirner inadvertently set himself up as an enemy of the people.[12] His uncompromising stance

---

9   See Cioran, *The Trouble with Being Born*, 85: "[Nietzsche] demolished so many idols only to replace them with others: a false iconoclast, with adolescent aspects and a certain virginity, a certain innocence inherent in his solitary's [*sic*] career."

10   Stirner resigned from his teaching job on October 1, 1844, shortly before publication of *Der Einzige*, possibly in anticipation of achieving fame and success. See Mackay, *Max Stirner*, 183.

11   See *EO*, 139; *EE*, 162.

12   See Harari, *Sapiens*, 42: "The real difference between us and chimpanzees is the mythical glue that binds together large numbers of individuals, families and groups. This glue has made us the masters of creation." For Feuerbach, the difference was religion (Feuerbach, *The Essence of Christianity*, 1); for Aristotle, reason or the rational soul (Aristotle, *De Anima*, 59–65, 151–55); for Descartes, variously reason, language, self-consciousness, or the soul (Descartes, *A Discourse on Method*, 1, 3–4, 36–37, 45–46, 149). Dostoevsky has Razumikhin say cynically

led to him acquiring a reputation as a pariah and a misfit, despised by the political right as a dangerous anarchist and by the political left as a proto-fascist, though in fact he was just a man who held up a mirror to *Homo mythologicus* in all its nakedness.[13] Stirner exposes what he considers to be the mendacity of man's fictional abstractions by endeavoring to divest language of its ideological prejudices to reveal what he calls "the nakedness and barrenness of concepts and ideas."[14] As a philosophical approach, demythologization arguably has many positive qualities—the elimination of deception, the condemnation of hypocrisy, the establishment of personal autonomy—but it overlooks the importance of mythology for mankind. The history of mythology may be, in the words of James Frazer (1854–1941), "the melancholy record of human error and folly," but that does not, in any way, affect the success or durability of mythopoeia.[15] As Onfray explains: "Human credulity is beyond imagining. Man's refusal to see the obvious, his longing for a better deal even if it is based on pure fiction, his determination to remain blind have no limits. Far better to swallow fables, fictions, myths, or fairy tales than to see reality in all its naked cruelty."[16]

Myth is the answer, however imperfect, to many of man's existential problems, not least that of the gloomy consciousness of his own death. It is, moreover, the expression of the power of the human spirit, the inspiration of art and culture, the engine of human progress, and the driving force of history. For a species whose coherence, identity, self-belief, sense of security, and evolutionary success depend crucially on its unique capacity to create (and believe in) myths, a demythologizer appears instinctively to be an existential threat.[17] From the point of view of the welfare of

---

that this difference is found in "talking nonsense." Dostoevsky, *Crime and Punishment*, 242.

13   For Stirner's reception by the political right and left, see Laska, *Ein dauerhafter Dissident*, 42–52 and 84–87, respectively. For *Homo mythologicus*, see Brockway, *Myth from the Ice Age to Mickey Mouse*, 7: "Modern people are no less prone to create myths than our archaic ancestors. Perhaps we should speak of *Homo Mythologicus* in the way we speak of *Homo Religiosus* or *Homo Ludens* meaning 'religious man' and 'playful man,' implying that these traits are natural to us as human beings. It is our nature to weave myths and to think in mythic terms."

14   Stirner, *Stirner's Critics*, 56–57; Stirner, *Max Stirner's Kleinere Schriften*, 115: "die Nacktheit und Kahlheit der Begriffe und Ideen."

15   Frazer, *Balder the Beautiful*, 2:304.

16   Onfray, *Atheist Manifesto*, 2.

17   See Roszak, *The Making of a Counter Culture*, 214: "The myth has, after all, been identified as a universal phenomenon of human society, a constitutive factor so critical in importance that it is difficult to imagine a culture having any coherence at all if it lacked the mythological bond."

humanity, Stirner's iconoclasm is inexcusable, which is why so many writers, philosophers, and historians of ideas have never forgiven him, while simultaneously doing their level best to forget him.[18] Stirner's outlaw status as a desecrator of sacred beliefs thus plays the decisive role in his enemies' portrayal of him as a nihilist, a term that is sufficiently vague, at least in its unqualified form, to be acceptable to adversaries and critics of all persuasions as a catch-all expression of contempt. Christians, communists, and conservatives are all united in their condemnation of Stirner as a nihilist. If he is to be saved from unwarranted oblivion or infamy, a reassessment is needed of this misleading association of demythologization with nihilism, misleading, at least, in that it gives the impression that its results are exclusively negative.

However, with a word as prevalent in modern parlance as nihilism is and yet so ambiguous, it must be conceded that the answer to the question posed by this study ultimately comes down to semantics. Returning to the reference work definitions of nihilism encountered in chapter 2, there is one—and perhaps only one—that fits Stirner exactly, namely *Collins Cobuild Advanced Learner's Dictionary*'s: "a belief which rejects all political and religious authority . . . in favour of the individual." It almost seems as if the author were basing the definition on a description of Stirner, the well-known nihilist. In this sense of the word, assuming it is a valid definition, the first association of Stirner with nihilism in Rosenkranz's diary entry soon after publication of *Der Einzige* is unimpeachable. Employing the epithet in this way effectively retraces its steps to its origins in the eighteenth century as a cautionary warning of the dangers of Enlightenment thought. It would mean that, just as, to paraphrase Stirner, Nero is only bad for those who are good, Stirner is only a nihilist (in this sense) for those who believe in an ideology that he threatens. If this is really what Stirner's critics mean when they call him a nihilist, it perhaps explains why many of them do not specify what type of nihilism they have in mind, as this usage of the term predates nihilism's categorization. It is like the ghost of nihilism past returning to haunt his memory.

Nihilism employed in this manner is almost more revealing about the accusers' fears than it is about Stirner's ideas. It indicates, above all else, that Stirner does not share their treasured beliefs in certain narratives, or,

---

18   See Laska, *Ein dauerhafter Dissident*, 7: "In the history of philosophy, he [Stirner] is mostly passed over or mentioned only in passing. He is rarely to be found in the indexes of specialist journals, in the programs of publishing houses, in the schedules of university lectures; he hardly even plays a role in non-academic discourse. There is not and never has been one single philosopher who refers positively and specifically to Stirner."

in Stirner's terminology, their *idées fixes*.[19] It is tantamount to using nihilism as a malediction rather than a useful description, which is indeed, as we have seen, how the word was generally employed until Turgenev and Nietzsche transformed its meaning.[20] The accusation against Stirner of nihilism in this sense is, arguably, based on the Ionian fallacy of assuming that everything that exists belongs to a single coherent structure and that the only alternative to monism, therefore, is nihilism.[21] It is certainly noticeable that many of Stirner's staunchest critics, foremost among them Paterson and Helms, are devoted monists. Stirner, on the other hand, has all the hallmarks of being a pluralist, taking pluralism to the utmost extreme of a plurality consisting of every individual voice, entirely without the synthetic formation of groups, let alone one single, self-anointed group governed by a virtually unchallengeable doctrine.

The essence of Stirner's pluralism is captured unwittingly (though logically enough in a satire on blind belief in dogma), by Monty Python's fictional character, Brian, who beseeches his followers to exercise their critical faculties: "You've got it all wrong. You don't need to follow me. You don't need to follow anyone. You've got to think for yourselves. You're all individuals."[22] The comparison of Stirner's philosophy with the comedy of Monty Python is not intended to be flippant: they have much in common, not just in their derisive irreverence but also in their merciless targeting of established institutions and orthodox ideologies. Indeed, the scathing reaction of the political and religious establishment to the release of *Life of Brian*, typified by the attacks of Malcolm Muggeridge and Mervyn Stockwood in the famous TV debate with John Cleese and Michael Palin on November 9, 1979, was not dissimilar in nature to the monistic condemnation of *Der Einzige*.[23] As with Wiersma's censure of the Python film mentioned in chapter 2 above, the rejection of Stirner's book using the extreme imprecation of nihilism can be seen as the result of a conflict between the dogmatic defenders of various doctrinaire ideologies and their perceived enemy in the form of the ultimate demythologizer, be it Stirner or Monty Python, whose denial of

19 See Rosenkranz, *Aus einem Tagebuch*, 133.

20 Onfray makes a similar point about the polemical use of the word atheist, which he calls "this single weak epithet, tailored to discredit." Onfray, *Atheist Manifesto*, 20.

21 See Berlin, *Concepts and Categories*, 76–77.

22 Monty Python, "He's Not the Messiah—Life of Brian," YouTube, accessed June 30, 2023, https://www.youtube.com/watch?v=DBbuUWw30N8. Tellingly, the crowd's response, chanting in metronomic unison, "yes, we're all individuals . . . yes, we are all different," highlights the social impracticality of a doctrine based on radical individualism.

23 See "Life of Brian Debate," BBC Archive, accessed June 30, 2023, http://www.bbc.co.uk/archive/life-of-brian-debate-1979/z4dqrj6.

the validity of absolutes discredits and fatally undermines their fictional structures of belief. As a label, nihilism, when applied in this manner, is not intended to have a specific meaning: its purpose is simply to act as an anathema.

Although the chorus of monist cries of "nihilist" is misleading for anyone who wishes to approach Stirner with an open mind, perhaps the greater issue in the history of such accusations is the extension of the practice of associating Stirner with nihilism beyond the time of the term's fundamental shift in meaning in the middle of the nineteenth century, thus transposing nihilism's etymological transmutation to Stirner's thought. This process was, to some extent, made inevitable by the concurrence in the 1890s of Nietzsche's sudden popularity and the first Stirner renaissance, which largely sealed the fate of Stirner's legacy. The fact is that if the allegations of nihilism against Stirner were to be seen as no more than an excessively disparaging response to his rejection of dogma and ideology, they could be considered almost harmless; but couched as they now are in the context of nihilism's modern terminology, with all its connotations and associations, the word takes on a far more sinister meaning that contributes both to Stirner's continued ostracism and the failure on the part of scholars and other critics to engage seriously with his ideas.

This book has attempted to show that the common understanding of Stirner is based on an accumulation of false assumptions and misguided criticism that has distorted, or even disfigured beyond recognition, the meaning of his ideas. The Stirner who lies largely concealed beneath countless layers of misinterpretation deserves to be rediscovered for what he has to say on mythology, egoism, and individual autonomy— all subjects of enduring significance for human society and culture. In this way, Stirner can perhaps be rescued from the margins of intellectual and scholarly discourse, especially in the anglophone world, where Paterson's largely unchallenged interpretation has done immeasurable damage to Stirner's standing. If the present study succeeds in supplanting Paterson's book as a reference work for Stirner studies in English, it will have achieved one worthwhile objective. This undertaking with regard to Stirner's legacy should be seen not so much as a rehabilitation, as Stirner has never been truly accepted as a serious philosophical protagonist, nor a rediscovery, as he has never been completely buried either, but rather as a reevaluation of his worth as a thinker.

This is not, however, to promise Stirner a place at the top table; his overall contribution to the history of ideas is plainly not comparable with that of Socrates, Kant, or Nietzsche, or the other giants that dominate the annals of Western philosophy. Stirner's written output is meager and the range of his ideas is limited; his writing is readable, especially compared to that of his predecessors, although it is neither poetic nor cerebral; his social theory seems rudimentary and alarmingly naïve; and he has nothing to say about the transcendental, not even how to deal with its absence. But his original ideas on the antagonistic relationship between the egoistic individual and sacred heteronomous abstractions have hardly been surpassed in the ensuing period of nearly two centuries. Stirner was the first, and is, arguably, the only thinker to deconstruct entirely man's urge to mythologize, not only in terms of extant myths like monarchy, state, and religion, but also with regard to the process of mythologization itself.

One final question to be asked before reaching a concluding verdict on the question of the relationship between Stirner's thought and nihilism is whether a version of that opaque term nihilism might exist that reconciles the affirmatory and annihilatory aspects of Stirner's thought, in other words, whether Stirner, even if he is not specifically a political, moral, or existential nihilist, might be described as a happy nihilist. Camus appears to hint at such a possibility in *L'Homme révolté*, where he compares and contrasts Stirner's nihilism with Nietzsche's: "But, unlike with Nietzsche, his nihilism is a satisfied one. Stirner laughs in the impasse, Nietzsche rushes against the walls."[24] However, while this statement is admirably poetic, its accuracy is more questionable. Camus seems to have derived the image of a laughing Stirner from one solitary passage which he quotes from *Der Einzige*, where Stirner describes his own position using the idiom *der lachende Erbe* (the laughing heir) while poking fun at the notion of the thousand-year existence of the German nation. True to his provocative style, Stirner describes the death and burial of the German people, but far from plotting their premeditated murder, as Camus (perhaps influenced by the horrors of the recent war) goes on to suggest, Stirner is predicting—in entirely metaphorical terms—the demise of German nationalism as a tyrannical absolute and celebrating the envisioned liberation of the individual from its yoke:[25]

> The German nation and German peoples have behind them a history of a thousand years: what a long life! O, go to rest, never to rise again—that all may become free whom you so long have held in fetters.—The *people* is dead.—Up with *me*! . . . Tomorrow they carry thee to the grave; soon thy sisters, the peoples, will follow thee. But,

---

24 Camus, *L'Homme révolté*, 84. The short section on Stirner is omitted from Anthony Bower's English translation in the Penguin edition.

25 See Camus, *L'Homme révolté*, 87: "Since every individual in and of itself is fundamentally criminal towards the state and the people, we must recognize that living is synonymous with transgressing. To be unique, he who does not take it upon himself to die, must take it upon himself to kill." Concerning Camus' state of mind around that time, see Camus, "The Human Crisis," a lecture delivered at Columbia University in 1946, quoted in Isaac, *Arendt, Camus and Modern Rebellion*, 21.

when they have all followed, then—mankind is buried, and I am my own, I am the laughing heir!

[Deutsches Volk und deutsche Völker haben eine Geschichte von tausend Jahren hinter sich: welch langes Leben! Geht denn ein zur Ruhe, zum Nimmerauferstehen, auf dass alle frei werden, die Ihr so lange in Fesseln hieltet.—Tot ist das *Volk*.—Wohlauf *Ich*! . . . Morgen trägt man Dich zu Grabe; bald werden deine Schwestern, die Völker, Dir folgen. Sind sie aber alle gefolgt, so ist—die Menschheit begraben, und Ich bin mein eigen, Ich bin der lachende Erbe!][26]

Camus' flawed, literal interpretation of Stirner's colorful language leads him to conclude: "Thus, on the ruins of the world, the desolate laughter of the king of individuals depicts the last victory of the spirit of revolt. But at this extremity, nothing else is possible but death or resurrection."[27] The "king of individuals" that Camus describes sounds more like the murderer, Mersault, in *A Happy Death*, than Stirner, whose philosophical endeavors were directed instead towards the attainment of a happy life. The impression Camus gives of Stirner is of a bitter and twisted, apocalyptic rebel, laughing demonically at his acts of destruction. It is unfortunate that one of Stirner's best-known critics has given such a misleading account of his work, thereby perpetuating the myth of Stirner, the happy, or at least laughing, nihilist, though not laughing like Rembrandt's portrait of Democritus, but more like Doré's Lucifer on his descent to hell.

It is clear that Camus' description of Stirner as a laughing nihilist does not achieve a balance between the constructive and destructive elements in Stirner's thought, as it relies too heavily on a negative reading of *Der Einzige*. He exaggerates the significance of Stirner's apparent condoning of murder, while ignoring the positive themes of self-mastery, individual autonomy, and liberation from external subjugation,[28] thus allowing him to declare: "With Stirner, the negation that animates revolt irresistibly overwhelms all affirmation."[29] Paterson would later echo Camus' sentiment: "To seek in Stirner a positive moral or social philosophy . . . is

---

26   *EO*, 193; *EE*, 222–23. Camus only quotes the last sentence, which ends with the idiom in question.

27   Camus, *L'Homme révolté*, 87–88.

28   See Camus, *L'Homme révolté*, 87–88.

29   Camus, *L'Homme révolté*, 85–86. Camus is effectively focusing on the shorter first part of *Der Einzige* and disregarding the longer second part. See Leopold, "Introduction," xxii: "Whereas the negative project of the First Part of *The Ego and Its Own* was to demonstrate that modernity had striven unsuccessfully to overcome religious modes of thought, the positive project of the Second Part is to characterize the future epoch of egoism."

to seek in vain."[30] In truth, the label "happy nihilist" is of little use as a description of Stirner, mainly because, like Paterson's unfortunate phrase "the nihilistic egoist," it is too oxymoronic to make any real sense, but also because it would satisfy neither side of the debate, neither those who wish to demonize Stirner for his acts of desecration nor those who consider his message to be both positive and valuable.

There is an alternative reading of Stirner's project that deserves attention because of its potential relevance to the question of his alleged connection to nihilism. The idea was first proposed by Engels in a letter to Marx on November 19, 1844: "This egoism is simply the essence of present society and present man brought to consciousness."[31] It resurfaced in an article by Keben in 1890: "Stirner's radical individualism contains the logical justification of existing conditions! Yes, certainly—the egoism of all is only limited by the victorious, overpowering egoism of a few."[32] Five years later, Zenker observed with reference to Stirner's union of egoists, "that here . . . we only have to do, at bottom, with the logical extension of the present order of society that rests on free competition."[33] Likewise, Schultheiss, in his 1905 doctoral dissertation, perhaps borrowing from Zenker, also writes about Stirner's theory of egoistic social organization being a reflection of current reality.[34] More than a century later, Stulpe took up the idea again, speculating that Stirner was now forgotten, "because the unique individual has become, in a way, ubiquitous and is taken for granted."[35] Despite the apparent incoherence of Stulpe's proposition that a writer's popularity is inversely proportional to the prevalence of her or his ideas, this is a more subtle argument than Helms's elaborate but clumsy and implausible attempt to establish a connection between Stirner, fascism, and the West Germany of the 1960s via the ideology of the lower-middle class, leading him too to observe: "Stirner has never been more actual, never more contemporary than today."[36] A more recent declaration of Stirner's modernity can be found in Jacob Blumenfeld's 2018 monograph, where he remarks that "Stirner's . . . philosophy is especially in vogue today," as evidenced by Engels's sketch of Stirner's face having been "revived as a meme, popping up in the stranger corners of the Internet."[37]

All of the above examples, stretching back to the late nineteenth century, demonstrate the enduring relevance of Stirner's focus on egoism,

30 Paterson, *The Nihilistic Egoist*, 316.
31 Marx and Engels, *Collected Works*, 38:11.
32 Keben, "John Henry Mackay und sein Philosoph," 190.
33 Zenker, *Anarchism*, 106.
34 See Schultheiss, *Stirner*, 129.
35 Stulpe, *Gesichter des Einzigen*, 28.
36 Helms, *Die Ideologie der anonymen Gesellschaft*, 499.
37 Blumenfeld, *All Things are Nothing to Me*, 1.

individualism, and anti-establishmentarianism (although Stirner himself might say that his view is of course perpetually relevant because it describes human nature). The majority of such comments about Stirner's actuality have been critical in nature, attacking the perceived excesses of amoral libertarianism or radical anarchism allegedly reflected in modern social trends, but, more recently, there has been a resurgence of interest in the political implications of Stirner's ideas because of their pertinence to a contemporary Western society that is increasingly fractured, individualistic, and skeptical of authority, government, and the shifting ideologies of the political right and left.[38] Stirner's outline of an alternative both to socialism and to conservative orthodoxy, as well as his mistrust of all power structures and their mechanisms of indoctrination, resonates with those who are disaffected by the development of modern capitalist society, but are also unconvinced of the practical benefits of Marxism. Newman thus insists that Stirner should not simply be seen as constituting a historical and philosophical curiosity.[39] By applying Foucault's concept of voluntary inservitude to Stirner, Newman reveals a link between Stirner's egoism and postmodern individualism, which leads him to declare: "There emerges, from Stirner's thought, a certain kind of micropolitical ethics that has important implications for any consideration of radical politics today."[40] Indeed, Stirner, in challenging the tyranny of absolute abstractions and sacred myths, paves the way for a reassessment of the individual's relationship to the self and others, as well as offering an entirely new perspective on the mechanisms of power and alienation.

Extrapolating from these analyses of Stirner's thought in the light of the growth of individualism in Western society, one might regard Stirner as the archetype of a mutant adaptation which, arguably, is becoming increasingly widespread almost to the point of ubiquity, as mankind moves ever further away from the generations that felt powerfully the loss of faith, for the simple reason that there is ever less faith to lose: a calm, quiet, easy-going, self-composed, almost anonymous, even serene individual, not overly concerned with personal survival, unimpressed by authority of any kind, skeptical of dogma in all its guises, protective of his personal autonomy, happy to enjoy the moment for as long as it lasts, and ready to disappear at any time into the anonymity of the crowd, or

---

38 As examples of the renewed interest in Stirner's political significance, see, for instance, Welsh, *Max Stirner's Dialectical Egoism: A New Interpretation*; Saul Newman, "Stirner's Ethics of Voluntary Inservitude"; and Ferguson, "Why Anarchists Need Stirner."
39 See Newman, "Introduction," 4–5.
40 Newman, "Stirner's Ethics of Voluntary Inservitude," 189. See Welsh, *Max Stirner's Dialectical Egoism: A New Interpretation*, 5: "Max Stirner was a theorist of modernity . . . rooted in his unique concept of egoism."

into the sunset if necessary.[41] Such a type is, in other words, a twenty-first-century version of Nietzsche's last man, or the personification of Peter Watson's untroubled ones, who, like Dürer's knight, are unconcerned by Death and the Devil, though not because of a supernatural myth that guarantees salvation, but because of an apparent insensitivity to Death's sting:

> Such individuals may call into question Robert Musil's claim that even people who scoff at metaphysics feel a strange cosmic presence, or Thomas Nagel's comment that we all have a sense of looking down on ourselves as if from a great height. But such individuals are not "metaphysical types" and seek no "deep" meaning in existence. They just get on with their lives, making ends meet, living from day to day and season to season, enjoying themselves where they can, untroubled by matters that so perplex their neighbours. . . . In some ways, they are the most secular people of all and perhaps the most content.[42]

According to such a view, Stirner would represent the premature beginning of the end of angst, the incipient transition from transcendental homelessness to transcendental obliviousness, and the potential for the start of a new era based on realistic, earthly expectations and belief in the power of practical, as opposed to sacred, reason. He would, however unintentionally, be a solution to nihilism rather than a nihilist, the herald of a secular, post-postmodern epoch of satisfied, if subversive, nominalism, as man evolves in a new world which is not so much brave as indifferent. Indifferent, that is, not to life, but to the collision between individual consciousness and personal mortality. This interpretation would give us a Stirner who could be seen as a guide to the future beyond Nietzsche's ominous prediction for the next two centuries; a Stirner who could be described, in short, as an *anti*-nihilist.[43]

What, then, can be concluded about the relationship between Stirner's thought and nihilism? In essence, Stirner's philosophy seems to have more in common with Democritus and Epicurus, or Adam Smith and Alexander Herzen for that matter, than with anyone who, like Mainländer, Heidegger, or Cioran, might generally be considered a nihilist. Indeed, it is clear that calling Stirner the Nihilist, as one might call

---

41   Cf. Joyce, *A Portrait of the Artist*, 191: "I will not serve that in which I no longer believe, whether it call itself my home, my fatherland, or my church: and I will try to express myself in some mode of life or art as freely as I can and as wholly as I can, using for my defence the only arms I allow myself to use—silence, exile, and cunning."
42   Watson, *The Age of Nothing*, 542.
43   See Nietzsche, *The Will to Power*, 7.

Schopenhauer the Pessimist, or Sartre the Existentialist, is highly problematic. Not only are there, as outlined above, a number of more appropriate labels, with one possible interpretation even making Stirner the exact opposite of a nihilist, but the word nihilism without a qualifying adjective generally means, in current usage, existential nihilism, which is completely unsuitable as a description of Stirner's life-affirming philosophy, which is utterly devoid of the negative aspects of existentialism.

Furthermore, even though there may be some elements of Nietzschean active nihilism in Stirner's iconoclasm, there is no hint of passive nihilism, nor of pessimism, anti-natalism, or suicidal tendencies. Stirner follows the Enlightenment principle of searching for the rational improvement of human life, rather than delving into the mysterious depths of the unconscious will, even if his analysis of human behavior does take account of the irrational. He was not swayed by the Counter-Enlightenment ideas of German Romanticism; for Stirner, the world of human experience is plainly discoverable rather than unfathomable. And this, finally, is the point to be made about his pitiful biography: only his fundamentally positive outlook can explain the untroubled, almost playful equanimity that he displays in his writing. Stirner follows Hegel in emphasizing the importance of the negative impulse as the indispensable engine of progress, non-eschatological progress in Stirner's case, to be sure, but progress, nonetheless. This appreciation of the creative power of negation should not be mistaken for negativity.

Nonetheless, Stirner seems to have become caught between the two nothings that flank his magnum opus, a victim of his own lust for irreverent provocation, his ghost condemned to walk the earth as a case of (often intentionally) mistaken identity. If, despite all the evidence to the contrary assembled in this study, one were to persist in using the term nihilist in its original sense as a way of expressing disapprobation of Stirner's dismantling of cherished beliefs and institutions, it would be at the risk of misrepresenting his ideas, ignoring his positive message, and giving a one-sided and jaundiced view of his thought. It would effectively mean applying to Stirner's thought the label of nihilism, when what is at least equally if not more nihilistic is the accuser's horror at the vision of Stirner's brave (or indifferent) new world devoid of absolute values and metaphysical certainty. Were one nonetheless to do so, focusing, however tendentiously, solely on Stirner's sacrilege, impiety, and antagonism towards heteronomous abstractions, would not atheist, iconoclast, or nominalist be more apposite terms than nihilist?

Regarding Stirner and the specific types of nihilism with which this study has been concerned, a tenuous connection to political nihilism has been established, not least because of Stirner's modest (and partly hypothetical) influence on Bakunin, Herzen, Belinsky, and Speshnev, as well as, conceivably, on Pisarev and Chernyshevsky. Political nihilism is not, however, defined simply as the rejection of the state, a position that Stirner certainly holds, but which is better described as anarchism. Political nihilism refers instead to the specific doctrine prevalent in mid-nineteenth-century Russia that promoted the annihilation of Tsarist political authority without much consideration for what would follow, a context with which Stirner clearly had no direct involvement. Political nihilism is violent and revolutionary; Stirner's thought, despite its unwarranted reputation, is neither.

There is a deeper and closer connection between Stirner's thought and moral nihilism, insofar as his explicit rejection of *Sittlichkeit* (ethicality) and his relegation of the notion of good and evil, along with all evaluative judgment, to the status of a relative expression of personal preference, is entirely compatible with moral nihilism. Nonetheless, to call Stirner a moral nihilist is to highlight just one corollary aspect of his thought and is therefore wholly inadequate as an overall account of his philosophy. More inappropriate still is Stirner's classification as an existential nihilist, a designation for which no cogent justification can be found despite some general characteristics shared by Stirner and the existentialists. Above all, Stirner's positive outlook on human existence disqualifies him from representing, or indeed personifying, existential nihilism.

None of the specific types of nihilism most frequently associated with Stirner, nor any others encountered in the course of this investigation, can reasonably be claimed to encapsulate his philosophy as a whole. As a comprehensive description of his thought, nihilism would only be appropriate in the unlikely event that the word were one day to lose its negative connotations, and a new variety, mythological nihilism, were coined. In the meantime, and in the light of this study, it is more reasonable to conceive of Stirner as a hedonistic, pluralistic, quasi-nominalistic, anti-heteronomous, iconoclastic demythologizer, whose ethics are consistent with moral nihilism, and whose philosophy is based on the oft-misconstrued concept of egoism. Admittedly, this is not a simple characterization of Stirner's thought, but nor is it a simplistic misinterpretation or, worse still, a sophisticated falsification.

Bibliography

Works by Max Stirner

Stirner, Max. *The Ego and His Own*. Translated by Steven T. Byington. New York: Benj. R. Tucker, 1907.
———. *The Ego and His Own*. Edited by John Carroll and translated by Steven T. Byington. London: Jonathan Cape, 1971.
———. *The Ego and His Own: The Case of the Individual Against Authority*. Edited by James J. Martin and translated by Steven T. Byington. New York: Libertarian Book Club, 1963.
———. *The Ego and Its Own*. Edited by David Leopold and translated by Steven T. Byington. Cambridge: Cambridge University Press, 2006.
———. *Der Einzige und sein Eigenthum*. Leipzig: Otto Wigand, 1845.
———. *Der Einzige und sein Eigentum*. Edited by Paul Lauterbach. Leipzig: Reclam, 1893.
———. *Der Einzige und sein Eigentum und andere Schriften*. Edited by Hans G. Helms. Munich: Hanser, 1968.
———. *Der Einzige und sein Eigentum: Ausführlich kommentierte Studienausgabe*. Edited by Bernd Kast. Freiburg and Munich: Verlag Karl Alber, 2016.
———. *The False Principle of Our Education or Humanism and Realism*. Translated by Robert H. Beebe. Colorado Springs, CO: Ralph Myles, 1967.
———. *Max Stirner's Kleinere Schriften und seine Entgegnungen auf die Kritik seines Werkes: "Der Einzige und sein Eigenthum"; Aus den Jahren 1842–1847*. Edited by John Henry Mackay. Berlin: Schuster & Loeffler, 1898.
———. "Recensenten Stirners." *Wigand's Vierteljahrsschrift* 3, no. 4 (1845): 147–94.
———. *Stirner's Critics*. Translated by Wolfi Landstreicher. Berkeley, CA: LBC Books, 2012.
———. *The Unique and Its Property*. Translated by Wolfi Landstreicher. [n.p.]: Underworld Amusements, 2017.

Works by Friedrich Nietzsche

Nietzsche, Friedrich. *Beyond Good and Evil: Prelude to a Philosophy of the Future*. Translated by R. J. Hollingdale. Harmondsworth: Penguin, 1975.

---. *Briefwechsel: Kritische Gesamtausgabe.* Edited by Giorgio Colli and Mazzino Montinari. Berlin and New York: De Gruyter, 1975–.

---. *The Complete Works of Nietzsche.* Edited by Oscar Levy and translated by Anthony M. Ludovici and others, 18 vols. New York: Macmillan, 1909–1913.

---. *Ecce Homo: How One Becomes What One Is.* Translated by R. J. Hollingdale. Harmondsworth: Penguin, 1988.

---. *The Gay Science.* Translated by Walter Kaufmann. New York: Vintage, 1974.

---. *On the Genealogy of Morals.* Translated by Walter Kaufmann and R. J. Hollingdale; *Ecce Homo.* Translated by Walter Kaufmann. New York: Vintage, 1989.

---. *Human, All Too Human.* Translated by R. J. Hollingdale. Cambridge: Cambridge University Press, 1996.

---. *The Portable Nietzsche.* Translated by Walter Kaufmann. Harmondsworth: Penguin, 1988.

---. *Thoughts out of Season II: The Use and Abuse of History; Schopenhauer as Educator.* Translated by Adrian Collins. London: George Allen & Unwin, 1910.

---. *Thus Spoke Zarathustra: A Book for Everyone and No One.* Translated by R. J. Hollingdale. Harmondsworth: Penguin, 1975.

---. *Twilight of the Idols and The Anti-Christ.* Translated by R. J. Hollingdale. Harmondsworth: Penguin, 1975.

---. *Werke: Kritische Gesamtausgabe.* Edited by Giorgio Colli and Mazzino Montinari. Berlin and New York: De Gruyter, 1967–.

---. *The Will to Power: Selections from the Notebooks of the 1880s.* Translated by Michael A. Scarpitti and R. Kevin Hill. London: Penguin, 2017.

---. *Der Wille zur Macht: Versuch einer Umwerthung aller Werthe; aus dem Nachlaß 1884–1888.* Leipzig: C. G. Naumann, 1906.

Other Sources

Achelis, Thomas. "Ethische Probleme." *Die Gegenwart* 27, no. 53 (1898): 150–52.

Adorno, Theodor W. *Die musikalischen Monographien.* Frankfurt am Main: Suhrkamp, 1971.

Annenkov, P. V. *The Extraordinary Decade: Literary Memoirs.* Edited by Arthur P. Mendel and translated by Irwin R. Titunik. Ann Arbor: University of Michigan Press, 1968.

Arendt, Dieter. *Der "poetische Nihilismus" in der Romantik.* Berlin and New York: De Gruyter, 1972.

---. "Die Überwindung des Nihilismus." In *Der Nihilismus als Phänomen der Geistesgeschichte in der Wissenschaftlichen Diskussion unseres Jahrhunderts,* edited by Dieter Arendt, 350–54. Darmstadt: Wissenschaftliche Buchgesellschaft, 1974.

———. "Introduction." In *Nihilismus: Die Anfänge von Jacobi bis Nietzsche*, edited by Dieter Arendt, 9–106. Cologne: Hegner, 1970.
Aristotle. *De Anima*. Translated by R. D. Hicks. Cambridge: Cambridge University Press, 1907.
Arvon, Henri. *Aux sources de l'existentialisme: Max Stirner*. Paris: Presses Universitaires de France, 1954.
Artzibashef, Michael. "Introduction." In *The Millionaire*, translated by Percy Pinkerton, 5–10. New York: Huebsch, 1915.
Aubrey, John. *"Brief Lives," chiefly of Contemporaries, set down by John Aubrey, between the Years 1669 and 1696*. Oxford: Clarendon Press, 1898.
Auerbach, Berthold. *Schrift und Volk: Grundzüge der volksthümlichen Literatur*. Leipzig: F. A. Brockhaus, 1846.
Ayer, A. J. *Language, Truth and Logic*. Harmondsworth: Penguin, 1975.
Baader, Franz von. "Über die Freiheit der Intelligenz." In *Nihilismus: Die Anfänge von Jacobi bis Nietzsche*, edited by Dieter Arendt, 275–89. Cologne: Hegner, 1970.
Bakunin, Mikhail. "The Reaction in Germany." In *Bakunin on Anarchy: Selected Works by the Activist-Founder of World Anarchism*, edited by Sam Dolgoff, 55–57. New York: Vintage, 1972.
———. *Statism and Anarchy*. Edited and translated by Marshall S. Shatz. Cambridge: Cambridge University Press, 1990.
Ball, Hugo. *Die Folgen der Reformation: Zur Kritik der deutschen Intelligenz*. Göttingen: Wallstein, 2005.
Barnes, Jonathan. *Early Greek Philosophy*. London: Penguin, 1987.
Basch, Victor. *L'Individualisme anarchiste: Max Stirner*. Paris: Félix Alcan, 1904.
Bauer, Bruno. *Christus und die Caesaren: Der Ursprung des Christenthums aus dem römischen Griechenthum*. Berlin: Eugen Grosser, 1877.
Baum, Günther. *Vernunft und Erkenntnis: Die Philosophie F. H. Jacobis*. Bonn: Bouvier, 1969.
Baxa, Jakob. *Gesellschaftslehre von Platon bis Friedrich Nietzsche: Eine dogmengeschichtliche Einführung in die gesellschaftswissenschaftlichen Theorien*. Leipzig: Quelle & Meyer, 1927.
Benatar, David. *Better Never to Have Been: The Harm of Coming into Existence*. Oxford: Oxford University Press, 2006.
———. *The Human Predicament: A Candid Guide to Life's Biggest Questions*. New York: Oxford University Press, 2017.
Berber, Friedrich. *Das Staatsziel im Wandel der Weltgeschichte*. Munich: C. H. Beck, 1978.
Berg, Leo. *Der Übermensch in der modernen Litteratur: Ein Kapitel zur Geistesgeschichte des 19. Jahrhunderts*. Paris, Leipzig, and Munich: Albert Langen, 1897.
Berlin, Isaiah. *Concepts and Categories: Philosophical Essays*. Edited by Henry Hardy. New York: Viking Press, 1979.

———. "Fathers and Children, the Romanes Lecture 1970." In Ivan Turgenev, *Fathers and Sons*, translated by Rosemary Edmonds, 7–61. Harmondsworth: Penguin, 1977.

———. "Introduction." In Alexander Herzen, *My Past and Thoughts: The Memoirs of Alexander Herzen*, translated by Humphrey Higgens, xix–xliii. Berkeley and Los Angeles: University of California Press, 1982.

———. "Introduction." In Franco Venturi, *Roots of Revolution: A History of the Populist and Socialist Movements in Nineteenth Century Russia*, translated by Francis Haskell, vii–xxx. New York: Grosset & Dunlap, 1966.

———. *Russian Thinkers*. Edited by Henry Hardy and Aileen Kelly. London: Penguin, 2013.

———. *The Roots of Romanticism: The A. W. Mellon Lectures in the Fine Arts, 1965; The National Gallery of Art, Washington, DC*. Edited by Henry Hardy. London: Pimlico, 2000.

———. *Two Concepts of Liberty: An inaugural lecture delivered before the University of Oxford on 31 October 1958*. Oxford: Clarendon Press, 1958.

Bernoulli, Carl Albrecht. *Franz Overbeck und Friedrich Nietzsche—eine Freundschaft*. 2 vols. Jena: E. Diederichs, 1908.

Bernstein, Eduard. "Die Soziale Doktrin des Anarchismus. II. Max Stirner und 'Der Einzige.'" *Die Neue Zeit: Revue des geistigen und öffentlichen Lebens* 10, no. 1 (1891–1892): 421–28.

Biedermann, Karl. *1840–1870: Dreißig Jahre deutscher Geschichte; Vom Thronwechsel in Preußen 1840 bis zur Aufrichtung des neuen deutschen Kaiserthums; Nebst einem Rückblick auf die Zeit von 1815–1840*. 2 vols. Breslau: S. Schottlaender, 1881.

Billington, James H. *The Icon and the Axe: An Interpretive History of Russian Culture*. New York: Vintage, 1970.

Binswanger, Ludwig. *Grundformen und Erkenntnis menschlichen Daseins*. Zürich: Max Niehmann, 1942.

Blake, William. *Poems of William Blake*. Edited by W. B. Yeats. London: George Routledge and Sons, 1920.

Bloom, Harold. *Wallace Stevens: The Poems of our Climate*. Ithaca, NY and London: Cornell University Press, 1977.

Blumenfeld, Jacob. *All Things are Nothing to Me: The Unique Philosophy of Max Stirner*. Alresford: Zero Books, 2018.

Bonsiepen, Wolfgang. *Der Begriff der Negativität in den Jenaer Schriften Hegels*. Hamburg: Felix Meiner, 2016.

Brassier, Ray. *Nihil Unbound: Enlightenment and Extinction*. Basingstoke: Palgrave Macmillan, 2007.

Brobjer, Thomas H. "A Possible Solution to the Stirner-Nietzsche Question." *Journal of Nietzsche Studies* 25 (2003): 109–14.

Brock, Eike. *Nietzsche und der Nihilismus*. Berlin, Munich, and Boston: De Gruyter, 2015.

Brockway, Robert W. *Myth from the Ice Age to Mickey Mouse*. Albany: State University of New York Press, 1993.

Bruce, Steve. *God is Dead: Secularization in the West.* Hoboken, NJ: Wiley-Blackwell, 2002.
Buber, Martin. *Between Man and Man.* Translated by Ronald Gregor Smith. New York: Collier Books, 1965.
Büchner, Georg. *Werke und Briefe.* Munich: Deutscher Taschenbuch Verlag, 1965.
Bull, George. "Introduction." In Niccolò Machiavelli, *The Prince,* translated by George Bull, 9–26. Harmondsworth: Penguin, 1977.
Calvez, Jean-Yves. *Karl Marx: Darstellung und Kritik seines Denkens.* Translated by Theodor Sapper. Olten and Freiburg: Walter, 1964.
Camus, Albert. *L'Homme révolté.* Paris: Gallimard, 1951.
———. *The Myth of Sisyphus.* Translated by Justin O'Brien. Harmondsworth: Penguin, 1976.
———. *The Rebel.* Translated by Anthony Bower. Harmondsworth: Penguin, 1975.
Carr, Karen L. *The Banalization of Nihilism: Twentieth-Century Responses to Meaninglessness.* New York: State University of New York Press, 1992.
Carroll, John. *Break-Out from the Crystal Palace: The anarcho-psychological critique; Stirner, Nietzsche, Dostoevsky.* London and Boston: Routledge & Kegan Paul, 1974.
———. "Introduction." In Max Stirner, *The Ego and His Own,* edited by John Carroll and translated by Steven T. Byington, 11–36. London: Jonathan Cape, 1971.
Carus, Paul. *Nietzsche and Other Exponents of Individualism.* Chicago and London: Open Court Publishing, 1914.
Chalybäus, Heinrich Moritz. *Historical Development of Speculative Philosophy from Kant to Hegel.* Translated by Alfred Edersheim. Edinburgh: T. & T. Clark, 1854.
Chernyshevsky, Nikolai. *Polnoe sobranie sochinenii.* Edited by B. Koz'min and others. 16 vols. Moscow: Goslitizdat, 1939–1953.
———. *What Is to Be Done?* Translated by Michael R. Katz. Ithaca, NY and London: Cornell University Press, 1989.
Cioran, E. M. *The Trouble with Being Born.* Translated by Richard Howard. New York: Arcade Publishing, 1998.
Clark, John P. *Max Stirner's Egoism.* London: Freedom Press, 1976.
Coates, Ken. *Anti-Natalism: Rejectionist Philosophy from Buddhism to Benatar.* Sarasota: First Edition Design Publishing, 2014.
Confino, Michael, ed. *Daughter of a Revolutionary: Natalie Herzen and the Bakunin-Nechayev Circle.* Translated by Hilary Sternberg and Lydia Bott. London: Alcove Press, 1974.
Copleston, Frederick. *A History of Philosophy.* 9 vols. New York: Image, 1946–1975.
Cornu, Auguste. *Karl Marx und die Entwicklung des modernen Denkens: Beitrag zum Studium der Herausbildung des Marxismus.* Translated by Josef Schlesinger. Berlin: Dietz, 1950.

Crosby, Donald A. *The Specter of the Absurd: Sources and Criticisms of Modern Nihilism*. Albany: State University of New York Press, 1988.
Cunningham, Conor. *Genealogy of Nihilism: Philosophies of Nothing and the Difference of Theology*. London: Routledge, 2002.
Dawkins, Richard. *The God Delusion*. London: Bantam Press, 2006.
———. *The Selfish Gene*. Oxford and New York: Oxford University Press, 1991.
Deleuze, Gilles. *Nietzsche and Philosophy*. Translated by Hugh Tomlinson. London and New York: Continuum, 2002.
———. *The Logic of Sense*. Edited by Constantin V. Boundas and translated by Mark Lester. New York: Columbia University Press, 1990.
De Ridder, Widukind. "Max Stirner: The End of Philosophy and Political Subjectivity." In *Max Stirner*, edited by Saul Newman, 143–64. Basingstoke: Palgrave Macmillan, 2011.
Descartes, René. *A Discourse on Method*. Translated by John Veitch. London and Toronto: J. M. Dent, 1920.
Diamond, Jared. *Guns, Germs and Steel: A Short History of Everybody for the Last 13,000 Years*. London: Vintage, 2017.
Dod, Elmar. *Der unheimlichste Gast wird heimisch: Die Philosophie des Nihilismus; Evidenzen der Einbildungskraft*. Baden-Baden: Tectum Verlag, 2019.
Dostoevsky, Fyodor. *The Brothers Karamazov*. Translated by Richard Pevear and Larissa Volokhonsky. New York: Farrar, Straus and Giroux, 2002.
———. *The Brothers Karamazov*. Translated by David McDuff. London: Penguin, 2003.
———. *Crime and Punishment*. Translated by David McDuff. London: Penguin, 2003.
———. *Demons*. Translated by Robert A. Maguire. London: Penguin, 2008.
Dreier, James. "Moral Relativism and Moral Nihilism." In *The Oxford Handbook of Ethical Theory*, edited by David Copp, 240–62. Oxford: Oxford University Press, 2007.
Drews, Arthur. *Die deutsche Spekulation seit Kant mit besonderer Rücksicht auf das Wesen des Absoluten und die Persönlichkeit Gottes*. 2 vols. Leipzig: Fock, 1895.
———. *Geschichte der Philosophie*. Berlin and Leipzig: G. J. Göschen, 1913.
Droz, Jacques. *Europe between Revolutions 1815–1848*. Translated by Robert Baldick. Glasgow: Collins, 1967.
Dubois, Félix. *Die anarchistische Gefahr*. Translated by Max Tüdjen. Amsterdam: Dieckmann, 1894.
Düsing, Edith. "Gottestod-Nihilismus-Melancholie. Nietzsches Denkweg als Diagnose und Therapie des Nihilismus." In *Der Tod Gottes und die Wissenschaft: Zur Wissenschaftskritik Nietzsches*, edited by Carlo Gentili and Cathrin Nielsen, 31–66. Berlin and New York: De Gruyter, 2010.
Emmelius, Johann-Christoph. "'Ich hab' mein' Sach' auf nichts gestellt.' Zu Herkunft, Funktion und Vorgeschichte eines Zitats in Franz Overbecks

Brief an Friedrich Nietzsche vom 15. April 1883." *Nietzsche-Studien* 33 (2008): 306–34.
Epicurus. *The Art of Happiness*. Translated by George K. Strodach. New York: Penguin, 2013.
Fay, Laurel. *Shostakovich: A Life*. Oxford and New York: Oxford University Press, 2000.
Ferguson, Kathy E. "Why Anarchists Need Stirner." In *Max Stirner*, edited by Saul Newman, 167–88. Basingstoke: Palgrave Macmillan, 2011.
Feuerbach, Ludwig. *Gesammelte Werke*. Edited by Werner Schuffenhauer. 21 vols. Berlin: Akademie Verlag, 1973–1996.
———. *Sämmtliche Werke*. 10 vols. Leipzig: Otto Wigand, 1846–1866.
———. *The Essence of Christianity*. Translated by Marian Evans. London: John Chapman, 1854.
———. "*The Essence of Christianity* in Relation to *The Ego and Its Own*." Translated by Frederick M. Gordon. *The Philosophical Forum* 8, nos. 2–4 (1978): 81–91.
Fichte, Johann Gottlieb. "On the Basis of our Belief in a Divine Governance of the World." In J. G. Fichte, *Introductions to the Wissenschaftslehre and Other Writings (1797–1800)*, translated by Daniel Breazeale, 141–54. Indianapolis, IN and Cambridge: Hackett Publishing, 1994.
Fisher, H. A. L. *A History of Europe*. 3 vols. London and Glasgow: Collins, 1971.
Forberg, Friedrich Karl. "Entwicklung des Begriffs der Religion." *Philosophisches Journal einer Gesellschaft Teutscher Gelehrten* 8 (1798): 21–46.
Förster-Nietzsche, Elisabeth. "Introduction." In Henri Lichtenberger, *Die Philosophie Friedrich Nietzsches*, translated by Elisabeth Förster-Nietzsche, v–lxiv. Dresden and Leipzig: Carl Reißner, 1899.
———. "Nietzsche und Stirner." *Die Zukunft* 15, no. 24 (March 16, 1907): 407–8.
Frank, Joseph. *Dostoevsky: A Writer in His Time*. Princeton, NJ and Oxford: Princeton University Press, 2012.
Frazer, James George. *Balder the Beautiful: The Fire-Festivals of Europe and the Doctrine of the External Soul*. 2 vols. London: Macmillan, 1919.
Frede, Victoria. *Doubt, Atheism, and the Nineteenth-Century Russian Intelligentsia*. Madison: University of Wisconsin Press, 2011.
Frege, Gottlob. "Über Sinn und Bedeutung." *Zeitschrift für Philosophie und philosophische Kritik* 100, no. 1 (1892): 25–50.
Freud, Sigmund. *Civilization and Its Discontents*. Translated by Joan Riviere. London: Hogarth Press, 1930.
Friedell, Egon. *A Cultural History of the Modern Age: The Crisis of the European Soul from the Black Death to the World War*. Translated by Charles Francis Atkinson. 3 vols. New York: Alfred A. Knopf, 1954.
Friedlaender, Salomo. *Friedrich Nietzsche: Eine intellektuelle Biographie*. Leipzig: G. J. Göschen, 1911.
Garff, Joakim. *Søren Kierkegaard: A Biography*. Translated by Bruce H. Kirmmse. Princeton, NJ and Oxford: Princeton University Press, 2005.

Garland, Henry, and Mary Garland. *The Oxford Companion to German Literature.* Oxford: Clarendon Press, 1976.
Gass, William H. *Reading Rilke: Reflections on the Problems of Translation.* New York: Alfred A. Knopf, 1999.
Gast, Peter. "Nietzsche und Stirner." *Die Zukunft* 15, no. 30 (April 6, 1907): 146.
Gawoll, Hans-Jürgen. *Nihilismus und Metaphysik: Entwicklungsgeschichtliche Untersuchung vom deutschen Idealismus bis zu Heidegger.* Stuttgart: Frommann-Holzboog, 1989.
Gertz, Nolen. *Nihilism.* Cambridge, MA: The MIT Press, 2019.
Gillespie, Gerald, ed. *Die Nachtwachen des Bonaventura/The Night Watches of Bonaventura.* Translated by Gerald Gillespie. Austin: University of Texas Press, 1971.
Gillespie, Michael Allen. *Nihilism before Nietzsche.* Chicago: University of Chicago Press, 1996.
———. "Nihilism in the Nineteenth Century: From Absolute Subjectivity to Superhumanity." In *The Edinburgh Critical History of Nineteenth-Century Philosophy*, edited by Alison Stone, 278–93. Edinburgh: Edinburgh University Press, 2011.
Gillis, Alan. *Irish Poetry of the 1930s.* Oxford: Oxford University Press, 2005.
Gilman, Sander L., ed. *Conversations with Nietzsche: A Life in the Words of his Contemporaries.* New York and Oxford: Oxford University Press, 1987.
Glassford, John. "Did Friedrich Nietzsche Plagiarize from Max Stirner?" *Journal of Nietzsche Studies* 18 (1999): 73–79.
Gleichen-Rußwurm, Alexander von. "Der Einzige und sein Eigentum. Eine Erinnerung zu Max Stirners hundertstem Geburtstag." *Die Nation* 24 no. 3 (October 20, 1906): 41–43.
Goethe, Johann Wolfgang von. *Goethe's Gedichte.* 2 vols. Stuttgart and Tübingen: Cotta, 1845.
———. *The Poems of Goethe.* Translated by Edgar Alfred Bowring. New York: Hurst & Co., 1853.
Goldschmidt, Arthur. "Max Stirner, sein Leben und sein Werk." *Die Gesellschaft: Halbmonatsschrift für Litteratur, Kunst und Socialpolitik* 3 (1898): 227–39.
Gottlieb, Anthony. *The Dream of Reason: A History of Western Philosophy from the Greeks to the Renaissance.* London: Penguin, 2016.
Gottschall, Rudolf von. "Die deutsche Philosophie seit Hegel's Tode." In *Die Gegenwart: Eine encyclopädische Darstellung der neuesten Zeitgeschichte für alle Stände*, vol. 6, 292–340. Leipzig: F. A. Brockhaus, 1851.
Goudsblom, Johan. *Nihilism and Culture.* Oxford: Blackwell, 1980.
Green, Ronald. *Nothing Matters: A Book about Nothing.* Alresford: iff Books, 2011.
Grün, Karl, ed. *Ludwig Feuerbach in seinem Briefwechsel und Nachlass sowie in seiner Philosophischen Characterentwicklung.* 2 vols. Leipzig and Heidelberg: C. F. Winter, 1874.
Gutzkow, Karl. *Gesammelte Werke.* 12 vols. Jena: Costenoble, 1879.

Hamann, Richard, and Jost Hermand. *Naturalismus*. Berlin: Akademie Verlag, 1968.
Hamilton, Sir William. *Lectures on Metaphysics and Logic*. Edinburgh and London: Blackwood, 1861.
Hanne, Johann Wilhelm. *Der moderne Nihilismus und die Strauß'sche Glaubenslehre im Verhältnis zur Idee der christlichen Religion*. Bielefeld: Velhagen & Klasing, 1842.
Harari, Yuval Noah. *21 Lessons for the 21st Century*. London: Jonathan Cape, 2018.
———. *Sapiens: A Brief History of Humankind*. London: Vintage, 2014.
Harman, Gilbert. *The Nature of Morality: An Introduction to Ethics*. New York: Oxford University Press, 1977.
Hart, Julius. *Der neue Gott: Ein Ausblick auf das kommende Jahrhundert*. Florence and Leipzig: E. Diederichs, 1899.
Hartmann, Eduard von. *Ethische Studien*. Leipzig: Hermann Haacke, 1898.
———. "Nietzsches 'neue Moral.'" *Preussische Jahrbücher* 67, no. 5 (1891): 501–21.
———. *Phänomenologie des sittlichen Bewusstseins: Prolegomena zu jeder künftigen Ethik*. Berlin: Duncker, 1879.
———. *Philosophy of the Unconscious*. Translated by William Chatterton Coupland. 3 vols. New York: Macmillan & Co., 1884.
Hegel, Georg Wilhelm Friedrich. *Faith & Knowledge*. Translated by Walter Cerf and H. S. Harris. Albany: State University of New York Press, 1977.
———. *Hegel's Philosophy of Right*. Translated by S. W. Dyde. London: George Bell, 1896.
———. *Hegel's Science of Logic*. Translated by A. V. Miller. Amherst, NY: Humanity Books, 1998.
———. *The Logic of Hegel translated from the Encyclopaedia of the Philosophical Sciences*. Translated by William Wallace. Oxford: Clarendon Press, 1892.
Heidegger, Martin. *Being and Time*. Translated by John Macquarrie and Edward Robinson. Oxford: Basil Blackwell, 1978.
———. *Nietzsche*. Translated by David Farrell Krell. 2 vols. New York: Harper Collins, 1991.
Helms, Hans G. *Die Ideologie der anonymen Gesellschaft: Max Stirners "Einziger" und der Fortschritt des demokratischen Selbstbewusstseins vom Vormärz bis zur Bundesrepublik*. Cologne: M. DuMont Schauberg, 1966.
Heman, Friedrich. "Der Philosoph des Anarchismus und Nihilismus. Zum hundertjährigen Geburtstag Max Stirners." *Der Türmer* 9, no. 1 (1906): 67–74.
Herzen, A. I. *Sobranie sochinenii*. Edited by Semen Iosifovich Mashinskii. 30 vols. Moscow: Izd-vo Akademii nauk SSSR, 1954–1965.
Hingley, Ronald. *Nihilists: Russian Radicals and Revolutionaries in the Reign of Alexander II (1855–81)*. London: Weidenfeld and Nicolson, 1967.
Hitchens, Christopher. *Arguably*. London: Atlantic Books, 2012.

———. *God Is Not Great: How Religion Poisons Everything*. London: Atlantic Books, 2007.
Hobbes, Thomas. *Leviathan*. London: Penguin, 1987.
Hoffmann, David Marc. *Zur Geschichte des Nietzsche-Archivs*. Berlin and New York: De Gruyter, 1991.
———, ed. *Franz Overbeck, Heinrich Köselitz: Briefwechsel*. Berlin and New York: De Gruyter, 1998.
Hoffmann, Henryk. "The Development of Religious Studies in Poland: History and the Present State." In *Studying Religions with the Iron Curtain Closed and Opened: The Academic Study of Religion in Eastern Europe*, edited by Tomáš Bubík and Henryk Hoffmann, 87–121. Leiden and Boston: Brill, 2015.
Holbrook, David. "A Philosopher for Today? Max Stirner's Egoistical Nihilism." *New Blackfriars* 58, no. 687 (1977): 382–90.
Hölderlin, Friedrich. *Hyperion or The Hermit in Greece*. Translated by Willard R. Trask. New York: Frederick Ungar Publishing, 1984.
Holz, Hans Heinz. *Der französische Existentialismus: Theorie und Aktualität*. Munich and Speyer: Dobbeck, 1958.
Hook, Sidney. *From Hegel to Marx: Studies in the Intellectual Development of Karl Marx*. Ann Arbor: University of Michigan Press, 1962.
Horkheimer, Max, and Theodor W. Adorno. *Dialectic of Enlightenment*. Translated by John Cumming. New York: Herder and Herder, 1972.
Hugo, Victor. *Les Miserables*. Translated by Charles E. Wilbour. New York: The Modern Library, 1902.
Hume, David. *A Letter from a Gentleman to His Friend in Edinburgh; Containing Some Observations on a Specimen of the Principles Concerning Religion and Morality Said to be Maintain'd in a Book Lately Publish'd Intituled [sic], "A Treatise on Human Nature", etc*. Edited by Ernest C. Mossner and John V. Price. Facsimile reprint. Edinburgh: Edinburgh University Press, 1967.
Huszar, George de. "Nietzsche's Theory of Decadence and the Transvaluation of all Values." *Journal of the History of Ideas* 6 (1945): 259–72.
Immermann, Karl Leberecht. *Die Epigonen*. Berlin: Ehle, 1854.
Index Librorum Prohibitorum: Katalog über die in den Jahren 1844 und 1845 in Deutschland verbotenen Bücher; Beitrag zur Geschichte der Presse; Erste Hälfte. Jena: Luden, 1845.
Inwagen, Peter van. *Material Beings*. Ithaca, NY and London: Cornell University Press, 1990.
Isaac, Jeffrey C. *Arendt, Camus and Modern Rebellion*. London and New Haven, CT: Yale University Press, 1992.
Jacobi, Friedrich Heinrich. *Friedrich Heinrich Jacobi's Werke*. 6 vols. Leipzig: Gerhard Fleischer, 1812–1825.
Jean Paul Richter, Friedrich. *School for Aesthetics*. In *German Romantic Criticism*, edited by A. Leslie Willson and translated by Margaret R. Hale, 31–61. New York: Continuum, 1982.

———. *Clavis Fichtiana seu Leibgeberiana*. In *Sämtliche Werke*, vol. 1.3:1011–56. Munich and Vienna: Carl Hanser Verlag, 1996.
Jenisch, Daniel. *Ueber Grund und Werth der Entdeckungen des Herrn Professor Kant in der Metaphysik, Moral und Aesthetik*. Berlin: Vieweg, 1796.
Joël, Karl. "Nietzsche und Stirner." *Die Zukunft* 15, no. 27 (April 6, 1907): 34–35.
———. *Wandlungen der Weltanschauung: Eine Philosophiegeschichte als Geschichtsphilosophie*. 2 vols. Tübingen: J. C. B. Mohr, 1934.
Joyce, James. *A Portrait of the Artist as a Young Man*. Ware: Wordsworth Editions, 1992.
Kahlefeld, Susanna. *Dialektik und Sprung in Jacobis Philosophie*. Würzburg: Königshausen & Neumann, 2000.
Kant, Immanuel. "Answer to the Question: What Is Enlightenment." In *Basic Writings of Kant*, edited by Allen W. Wood and translated by Thomas K. Abbott, 133–41. New York: The Modern Library, 2001.
Kast, Bernd. *Max Stirners Destruktion der spekulativen Philosophie: Das Radikal [sic] des Eigners und die Auflösung der Abstrakta Mensch und Menschheit*. Freiburg and Munich: Verlag Karl Alber, 2016.
———. "Afterword." In Max Stirner, *Der Einzige und sein Eigentum: Ausführlich kommentierte Studienausgabe*, edited by Bernd Kast, 371–95. Freiburg and Munich: Verlag Karl Alber, 2016.
———. "Afterword." In Henri Arvon, *Max Stirner: An den Quellen des Existentialismus*, edited by Armin Geus and translated by Gerhard H. Müller, 204–19. Rangsdorf: Basilisken-Presse, 2012.
———. "Rechtfertigt Stirner Mord, Selbstmord, Inzest und Prostitution? Überlegungen zu provozierenden Aspekten von Stirners Ethik." *Der Einzige: Jahrbuch der Max Stirner Gesellschaft* 6 (2013): 28–45.
Katkov, M. N. "Sochineniia v stikhakh I proze grafini S. F. Tolstoi." *Otechestvennyia zapiski* 12, no. 10 (1840): 17.
Katz, Martin. *Mikhail N. Katkov: A Personal Biography 1818–1887*. The Hague: Mouton, 1966.
Keben, Georg. "John Henry Mackay und sein Philosoph." *Monatsblätter: Organ der Breslauer Dichterschule* 16, no. 12 (1890): 172–90.
Keyserling, Hermann Graf. *Unsterblichkeit: Eine Kritik der Beziehungen zwischen Naturgeschehen und menschlicher Vorstellungskraft*. Darmstadt: Otto Reich, 1920.
Khawaja, Noreen. "Heidegger's Kierkegaard: Philosophy and Religion in the Tracks of a Failed Interpretation." *The Journal of Religion* 95 (2015): 295–317.
Kierkegaard, Søren. *The Concept of Dread*. Translated by Walter Lowrie. Princeton, NJ: Princeton University Press, 1973.
———. *Fear and Trembling*. Translated by Alastair Hannay. London: Penguin, 2005.
———. *Philosophical Fragments or A Fragment of Philosophy*. Translated by David F. Swenson. Princeton, NJ: Princeton University Press, 1962.

———. *The Sickness unto Death.* Translated by Alastair Hannay. London: Penguin, 1989.

Kirk, Robert. *Translation Determined.* Oxford: Clarendon Press, 1986.

Koepke, Wulf. "Nothing but the Dark Side of Ourselves? The Devil and Aesthetic Nihilism." In *The Fantastic Other, an Interface of Perspectives*, edited by Brett Cooke, George E. Slusser, and Jaume Marti-Olivella, 143–63. Amsterdam: Rodopi, 1998.

Kohlschmidt, Werner. "Nihilismus der Romantik." In *Der Nihilismus als Phänomen der Geistesgeschichte*, edited by Dieter Arendt, 79–98. Darmstadt: Wissenschaftliche Buchgesellschaft, 1974.

Kołakowski, Leszek. *Main Currents of Marxism: Its Rise, Growth, and Dissolution.* Translated by P. S. Falla. 3 vols. Oxford: Clarendon Press, 1978.

Köppen, Friedrich. *Schellings Lehre oder das Ganze der Philosophie des absoluten Nichts.* Hamburg: Friedrich Perthes, 1803.

Künneth, Walter. *Politik zwischen Dämon und Gott: Eine christliche Ethik des Politischen.* Berlin: Lutherisches Verlagshaus, 1954.

Kurtschinsky, M. *Der Apostel des Egoismus: Max Stirner und seine Philosophie der Anarchie.* Translated by Gregor von Glasenapp. Berlin: R. L. Prager, 1923.

Laas, Ernst. *Idealismus und Positivismus: Eine kritische Auseinandersetzung.* 2 vols. Berlin: Weidmannsche Buchhandlung, 1882.

Lachmann, Benedict. *Protagoras, Nietzsche, Stirner: Ein Beitrag zur Philosophie des Individualismus und Egoismus.* Berlin: Leonhard Simion Nf., 1914.

Laforgue, Jules. *Oeuvres complètes de Jules Laforgue.* 3 vols. Paris: Société du Mercure de France, 1902–1903.

Lampert, E. *Sons against Fathers: Studies in Russian Radicalism and Revolution.* London: Oxford University Press, 1965.

———. *Studies in Rebellion.* London: Routledge & Kegan Paul, 1957.

Landstreicher, Wolfi. "Introduction." In Max Stirner, *The Unique and Its Property.* Translated by Wolfi Landstreicher, 4–13. [n.p.]: Underworld Amusements, 2017.

Lange, Friedrich Albert. *The History of Materialism and Criticism of its Present Importance.* Translated by Ernest Chester Thomas. London: Routledge & Kegan Paul, 1950.

Lantz, Kenneth. *The Dostoevsky Encyclopedia.* Westport, CT and London: Greenwood Press, 2004.

Larkin, Philip. *Collected Poems.* London: Faber & Faber, 1988.

Laska, Bernd A. *Ein dauerhafter Dissident: 150 Jahre Stirners "Einziger"; Eine kurze Wirkungsgeschichte.* Nuremberg: LSR-Verlag, 1996.

———. *Ein heimlicher Hit: 150 Jahre Stirners "Einziger"; Eine kurze Editionsgeschichte* Nuremberg: LSR-Verlag, 1994.

———. *"Katechon" und "Anarch": Carl Schmitts und Ernst Jüngers Reaktionen auf Max Stirner.* Nuremberg: LSR-Verlag, 1997.

———. "Nietzsches initiale Krise. Die Stirner-Nietzsche-Frage in neuem Licht." *Germanic Notes and Reviews* 33, no. 2 (2002): 109–33.

Leopardi, Giacomo. *Moral Fables, followed by Thoughts.* Translated by J. G. Nichols. Richmond: Alma Books, 2017.
———. *Zibaldone.* Edited by Michael Caesar and Franco D'Intino and translated by Kathleen Baldwin. New York: Farrar, Straus and Giroux, 2013.
Leopold, David. "Introduction." In Max Stirner, *The Ego and Its Own*, edited by David Leopold, xi–xxxii. Cambridge: Cambridge University Press, 1995.
———. "'The State and I:' Max Stirner's Anarchism." In *The New Hegelians: Politics and Philosophy in the Hegelian School*, edited by Douglas Moggach, 176–99. Cambridge: Cambridge University Press, 2006.
Lévy, Albert. *Stirner et Nietzsche.* Paris: Société Nouvelle de Librairie et d'Édition, 1904.
Lichtenberg, Georg Christoph. *Schriften und Briefe.* Edited by Wolfgang Promies. 4 vols. Frankfurt am Main: Zweitausendeins, 1994.
Lichtenberger, Henri. *Die Philosophie Friedrich Nietzsches.* Translated by Elisabeth Förster-Nietzsche. Dresden and Leipzig: Carl Reißner, 1899.
Ligotti, Thomas. *The Conspiracy against the Human Race: A Contrivance of Horror.* New York: Penguin, 2018.
Löwith, Karl. *Das Individuum in der Rolle des Mitmenschen.* Munich: Drei Masken-Verlag, 1928.
———. *From Hegel to Nietzsche: The Revolution in Nineteenth-Century Thought.* Translated by David E. Green. London: Constable, 1965.
Lucchesi, Matteo Johannes Paul. *Die Individualitätsphilosophie Max Stirners.* Leipzig-Reudnitz: Hoffmann, 1897.
Lucretius. *On the Nature of The Universe.* Translated by R. E. Latham. London: Penguin, 1994.
Ludwig, Franz. *Kommunismus, Anarchismus, Sozialismus: Geschichtliches und Kritisches.* Berlin: Verlag des Reichsverbands gegen die Sozialdemokratie, 1908.
Lütgert, Wilhelm. "Die Religion des deutschen Idealismus und ihr Ende. Dritter Teil: Höhe und Niedergang des Idealismus." *Beiträge zur Förderung der christlichen Theologie* 2, no. 10 (1926): 212–20.
Lütkehaus, Ludger. *Nichts: Abschied vom Sein, Ende der Angst.* Leipzig: Zweitausendeins, 2014.
Macaulay, Thomas Babington. *Readings from Macaulay: Italy.* Boston, MA: Chautauqua Press, 1885.
Machiavelli, Niccolò. *Discourses on the First Decade of Titus Livius.* Translated by Ninian Hill Thomson. London: Kegan Paul, Trench & Co., 1883.
———. *The Prince.* Translated by George Bull. Harmondsworth: Penguin, 1977.
Mackay, John Henry. *Max Stirner: His Life and His Work.* Translated by Hubert Kennedy. Concord, CA: Peremptory Publications, 2005.
Mackie, J. L. *Ethics: Inventing Right and Wrong.* London: Penguin, 1990.
Macquarrie, John. *An Existentialist Theology: A Comparison of Heidegger and Bultmann.* Harmondsworth: Penguin, 1973.
———. *Existentialism.* Harmondsworth: Penguin, 1977.

Mainländer, Philipp. *Die Philosophie der Erlösung.* Berlin: Theobald Grieben, 1876.
Malia, Martin E. *Alexander Herzen and the Birth of Russian Socialism.* New York: Grosset & Dunlap, 1965.
Marmysz, John. *Laughing at Nothing: Humor as a Response to Nihilism.* Albany: State University of New York Press, 2003.
Martin, Glen T. *From Nietzsche to Wittgenstein: The Problem of Truth and Nihilism in the Modern World.* New York: Peter Lang, 1989.
Martin, James J. "Introduction." In Max Stirner, *The Ego and His Own: The Case of the Individual Against Authority*, edited by James J. Martin and translated by Steven T. Byington, xi–xx. New York: Libertarian Book Club, 1963.
Martin, Nicholas. *Nietzsche and Schiller: Untimely Aesthetics.* Oxford: Clarendon Press, 1996.
Marx, Karl, and Friedrich Engels. *Collected Works.* Translated by Peter and Betty Ross, etc. 50 vols. Moscow: Progress Publishers, 1975–2004.
Masaryk, Tomáš Garrigue. *Masaryk on Marx.* An abridged edition of T. G. Masaryk, *The Social Question: Philosophical and Sociological Foundations of Marxism.* Edited and translated by Erazim V. Kohák. Lewisburg, PA: Bucknell University Press, 1972.
———. *The Spirit of Russia: Studies in History, Literature and Philosophy.* Translated by Eden and Cedar Paul. 3 vols. London: George Allen & Unwin, 1919–1967.
———. *Zur russischen Geschichts- und Religionsphilosophie: Soziologische Skizzen.* 2 vols. Jena: E. Diederichs, 1913.
Mauthner, Fritz. "Hat Nietzsche Stirner's *Einzigen* gekannt?" *Der Einzige—Vierteljahresschrift des Max-Stirner-Archivs Leipzig* 4, no.4 (2001): 21–23.
Mautz, Kurt Adolf. *Die Philosophie Max Stirners im Gegensatz zum Hegelschen Idealismus.* Berlin: Junker & Dünnhaupt, 1936.
May, Gerhard. *Creatio Ex Nihilo: The Doctrine of "Creation out of Nothing" in Early Christian Thought.* Translated by A. S. Worrall. Edinburgh: T. & T. Clark, 1994.
McLaughlin, Paul. *Mikhail Bakunin: The Philosophical Basis of His Anarchism.* New York: Algora Publishing, 2002.
McLellan, David. *Karl Marx: His Life & Thought.* London and Basingstoke: Macmillan, 1973.
———. *The Young Hegelians and Karl Marx.* London: Macmillan, 1969.
Messer, Max. *Max Stirner.* Berlin: Bard, Marquardt & Co., 1907.
Milkov, Nikolay. *A Hundred Years of English Philosophy.* Dordrecht: Springer, 2003.
Molderings, Herbert. *Duchamp and the Aesthetics of Chance.* Translated by John Brogden. New York: Columbia University Press, 2010.
Müller-Lauter, Wolfgang. "Nihilismus als Konsequenz des Idealismus." In *Denken im Schatten des Nihilismus: Festschrift für W. Weischedel zum 70.*

Geburtstag, edited by A. Schwan, 113–63. Darmstadt: Wissenschaftliche Buchgesellschaft, 1975.

Nathanson, Hugo. "Max Stirner. (Zum hundertsten Geburtstag)." *Das Blaubuch: Wochenschrift für öffentliches Leben, Literatur und Kunst* 1, no. 42 (October 25, 1906): 1636–38.

Newman, Saul. "Introduction: Re-encountering Stirner's Ghosts." In *Max Stirner*, edited by Saul Newman, 1–18. Basingstoke: Palgrave Macmillan, 2011.

———. "Stirner's Ethics of Voluntary Inservitude." In *Max Stirner*, edited by Saul Newman, 189–209. Basingstoke: Palgrave Macmillan, 2011.

Nicholson, Reynold Alleyne. *Studies in Islamic Poetry*. Cambridge: Cambridge University Press, 1921.

Nishitani, Keiji. *The Self-Overcoming of Nihilism*. Translated by Graham Parkes with Setsuko Aihara. Albany: State University of New York Press, 1990.

Obereit, Jacob Hermann. *Der wiederkommende Lebensgeist der verzweifelten Metaphysik: Ein kritisches Drama zu neuer Grund-Critik vom Geist des Cebes*. Berlin: Georg Jacob Decker und Sohn, 1787.

Onfray, Michel. *A Hedonist Manifesto: The Power to Exist*. Translated by Joseph McClellan. New York: Columbia University Press, 2015.

———. *Atheist Manifesto: The Case Against Christianity, Judaism, and Islam*. Translated by Jeremy Leggatt. New York: Arcade Publishing, 2011.

Oswald, David. "Introduction." In Rainer Maria Rilke, *Duino Elegies*, translated by David Oswald, 7–23. Einsiedeln: Daimon Verlag, 1992.

Parker, S. *Cicero's Five Books De Finibus: or, Concerning the Last Object of Desire and Aversion*. Oxford: N. Bliss, 1812.

Pasley, Malcolm. "Nietzsche's Use of Medical Imagery." In *Nietzsche: Imagery and Thought*, edited by Malcolm Pasley, 123–58. London: Methuen, 1978.

Paterson, R. W. K. *The Nihilistic Egoist: Max Stirner*. London, New York, and Toronto: Oxford University Press, 1971.

Penzo, Giorgio. *Die existentielle Empörung: Max Stirner zwischen Philosophie und Anarchie*. Translated by Barbara Häußler. Frankfurt am Main: Peter Lang, 2006.

———. *Max Stirner: La rivolta esistenziale*. Turin: Marietti, 1971.

Pietsch, Ludwig. *Wie ich Schriftsteller geworden bin: Erinnerungen aus den Fünfziger Jahren*. Berlin: F. Fontane & Co., 1893.

Pinkard, Terry. "The Social Conditions of Philosophy in the Nineteenth Century." In *The Cambridge History of Philosophy in the Nineteenth Century (1790–1870)*, edited by Allen W. Wood and Songsuk Susan Hahn, 46–60. New York: Cambridge University Press, 2012.

Pinker, Steven. *Enlightenment Now: The Case for Reason, Science, Humanism and Progress*. London: Penguin, 2019.

Pisarev, Dmitry. *Collected Works*. Edited by V. Kirpotina. 2 vols. Moscow: Gos. izd-vo khudozh. lit-ry, 1934–1935.

Plato. *The Republic*. Harmondsworth: Penguin, 1964.

Pöggeler, Otto. "Hegel und die Anfänge der Nihilismus-Diskussion." In *Der Nihilismus als Phänomen der Geistesgeschichte*, edited by Dieter Arendt, 307–49. Darmstadt: Wissenschaftliche Buchgesellschaft, 1974.
Polturak, Aurélie. "Die Philosophie Max Stirners systematisch dargestellt." *Stirneriana* 6 (Leipzig: Verlag Max-Stirner-Archiv, 1998): 1–63.
Ponomarev, Alexey. *Der Nihilismus und seine Erfahrung in der Romantik*. Marburg: Tectum Verlag, 2010.
Prideaux, Sue. *Edvard Munch: Behind the Scream*. New Haven, CT and London: Yale University Press, 2005.
———. *I am Dynamite! A Life of Friedrich Nietzsche*. London: Faber & Faber, 2018.
Pypina, V. A. *Lyubov' v zhizni Chernyshevskogo (Po materiyalam semeynogo arkhiva)*. Petrograd: Put' k znaniu, 1923.
Radowitz, Joseph von. *Gespräche aus der Gegenwart über Staat und Kirche*. Stuttgart: Ad. Becher's Verlag, 1851.
Rauschning, Hermann. *Die Revolution des Nihilismus: Kulisse und Wirklichkeit im Dritten Reich*. Zürich: Europa Verlag, 1938.
Read, Herbert. *Existentialism, Marxism and Anarchism: Chains of Freedom*. London: Freedom Press, 1952.
———. *The Tenth Muse: Essays in Criticism*. London: Routledge & Kegan Paul, 1957.
Reginster, Bernard. *The Affirmation of Life: Nietzsche on Overcoming Nihilism*. Cambridge, MA: Harvard University Press, 2006.
———. "Nietzsche on Selflessness and the Value of Altruism." *History of Philosophy Quarterly* 17, no. 2 (2000): 177–200.
Reschika, Richard. *Philosophische Abenteurer*. Tübingen: J. C. B. Mohr, 2001.
Ridley, Matt. *The Origins of Virtue*. London: Penguin, 1997.
Riehl, Alois. *Friedrich Nietzsche: Der Künstler und der Denker*. Stuttgart: F. Frommann, 1898.
Robinson, Cedric J. *The Terms of Order: Political Science and the Myth of Leadership*. Albany: State University of New York, 1980.
Rosen, Stanley. *Nihilism: A Philosophical Essay*. New Haven, CT and London: Yale University Press, 1969.
Rosenkranz, Karl. *Aus einem Tagebuch: Herbst 1833 bis Frühjahr 1846*. Leipzig: F. A. Brockhaus, 1854.
Roszak, Theodore. *The Making of a Counter Culture: Reflections on the Technocratic Society and Its Youthful Opposition*. New York: Doubleday, 1969.
Ruest, Anselm. *Max Stirner: Leben—Weltanschauung, Vermächtnis*. Berlin and Leipzig: Hermann Seemann Nachfolger, 1906.
Ruge, Arnold. *Briefwechsel und Tagebuchblätter aus den Jahren 1825–1847*. Edited by Paul Nerrlich. Aalen: Scientia Verlag, 1985.
Russell, Bertrand. *A History of Western Philosophy*. London and Sydney: Unwin, 1988.
Safranski, Rüdiger. *Nietzsche: A Philosophical Biography*. Translated by Shelley Frisch. New York and London: W. W. Norton, 2003.

Santayana, George. *Egotism in German Philosophy*. London: J. M. Dent, 1940.
Sartre, Jean-Paul. *Being and Nothingness: An Essay on Phenomenological Ontology*. Translated by Hazel E. Barnes. London: Methuen, 1977.
———. *Existentialism and Humanism*. Translated by Philip Mairet. London: Methuen, 1960.
———. *Nausea*. Translated by Robert Baldick. Harmondsworth: Penguin, 1963.
———. *Saint Genet, Actor and Martyr*. Translated by Bernard Frechtman. New York: George Braziller, 1974.
Sawicki, Franz. *Das Problem der Persönlichkeit und des Übermenschen*. Paderborn: Ferdinand Schöningh, 1909.
Schaefer, Dirk. *Im Namen Nietzsches: Elisabeth Förster-Nietzsche und Lou Andreas-Salomé*. Frankfurt am Main: Fischer, 2001.
Schapiro, Leonard. *Turgenev, His Life and Times*. Cambridge, MA: Harvard University Press, 1982.
Scheibert, Peter. *Von Bakunin zu Lenin: Geschichte der russischen revolutionären Ideologien 1840–1895*. Leiden: E. J. Brill, 1956.
Scheit, Herbert. "Max Stirner—ein antipädagogischer Pädagoge." In *Stirner-Treffen: 21.–23. Juni 2002 in Hummeltal b. Bayreuth; Protokoll*, 5–19. Leipzig: Verlag Max-Stirner-Archiv, 2003.
Schellwien, Robert. *Max Stirner und Friedrich Nietzsche: Erscheinungen des modernen Geistes, und das Wesen des Menschen*. Leipzig: C. E. M. Pfeffer, 1892.
Schenk, H. G. *The Mind of the European Romantics*. Oxford: Oxford University Press, 1979.
Schiereck, Larry Alan. *Max Stirner's Egoism and Nihilism*. [n.p.]: Underworld Amusements, 2018.
Schirnhofer, Resa von. "Vom Menschen Nietzsche." *Zeitschrift für philosophische Forschung* 22 (1968), no. 2: 250–60; and no. 3: 441–58.
Schmitz, Hermann. *Selbstdarstellung als Philosophie: Metamorphosen der entfremdeten Subjektivität*. Bonn: Bouvier, 1995.
Schopenhauer, Arthur. *Essays and Aphorisms*. Translated by R. J. Hollingdale. Harmondsworth: Penguin, 1976.
———. *The World as Will and Representation*. Translated by E. F. J. Payne. 2 vols. New York: Dover, 1966.
Schröder, Winfried. "Introduction." In Matthias Knutzen, *Schriften, Dokumente*, edited by Winfried Schröder, 7–32. Stuttgart: Frommann-Holzboog, 2010.
———. *Moralischer Nihilismus: Radikale Moralkritik von den Sophisten bis Nietzsche*. Stuttgart: Reclam, 2005.
Schuffenhauer, Werner. *Feuerbach und der junge Marx: Zur Entstehungsgeschichte der marxistischen Weltanschauung*. Berlin: Deutscher Verlag der Wissenschaften, 1972.
Schultheiss, Hermann. *Stirner: Grundlagen zum Verständnis des Werkes "Der Einzige und sein Eigentum."* Ratibor: F. Lindner, 1906.

Seife, Charles. *Zero: The Biography of a Dangerous Idea.* London: Souvenir Press, 2000.
Sextus Empiricus. *Against the Logicians.* Translated by R. G. Bury. Cambridge, MA: Harvard University Press, 1935.
Shafer-Landau, Russ. *The Fundamentals of Ethics.* New York and Oxford: Oxford University Press, 2012.
Simmel, Georg. *Schopenhauer und Nietzsche: Ein Vortragszyklus.* Leipzig: Duncker & Humblot, 1907.
Slocombe, Will. *Nihilism and the Sublime Postmodern: The (Hi)Story of a Difficult Relationship from Romanticism to Postmodernism.* New York and London: Routledge, 2006.
Sloterdijk, Peter. *Kritik der zynischen Vernunft.* 2 vols. Frankfurt am Main: Suhrkamp, 1983.
Smith, Adam. *An Inquiry into the Nature and Causes of the Wealth of Nations.* Edited by Edwin Cannan. New York: Random House, 1937.
———. *The Theory of Moral Sentiments.* London: A. Millar, 1761.
Sophocles. *The Theban Plays.* Translated by E. F. Watling. Harmondsworth: Penguin, 1985.
Spann, Othmar. *Kurz gefaßtes System der Gesellschaftslehre.* Berlin: J. Guttentag, 1914.
Spinoza, Benedict de. *Ethics.* Edited and translated by Edwin Curley. London: Penguin, 1996.
Stein, Ludwig. *Philosophische Strömungen der Gegenwart.* Stuttgart: Ferdinand Enke, 1908.
Steiner, Rudolf. "Das Nietzsche-Archiv und seine Anklagen gegenüber dem bisherigen Herausgeber. Eine Enthüllung." *Magazin für Literatur* 69, no. 6 (1900): 505–28.
———. *Friedrich Nietzsche: Fighter for Freedom.* Translated by Margaret Ingram deRis. Englewood, NJ: Rudolf Steiner Publications, 1960.
Stepelevich, Lawrence S. "Hegel and Stirner: Thesis and Antithesis." *Idealistic Studies* 6, no. 3 (1976): 263–78.
———. "Letter from Edgar Bauer (duplicate)." Translated by Lawrence S. Stepelevich. *The Philosophical Forum* 8, nos. 2–4 (1978): 171.
———. "Max Stirner and the Last Man." *The Heythrop Journal* 48, no. 8 (2011): 1–11.
———. "Max Stirner as Hegelian." *Journal of the History of Ideas* 46, no. 4 (1985): 597–614.
———. *Max Stirner on the Path of Doubt.* Lanham, MD: Lexington Books, 2020.
Stern, J. P. *A Study of Nietzsche.* Cambridge: Cambridge University Press, 1979.
———. "Nietzsche and the Idea of Metaphor." In *Nietzsche: Imagery and Thought*, edited by Malcolm Pasley, 64–82. London: Methuen, 1978.
Stewart, Jon. *A History of Nihilism in the Nineteenth Century: Confrontations with Nothingness.* Cambridge: Cambridge University Press, 2023.

Strauss, David Friedrich. *Streitschriften zur Verteidigung meiner Schrift über das Leben Jesu und zur Charakteristik der gegenwärtigen Theologie.* Tübingen: Osiander, 1837.
Strauss, Leo. "German Nihilism." *Interpretation: A Journal of Political Philosophy* 26, no. 3 (1999): 353–78.
———. *The City and Man.* Chicago: University of Chicago Press, 1978.
Ströbel, Heinrich. "Stirners 'Einziger und sein Eigentum.'" *Neuland: Monatsschrift für Politik, Wissenschaft, Literatur und Kunst* 2, no. 2 (1897): 82–92.
Stulpe, Alexander. *Gesichter des Einzigen: Max Stirner und die Anatomie moderner Indivdualität.* Berlin: Duncker & Humblot, 2010.
Sveistrup, Hans. "Stirner als Soziologe." *Stirneriana* 29 (2006): 17–40.
Tartaglia, James. *Philosophy in a Meaningless Life.* London: Bloomsbury, 2015.
———. *Nihilism and the Meaning of Life: A Philosophical Dialogue with James Tartaglia.* Edited by Masahiro Morioka. Saitama: Journal of Philosophy of Life, 2017.
Thacker, Eugene. *Infinite Resignation.* London: Repeater Books, 2018.
———. *Starry Speculative Corpse.* Winchester and Washington, DC: Zero Books, 2015.
Thielicke, Helmut. *Nihilism: Its Origin and Nature—with a Christian Answer.* Translated by John W. Doberstein. New York: Harper & Brothers, 1961.
Timm, H. "Die Bedeutung der Spinoza-Briefe für die Entwicklung der idealistischen Religionsphilosophie." In *Friedrich Heinrich Jacobi: Philosoph und Literat der Goethezeit*, edited by Klaus Hammacher, 35–81. Frankfurt am Main: Vittorio Klostermann, 1971.
Tolstoy, Leo. *Anna Karenina.* Translated by Louise and Aylmer Maude. Oxford: Oxford University Press, 1998.
Tongeren, Paul van. *Friedrich Nietzsche and European Nihilism.* Translated by David Versteeg and Vasti Calitz. Newcastle upon Tyne: Cambridge Scholars Publishing, 2018.
Tucker, Benjamin. "Publisher's Preface." In Max Stirner, *The Ego and His Own*, translated by Steven T. Byington, vii–xi. New York: Benj. R. Tucker, 1907.
Turgenev, Ivan. *Fathers and Sons.* Translated by Rosemary Edmonds. Harmondsworth: Penguin, 1977.
Türkdogan, Halil Ibrahim. "Fragmentarisches über die Revolte." *Der Einzige: Vierteljahresschrift des Max-Stirner-Archivs Leipzig*, 3, no. 3 (2000): 45–47.
Ulrich, Jörg. *Individualität als politische Religion: Theologische Mucken und metaphysische Abgründe (post)moderner Subjektivität.* Albeck bei Ulm: Verlag Ulmer Manuskripte, 2002.
Unamuno, Miguel de. *The Tragic Sense of Life in Men and in Peoples.* Translated by J. E. Crawford Flitch. London: MacMillan, 1921.

Venturi, Franco. *Roots of Revolution: A History of the Populist and Socialist Movements in Nineteenth Century Russia*. Translated by Francis Haskell. New York: Grosset & Dunlap, 1966.

Vercellone, Frederico. *Einführung in den Nihilismus*. Munich: Fink, 1988.

Vogel, Martin. *Apollinisch und Dionysisch: Geschichte eines genialen Irrtums*. Regensburg: G. Bosse, 1966.

Vordtriede, Werner. "Das nihilistische Geburtstagskind." In *Der Nihilismus als Phänomen der Geistesgeschichte*, edited by Dieter Arendt, 210–12. Darmstadt: Wissenschaftliche Buchgesellschaft, 1974.

Weier, Winfried. *Nihilismus: Geschichte, System, Kritik*. Paderborn: Ferdinand Schöningh, 1980.

Weiße, C. H. *Die Idee der Gottheit: Eine philosophische Abhandlung; Als wissenschaftliche Grundlegung zur Philosophie der Religion*. Dresden: Ch. F. Grimmer'sche Buchhandlung, 1833.

Welsh, John F. *Max Stirner's Dialectical Egoism: A New Interpretation*. Lanham, MD: Lexington Books, 2010.

Wendel, Hermann. "Die Generation um Conradi." *Sozialistische Monatshefte* 10, no. 5 (1906): 413–20.

Whitmarsh, Tim. *Battling the Gods: Atheism in the Ancient World*. London: Faber & Faber, 2017.

Wiersma, Hans. "Redeeming *Life of Brian*: How Monty Python (Ironically) Proclaims Christ *Sub Contrario*." *Word & World* 32, no. 2 (2012): 166–77.

Wittgenstein, Ludwig. *Tractatus Logico-Philosophicus*. London: Kegan Paul, Trench, Trübner & Co., 1933.

Woodcock, George. *Anarchism: A History of Libertarian Ideas and Movements*. Cleveland, OH: The World Publishing Company, 1962.

Zenker, E. V. *Anarchism: A Criticism and History of the Anarchist Theory*. London: Methuen, 1898.

Zepler, Wally. "Individualismus." *Sozialistische Monatshefte* 13, no. 2 (1909): 888–901.

Index

Abbagnano, Nicola, 226
abortion, 159
abstractions, 4, 7, 129, 138, 168, 180, 198, 210, 216–19, 225, 230, 242
absurdity, 83–84, 187–88, 197, 235
Achelis, Thomas, 91
Adorno, Theodor, 123, 183
Alexander II (tsar), 51, 124–26, 147
Alexander III (tsar), 51
alienation, 108, 120, 130, 187, 194–96, 245
altruism, 111–17, 133, 142, 158–59, 171, 193
amoralism, 138, 163, 176
anarchism, 6, 8, 51, 89–94, 96–99, 128, 148, 152, 177
angst, 84–85, 194, 196–97, 202, 217, 226–27, 246
Annenkov, Pavel, 132
annihilation, 90, 143, 178, 182, 210, 218–19, 222
anthropocentrism, 91
anti-authoritarianism, 131, 145–46, 166
anti-establishmentarianism, 126, 146, 245
anti-natalism, 57, 227–28, 247
anti-nihilism, 50–51, 61, 79–80, 131, 161, 246
antinomianism, 163
anti-Platonism, 32, 235, 236
anxiety, 31, 84, 95, 186, 194, 197, 217
apathy, 105, 145
Aquinas, Thomas (Saint), 190
Arendt, Dieter, 43, 98
Arent, Wilhelm, 88
Aristotle, 34, 111, 190, 204n102, 237n12
Arvon, Henri, 104, 203–4, 206
Aston, Louise, 17

ataraxia, 33, 101
atheism, 15, 17–18, 37–38, 57, 65, 84, 94, 101, 104, 108–9, 200, 207–9, 212–13; and nothingness, 26, 29–31, 39, 44
atomistic-Epicurean tradition, 235
Auerbach, Berthold, 46
authenticity, 190–91, 199, 204
authority/authoritarianism, 7, 8, 51, 60, 77, 125, 131, 158, 166, 239
autonomy, 8, 103, 110, 115, 133, 164–65, 174, 176, 182, 210, 215, 222, 235–45 *passim*
Avicenna (Ibn Sina), 190
Ayer, Alfred Jules, 156–57, 162, 178

Baader, Franz von, 43
Bahnsen, Julius, 80, 81, 149
Bakunin, Mikhail, 70, 127–31, 136, 140, 147, 148, 247
Bakunin, Mikhail, works: "The Reaction in Germany," 127, 136; *Statism and Anarchy*, 130
Ball, Hugo, 8, 94
Basch, Victor, 19n56, 153
Bataille, Georges, 82
Baudelaire, Charles, 65, 205
Baudrillard, Jean, 82
Bauer, Bruno, 11–12, 15–18, 45, 47, 95, 107–8, 130, 139, 144–45, 184
Bauer, Edgar, 14, 15, 17, 130
Baumgartner, Adolf, 68–70, 72
Baxa, Jakob, 94
Beckett, Samuel, 82, 227
becoming, 218
being, 84, 96, 216–18, 220–21
Belinsky, Vissarion, 127, 132–33, 135–37, 139, 141, 144, 247
Benatar, David, 28n10, 227
Bentham, Jeremy, 235
Berber, Friedrich, 98

Berg, Alban, 82
Berg, Franz, 43
Berg, Leo, 90
Bergerac, Cyrano de, 235
Berlin, Isaiah, 131–32, 151–52, 205–6
Bernoulli, Carl Albrecht, 68–70
Bernstein, Eduard, 89–90, 104–5, 155, 212
Beta, Heinrich, 110
Bey, Nimet Eloui, 13
Biedermann, Karl, 88, 104, 124
Billington, James, 140, 140n67
Binswanger, Ludwig, 95, 173
Bismarck, Otto von, 14
Blumenfeld, Jacob, 244
Böhme, Jakob, 46
Bolshevism, 92
Bonaparte, Napoleon, 10
boredom, 95, 194
Brobjer, Thomas H, 77
Buber, Martin, 1, 123, 201–3
Büchner, Georg, 45
Buddhism, 46, 60, 64
Buhl, Ludwig, 11, 15–17
Bull, George, 159
Bülow, Hans von, 69–70, 69n79
Burtz, Agnes Clara Kunigunde, 10
Byington, Steven Tracy, 3–4, 115n124, 149n101, 212, 214, 215

Callicles, 89
Calvez, Jean-Yves, 97
Camus, Albert, 1, 8, 82–84, 103–4, 145, 148, 150, 187, 192–93, 197–98, 212, 242–43
Camus, Albert, works: *L'Étranger* (The Outsider), 195; *A Happy Death*, 243; *L'Homme révolté* (The Rebel), 97, 108n87, 242, 242nn24–25; *La Peste* (The Plague), 195
capitalism, 7, 113, 154n3, 245
Carr, Karen Leslie, 28–29, 41, 60, 100–101, 155–56, 186–87
Carroll, John, 75–76, 122, 139, 164–65, 168–69, 179, 199, 215, 235
Carus, Paul, 81, 81n149

Catholicism, 11, 30, 43
censorship, 10–11, 123, 173, 180–81, 184
Chalybäus, Heinrich Moritz, 218
Chamfort, Nicolas, 227
chastity, 168–69, 172
Chernyshevsky, Nikolay, 49, 126–27, 132, 139, 141–44, 146; influence of Stirner on, 49–50
Chernyshevsky, Nikolay, works: *What Is to Be Done?* 141–42, 143n78
Christ, Jesus, 16, 36
Christianity, 7, 8, 15, 18–19, 107–8, 121, 161; as anthropological phenomenon, 15, 57; miracles, 15, 148; Nietzsche on, 61, 63–64, 76–78, 90–91, 168–69; Stirner on, 77–78, 90–91, 165, 169–70, 177, 189, 228, 231–32
Cicero, 231
Cioran, Emil Mihai, 82, 226–27, 237n9, 246
Clark, John P, 99, 193, 200
Cleese, John, 240
communism, 3, 6, 19, 51, 78, 94, 118, 128, 150, 239
compassion, 64, 92, 112, 115–17, 121, 231–32
Comte, Auguste, 111, 116
Comte, Auguste, works: *Cours de philosophie positive* (The Course of Positive Philosophy), 111
Conrad, Joseph, 82
Conradi, Hermann, 67n69, 88
consciousness, 8, 43, 53, 83, 99, 108, 180, 210, 232
consequentialism, 155, 171
Copernicus, Nicolaus, 62
Copleston, Frederick, 191, 216
Cornu, Auguste, 96
Cramer, Johann Andreas, 38
creatio ex nihilo, 107
creative nothing, 24, 107, 189, 195–96, 203, 215–17, 234
Crevier, Jean-Baptiste Louis, 36
criticism, biblical, 16
Crosby, Donald Allen, 28, 176–77, 187–88, 191, 226

Dadaism, 93–94
Daehnhardt, Marie, 11, 13, 17
Darwin, Charles, 14
Darwinism, 122, 123, 144
Dasein, 84, 217, 220
Dawkins, Richard, 112, 235
Dawkins, Richard, works: *The Selfish Gene*, 112
death, 49, 83–85, 106, 194–97, 217, 231–32
Death Metal, 82
death penalty, 159
decision, 190
definitions of nihilism, 2, 23–32, 48, 54, 59–60, 144, 186, 239; dictionary definitions and interpretations, 27–28; Nietzsche's definition (*see* Nietzschean nihilism)
deicide, 56–57, 77
deism, 43–44
Dejacque, Joseph, 148
Deleuze, Gilles, 8, 76, 97–98, 108, 235, 236
democracy, 49, 76
Democritus, 230–31, 235, 243, 246
demythologization, 13, 76, 151, 178, 182, 215, 236–40, 248
De Ridder, Widukind, 199
Derrida, Jacques, 82
Descartes, René, 120, 191, 237n12
despair, 41, 46, 82–84, 95, 107, 187, 194, 196–97, 199, 220, 235–36
Deutsche Jahrbücher für Wissenschaft und Kunst, 127
Diamond, Jared, 122
Diogenes the Cynic (Diogenes of Sinope), 56, 235, 236–37
divine, the, 4, 56, 96, 184, 214, 228
Dobrolyubov, Nikolai, 132, 139
Doctors' Club (*Doktorenklub*), 130
Dod, Elmar, 102, 105, 212
dogma, 5, 7, 8, 60, 74, 93, 101, 114, 152, 164, 179–80, 184, 198–99, 237
Dostoevsky, Fyodor, 30–31, 50–51, 117, 127, 132, 148, 162, 187, 197, 199; Stirner's influence on, 137–40
Dostoevsky, Fyodor, works: *The Brothers Karamazov*, 30n25, 31, 117, 127, 138, 138n59; *Crime and Punishment*, 138, 237n12; *Demons*, 50, 50n115, 138, 148
dread. *See* angst
Dreier, James, 156–57
Drews, Arthur, 94, 110
Droz, Jacques, 97
Droz, Théophile, 70
Dubois, Félix, 90, 104
Duchamp, Marcel, 82, 122–23
Duchamp, Marcel, works: *Fountain*, 122–23
Düsing, Edith, 59

education, 10, 166–68
ego, 4, 74, 93, 96, 99, 105, 108, 191, 193, 197, 203, 219, 233
egoism, 4, 7, 8, 41, 95, 146, 184, 202; and moral nihilism, 158–59, 172–77, 179–82; psychological, 112; rational, 141–43; in Stirner's thought, 95–96, 98, 106, 110–23, 191, 193
egoism-altruism dichotomy, 112, 184, 231
egosystem, 8, 121. *See also* union of egoists
Eigenheit (ownness), 8, 133, 150
Einzige, Der (periodical), 93
Einzige und sein Eigentum, Der (The Ego and Its Own), 1, 3, 6–8, 10–11, 87–90, 94–95, 97–99, 101–2, 107–8, 112, 114, 122, 124, 132, 137, 142, 164–68, 172, 189, 192, 197–98, 202; ban, 10; Lauterbach edition, 54; liberalism in, 18–19; nothingness in, 105–10, 211; prologue, 105–7, 192, 222; reviews, 118, 223–24; section 1 "Man" (*Der Mensch*), 7; section 2 "I" (*Ich*), 8, 152, 182–83; title, 3–4, 100–101; translation of, 3, 4, 215–16; translations, 3–4, 75;

Einzige und sein Eigentum, Der (*continued*):
  two nothings, 212–26; Young Hegelians and, 118
emancipation, 8, 120, 126, 129, 141, 147, 150–51, 176, 179, 204, 228
Emmelius, Johann-Christoph, 73–74
emotivism, 157
empathy, 112, 115
Empedocles, 80, 81
empiricism, 114
emptiness, 28, 31, 38, 63, 83, 149, 186, 196, 210, 215, 218, 226, 234
Engels, Friedrich, 1, 12, 14–17, 96, 118, 122, 128, 244
Engels, Friedrich, works: [with Marx] *Manifest der Kommunistischen Partei* (The Communist Manifesto), 122; *Der Triumph des Glaubens* (The Triumph of Faith), 14
Engert, Rolf, 23
Enlightenment, The, 4, 7, 15, 18, 36, 58, 120–22, 152, 183–84, 237, 239, 247. *See also* Scottish Enlightenment
Epicureanism, 212–13, 235–36
Epicurus, 197, 212, 230–32, 235, 246
Epicurus, works: *De rerum natura* (On the Nature of the Universe), 212, 236n7
Ernst, Max, 1, 122, 122n156
error theory of ethics, 157–58, 162, 182; argument from queerness, 158, 172; argument from relativity, 158, 170
essence, 188–90, 203, 211, 225
ethics, 37, 90, 154, 156–58, 162–63, 171, 173–74, 176–77, 182, 197
etymology of nihilism, 23, 27, 32, 34–35, 47, 82, 104, 241; *Annihilation*, 37; *nihil*, 23, 27, 144, 146; *Nihilianismus*, 35, 38; *Nihilisme*, 36; *Nihilismus*, 21, 36, 37, 39, 40, 41, 43, 44, 46, 47, 52, 87. *See also* definitions of nihilism; genealogy of nihilism

eudaemonism, 226–33
euthanasia, 159
evolution of nihilism. *See* genealogy of nihilism
ex nihilo nihil fit, 89, 89n7
existence, 188–91, 196–97, 199, 203, 225, 232
existentialism, 82–85, 108, 145, 186–211, 221, 225–26, 232; positive and negative themes, 190–98, 203; Stirner and, 186–206
existential nihilism, 28, 31, 63, 82, 85, 98, 104, 123, 186–236; the existential question, 186–90; Stirner and, 186–233

faith, 40, 83, 137, 188, 208–9, 245
Fallersleben, Hoffmann von, 17
fascism, 21, 102, 154, 183, 204, 238, 244
Feder, Johann Georg Heinrich, 36
feelings, 113, 157, 162, 166
Feuerbach, Ludwig, 7, 14–16, 45–46, 57, 76, 78, 87–88, 107–8, 118, 120, 131, 141, 147, 184, 190, 216–17
Feuerbach, Ludwig, works: *Das Wesen des Christhenthums* (The Essence of Christianity), 14, 45, 217; review of *Der Einzige*, 223–24
Fichte, Johann Gottlieb, 15, 35–43, 45, 47, 100, 120, 191, 197, 220
Fichte, Johann Gottlieb, works: *Grundlage der gesamten Wissenschaftslehre* (Foundations of the Entire Science of Knowledge), 37, 41; "Ueber den Grund unseres Glaubens an eine göttliche Weltregierung" (On the Basis of our Belief in a Divine Governance of the World), 37
finitude, 107, 194, 196–97
Fisher, Herbert Albert Laurens, 125
fixed ideas (*fixe Ideen*), 6, 19, 79, 129, 147, 150, 165, 179, 184, 192, 240
Fleming, Kurt W, 103, 232, 236
Forberg, Friedrich Karl, 37

Förster-Nietzsche, Elisabeth, 69, 72–74, 73n93, 77, 123
Foucault, Michel, 20, 235, 245
Fourier, Charles, 137
Frank, Joseph, 137–38, 152
Frazer, James, 238
freedom, 6, 8, 20, 79, 84, 103, 131, 163, 167, 190–94, 202
Freien, Die (the Free Ones), 14–19, 88, 120, 128, 130, 133, 140
Frege, Gottlob, 221
French Revolution, 149–50
Freud, Sigmund, 71, 122–23, 142, 230
Friedell, Egon, 80, 116
Friedlaender, Salomo, 93

Galotti, Emilia, 172–73
Garve, Christian, 113
Gassendi, Pierre, 235
Gast, Peter (Heinrich Köselitz), 52, 55n7, 72–74, 77
gender inequality, 142
genealogy of nihilism, 24, 40–47, 54, 85, 102, 144, 241; existential manifestation, 82–86, 186; polemical use, 24, 41, 43, 45, 85, 87–88, 100, 144–45, 155, 178; political watchword, 49–52, 85. *See also* definitions of nihilism; etymology of nihilism
generosity. *See* kindness
Gersdorff, Carl von, 68
Gertz, Nolen, 186, 226
Gillespie, Gerald, 41, 54, 102, 145, 148
Glassford, John, 77, 79, 81n148
Gleichen-Rußwurm, Alexander von, 92
God, 18, 27–31, 36–40, 79, 107, 183, 194, 202, 207; death of, 56–58, 63, 76–78, 84, 109, 178, 183–84, 196, 226
Goethe, Johann Wolfgang von, 73–74, 80–81, 105–7, 143, 222
Goethe, Johann Wolfgang von, works: *Satyros oder der vergötterte Waldteufel* (Satyros or the Deified Forest Devil), 107n84; "Vanitas! vanitatum vanitas!," 73–74, 105, 222
Goldschmidt, Arthur, 91
Goncharov, Ivan, 136
goodness, 6, 154–56, 163–65, 169–71, 175, 178
Gorgias, 33
Gorgias, works: *Concerning the Nonexistent*, 33
Gottschall, Rudolf, 189–90
Götze, Friedrich Lebrecht, 35
Goudsblom, Johan, 59, 98; meanings of nihilism in Nietzsche, 59–60
Grenzboten, Die (The Border Messenger), 22
Grün, Karl, 87–88, 104
guilt, 194
Gutzkow, Karl, 45–46, 88

habit, 173, 180n103
Hallesche Jahrbücher, 16
Hanne, Johann Wilhelm, 45
Harari, Yuval Noah, 31n26, 181, 216, 237
Harman, Gilbert, 157, 161–62, 178
Hart, Heinrich, 88
Hart, Julius, 88, 91
Hartmann, Eduard von, 46, 54, 66–67, 74, 81, 87, 94, 110, 121, 123, 149, 205, 230
Hartmann, Eduard von, works: *Philosophie des Unbewussten* (Philosophy of the Unconscious), 46, 66
hedonism, 89, 213, 226–33, 235–36, 248
Hegel, Gottfried Wilhelm Friedrich, 3, 6, 10, 17, 22, 39–40, 43, 45, 56–57, 80, 120, 154, 190, 203; being-nothing-becoming, 217–20; dialectical theory, 19, 57, 76, 106, 218–20; political views, 127
Hegel, Gottfried Wilhelm Friedrich, works: *Die Phänomenologie des Geistes* (The Phenomenology of Mind), 10; *Wissenschaft der Logik* (Science of Logic), 218

Hegelianism, 76, 101, 203; Old/New, 21–22, 21n67; post-Hegelianism, 6, 77, 104, 200, 219; Right/Left, 16, 21n67, 100, 130, 137, 144–45, 218. *See also* Young Hegelians
hegemony, 4, 6, 150, 152, 183, 192
Heidegger, Martin, 31, 84, 194, 197, 204, 216–17, 246
Heidegger, Martin, works: *Sein und Zeit* (Being and Time), 84
Heine, Heinrich, 45, 57n16
Helms, Hans G, 21, 98, 120, 123, 138, 154, 162, 183, 204, 240, 244
Heman, Friedrich, 92, 105, 124, 212
Henckell, Karl, 88
Herder, Johann Gottfried von, 80–81
heresy, 35, 36, 38, 39
Herwegh, Georg, 17
Herzen, Alexander, 127, 131, 136, 139, 141, 144, 146, 246–47
Hess, Moses, 18, 118, 184
heteronomy, 7–8, 119n141, 131, 133, 135, 150, 168, 176, 184, 230, 237, 242
Higgins, C. Francis, 33
Hildebrand, Max, 12, 15
Hingley, Ronald, 126, 141, 144, 147
Hippels Weinstube, 14, 16
history, 7, 63, 96, 122, 152, 187, 238
history of nihilism. *See* genealogy of nihilism
Hitchens, Christopher, 31n26, 85, 235
Hobbes, Thomas, 13, 69, 117, 163, 179, 231
Hobbes, Thomas, works: *Leviathan*, 231
Holbach, Baron d', 18, 235
Holbrook, David, 99
Hölderlin, Friedrich, 42
Holz, Hans Heinz, 97, 204
Homer, 111
Homer, works: *Odyssey*, 111
Hook, Sidney, 163–64, 174, 176, 177
Horkheimer, Max, 183
horror vacui, 31, 84, 196
Hugo, Victor, 46–47

humanism, 57, 88, 163, 170, 183, 194, 199, 231
Hume, David, 18, 85, 114; Hume's law, 177
hyperbole, 3, 89, 168, 225n195

Ibsen, Henrik, 205
idealism, 7, 36–40, 42–45, 77, 88, 100, 107, 191
idées fixes. *See* fixed ideas
Immermann, Karl Leberecht, 44
immortality, 28, 30n25, 52, 83, 107, 208, 210, 218
incest, 102, 134–35, 155
individualism, 7, 74, 77, 89–97, 122, 129, 147, 179, 245
infanticide, 102, 134–35, 147, 155, 160
infinity, 34, 39, 47, 56, 57n13, 58, 196, 236
insurrection (*Empörung*), 147–53
Ionesco, Eugène, 82
Ionian fallacy, the, 240
is-ought problem, 177
italicization, 3, 226n195
Ivanov, Ivan, 50, 147–48

Jacobi, Friedrich Heinrich, 15, 34–40, 47, 145, 154
Jaspers, Karl, 204
Jean Paul, 40, 42, 45, 106–7
Jenisch, Daniel, 36, 145
Joël, Karl, 69, 72, 95
Joubert, Joseph, 227
Judaism, 16, 217
Junges Deutschland (Young Germany), 45; *das jüngste Deutschland* (Youngest Germany), 88
justice, 6, 46, 79, 129, 157, 178, 192, 214

Kafka, Franz, 82
Kahlefeld, Susanna, 38
Kant, Immanuel, 7, 35–37, 101, 120, 169, 218, 241
Kant, Immanuel, works: *Was ist Aufklärung?* (What Is Enlightenment?), 7

Karakozov, Dmitry, 51, 126
Kast, Bernd, 8, 23, 90, 104, 108, 110, 119–21, 173, 202, 220, 226, 232
Katkov, Mikhail, 144–45
Keben, Georg, 89, 154, 244
Keyserling, Hermann Graf, 94
Khawaja, Noreen, 84
Kierkegaard, Søren, 83–84, 95, 98, 105, 190–92, 197, 199–203, 208, 220, 227
Kierkegaard, Søren, works: *The Concept of Dread*, 84; *Fear and Trembling*, 83; *Journals*, 105; *The Sickness unto Death*, 83
kindness, 111–13, 232
Kleist, Heinrich von, 98
Klingemann, August, 41–43, 106–7
Klingemann, August, works: *Die Nachtwachen des Bonaventura* (The Night Watches of Bonaventura), 41–43, 47, 106
Klutentreter, Wilhelm, 97
Knutzen, Matthias, 18
Kohlschmidt, Werner, 41, 41n70
Kołakowski, Leszek, 75, 138, 151
Köppen, Carl Friedrich, 15, 17, 130
Köppen, Friedrich, 39
Köselitz, Heinrich. *See* Gast, Peter
Kotzebue, August Friedrich Ferdinand von, 171
Kropotkin, Peter, 48
Krug, Wilhelm Traugott, 43
Künneth, Walter, 97
Kurtschinsky, Mikhail, 128

Laas, Ernst, 88–89, 104, 155
Lachmann, Benedict, 75, 177
La Mettrie, Julien Offray de, 235
Lampert, Eugene, 125, 127, 129, 136, 137, 146
Landstreicher, Wolfi, 3, 216
Lange, Friedrich Albert, 67–68, 72, 87
Lange, Friedrich Albert, works: *Geschichte des Materialismus* (History of Materialism), 67, 72, 87
Larkin, Philip, 84–85, 227, 228n206
Larkin, Philip, works: "Aubade," 85

Laska, Bernd, 8, 19–20, 23, 55, 70–72, 81, 88, 98, 102–4, 139–40, 152, 154, 184, 226, 232
Lauterbach, Paul, 54, 74n100, 123
Leibniz, Gottfried Wilhelm, 228
Leopardi, Giacomo, 65, 205, 220, 227, 235
Leopold, David, 3–4, 20, 112, 133, 174–77, 179, 182, 203, 235, 243n29
Leskov, Nikolai, 51
Lessing, Gotthold Ephraim, 38
Lévy, Albert, 66n63, 68, 70, 76
liberalism, 18–19, 78, 88
libertarianism, 130, 245
Lichtenberger, Henri, 72, 74–75
Life of Brian (Monty Python), 44n91, 240
Ligotti, Thomas, 85
Ligotti, Thomas, works: *The Conspiracy against the Human Race*, 85
Locke, John, 157
logical positivism. *See* positivism
Lombard, Peter, 38
love, 8, 49, 112–17, 119, 159, 202; sacred love (*heilige Liebe*), 119, 231; self-love (*Eigenliebe*), 113, 115, 228–29, 231–32
Löwith, Karl, 8, 18, 75, 77, 95, 104–5, 123, 200–2, 212
Lucchesi, Matteo Johannes Paul, 90–93, 105, 212
Lucretius, 85, 90n7, 212, 236n7
Lucretius, works: *De rerum natura*, 212
Ludwig, Franz, 93
Lütgert, Wilhelm, 94
Luther, Martin, 51, 80, 81
Lütkehaus, Ludger, 101, 105, 212, 218n164
Łyszczyński, Kazimierz, 18

Macaulay, Thomas Babington, 159–60
Machiavelli, Niccolò, 159–62, 164, 171, 178–80, 237
Machiavelli, Niccolò, works: *Discourses*, 160; *The Prince*, 160–61

Mackay, John Henry, 9–17, 20, 22–23, 75, 139–40, 153, 203
Mackie, John, 157–59, 162, 172, 178–79, 182
Macquarrie, John, 188–92, 194, 198–99
Mahler, Gustav, 227
Mainländer, Philipp, 57, 65, 80–81, 140, 149, 227, 246
Malia, Martin, 131
Mann, Thomas, 30
Marmysz, John, 101–2
Maron, Hermann, 17
Marot (church councilor), 11–12
Martin, Nicholas, 78, 81
Marx, Karl, 7, 13, 15, 190, 204; on Stirner, 1, 2–3, 20, 96, 102–3, 121–22
Marx, Karl, works [with Engels]: *Die deutsche Ideologie* (The German Ideology), 15, 20, 96, 121; *Manifest der Kommunistischen Partei* (The Communist Manifesto), 122
Marxism, 21, 96–97, 128, 154, 204, 245
Masaryk, Tomáš Garrigue, 8, 47, 91, 124, 131, 138, 144, 147, 151n106, 152
materialism, 38, 49, 67, 121, 126, 144–46, 231
mathematics, 33–34, 84
matricide, 49, 147
Mautz, Kurt Adolf, 95
Max Stirner Society, 23, 102–4
Mazzini, Giuseppe, 131
McLaughlin, Paul, 128, 130
McLellan, David, 19n59, 98
Mendelssohn, Moses, 36, 38, 100
Meslier, Jean, 18, 235
mesomidenika, 213
Messer, Max, 92–93, 174, 176–77
metaphysics, 37, 109, 138, 144, 148, 155, 158, 194, 207, 216
Meyen, Eduard, 15, 17, 18
might. *See* power
Mill, John Stuart, 235
mineness, 191, 198

modernity, 7, 54, 59, 64, 80, 243n29, 244, 245n40
Molderings, Herbert, 123
monarchy, 6, 124, 242
monism, 240
Monty Python, 44n91, 240
morality, 78, 156–79, 182, 184; Stirner and, 57, 61, 78–79, 91, 154–59, 161–72, 174–76, 178–82
moral nihilism, 28, 63, 90, 104, 121, 154–86, 228, 234; and atheism, 178; definition, 154–59, 162; and egoism, 158–59, 172–77, 179–82; Machiavelli and, 159–61, 164, 171, 178–80; Nietzsche and, 161–62
moral relativism, 114, 152, 156–57, 161, 173, 188
Muggeridge, Malcolm, 44n91, 240
Müller, Max, 46
Müller-Lauter, Wolfgang, 37–40
Munch, Edvard, 82–83, 227
Muravyov, Count Mikhail, 126
murder, concept of, 89, 102, 155, 159–61, 171–72, 178–79; of God (*see* God, death of); political, 50–51, 124–26, 147–48, 171
Mushacke, Eduard, 17, 70–71
Mushacke, Hermann, 68, 70–71
Musil, Robert, 246
mysticism, 35–36, 46, 132, 144n85, 178, 224, 232
myth/mythology, 4, 6, 8, 119n141, 150, 152, 180–81, 199, 210, 216, 227, 236–38, 242

Nagel, Thomas, 246
Narodnaya Volya (People's Will), 51, 147
Nathanson, Hugo, 92
nationalism, 6, 78, 181n106, 242
Naturalism, 88, 107, 236
nausea, 172, 194–95, 197n68
Nauwerck, Karl, 15, 17
Nazism, 30–32, 183
Nechaev, Sergey Gennadiyevich, 50, 126, 147–53, 247; and Stirner, 147–53

Nechaev, Sergey Gennadiyevich, works: "Revolutionary Catechism," 50, 147
negation/negativity, 21, 29, 95, 98, 105, 127, 136, 144, 147
Neoplatonism, 105
Newman, Saul, 20–22, 103, 245
New People (Russian nihilists), 126
Newton, Sir Isaac, 14
Nicholas I (tsar), 125, 144
Nichts/nichts (nothing), 34, 106–8, 213–15, 218, 220–25
Nietzsche, Friedrich, 111–12, 165, 168, 174, 181, 187, 198–99, 229, 237, 241–42; *amor fati*, 229; anti-nihilism, 61, 79, 161; on compassion, 64, 117; death of God, 56–58, 63, 77–78, 80, 178; Hartmann's attack on, 54, 66–67, 74; *Lust* (joy), 230; mental illness, 67, 71, 72, 82; nihilism (*see* Nietzschean nihilism); order, universal, 62; parable of the madman (*Der Tolle Mensch*), 56; plagiarism, 55, 57, 66, 69–70, 74, 77, 81; relativism, 62; right and wrong, 62; rise to fame, 54; sources, 57, 81; tragic age for Europe, 58–59, 80, 84–85; will to power, 79; writing style, 6, 55, 75–77. *See also* Förster-Nietzsche, Elisabeth; Stirner-Nietzsche question
Nietzsche, Friedrich, works: *Also sprach Zarathustra* (Thus Spoke Zarathustra), 65; *Der Antichrist. Fluch auf das Christenthum* (The Anti-Christ: A Curse on Christianity), 61; *Dionysus-Dithyrambs*, vi, 213; *Ecce Homo*, 64, 80, 116n129, 168; *Die fröhliche Wissenschaft* (The Gay Science), 56; *Götzen-Dämmerung oder wie man mit dem Hammer philosophirt* (Twilight of the Idols or How to Philosophize with a Hammer), 61, 161; *Jenseits von Gut und Böse* (Beyond Good and Evil, 1886), 78; "Lenzer Heide" text, 56, 61, 64n42; *Ueber Wahrheit und Lüge im außermoralischen Sinne* (On Truth and Lie in an Extra-Moral Sense), 62; *Vom Nutzen und Nachteil der Historie für das Leben* (On the Use and Abuse of History for Life), 66; *Der Wille zur Macht* (The Will to Power), 55–56, 90, 187
Nietzschean nihilism, 26, 51–86, 234–35; active/passive, 60–61, 64; evolution of, 54–59; features/typology of, 59–65; meaninglessness of life, 56, 61, 63, 65, 82
Nietzsche Archive, 55, 69, 72
nihilism, 2; aesthetic, 28; alethiological, 28, 29, 90, 178; antecedents (*see* origins of nihilism); atheism and, 29; axiological (existential), 28; cosmic, 28, 63, 186; epistemological, 28, 33, 186; ethical (moral), 22, 28, 31, 90, 154–56, 186; existential (*see separate entry*); extreme, 76, 97, 162; historical, 27; logical (alethiological), 29, 90; mereological, 28, 29; metaphysical (ontological), 28; moderate, 157, 162; moral (*see separate entry*); ontological, 28, 33, 96; as pathology, 31, 64–65; philosophical, 27; political (*see separate entry*); popularization of, 35, 47, 52; Russian (*see separate entry*); semantic, 29; social (political), 90, 94; theological, 29, 178. *See also* definitions of nihilism; etymology of nihilism; genealogy of nihilism; origins of nihilism; Stirner, Max, status as nihilist
Nishitani, Keiji, 97, 105
nominalism, 201, 204, 214, 246
nothing, 24, 33, 34, 36, 42, 73, 146, 216

nothingness, 22, 30, 33–34, 38, 40–42, 44, 62–64, 83–85, 101, 194–96, 200, 208, 216

Obereit, Jacob Hermann, 35–36, 38, 44, 145
Obereit, Jacob Hermann, works: *Der wiederkommende Lebensgeist* (The Returning Life Spirit), 36, 38
Onfray, Michel, 136n45, 184, 213, 235–36, 238, 240n20
ordinary language philosophy, 31
origins of nihilism, 33–40
oudenophobia, 227
Overbeck, Franz, 69–70, 72–75
Overbeck, Ida, 69–70, 73, 75, 81
ownership (*Eigentum*), 8, 20, 192, 219, 231
ownness (*Eigenheit*), 8, 133, 150, 163, 192, 199

Palin, Michael, 240
pantheism, 36–38, 43–45
paradox of negative existentials, 221
Parmenides, 33, 89n7, 212, 218, 221
Pascal, Blaise, 227
Paterson, Ronald William Keith, 8–9, 19, 77, 98–99, 108–10, 113–15, 119–20, 129, 148–49, 162–64, 193, 200, 204–12, 227, 235, 241, 243–44
Pecherin, Vladimir Sergeyvich, 140
Penzo, Giorgio, 98, 105, 196, 204–7, 212, 223
pessimism, 29, 57, 65, 90, 106, 149, 179, 194, 212–13, 227–28, 230, 232, 235, 247
Peter of Poitiers, 38
Petrashevsky, Mikhail, 137–38; Petrashevsky Circle, 137–38
Pietsch, Ludwig, 16
Pindar, 80, 81
Pinker, Steven, 183, 235
Pisarev, Dmitry, 49, 139, 141, 143, 146–47, 179, 247; Stirner's influence on, 49, 148
Pisemsky, Aleksey, 51
Plato, 31, 111, 190

Platonism, 31–32, 64, 235–36
pleasure, 46, 116, 142, 229–30, 236
pleasure principle (Freud), 230
pluralism, 240, 248
Poe, Edgar Allan, 205
Pöggeler, Otto, 43
polemics, anti-nihilist, 32
political nihilism, 28, 30, 90, 104, 123–53, 219, 247–48; definitions, 28, 125; meaning and history, 124–27; populism, 127–36, 151. *See also* Russian nihilism
Polturak, Aurélie, 94
polygamy, 134, 135, 155
populism, Russian, 127–36, 127n13
positivism, 49, 88, 126, 145–46, 152, 161–62, 226
possessedness, 115, 165, 199, 232
possessions. *See* property
postmodernism, 1, 191
power, 8, 79, 148, 179, 192, 228, 245
Praz, Mario, 84
privatio boni theory of evil, 105
proletariat, 93, 131
property, 4, 8, 18, 50, 92, 96, 108, 137, 181, 191, 197, 219, 222
Protagoras, 232, 235
Protestantism, 30, 43
Proudhon, Pierre-Joseph, 90, 128, 137, 170
psychology, 122, 181, 187, 199
Ptolemy, Claudius, 34
Pyrrho of Elis, 33, 101, 170
Pythagoras, 34, 47, 80, 81

quietism, 46

radicalism, 7, 14, 22, 46, 88, 95, 98, 104, 132–33, 152
Radowitz, Joseph von, 46
rationalism, 38
Rauschning, Hermann, 30–32
Read, Herbert, 1, 75, 109, 113, 196, 202–3
realism, 39, 146, 166, 179
reason, 40, 53, 184, 202; Platonic-Aristotelian conception of, 31–32

rebellion, 19, 105, 128n15, 149n101, 150, 198, 237
Reginster, Bernard, 82, 111
relations, social, 7, 151
religion, 6, 8, 11, 15, 31, 37, 61, 64, 107–8, 135, 138, 174, 208, 223–24, 242. *See also* Buddhism; Christianity; Judaism
repression, primary, 71
Reschika, Richard, 103–4
responsibility, 172, 190, 193, 201–2
revelation, 38, 57, 166
revolution, 22, 49–50, 125–32, 136, 139, 144, 148–52
Rilke, Rainer Maria, 13
Rimbaud, Arthur, 205
Robinson, Cedric, 148
Romanticism, 40–42, 45–46, 191, 195, 205, 220, 247
Romulus and Remus, 160
Rosen, Stanley, 31–32, 53
Rosenkranz, Karl, 21–22, 44–45, 87, 104, 110, 123, 145, 154–55, 162, 239
Rousseau, Jean-Jacques, 179
Rovelli, Carlo, 235
Ruest, Anselm, 8, 23, 68n72, 75, 92–93, 177
Ruge, Arnold, 15–18, 127, 225
Russian nihilism, 28, 35, 47–52, 58, 60, 88–89, 124–53, 227, 234; Stirner and, 126–53. *See also* political nihilism
Russkoe Slovo (Russian Word), 49, 143
Rutenberg, Adolf, 17, 130

Safranski, Rüdiger, 75
Salat, Jakob, 43
Sand, Karl-Ludwig, 171
Santayana, George, 112
Sartre, Jean-Paul, 30n25, 82, 84, 99, 145, 177n95, 187–97, 202–3, 208, 211, 215, 216, 221, 225n197, 247
Sartre, Jean-Paul, works: *La Nausée* (Nausea), 192, 195, 197
Sawicki, Franz, 93
Say, Jean-Baptiste, 113

Scheit, Herbert, 103
Schelling, Friedrich Wilhelm Joseph, 39, 43, 45, 80–81, 139–40, 189
Schellwien, Robert, 74–75, 89
Schiereck, Larry Alan, 109–10
Schiller, Johann Friedrich (translator), 113
Schiller, Johann Christoph Friedrich von, 62n41, 92
Schiller, Johann Christoph Friedrich von, *Don Karlos, Infant von Spanien* (Don Carlos), 62n41
Schirnhofer, Resa von, 72
Schlegel, Friedrich, 43
Schleiermacher, Friedrich, 10, 45, 81
Schmidt, Johann Caspar. *See* Stirner, Max
Schmitt, Carl, 20n60
Schmitz, Hermann, 23, 99
Schopenhauer, Arthur, 51, 60, 65, 68, 71, 76, 80–81, 87–88, 106–7, 133, 149, 205, 212–13, 226–27
Schopenhauer, Arthur, works: *Parerga und Paralipomena*, 106, 212; *Die Welt als Wille und Vorstellung* (The World as Will and Representation), 106
Schröder, Rudolf, 96
Schröder, Winfried, 101, 120, 155
Schuffenhauer, Werner, 98
Schultheiss, Hermann, 244
Scientific Revolution, 15, 34, 62
scientism, 49
Scottish Enlightenment, The, 114
Second World War. *See* World War II
Seife, Charles, 33–34
self, the, 8, 107, 163, 193–94, 197, 210–11, 215, 218–20, 228–29, 232, 245
self-consciousness, 120, 196
self-determination, 121n149, 163, 176, 237
self-enjoyment (*Selbstgenuss*), 8, 114, 229
self-fulfillment, 7, 135
self-interest, 18, 111, 113, 115, 141–42, 147, 151, 178, 182, 184, 231–32

selfishness, 110–15, 120
self-realization, 101, 103, 189, 203
self-sacrifice. *See* altruism
Shakespeare, William, 89n7, 117n133, 159, 170n71
Shakespeare, William, works: *Hamlet*, 42, 140, 170n71; *King Lear*, 89n7; *Macbeth*, 108; *Merchant of Venice, The*, 117
Shatz, Marshall Sharon, 130
Simmel, Georg, 76
sin, 84, 109, 118–19, 132–33, 209
Sinnott-Armstrong, Walter, 155
Sittlichkeit (morality, ethicality), 134, 154, 165, 170–71, 173–74, 176, 220, 248
skepticism, 7, 29, 33, 46, 60, 77–78, 114, 156–58, 178, 232, 234, 237
Slocombe, Will, 101, 144–45
Sloterdijk, Peter, 120–21
Smith, Adam, 113–14, 116–17, 246
Smith, Adam, works: *An Inquiry into the Nature and Causes of the Wealth of Nations*, 113; *The Theory of Moral Sentiments*, 116
socialism, 78, 88, 93, 119, 125, 130, 136–37, 143–44, 245
society/social organization, 7, 8, 141, 244
socioeconomics, 113, 121
sociopolitics, 21, 28, 44, 51, 90, 93, 121, 151–53, 181, 227
Socrates, 36, 241
solipsism, 2, 21, 37, 40, 98, 104, 129, 147, 154
Solovyov, Alexander, 126
sophism, 33, 76
Sovremennik (The Contemporary), 49, 126, 132, 139, 141
Spann, Othmar, 94
speculative philosophy, 237
Speshnev, Nikolay, 137–38, 152, 247
Spinoza, Baruch, 36, 38, 45, 231
Spinoza, Baruch, *Ethics*, 231
Spinozism, 38, 44
Spir, Afrikan, 81
spooks (*Spuke*). *See* fixed ideas

state, the, 18, 30, 74, 76, 90, 94, 124, 127, 136, 148–49, 161, 176, 218–19, 242
Stein, Ludwig, 93
Steiner, Rudolf, 73n93, 76
Stepelevich, Lawrence, 10, 19n56, 22n67, 65n59, 99
Stern, Joseph Peter, 56, 59
Stevens, Wallace, 82
Stewart, Jon, 102
Stirner, Max, life (chronologically): childhood, 9–10; marriages, 10, 11–12; teaching, 10, 77; intellectual milieu, 14–21; personality, 20, 100, 133; death, 12–13, 77; grave, 9, 70n79; obscurity, 2, 6–9, 87; renaissance(s), 22, 23, 54, 87, 89, 98, 105, 241
Stirner, Max, philosophy: anarchism, 21, 124, 128–30, 137, 177, 198, 203, 238; anti-Christianity, 77–78, 90–91, 133, 165, 169–70, 177, 189, 228, 231–32; atheism, 151, 203, 207–9, 213, 224; on chastity, 168–69, 172; critics, 89, 91–94, 98, 105, 110, 118–23, 234–41; death of God, 57, 65, 76–78; on education, 166–68; egoism, 21, 95–96, 98, 103, 106, 110–23, 129, 131, 133, 135, 138–39, 142–43, 150–51, 182, 191, 193, 199, 229–31; eudaemonism, 226–33; on existentialism, 186–206; hedonism, 226–33; as iconoclast, 61, 96, 131, 133, 151, 178, 206, 225, 236–39; on incest, 102, 134–35, 155; on infanticide, 102, 134–35, 147, 155, 160; influence on Dostoevsky and Turgenev, 137–40; influence on Nietzsche, 22, 55, 65–82, 86; and morality, 57, 61, 67, 78–79, 91, 135, 154–59, 161–72, 174–76, 178–82; on murder, 133, 135, 155, 159–60, 197–98, 243; naivety, 121–22, 151, 181, 228, 241; optimism, 93, 121, 179, 226–33, 236; place in

history of philosophy, 2, 19–20, 116, 234–37, 241; and political nihilism, 124–53; on polygamy, 134–35, 155; radicalism, 6–8, 92, 95, 98, 133, 206, 236; and Russian nihilism, 140–53; on suicide, 133, 135, 140, 155, 160, 195, 197–98; writing style, 2, 3, 6, 75–78, 95, 225
Stirner, Max, status as nihilist, 1–2, 8, 21–25, 86: challenges to accusations, 23, 96, 98–99, 102–4, 139–40; first hundred years, 87–95; post-WWII, 95–104
Stirner, Max, works: *Der Einzige und sein Eigentum* (*see separate entry*); "Recensenten Stirners" (Stirner's Critics), 118–19, 174, 224–25; translation of Adam Smith, 113; "Das unwahre Prinzip unserer Erziehung oder Humanismus und Realismus" (The False Principle of Our Education or Humanism and Realism), 166, 167–68
Stirner-Jahrbuch, 104
Stirner-Nietzsche question, 65–81, 91n17
Stockgänger, W, 94
Stockwood, Mervyn, 44n91, 240
Stoics, the, 80, 85
Stoppard, Tom, 221
Stoppard, Tom, works: *Rosencrantz and Guildenstern are Dead*, 221
Strauss, David Friedrich, 14–16, 45, 78, 81, 107–8, 127, 137, 184
Strauss, David Friedrich, works: *Das Leben Jesu* (The Life of Jesus), 14, 45, 139n64
Strauss, Leo, 32
Stravinsky, Igor, 82
Strindberg, August, 83n155, 205
Ströbel, Heinrich, 89, 155
Stulpe, Alexander, 21n66, 177, 244
subjectivism, 22, 36–37, 40–44, 47, 91, 104, 154, 176, 191, 203, 225
sublation (*Aufhebung*), 127, 219
suicide, 133, 134n39, 135, 140, 155, 159–60, 172, 195, 197–98, 247

Sveistrup, Hans, 182
Szeliga (Franz Friedrich Szeliga von Zychlinsky), 118, 224

Tartaglia, James, 24, 232
Telegraph für Deutschland, 45
terrorism, 27, 51, 148, 152
Thacker, Eugene, 178n97, 227
Thales, 227
theism, 121, 200–202, 204–5
Thielicke, Helmut, 30–32, 38, 84
Thrasymachus, 179
Tieck, Ludwig, 41, 43
Tieck, Ludwig, works: *William Lovell*, 41
Timon of Phlius, 170
Tolstoy, Leo, 51, 52n117
Tolstoy, Leo, works: *Anna Karenina*, 48n109
totalitarianism, 30
Trepov, Colonel Fyodor, 51
truth, 6, 53, 61–64, 77–79, 84, 98, 146, 161–66, 178, 201
Tucker, Benjamin, 1, 3
Turgenev, Ivan, 35, 47–52, 125, 127, 132, 136, 145, 213, 240; Stirner's influence on, 137–40
Turgenev, Ivan, works: *Fathers and Sons*, 35, 47–50, 127, 141, 145, 213
Türkdogan, Halil Ibrahim, 103

Ulrich, Jörg, 101, 105, 212
Unamuno, Miguel de, 213, 227
union of egoists (*Verein von Egoisten*), 8, 98, 121–22, 130, 148, 151, 174, 176, 244
Unique One, the, 8, 23, 89, 96, 107, 109, 115, 163, 182, 189, 193, 200–201, 209–10, 212, 233
universalism, 120
utilitarianism, 49, 78

values, 60, 84, 96–99, 154–58, 162–64, 172, 174–75, 183, 187–88, 235
Venturi, Franco, 127n13, 144–45
Vercellone, Frederico, 82, 101

virtue, 30n25, 111, 113n116, 120, 165, 231
void, the, 34, 38, 40, 105, 216, 222
Vordtriede, Werner, 41
Vormärz, 6, 17, 45, 226

Wagner, Cosima, 69
Wagner, Richard, 70
Walter of St. Victor, 35
Warnock, Geoffrey, 159
Watson, Peter, 246
Webster, John, 212
Webster, John, works: *The Duchess of Malfi*, 212
Weiller, Cajetan, 43
Weiße, Christian Hermann, 43
Welsh, John, 7, 245n40
Werder, Karl Friedrich, 128n15, 139
Wigand, Otto, 15, 17
Wigand, Otto, works: *Wigand's Vierteljahrsschrift*, 118n138, 223–24

Wilde, Oscar, 51
Wilde, Oscar, works: *Vera; or, the Nihilists*, 51
Winkler, Paula, 201
Wittgenstein, Ludwig, 29n14, 31, 82, 156
Wizenmann, Thomas, 36
Woodcock, George, 76
words, meanings of, 205–6
World War II, 1, 32, 96, 234

Yeats, William Butler, 82
Young Hegelians, 7, 11, 14–22, 40, 45, 47, 70, 88, 118, 123, 127–28, 130, 136, 139, 144, 152, 184, 237

Zasulich, Vera, 51
Zenker, Ernst Viktor, 137, 244
Zeno of Citium, 34, 80, 81
Zepler, Wally, 93
zero, 33–34, 47

Printed in the United States
by Baker & Taylor Publisher Services